OLD LONDON
Charterhouse to Holborn

THE
'VILLAGE LONDON'
SERIES
from
THE ALDERMAN PRESS

THE VILLAGE LONDON SERIES

Other titles already published in hard back are:

VILLAGE LONDON Volume I
VILLAGE LONDON Volume II
LONDON RECOLLECTED Volume I
LONDON RECOLLECTED Volume II
LONDON RECOLLECTED Volume III
LONDON RECOLLECTED Volume IV
LONDON RECOLLECTED Volume V

Other titles already published in paperback:

VILLAGE LONDON Pt. 1 West and North
VILLAGE LONDON Pt. 2 North and East
VILLAGE LONDON Pt. 3 South-East
VILLAGE LONDON Pt. 4 South-West

OLD FLEET STREET
CHEAPSIDE AND ST. PAUL'S
THE TOWER AND EAST END
SHOREDITCH to SMITHFIELD
CHARTERHOUSE to HOLBORN
STRAND to SOHO
COVENT GARDEN and the THAMES to WHITEHALL

*The above seven titles are extracts from the
hardback edition of London Recollected.*

OLD LONDON

Charterhouse to Holborn

by

WALTER THORNBURY

THE ALDERMAN PRESS

British Library Cataloguing in Publication Data.

Thornbury, Walter.
    Old London: Charterhouse to Holborn.
    1. London (England)_____History
    I. Title II. Thornbury, Walter. Old and
    new London
    942.1   DA677

ISBN 0-946619-29-8

This edition published 1987.

The Alderman Press, 1/7 Church Street,
Edmonton, London, N9 9DR

Printed and bound in Great Britain
by Robert Hartnoll (1985) Ltd., Bodmin.

CONTENTS.

CHAPTER XLVII.
THE CHARTERHOUSE.

PAGE

The Plague of 1348—Origin of the Charterhouse—Sir Thomas More there—Cromwell's Commissioners—Prior Houghton—The Departure of the Carthusians from London—A Visit from the Grave—Effect of the Dissolution on the Charterouse Priory—The Charterhouse and the Howards—Thomas Sutton—Bishop Hall's Letter and its Effect—Sutton's Death—Baxter's Claim defeated—A Letter from Bacon—Settlement of the Charterhouse : its Constitution—Sutton's Will—His Detractors—Funeral Sermon 380

CHAPTER XLVIII.
THE CHARTERHOUSE (*continued*).

Archdeacon Hale on the Antiquities of the Charterhouse—Course of the Water Supply—The "Ave"—John Houghton's Initials—The Entrances—The Master's Lodge—Portraits—Sheldon—Burnet—Mann and his Epitaph—The Chapel—The Founder's Tomb—The Remains of Norfolk House—The Great Hall and Kitchens—Ancient Monogram—The Cloisters—The School—Removal to Godalming—Experiences of Life at Charterhouse—Thackeray's Bed—The Poor Brothers—A Scene from "The Newcomes"—Famous Poor Brothers —The Charterhouse Plays—Famous Carthusians 388

CHAPTER XLIX.
THE FLEET PRISON.

An Ancient Debtors' Prison—Grievous Abuses—Star Chamber Offenders in the Fleet—Prynne and Lilburne—James Howell, the Letter-writer—Howard, the Philanthropist, at the Fleet—The Evils of Farming the Fleet—The Cases of Jacob Mendez Solas and Captain Mackpheadris—A Parliamentary Inquiry into the State of Fleet Prison—Hogarth's Picture on the Subject—The Poet Thomson's Eulogy of Mr. Oglethorpe—The Fleet Prison before and after it was Burnt in 1780—Code of Laws enforced in the Fleet—The Liberty of the "Rules"—The Gordon Rioters at the Fleet—Weddings in the Fleet—Scandalous Scenes—Mr. Pickwick's Sojourn in the Fleet—Famous Inmates of the Prison 404

CHAPTER L.
THE FLEET RIVER AND FLEET DITCH.

Origin of the Name—Rise of the Fleet—Its Course—Early Impurity—The Holebourne—Antiquities found in the Fleet—How far Navigable for Ships—Early mention of it—Clearing of the Fleet Valley—A Deposit of Pins—The Old Bridges—Fleet Bridge—Holborn Bridge—Historical Associations—Discovery of the Arches of the Old Bridge—Thieves' Houses—Pope on the "Fleet"—The River arched over —Floods on the Fleet—Disaster in 1846—The Fleet under the Main Drainage System—Dangers of Exploring the Sewer—A Strange Denizen of the Ditch—Turnmill Street and the Thieves' Quarter—West Street—Chick Lane—The Old "Red Lion," known as "Jonathan Wild's House" 416

CHAPTER LI.
NEWGATE STREET.

Christ Church, Newgate Street: as it was, and as it is—Exorbitant Burial Fees—Richard Baxter—Dr. Trapp and Sir John Bosworth—The Steeple of Christ Church—The Spital Sermons—A Small Giant and a very Great Dwarf—The Adventures of Sir Jeffrey Hudson—Coleridge at the "Salutation and Cat"—The "Magpie and Stump"—Tom D'Urfey at the "Queen's Arms Tavern"—The College of Physicians in Warwick Lane—Some Famous Old Physicians—Dr. Radcliffe—The College of Physicians cruelly duped—Dr. Mead—Other Famous Physicians : Askew, Pitcairne, Sir Hans Sloane—A Poetical Doctor—Monsey and his Practical Dentistry—The Cauliflower Club : the President's Chair—The Bagnio in Bath Street—Cock Lane and the Famous Ghost : Walpole : Dr. Johnson : the Imposture detected : Scratching Fanny : Coffin—Old Inns in the Neighbourhood : the "Old Bell :" the "Oxford Arms"—Snow Hill and John Bunyan—Dobson 427

CHAPTER LII.
NEWGATE.

The Fifth City Gate—Howard's Description of Newgate—The Gordon Riots—The Attack on Newgate—The Mad Quaker—Crabbe, the Poet —His Account of the Burning of Newgate—Dr. Johnson's Visit to the Ruins 441

CHAPTER LIII.
NEWGATE (*continued*).

Methodist Preachers in Newgate—Silas Told—The Surgeons' Crew—Dr. Dodd, the Popular Preacher—His Forgery—Governor Wall at Goree flogs a Soldier to Death—His Last Moments—Murder of Mr. Steel—Execution of the Cato Street Conspirators—Fauntleroy, the Banker—The Murder of the Italian Boy—Greenacre—Müller—Courvoisier—His Execution—Mrs. Brownrigg—Mr. Akerman and the Fire in Newgate—Mrs. Fry's Good Work in Newgate—Escapes from Newgate—Jack Sheppard—A Good Sermon on a Bad Text—Sanitary Condition of Newgate—Effect upon the Prisoners 447

CONTENTS.

CHAPTER LV.
ST. SEPULCHRE'S AND ITS NEIGHBOURHOOD.

PAGE

The Early History of St. Sepulchre's—Its Destruction in 1666—The Exterior and Interior—The Early Popularity of the Church—Interments here—Roger Ascham, the Author of the "Schoolmaster"—Captain John Smith and his Romantic Adventures—Saved by an Indian Girl—St. Sepulchre's Churchyard—Accommodation for a Murderess—The Martyr Rogers—An Odd Circumstance—Good Company for the Dead—a Leap from the Tower—A Warning Bell and a Last Admonition—Nosegays for the Condemned—The Route to the Gallows-tree—The Deeds of the Charitable—The "Saracen's Head"—Description by Dickens—Giltspur Street—Giltspur Street Compter—A Disreputable Condition—Pie Corner—Hosier Lane—A Spurious Relic—The Conduit on Snow Hill—A Ladies' Charity School—Turnagain Lane—Poor Betty:—A Schoolmistress Censured—Skinner Street—Unpropitious Fortune—William Godwin—An Original Married Life 477

CHAPTER LVI.
THE METROPOLITAN MEAT MARKET.

History of the Metropolitan Meat Market—Newgate Market and its Inconvenience—The Meat Market described—The Ceremony of Opening—A Roaring Trade—The Metropolitan Poultry Market—London Trade in Poultry and Game—French Geese and Irish Geese—Packed in Ice—Plover's Eggs for the Queen 491

CHAPTER LVII.
FARRINGDON STREET, HOLBORN VIADUCT, AND ST. ANDREW'S CHURCH.

Farringdon Without—A Notorious Alderman—Farringdon Within—Farringdon Street—Fleet Market—Farringdon Market—Watercress Sellers—On a November Morning—The Congregational Memorial Hall—Holborn Viaduct described—The City Temple—Opening of the Viaduct by the Queen—St. Andrew's, Holborn—Its Interior—Its Exterior—Emery, the Comedian—The Persecuting Lord Chancellor Wriothesley—Sacheverel: a Pugnacious Divine—The Registers of St. Andrew's—Marriages cried by the Bellman—Edward Coke's Marriage—Coke catches a Tartar—Colonel and Mrs. Hutchinson's Marriage—A Courtship worth reading—Christening of Richard Savage—The Unfortunate Chatterton—Henry Neele, the Poet—Webster, the Dramatist, and his White Devil—A Funeral Dirge—Tomkins, the Conspirator—Strutt, and "Sports and Pastimes"—"Wicked Will" Whiston—A Queen's Faults—Hacket, afterwards Bishop of Lichfield and Coventry—A Surprise for Dissenters—Stillingfleet: A Controversial Divine—Looking People in the Face—The Rev. Charles Barton—An Agreeable Surprise—St. George the Martyr, Queen Square, and St. Andrew's—St. Andrew's Grammar School 496

CHAPTER LVIII.
ELY PLACE.

Ely Place: its Builders and Bishops—Its Demolition—Seventy Years ago—"Time-honoured" Lancaster's Death—A King admonished—The Earl of Sussex in Ely Place—The Hatching of a Conspiracy—Ely Place Garden—The Duke of Gloucester's Dessert of Strawberries—Queen Elizabeth's Handsome Lord Chancellor—A Flowery Lease—A Bishop Extinguished—A Broken Heart—Love-making in Ely Place—"Strange Lady" Hatton shows her Temper—An Hospital and a Prison—Festivities in Ely Place—The Lord Mayor offended—Henry VII. and his Queen—A Five Days' Entertainment—The Last Mystery in England—A Gorgeous Anti-masque—Two Bailiffs baffled, and a Bishop taken in—St. Etheldreda's Chapel—Its Interior—The Marriage of Evelyn's Daughter—A Loyal Clerk 514

CHAPTER LIX.
HOLBORN TO CHANCERY LANE.

The Divisions of Holborn—A Miry Thoroughfare—Oldbourne Bridge—In the Beginning of the Century—Holborn Bars—The Middle Row—On the Way to Tyburn—A Sweet Youth in the Cart—Clever Tom Clinch—Riding up Heavy Hill—The Hanging School—Cruel Whippings—Statue to the late Prince Consort—The "Rose" Tavern—Union Court—Bartlett's Buildings—Dyer's Buildings—A Famous Pastry-cook—Castle Street—A Strange Ceremony—Cursitor Street—Lord Chancellor Eldon—A Runaway Match—Southampton House—An Old Temple—Southampton Buildings—Flying for Dear Life—Jacob's Coffee House—Ridiculous Enactments—Dr. Birkbeck and Mechanics' Institutions—An Extraordinary Well—Fulwood's Rents—Ned Ward and the "London Spy"—Selling a Horse—Dr. Johnson—A Lottery Office—Lotteries: their History and Romance—Praying for Luck—A £20,000 Prize—Lucky Numbers—George A. Stevens—Gerarde the Old Herbalist, and his Garden—The Flying Pieman of Holborn Hill—An Old Bellman of Holborn. 526

CHAPTER LX.
THE NORTHERN TRIBUTARIES OF HOLBORN.

Field Lane—A Description by Dickens—Saffron Hill—Old Chick Lane—Thieves' Hiding Places—Hatton Garden—A Dramatist's Wooing—The Celebrated Dr. Bate—Charles Street—Bleeding Heart Yard—Love or Murder—Leather Lane—George Morland, the Painter—Robbing One's Own House—Brooke Street—The Poet Chatterton—His Life in London, and his Death—The Great Lord Hardwicke—A Hardworking Apprenticeship—A Start in Life—Offices of the Prudential Assurance Company—Greville Street—Lord Brooke's Murder—A Patron of Learning—Gray's Inn Road—Tom Jones's Arrival in Town—"Your Money or Your Life!"—Poets of Gray's Inn Road—James Shirley, the Dramatist—John Ogilby—John Langhorne—The "Blue Lion"—Fox Court—The Unfortunate Richard Savage . 542

CHAPTER LXI.
THE HOLBORN INNS OF COURT AND CHANCERY.

Gray's Inn—Its History—The Hall—A Present from Queen Elizabeth—The Chapel—The Library—Divisions of the Inn—Gray's Inn Walks—Bacon on Gardens—Observing the Fashions—Flirts and Flirtations—Old Recollections—Gray's Inn Gateway—Two Old Booksellers—Alms for the Poor—Original Orders—Eggs and Green Sauce—Sad Livery—Hats off!—Vows of Celibacy—Mootings in Inns of Court—Joyous Revels—Master Roo in Trouble—Rebellious Students—A Brick Fight—An Address to the King—Sir William Gascoigne—A Prince imprisoned—Thomas Cromwell—Lord Burleigh—A Call to Repentance—Simon Fish—Sir Nicholas Bacon—Lord Bacon—A Gorgeous Procession—An Honest Welsh Judge—Bradshaw—Sir Thomas Holt—A Riot suppressed—Sir Samuel Romilly 553

CHAPTER LIV.
THE OLD BAILEY.

Origin of the Name—The Old Sessions House—Constitution of the Court in Strype's Time—The Modern Central Criminal Court—Number of Persons tried here annually—Old Bailey Holidays—Speedy Justice—A Thief's Defence—The Interior of the Old Court—Celebrated Criminals tried here—Trial of the Regicides—Trial of Lord William Russell—The Press-yard—The Black Sessions of 1750—Sprigs of Rue in Court—Old Bailey Dinners—The Gallows in the Old Bailey—The Cart and the New Drop—Execution Statistics—Execution Customs—Memorable Executions—A Dreadful Catastrophe—The Pillory in the Old Bailey—The Surgeons' Hall—A Fatal Experiment—The Dissection of Lord Ferrers—Goldsmith as a Rejected Candidate—Famous Inhabitants—The Little Old Bailey—Sydney House—Green Arbour Court and Breakneck Steps—Goldsmith's Garret—A Region of Washerwomen—Percy's Visit to Goldsmith . . 461

CONTENTS.

CHAPTER LXII.
THE HOLBORN INNS OF COURT AND CHANCERY (*continued*).

Ecclesiastics of Gray's Inn—Stephen Gardiner—Whitgift—Bishop Hall, the "Christian Seneca"—Archbishop Laud—William Juxon—On the Scaffold—The "Bruised Reed"—Baxter's Conversion—Antiquaries and Bookworms—The Irritable Joseph Ritson—John Britton—Hall and his "Chronicles"—Rymer and his "Fœdera"—The Original of "Tom Folio"—George Chapman—A Celebrated Translation—Oliver Goldsmith—A Library of One Book—William Cobbett—Holborn Town Hall—What are Inns of Chancery?—Furnivals' Inn—A Street Row—Sir Thomas More—Snakes and Eels—A Plague of a Wife—A Scene in the Tower—Scourges and Hair Shirts—No Bribery—Charles Dickens and "Pickwick"—Thavie's Inn—Barnard's Inn—The Old Hall—The Last of the Alchemists—A given Quantity of Wine—The "No Popery" Riots—Staple Inn—Steevens correcting his Proof Sheets—Dr. Samuel Johnson—A "Little Story Book"—Fire! Fire! 566

LIST OF ILLUSTRATIONS.

The Charterhouse, from the Square: from a View by
    Grey, published in 1804 384
The Exterior of the Hall, Charterhouse . . . 385
Charterhouse—The Upper Green, from a View taken
    in 1805 390
Charterhouse Square, from an Old Print . . . 391
Thomas Sutton, from an Engraving, by Virtue, of the
    Charterhouse Portrait 396
Street Front of the Fleet Prison 397
Courtyard in the Fleet Prison 402
Interior of the Fleet Prison—The Racket Court . 403
The last Remains of the Fleet Prison . . . 408
A Wedding in the Fleet, from a Print of the
    Eighteenth Century 409
Remains of Old Holborn Bridge, from a Sketch taken
    during the Alterations, 1844 414
Holborn Valley and Snow Hill previous to the Con-
    struction of the Viaduct 415
The Fleet Ditch near West Street, from a Sketch
    taken in 1844 420
The Old "Red Lion," from the Front—Back of the
    "Red Lion," from the Fleet—The Fleet Ditch,
    from the "Red Lion," from Sketches taken
    before the Demolition 421
Old Newgate 426
King Charles's Porter and Dwarf, from the Old Bas-
    relief 427
College of Physicians, Warwick Lane—The Quad-
    rangle 432
Cock Lane 433
The "Ghost's" House in Cock Lane . . . 438
The "Saracen's Head," Snow Hill, from a Sketch
    taken during its Demolition . . . 439
Door of Newgate 444
Burning of Newgate, from a Contemporary Print . 445
The Condemned Cell in Newgate . . . 450
The Old Sessions House in the Old Bailey in 1750 451
Cato Street, from a View published in 1820 . 456
Mrs. Brownrigg, from the Original Print . . 457
The Chapel in Newgate 462
Jack Sheppard's Escapes 463

Front of Newgate from the Old Bailey . . . 468
Surgeons' Hall, Old Bailey (1800) . . . 469
Jonathan Wild's House 474
Jonathan Wild in the Cart, from a Contemporary Print 475
Goldsmith's House, Green Arbour Court, about 1800 480
St. Sepulchre's Church in 1737, from a View by Toms 481
Porch of St. Sepulchre's Church . . . 486
Giltspur Street Compter (1840) 487
Map of Farringdon Ward Without (1750) . . 492
The Metropolitan Meat Market 493
Fleet Market, about 1800, from a Drawing in Mr.
    Gardner's Collection 498
Field Lane about 1840 499
The West End of St. Andrew's 504
Interior of St. Andrew's Church 505
St. Andrew's Church, from Snow Hill, in 1850 . 510
"Sacheverell" Cards, selected from a Pack illus-
    trating the reign of Queen Anne . . . 511
William Whiston 516
Ely House—The Hall, from Grose's "Antiquities"
    (1772) 517
Ely Chapel, from a View by Malcolm (1800) . 522
Ely House, from a Drawing made in 1772 . . 523
Middle Row, Holborn, from a Drawing taken shortly
    before its Demolition 528
Staircase in Southampton House . . . 529
Room of a House in Fulwood's Rents, after
    Archer 534
Drawing the State Lottery at Guildhall, from a Print
    of about 1750 535
Old Houses in Holborn, opposite Gray's Inn Road . 540
Bleeding Heart Yard 541
Leather Lane 546
Chatterton's House in Brooke Street . . . 547
The Hall of Gray's Inn 553
Gray's Inn Gardens (1770) 558
Barnard's Inn 559
Staple Inn 564
Doorway in Staple Inn 565
Exterior of Furnival's Inn (1754) . . . 570
Interior of Furnival's Inn, after Nicholls (1754) . 571

OLD LONDON
Charterhouse to Holborn

CHARTERHOUSE—THE UPPER GREEN. *From a View taken in* 1805. (*See page* 395.)

CHAPTER XLVII.

THE CHARTERHOUSE.

The Plague of 1348—The Origin of the Charterhouse—Sir Thomas More there—Cromwell's Commissioners—Prior Houghton—The Departure of the Carthusians from London—A Visit from the Grave—Effect of the Dissolution on the Charterhouse Priory—The Charterhouse and the Howards—Thomas Sutton—Bishop Hall's Letter and its Effect—Sutton's Death—Baxter's Claim defeated—A Letter from Bacon—Settlement of the Charterhouse : its Constitution—Sutton's Will—His Detractors—Funeral Sermon.

IN the year 1348 (Edward III.) a terrible pestilence devastated London. The dirt and crowding of the old mediæval cities made them at all times nurseries of infectious disease, and when a great epidemic did come it mowed down thousands. The plague of 1348 was so inappeasable that it is said grave-diggers could hardly be found to bury the dead, and many thousand bodies were carelessly thrown into mere pits dug in the open fields.

Ralph Stratford, Bishop of London, shocked at these unsanctified interments, in his zeal to amend the evil consecrated three acres of waste ground, called "No Man's Land," outside the walls, between the lands of the Abbey of Westminster and those of St. John of Jerusalem, at Clerkenwell. He there erected a small chapel, where masses were said for

the repose of the dead, and named the place Pardon Churchyard. The plague still raging, Sir Walter de Manny, that brave knight whose deeds are so proudly and prominently blazoned in the pages of Froissart, purchased of the brethren of St. Bartholomew Spital a piece of ground contiguous to Pardon Churchyard, called the Spital Croft, which the good Bishop Stratford also consecrated. The two burial-grounds, afterwards united, were known as New Church Hawe.

Stow, in his "Survey," mentions a stone cross in this cemetery, recording the burial there during the pestilence of 50,000 persons. In 1361, Michael de Northburgh, Bishop Stratford's successor, died, bequeathing the sum of £2,000, for founding and building a Carthusian monastery at Pardon Churchyard, which he endowed with all his leases, rents, and tenements, in perpetuity. He also bequeathed a silver enamelled vessel for the Host and one for the holy water, a silver bell, and all his books of divinity. Sir Walter de Manny, in the year 1371, founded here a Carthusian convent, which he called "The House of the Salutation of the Mother of God." This he endowed with the thirteen acres and one rod of land which Bishop Stratford had consecrated for burial, and, with the consent of the general of the order, John Lustote was nominated first prior. Sir Walter's charter of foundation was witnessed by the Earls of Pembroke, March, Sarum, and Hereford, by John de Barnes, Lord Mayor, and William de Walworth and Robert de Gayton, sheriffs.

The order of Carthusians, we may here remind our readers, was founded by Bruno, a priest in the church of St. Cunibert, at Cologne, and Canon of Rheims, in Champagne, in 1080 (William the Conqueror). Bruno, grieved at the sins of Cologne, withdrew with six disciples to the Chartreuse, a desert solitude among the mountains of Dauphine. A miracle hastened the retirement of Bruno. One of his friends, supposed to be of unblemished life, rose from his bier, and exclaimed, "I am arraigned at the bar of God's justice. My sentence is just now passed. I am condemned by the just judgment of God." Bruno died in 1101, and miracles soon after were effected by a spring that broke forth near his tomb.

"Not content," says a recent writer, "with the rigorous rule of St. Benedict, the founder imposed upon the order precepts so severe as to be almost intolerable, and a discipline so harsh, that it was long before the female sex could be induced to subject themselves to such repugnant laws. One of their peculiarities was, that they did not live in cells, but each monk had a separate house, in which were two chambers, a closet, refectory, and garden. None went abroad but the prior and procurator, on the necessary affairs of the house. They were compelled to fast, at least one day in a week, on bread, water, and salt; they never ate flesh, at the peril of their lives, nor even fish, unless it was given them; they slept on a piece of cork, with a single blanket to cover them; they rose at midnight to sing their matins, and never spoke to one another except on festivals and chapter days. On holy days they ate together at the common refectory, and were strictly charged to keep their eyes on the meat, their hands upon the table, their attention on the reader, and their hearts fixed upon God. Their laws professed to limit the quantity of land they should possess, in order to prevent the luxury and wealth so prevalent among the other orders. Their clothing consisted of two hair-cloths, two cowls, two pair of hose, and a cloak, all of the coarsest manufacture, contrived so as almost to disfigure their persons. Their rigorous laws seem to have prevented the increase of their order, for in the height of their prosperity they could not boast of more than 172 houses, of which five only were of nuns."

The London Charterhouse was the fourth house of the order founded in England, the first being at Witham, in Somersetshire, where Hugh, the holy Bishop of Lincoln, was the first prior. The grants to the new London monastery of the Carthusians were no doubt numerous; for, we find, among others enumerated in the "Chronicles of the Charterhouse," 260 marks given by Felicia de Thymelby, in the reign of Richard II., for the endowment of a monk "to pray and celebrate the divine offices for the souls of Thomas Aubrey and the aforesaid Felicia, his wife;" also a grant of one acre of land in Conduit-shote Field, near Trillemyle Brook, in the parish of St. Andrew, Holborn, lying between the pasture-land of the Convent of Charterhouse, the pasture of St. Bartholomew's Priory, and the king's highway leading from Holborn towards Kentish Town. The prior of St. John, Clerkenwell, also frequently exchanged lands, and we find the Prior of Charterhouse granting a trental of masses, to the end that "the soul of Brother William Hulles, the Prior of the Hospital of St. John of Jerusalem, might the sooner be conveyed, with God's providence, into Abraham's bosom."

"About the latter part of the fifteenth century," says an historian of the Charterhouse, "we find our convent the home of a future Lord Chancellor of England; for we read that Sir Thomas More 'gave himself to devotion and prayer, in the Charterhouse of London, religiously living there without vow about four years.'"

The Charterhouse had flourished for nearly three centuries in prosperity, its brethren retaining a good character for severe discipline and holy life, when the storm of the Dissolution broke upon them. Three of Cromwell's cruel commissioners visited the Charterhouse, and their merciless eyes soon found cause of complaint. In 1534 John Houghton, the prior, and Humfry Midylmore, procurator, after being sent to the Tower for a month, were released on signing a certificate of conditional conformity. The majority of the brethren refused to subscribe to Henry's supremacy. The exertions, however, of the Confessor to the Bridgetine Convent, at Sion House, gradually led the refractory monks to subscribe to the king's supremacy. In

April, 1535, the prior, Houghton, whose adhesion had been received with distrust, was arraigned on a vague charge of speaking too freely of the king's proceedings, and he and two other Carthusians, one a father of Sion, the other the vicar of Isleworth, were hung, drawn, and quartered at Tyburn. "As they were proceeding from the Tower to execution, Sir Thomas More, who was then confined for a similar offence, chanced to espy them from the window of his dungeon; and, as one longing in that journey to have accompanied them, said unto his daughter, then standing there beside him, 'Lo, dost thou not see, Megg, that these blessed fathers be now as cheerfully going to their deaths as bridegrooms to their marriage?' Not long after he followed their steps on his way to the scaffold."

The three heads were exposed on London Bridge, and the fragments of Prior Houghton's body were barbarously spiked over the principal gate of Charterhouse. The prior's fate, however, only roused the collective zeal of the brotherhood, and the very next month three more monks were condemned and executed. From the letter of Fylott, one of the king's assistant commissioners, we learn that though the Charterhouse monks claimed to be solitary, there had been found no less than twenty-four keys to the cloister doors, and twenty-two to the buttery. The monks plainly told the commissioners that they would listen to no preacher who denounced images and blasphemed saints; and that they would read their Doctors, and go no further.

The monks had not long to rest. In 1537 the Charterhouse brothers refused to renounce the Pope by oath, or acknowledge Henry as supreme head on earth of the English Church. Some of the order who had previously yielded now refused to obey, and were at once hurried to prison. The monastery was then dissolved, and Prior Trafford at once resigned. The majority of the monks consented to the surrender, the prior receiving an annual pension of £20, and the monks £5 each. Nine out of ten brothers, cruelly handled in Newgate, were literally starved to death. The survivor, after four years' misery, was executed in 1541.

"According to Dugdale," writes a Carthusian, "the annual revenues of this house amounted at the dissolution to £642 0s. 4d., whilst the united revenues of the nine houses of Carthusians in England were valued at the sum of £2,947 15s. 4¼d.

"Before the final departure of the convent from London, sundry miracles are said to have been wrought, and revelations to have been made, urging the brothers to abide in the faith, and to bear witness of the truth of the Christian religion at the expense of their lives. Unearthly lights were seen shining on their church. At the burial of one of their saints, when all things appeared mournful and solemn, a sudden flash of heavenly flame kindled all the lamps of their church, which were lighted only on great days; and a deceased father of the convent twice visited a living monk who had attended him in his last illness. The narrative of this last alleged miracle is given in the following letter, written by the favoured monk:—

"Item. The same day, at five of the clock at afternoon, I being in contemplation in our entry, in our cell, suddenly he appeared unto me in a monk's habit, and said to me, 'Why do ye not follow our father?' and I said, 'Wherefore?' He said, 'For he is entered in heaven, next unto angels;' and I said, 'Where be all our other fathers, which died as well?' He answered and said, 'They be well, but not so well as he?' And then I said to him, 'Father, how do you?'. And he answered and said, 'Well enough.' And I said, 'Father, shall I pray for you?' And he said, 'I am well enough, but prayer, both from you and others, doeth good;' and so suddenly vanished away.

"Item. Upon Saturday next after, at five of the clock in the morning, in the same place, in our entry, he appeared to me again, with a large white beard, and a white staff in his hand, lifting it up, whereupon I was afraid; and then, leaning upon his staff, said to me, 'I am sorry that I lived not till I had been a martyr.' And I said, 'I think that he, as well as ye, was a martyr.' And he said, 'Nay, Fox, my lord of Rochester, and our father, was next unto angels in heaven.' And then I said, 'Father, what else?' And then he answered and said, 'The angels of peace did lament and mourn without measure;' and so vanished away."

The remnant of the order sought refuge in Bruges. Returning in 1555, they were reinstated at Shene, near Richmond, by Cardinal Pole, but Elizabeth soon expelled them, and they fled to Nieuport, in Belgium, where they remained till the suppression of religious orders by Joseph II., in 1783. One of their chief treasures, an illuminated Bible, given the Shene monastery by Henry V., was in existence in the Tuileries in 1847.

The dissolution pressed heavily on the Charterhouse Priory, of which almost all that now remains is part of the south wall of the nave, incorporated in the present chapel. When the monasteries became lumber-rooms, stables, and heaps of mere history materials, Charterhouse was tossed (as Henry threw sops to his dogs) to John Brydges, yeoman, and Thomas Hale, groom of the king's "hales" and tents, as a reward for their care of Henry's nets and pavilions deposited in the old monastery. They retained the sacred property for three years, and then surrendered the grant for an annual pension of £10. The king then cast this portion of God's land to Sir Thomas Audley, Speaker of the House of Commons, from whom it passed to Sir Edward North, one of the king's serjeants-at-law, and a privy-councillor in high favour with the royal tyrant.

"But even he," says one historian, "was not free from Henry's suspicion and distrust, as the following anecdote will show:—One morning, a messenger from the king arrived at Charterhouse, commanding the immediate presence of Sir Edward at court. One of North's servants, a groom of the bedchamber, who delivered the message, observed his master to tremble. Sir Edward made haste to the palace, taking with him this said servant, and was admitted to the king's presence. Henry, who was walking with great earnestness, regarded him with an angry look, which Sir Edward received with a very still and sober carriage. At last the king broke out in these words: 'We are informed you have cheated us of certain lands in Middlesex.' Receiving a humble negative from Sir Edward, he replied, 'How was it then? did we give those lands to you?' To which Sir Edward responded, 'Yes, sire; your Majesty was pleased so to do.' The king, after some little pause, put on a milder countenance, and calling him to a cupboard, conferred privately with him for a long time; whereby the servant saw the king could not spare his master's service yet. From this period Sir Edward advanced still higher in the estimation of the king, and at his death received a legacy of £300, besides being included among the sixteen guardians appointed during the minority of his son, Edward VI. North was compelled to acknowledge Lady Jane Grey's right to the throne, but subsequently changed his opinions, and was one of the first to proclaim the Princess Mary queen. For his flexibility he was soon after re-elected to the Privy Council, and elevated to the peerage, 17th February, 1554, being then summoned to Parliament by the title of Baron North."

Sir Edward North conveyed Charterhouse to the Duke of Northumberland; but on the execution of the duke the house was granted again to Sir Edward North. In 1558, on her journey from Hatfield to London, Queen Elizabeth was met at Highgate by the Lord Mayor and corporation, and conducted to Charterhouse, where she stayed many days. In 1561 Elizabeth made another visit to Lord North, and remained with him four days. This visit is supposed to have crippled this nobleman, who lived in privacy the remainder of his days, but was, in compensation, appointed Lord Lieutenant of Cambridgeshire and the Isle of Ely. Lord North died in 1564; and his son Roger sold Charterhouse in 1565 to the Duke of Norfolk (without Pardon Chapel and Whitewell Beach) for £2,500, and for a further £320 eventually surrendered the rest of the estate.

"Here the duke," says the author of the "Chronicles of the Charterhouse," "resided till the year 1569, when he was committed to the Tower for being implicated in a conspiracy for the restoration of Mary Queen of Scots, and for engaging in a design of espousal between himself and fallen royalty. From the Tower he was released in the following year, and allowed to return to the Charterhouse; but he resumed his traitorous idea of marriage, and his papers and correspondence being discovered in concealment, some under the roof of his house, and others under the door-mat of his bedchamber, he was attainted of high treason, and again incarcerated in the Tower, on the 7th of September, 1571. This unfortunate nobleman suffered on the scaffold in the year 1572, when the Charterhouse, along with his other estates, escheated to the Crown. His son Philip, Earl of Arundel, was impeached in 1590, for also favouring Mary, and died in prison in the year 1595, most probably escaping by disease a more disgraceful and ignominious death by the hands of the executioner."

On the death of Mary Queen of Scots, that fair siren who had been so fatal to the House of Norfolk, Elizabeth generously returned the forfeited estates to the Norfolk family, Lord Thomas Howard, the duke's second son, receiving Charterhouse. The Howards flourished better under King James, who remembered they had assisted his mother, and he visited Charterhouse for several days, knighted more than eighty gentlemen there, and soon after made Lord Howard Earl of Suffolk. From this earl, Charterhouse—or Howard House, as it was now called—was purchased by that remarkable man, Thomas Sutton, the founder of one of London's greatest and most permanent charities.

"Of noble and worthy parentage, this gentleman," says the author of the "Chronicles of the Charterhouse," "descended from one of the most ancient families of Lincolnshire, was born at Knaith, in that county, in the year 1531. His father was Edward Sutton, steward to the courts of the Corporation of Lincoln, son of Thomas Sutton, servant to Edward IV.; and his mother, Jane, daughter of Robert Stapleton, Esq., a branch of the noble family of the Stapletons of Yorkshire, one of whom was Sir Miles Stapylton, one of the first Knights of the Garter, and Sir Bryan Stapylton, of Carleton, *tempore* Richard II., also a Knight of the Garter: 'ancestors,' as the learned antiquary, Hearne, justly observes, 'not so low, that his descent should be a shame to his virtues; nor yet so great, but that his virtue might be an ornament to his birth.' He was brought up for three years at Eton, under the tuition of Mr. Cox, afterwards Bishop of Ely, and two years in St. John's College, Cambridge.   In 1553, however, he removed from Cambridge, without having taken a degree, and became a student of Lincoln's Inn.   But here he did not remain long; his desire of travel increasing with his knowledge, and his principles (he being a member of the Anglican Church) compelling him to leave London, he determined to visit foreign parts.   He accordingly departed for Spain, and

had once held; and it appears that Mr. Sutton himself acted as a volunteer, and commanded a battery at the memorable siege of Edinburgh, when that city held out for the unfortunate Mary.   After a blockade of five weeks, the castle surrendered on the 28th May, 1573.   On his return from Scotland, Mr. Sutton obtained a lease of the manors of Gateshead and Wickham, near Newcastle.   This was the source of his immense wealth, for having 'several rich veins of coal,' which he worked with

THE CHARTERHOUSE, FROM THE SQUARE.   *From a View by G e, , pu lishe in 1804.*   (see p ge 389.)

having stayed there half a year, passed into Italy, France, and the Netherlands.   He is said to have taken a part in the Italian wars, and was present at the sacking of Rome, under the Duke of Bourbon. He returned to England in the year 1561, and through a recommendation from the Duke of Norfolk, he became secretary to the Earl of Warwick, who, 'in consideration of trewe and faithful service to us done by our well-beloved servant, Thomas Sutton,' appointed him Master of the Ordnance of Berwick-upon-Tweed, and granted him an annuity of £3 6s. 8d. for life.   When Lord Westmoreland's rebellion broke out in the North, the Earl of Warwick created Mr. Sutton Master-General of the Ordnance in that quarter, a post which he himself

great advantage, he had become, in 1585, worth £50,000.   The following year he left Newcastle for London, and assisted against the Spanish Armada, by fitting out a ship, named after himself, *Sutton*, which captured for him a Spanish vessel, worth £20,000.

"He brought with him to London the reputation of being a moneyed man, insomuch that it was reported 'that his purse returned from the North fuller than Queen Elizabeth's Exchequer.'   He was resorted to by citizens, so that in process of time he became the banker of London, and was made a freeman, citizen, and girdler of the City.

"Mr. Sutton, being now advanced in years, thought proper to retire from public life.   He relinquished his patent of Master-General of the Ordnance, and on the 20th of June following he executed a will, in which he surrendered all his estates in Essex to the Lord Chief Justice, Sir John Popham, and others (with power of revocation), in trust to found an hospital at Hallingbury Bouchers, in Essex, which place, as will be seen, he afterwards changed for London; and, 'as a proof of his trewe and faitheful heart borne to his dread sovereign, Queen Elizabeth, he bequeathed

insidious legacy-hunter and voluptuary whom the old poet has painted in the darkest colours, lived at this time in a house near Broken Wharf, and between Trig Stairs and Queenhithe, in Thames Street, an old City palace which had once belonged to the Dukes of Norfolk. The death of Sutton's wife seems to have first led the childless millionnaire to project some great and lasting work of charity. He was already surrounded by a swarm of carrion-crows, both from town and city, while a jackal

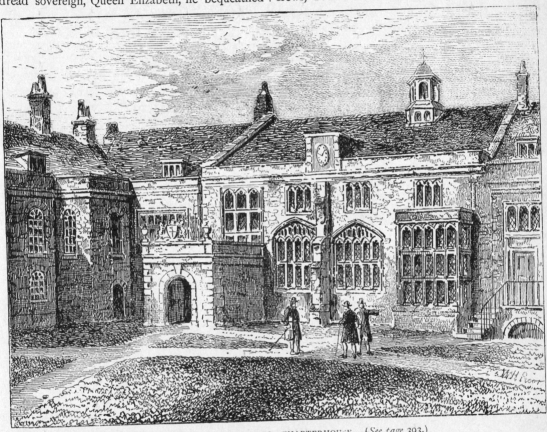

THE EXTERIOR OF THE HALL, CHARTERHOUSE. *(See page 393.)*

Her Majesty £2,000 in recompense of his over-sights, careless dealinge, and fearfulness in her service, most humbly beseeching her to stand a good and gracious lady to his poor wife.'" He also instituted a great many scholarships at Magdalen and Jesus Colleges, Cambridge; his generous will, in fact, being one long schedule of benevolent legacies.

Among other curious bequests in the interminable will of this great philanthropist, are the following:—£100 to the fishermen of Ostend, and £26 13s. 4d. for mending the highways between Islington and Newington, &c.

Sutton, who by many is thought to have been the original of Ben Jonson's Volpone, the Fox, that

pack of advisers followed untiringly at his heels. A Dr. Willet urged him to leave his money to the Controversial College at Chelsea, a ridiculous project encouraged by the king, or to assist James I. in bringing the water of the river Lea to London, by underground pipes.

The following passage in a letter from Mr. Hall, of Waltham, afterwards the celebrated Bishop of Exeter, served to fix the old man's determination :

"The very basest element yields gold. The savage Indian gets it, the servile apprentice works it, the very Midianitish camel may wear it ; the miserable worldling admires it, the covetous Jew swallows it, the unthrifty ruffian spends it. What are all these the better for it ? Only good use gives praise to earthly possessions. Hearing, therefore, you owe more to God, that He hath given you an heart to do good, a will to be as rich in good works as great in riches ; to be a friend to this Mammon is to be an enemy to God ; but to make friends with it is royal and Christian. . . . .

"Whatever, therefore, men either shew or promise, happy is that man that may be his own auditor, supervisor, executor. As you love God and yourself, be not afraid of being happy too soon. I am not worthy to give so bold advice ; let the wise man Syrach speak for me :—'Do good before thou die, and according to thine ability stretch out thine hand, and give. Defraud not thyself of thy good day, and let not the portion of thy good desires pass over thee. Shalt thou not leave thy travails to another, and thy labours to them that will divide thy heritage ?' Or, let a wiser than he speak, viz., Solomon :—'Say not, To-morrow I will give, if thou now have it ; for thou knowest not what a day will bring forth.' It hath been an old rule of liberality, 'He gives twice who gives quickly;' whereas slow benefits argue uncheerfulness, and lose their worth. Who lingers his receipts is condemned as unthrifty. He who knoweth both, saith, 'It is better to give than to receive.' If we are of the same spirit, why are we hasty in the worst, and slack in the better ? Suffer you yourself, therefore, good sir, for God's sake, for the Gospel's sake, for the Church's sake, for your soul's sake, to be stirred up by these poor lines to a resolute and speedy performing of your worthy intentions. And take this as a loving invitation sent from heaven by an unworthy messenger. You cannot deliberate long of fit objects for your beneficence, except it be more for multitude than want ; the streets, yea, the world is full. How doth Lazarus lie at every door ! How many sons of the prophets, in their meanly-provided colleges, may say, not '*Mors in ollá*,' but '*Fames !*' How many churches may justly plead that which our Saviour bad his disciples, 'The Lord hath need !'"

This letter fixed the wandering atoms of the old man's intentions. He at once determined to found a hospital for the maintenance of aged men past work, and for the education of the children of poor parents. He bought Charterhouse of the Howards for £13,000, and petitioned King James and the Parliament for leave and licence to endow the present hospital in 1609. This "triple good," as Bacon calls it—"this masterpiece of Protestant English charity," as it is called by Fuller, was also "the greatest gift in England, either in Protestant or Catholic times, ever bestowed by any individual."

Letters patent for the hospital were issued in June, 1611. Sutton himself was to be first master; but "man proposes, and God disposes." On December 12th of the same year Mr. Sutton died at his house at Hackney. His body was embalmed, and was borne to a vault in the chapel of Christchurch, followed by 6,000 persons. The procession of sable men from Dr. Law's house, in Paternoster Row, to Christchurch, lasted six hours. There was a sumptuous funeral banquet afterwards at Stationers' Hall, which was strewn with nine dozen bundles of rushes, the doors being hung with black cloth. Camden, as Clarencieux King of Arms, was on duty on the august

occasion. The sumptuous funeral feast in Stationers' Hall we have already mentioned.

But what greediness, envy, and hatred often lurk under a mourner's cloak ! The first act of Mr. Thomas Baxter, the chief mourner, at his cousin's funeral, was, as heir-at-law, to claim the whole of the property, and to attempt to forcibly take possession of Charterhouse. The case was at once tried, Sir Francis Bacon, Mr. Gaulter, and Mr. Yelverton appearing for the plaintiff, and Mr. Hubbard, Attorney-General, Mr. Serjeant Hutton, and Mr. Coventry arguing for the hospital. It was then adjourned to the Exchequer Chamber, where it was solemnly argued by all the judges of the land, except the Lord Chief Justice of the King's Bench, who was indisposed ; and, by Sir Edward Coke's exertions, a verdict was at last given for the defendants, the executors of Sutton. The rascally Baxter (although all impugners of the will were held by Sutton to forfeit their legacies) received the manor of Turback, in Lancashire, valued at £350 a year, a rectory worth £100, and £300 by will.

But the old man's money had still a greedy mouth open for it. Bacon, that wise but timid man, that mean courtier and false friend, was base enough to use all his eloquence and learning to fritter away, for alien purposes that would please and benefit the king, the money so nobly left. Hurt vanity also induced Bacon to make these exertions ; his name not having been included in Sutton's list of governors. Bacon's subtle letter opening the question is a sad instance of perverted talent. It begins—

"May it please your Majesty,—I find it a positive precept in the old law that there should be no sacrifice without salt ; the moral whereof (besides the ceremony) may be, that God is not pleased with the body of a good intention, except it be seasoned with that spiritual wisdom and judgment as it be not easily subject to be corrupted and perverted ; for salt, in the Scripture, is both a figure of wisdom and lasting. This cometh into my mind upon this act of Mr. Sutton, which seemeth to me as a sacrifice without salt ; having the materials of a good intention, but not powdered with any such ordinances and institutions as may preserve the same from turning corrupt, or, at least from becoming unsavoury and of little use. For though the choice of the feoffees be of the best, yet neither can they always live ; and the very nature of the work itself, in the vast and unfit proportion thereof, is apt to provoke a misemployment."

King James, though eager enough to lay his sprawling hands on the old man's money, which he had left to the poor of London, hardly dared to go so far as such a confiscation as Bacon had proposed ; but he dropped a polite hint to the governors that he would accept £10,000, to repair the bridge of Berwick-upon-Tweed, and this they reluctantly gave.

In 1614 the officers of the hospital were appointed, and the Rev. Andrew Perue chosen as master. Sutton's tomb in the Charterhouse Chapel being now completed, the corpse was carried there by torchlight on the shoulders of his pensioners and re-interred, a funeral oration being pronounced over the grave.

Malcolm gives the following summary of the property bequeathed in Mr. Sutton's will :—He left £12,110 17s. 8d. in legacies, and nearly £4,000 was found in his chest. His gold chain weighed fifty-four ounces, and was valued at £162. His damask gown, faced with wrought velvet, and set with buttons, was appraised at £10 ; his jewels at £59; and his plate at £218 6s. 4d. The total expenses of his funeral amounted to £2,228 10s. 3d., and his executors received, from the time of his decease to 1620, £45,163 9s. 9d.

At an assembly of governors in 1627, among other resolutions passed, it was agreed to have an annual commemoration of the founder every 12th of December, with solemn service, a sermon and "increase of commons," as on festival days. It was also decided that, except "the present physician, auditor, and receiver," no member of the foundation or lodger in the house should be a married man.

But the hospital had still another terrible danger to encounter. King James (who had no more notion of real liberty than an African king), at the instigation of his infamous favourite, Buckingham, demanded the revenues of Charterhouse to pay his army ; but Sir Edward Coke, who had saved the charity before, stepped to the front, and boldly repelled the king's aggression. The hospital at last reared its head serene as a harbour for poverty, an asylum for the vanquished in life's struggle. As an old writer beautifully says, " The imitation of things that be evil doth for the most part exceed the example, but the imitation of good things doth most commonly come far short of the precedent ; but this work of charity hath exceeded any foundation that ever was in the Christian world. Nay, the eye of time itself did never see the like. The foundation of this hospital is *opus sine exemplo*." A great school had arisen in London, as rich and catholic in its charity as Christ's Hospital itself.

The governors of Charterhouse are eighteen in number, inclusive of the master. The Queen and the archbishops are always in the list. The master was entitled to fine any poor brother 4s. 4d. or 8s. 8d. for any misdemeanour. He was to accept no preferment in church or commonwealth which would draw him from his care of the hospital.

The physician was to receive £20 a year, and not to exceed £20 a year for physic bills. The poor brethren were not to exceed four score in number, and were required to be either poor gentlemen, old soldiers, merchants decayed by piracy or shipwreck, or household servants of the king or queen.

Hearne, in his "Domus Carthusiana," a small 8vo volume published in 1677, shows that the world had not been kind to the founder's memory. Hearne, in his preface, says : " Sir Richard Baker, Dr. Heylin, Mr. Heylin, and Mr. Fuller say little of him, and that little very full of mistakes ; for they call him Richard Sutton, and affirm he lived a bachelor, and so by his single life had an opportunity to lay up a heap of money, whereas his dear wife is with much honour and respect mentioned in his will. Others give him bad words, say he was born of obscure and mean parents, and married as inconsiderable a wife, and died without an heir ; but then, to give some reason for his wealth (having no time nor desire to inquire into the means of his growing rich), to cut short the business, they resolve all into a romantic adventure. They say it was all got at a lump by an accidental shipwreck, which the kind waves drove to shore, and laid at his feet, whilst the fortunate Sutton was walking pensively upon the barren sands. They report that in the hulk coals were found, and under them an inestimable treasure, a great heap of fairy wealth. This I fancy may go for the fable, and his farming the coal-mines for the moral."

Percival Burrell, the preacher of Sutton's funeral sermon, thus describes the character of the generous man :—" He was," said the divine, "a great and good builder, not so much for his owne private as for the publicke. His treasures were not lavished in raysing a towre to his own name, or erecting stately pallaces for his owne pompe and pleasure, but the sustaining of living temples, the endowing of colledges, the enriching of corporations, the building causewayes, and repairing of high-wayes. Above all, the foundation of King James his Hospitall, at his sole and proper charge, were the happy monuments of his architecture. Surely this was to be a Megarensis in the best sense—that is, to build for ever. He did fulfill the letter of the apostle, in building *gold, silver, and precious stones;* for he commanded plate and jewels to bee sold and converted into money, for the expediting of our hospitall.

" I shall not mention thousands conferred upon friends and servants, but these legacies ensuing merit a lasting memory :—In the renowned University of Camb., to Jesus Colledge, 500 markes ;

to Magdalen, 500 pound; for the redemption of prisoners in London, 200 pound; for the encouragement of merchants, 1,000, to bee lent gratis unto ten beginners. Nor was his charity confined within these seas, but that western Troy, stout Ostend, shall receive 100 pound, for the relief of the poore, from his fountain. In all these his piety was very laudable; for in many of these acts of bounty, his prime repose was in the conscionable integrity of the priest, in those places where he sowed his benefits. Certes, this was to build as high as heaven."

CHAPTER XLVIII.

THE CHARTERHOUSE—(*continued*).

Archdeacon Hale on the Antiquities of the Charterhouse—Course of the Water Supply—The "Aye"—John Houghton's Initials—The Entrances—The Master's Lodge—Portraits—Sheldon—Burnet—Mann and his Epitaph—The Chapel—The Founder's Tomb—The Remains of Norfolk House—The Great Hall and Kitchens—Ancient Monogram—The Cloisters—The School—Removal to Godalming—Experiences of Life at Charterhouse—Thackeray's Bed—The Poor Brothers—A Scene from "The Newcomes"—Famous Poor Brothers—The Charterhouse Plays—Famous Carthusians.

IN a monograph on the Charterhouse, Archdeacon Hale, who held so long the post of master, entered deeply into its antiquities. "The monastery," wrote the archdeacon, in the *Transactions of the London and Middlesex Archæological Society* for October, 1869, "originally consisted of a number of cells, which, with the chapel, chapter-house, sacristan's cell, and little cloister, formed a quadrangle, to which some other irregular buildings were attached. The laundry was in the principal court; and near to it was the sacristan's washing-place, for washing the sacred utensils and vestments. The water-pipes entered under the cells on the north side of the quadrangle, and the water was received in an octangular building, and which is called the 'Aye,' the use and derivation of which word has not been discovered." The water was supplied by pipes running at the back of the cells, and the "lavoirs" were probably washing-places. The brewhouse is not shown in the old plan; its water-supply is only marked, and "the buttery-cock is shown without any building attached to it, whilst the water is described as passing on in two courses to the flesh-kitchen, one through the cloister, another through the gateway from the cistern at the kitchen-door, with a branch to a place or house called Elmys and the Hartes-Horne. We thus find two kitchens mentioned; the first denoted by the kitchen-door, and the remains of the second kitchen are to be found in the wall next the present gateway of the Charterhouse, formed of squares of flint and stone. The gateway of the old plan appears disconnected with the rest of the buildings, but it still exists." We have also the interesting fact, discovered by the diligence of Mr. Burtt, of the Record Office, that the Abbot of Westminster granted to the Prior and Convent of the Charterhouse three acres of land ("No Man's Land")

"probably a small piece by the wayside, the consideration for it being only the rendering of a red rose and the saying a mass annually for the sacred King and Confessor Edward."

The course by which the water was brought from Islington, across the fields, for the supply of the Charterhouse is shown in old vellum rolls, on which the course passes the windmill, of which the "Windmill" Inn, in St. John Street, was a remnant and a remembrance. The neighbouring Hospital of St. John was, in 1381, burnt by the Essex and Kent rebels, when the fire lasted seven days. The hospital does not appear to have been rebuilt before the end of the fifteenth century, and possibly the ruins of St. John's supplied some materials. Amongst other interesting fragments was the head of an Indian or Egyptian idol, which was found imbedded in the mortar amidst the rubble. The connection of the brethren of St. John of Jerusalem with the East suggests the idea that this little figure might have found its way to the Charterhouse from St. John's.

From a rough sketch accompanying Archdeacon Hale's paper, exhibiting the course of the conduit as it existed in 1624, it appears that "the 'Aye' in the centre of the quadrangle occupied by the monks had disappeared, and that, the water was brought to a reservoir still existing but now supplied from the New River instead of from the conduit. No record can be found of the time when this exchange took place. The drawing exhibits in a rude manner traces of buildings which still exist, as well as of those which were taken down for the erection of the new rooms for the pensioners some fifty years since. Three sides of a small quadrangle, an early addition to if not coeval with the building of the monastery, still remain; the windows and doorways give evidence of great variety of structure and of date, and the joints of the brickwork proofs of many alterations. There are letters on the west external wall, ' J. H.,' which we would willingly assume to be the initials of John Houghton, the last prior but one, and the wall itself as of his building. The cells of the monks, which were in the quadrangle, in the centre of which the conduit stood, have been all destroyed, with the exception of some few doorways still remaining. The buildings of the monastery now existing are on the south side of that quadrangle : they include the chapel, the small quadrangle above mentioned, and the courts of Howard House, including the Great Hall and the court called the Master's Court. At what time these buildings were erected between the ancient flesh-kitchen, the small quadrangle to the west, and the prior's lodgings on the north, has not been discovered. They were doubtless for the accommodation of strangers who resorted to and were received at the monastery. It has been said that much information respecting the temper and feelings of the people was obtained by Henry VII. from the knowledge which the Carthusian monks acquired through intercourse thus kept up with various classes."

Charterhouse Square has three entrances—Carthusian Street, Charterhouse Lane, and Charterhouse Street. The two first had originally each a gatehouse, and in Charterhouse Lane there was till recently a gate of iron surmounted by the arms of the hospital—arms that have never been blazoned with blood, but have been ever irradiated with a halo of beneficence and charity. Charterhouse Square is supposed to have been part of the ground first consecrated by Bishop Stratford, as a place of charitable burial. A town house belonging to the Earls of Rutland once adorned it, and in this mansion Sir William Davenant, wishing to win the gloom-struck Londoners from their Puritan severities, opened a sort of opera-house in 1656. Rutland Place, a court at the north-east corner of the square, still marks the spot, at the sight of which Cavaliers grew gayer, and Puritans sourer and more morose. A pleasant avenue of light-leaved limes traverses the square, for Charterhouse masters to pace under and archæologists to ponder beneath.

As we enter Charterhouse Square from Carthusian Street, the entrance to the old hospital is on the north side. The gateway is the original entrance of the monastery, and has been rubbed by many a monk's gown. This interesting relic is a Tudor arch, with a drip-stone, terminating in plain corbels. Above is a shelf, supported by two lions, grotesquely carved, and probably dating back to the early part of the sixteenth century. On the right stands the porter's lodge, on the left the house of the resident medical officer.

From the entrance court are two exits. The road straight from the entrance leads to the quadrangles, and the residences of the preacher, the reader, and other officers ; the left road points to the master's lodge, the hall, and the chapel. In the latter, turning under an archway leading to the principal court, is the entrance to the master's lodge. The fine hall of the lodge is adorned by a good portrait of the maligned but beneficent Sutton. In the noble upper rooms are some excellent portraits of illustrious past governors—men of all sects and of various fortunes. Prominent among these we note the following :—Black-browed, saturnine Charles II., and his restless favourite, George Villiers, second Duke of Buckingham ; the Earl of Shaftesbury, their dangerous Whig rival, and Charles Talbot, first Earl and afterwards Duke of Shrewsbury—a florid full-length, in robes of the Garter (the white rod the earl carries was delivered to him in 1714, by Queen Anne, with her dying hand) ; the ill-starred Duke of Monmouth, swarthy, like his father, in a long black wig, and in the robes of the Garter, and the charitable Sheldon, Archbishop of Canterbury, who is said to have expended more than £66,000 in public and private almsgiving, in relieving the sufferers by the Great Plague, and in redeeming Christian slaves from the Moors. The theatre Sheldon built at Oxford was a mark of his respect to the university, and a grateful remembrance of his time studiously spent as warden of the college of All Souls. There is also in an upper room a fine three-quarter length of the clever and learned but somewhat Darwinian divine, Dr. Thomas Burnet, who was elected Master of Charterhouse in 1685 ; he was the author of the "Sacred Theory of the Earth," a daring philosophical romance, which barred the rash writer's further preferment. As master, Burnet boldly resisted the intrusion of Andrew Popham, a Roman Catholic, into the house, by meddling James II. "Soon after Burnet's election," says Mr. Timbs, " James II. addressed a letter to the governors, ordering them to admit one Andrew Popham as pensioner into the hospital, upon the first vacancy, without tendering to him any oath, or requiring of him any subscription or recognition in conformity with Church of England doctrine, the king dispensing with any statute or order of the hospital to the contrary. Burnet, as junior governor, was called upon to vote first, when he maintained that, by express Act of Parliament, 3 Car. I., no officer could be admitted into that hospital without taking the oaths of allegiance and supremacy. An attempt was made, but without effect, to overrule this opinion. The Duke of Ormond supported Burnet, and, on the vote being put, Popham was rejected; and, notwithstanding the threats of the king and the Popish party, no member of the communion was ever admitted into the Charterhouse." This eccentric man—no relation of the great Whig friend of William of Orange—died in 1715. He appears here as a well-favoured man, in a black gown, and with short hair.

has over it a small tablet to Nicholas Mann, "Olim magister, nunc remistus pulvere." In the small square ante-chapel is a modern screen surmounted by the royal arms and those of the founder, Sutton. This ante-chapel is vaulted and groined; the bosses that bind the ribs being ornamented with roses, foliage, and shields, charged with the instruments of the Passion. The font is modern, and of the most Pagan period, contrasting painfully with the perpendicular of the ante-chapel, which bears the date 1512. The equilateral arch

CHARTERHOUSE—THE UPPER GREEN. *From a View taken in* 1805. (*See page* 395.)

An arched passage on the left of the master's court leads to Washhouse Court. A porch, surmounted by the royal arms, brings you to the great hall and kitchen, and a passage on the right conducts you to Chapel Court, which is surrounded by buildings to the south and west, by a piazza on the north, and by the chapel on the east. The chapel cloister consists of six Italian semi-classic arches, dull, clumsy, and exactly unsuited to the purpose of the place. Among the gravestones are those of a past organist, Richard John Samuel Stevens (1757), and Samuel Berdmore, master, (1802). Here also are memorials to three old Carthusians, Sir Henry Havelock, Thackeray, and John Leech. A door at the east end, leading to the ante-chapel,

at the east end, leading to the main chapel, is conjectured by the best authorities to have been the nave-arch of the original monastic church. It is filled up with a carved wooden screen, consisting of a series of pointed cinque-foiled arches.

The chapel is a thorough Jacobean structure, with the founder's tomb conspicuous in a proud position at the north-east corner, the rows of seats where the Charterhouse boys once sat with ill-concealed restlessness, and the pews of the old brotherhood arranged gravely by themselves. The present chancel, say the antiquarians, is part of the original nave. It is square, divided in the centre by two Tuscan pillars. An aisle (or, rather, recess) was added to the north side in 1826, and there is a

CHARTERHOUSE SQUARE. *From an old P int.* (*See page* 389.)

tower at the east end parallel with the ante-chapel. "The south wall alone is part of the original church; and it is supposed that the choir extended some way to the east beyond the present chapel." Behind a panel in the east wall the visitor is shown an aumbrye (cupboard), with some crumbling stone-work round it. "The pillars which divide the chapel in the centre support three semicircular arches, the keystones of which are embellished with the Charterhouse arms. The roof is flat, ceiled, and decorated after the style of the time of James I. At the west end, under the tower, is an open screen of wood, carved in a style corresponding with the date of the rest of the chapel. This supports a gallery containing the organ. Its principal orna-ments are grotesque, puffy-faced cherubim, helmets and swords, drums, and instruments of music; and in the centre is a shield, tied up with a thick cable charged with the arms of the hospital. The altar is of wood, and on each side in the corner of the chancel is a sort of stall, the one on the right being appropriated to the head-master, and that on the left to the second-master of the school."

The east window of five lights, filled with painted glass (the subject the Divine Passion), is the gift of the Venerable Archdeacon Hale, when master of the house. Another east window, represent-ing the Bearing of the Cross, was the result of a subscription among the boys themselves. In a southern window are some fragments of glass re-presenting the Charterhouse arms. "The pulpit and reading-desk," says the chronicler of the Charter house, "are against the south wall, as also are the master's and preacher's pews; the latter have small canopies over the seats allotted to them. The seats for the pensioners are open, and have at the side poppy-heads in the shape of greyhounds' heads, couped, ermine, collared gules, garnished and ringed, or, on the collar three annulets of the last, the crest of the hospital." The scholars formerly sat in the recess to the north.

"The founder's tomb on the north side of the chancel is a most superb specimen of the monu-mental taste in the reign of James I. It is composed of the most valuable marbles, highly carved and gilt, and contains a great number of quaint figures, of which the founder is the principal. His painted figure, in a gown, lies recumbent on the tomb. On each side is a man in armour, standing upright, supporting a tablet containing the inscription, and above is a preacher addressing a full congregation. The arms of the hospital are to be seen still higher, and above all a statue of Charity. It is also enriched with statues of Faith and Hope, Labour and Rest, and Plenty and Want,

and is surrounded by painted iron railings. The inscription is as follows :—

"Sacred to the glory of God, in grateful memory of Thomas Sutton, Esquire. Here lieth buried the body of Thomas Sutton, late of Castle-Camps, in the county of Cambridge, Esquire, at whose only costs and charges this hospital was founded and endowed with large possessions for the relief of poor men and children. He was a gentleman, born at Knaythe, in the county of Lincoln, of worthie and honest parentage. He lived to the age of seventy-nine years, and deceased the 12th of December, 1611."

This sumptuous tomb, still so perfect, cost £366 15s.

"In the return of the wall, opposite the founder's tomb, is a small monument to the memory of Francis Beaumont, Esq., formerly master of the hospital. He is represented kneeling before a desk, his hand resting on the Holy Scriptures, and habited in the costume of the period.

"The other monuments in the chapel are for the most part tasteless and inelegant; there are, however, a few exceptions. On the south wall is a full-sized figure of Edward, Lord Ellenborough, by Chantrey. He is represented sitting, in his robes as Chief Justice, with the following legend :—

"In the Founder's vault are deposited the remains of Edward Law, Lord Ellenborough, son of Edmund Law, Lord Bishop of Carlisle, Chief Justice of the Court of King's Bench from April, 1802, to November, 1818, and a Governor of the Charterhouse. He died December 13th, 1818, in the sixty-ninth year of his age; and, in grateful remembrance of the advantages he had derived through life from his education upon the Foundation of the Charterhouse, desired to be buried in this church."

The chapel contains monuments to Matthew Raine, one of the most eminent of the Charter-house masters; John Law, one of the founder's executors; Dr. Patrick, preacher to the house, who died in 1695; Andrew Tooke, master 1731; Thomas Walker, 1728; Dr. H. Levett, physician to the hospital in 1725; John Christopher Pepusch, organist to the house, and friend of Handel. In the Evidence Room behind the organ, in which the hospital records are kept, there are three doors, the three keys being kept by the master, the registrar, and one of the governors. A small door on the right of the cloisters communicates with a spiral staircase leading to the roof of the tower.

"The tower," writes a Carthusian, "is square, and is surmounted by a heavy Italian parapet, with a thing in the shape of a pinnacle at each angle. The whole is crowned with a wooden dome resting on pillars supporting semicircular arches. The dome carries on its top a vane representing the Charterhouse arms. Under this cupola is a bell, which bears the following legend :—

"T. S. Bartlet, for the Charterhouse made this bell, 1631."

In a vault beneath the chapel is the leaden coffin of Sutton, an Egyptian shaped case, with the date, 1611, in large letters on the breast, the face of the dead man being modelled with a square beard-case.

A small paved hall leading from the cloister is the approach to the great oak staircase of old Norfolk House, richly carved with shallow Elizabethan trophies and ornaments, the Sutton crest, a greyhound's head, showing conspicuously on the posts, probably additions to the original staircase, which is six feet wide, and consists of twenty-one steps. A large window midway looks into the master's court. The apartments of the reader are at the top of the staircase, on the right, and on the left an ante-chamber conducts to the terrace—a grand walk, eighty yards long, which commands a view of the green. Beyond this terrace, to the north, rises the great window of the hall of the new Merchant Taylors' school. The library, near the terrace, is a grave-looking room, containing a selection of divinity and old Jesuit books of travel, &c., given by Daniel Wray, Esq., whose portrait hangs over the fireplace.

The governor's room, part of old Norfolk House, which is next the library, is remarkable for its Elizabethan decorations, which are of the most magnificent description. " The ceiling," writes a Carthusian, " is flat, and is adorned with the armorial distinctions (three white lions) of Thomas, Duke of Norfolk, brilliantly painted and gilt. His motto, 'Sol a virtus invicta,' is inscribed on ornamental scrolls, tastefully arranged alternately with the date of the year (1838) in which this remnant of Elizabethan splendour was rescued from ruin. Previous to that time the emblazoned shields, which now glitter so brightly in gold and silver, were well-nigh obliterated with whitewash. The figures in the tapestry then presented a motley mixture of indistinguishable objects ; half of the beautifully-carved cornice which now supports the ceiling had vanished. The paintings of the ceiling consist of the following :—In the intercolumniations of the four pillars which form the basement are arabesque shields, containing paintings of Mars and Minerva, and over the space for the stove, representations of Faith, Hope, and Charity. Above this is a shield, charged with Mr. Sutton's arms, with his initials, T. S., one on each side. A large oval, containing the royal arms, supports this, with the emblems of the four evangelists in the spandrils formed by the square panel, of which it is the centre. On each side is an arch, supported by Ionic pillars, upon which are ovals, in which are portraits of the twelve apostles. The colours used are black, red, and gold. In this room

there are four square-headed windows, of five, four, and two lights, transomed.

" The tapestry on the walls consist of six pieces—three of large dimensions, the subjects of which are not known, though many conjectures have been hazarded. The largest piece represents a king, sitting enthroned, crowned, and sceptred ; behind him is a woman in plain attire, whilst at his feet kneels a queen, who is followed by a retinue, consisting of two black men, carrying a cushion, upon which rests a model of a fortress, another bearing the key of this citadel, and other attendants. This has been taken for the siege of Calais, and also the siege of Troy. The last supposition is, that it is a representation of the visit of the Queen of Sheba to Solomon. A second piece has been supposed to represent David, armed by Saul, in the act of sallying forth to meet 'the uncircumcised Philistine.' Two armies are seen in the background. Another appears to be a mixture of Scriptural subjects. A scene in the foreground does not much differ from the account of Deborah with Sisera's head, whilst the death of Abimelech is depicted behind. Three other pieces, containing figures of men, some of which are crowned, all which bear a striking resemblance the one to the other, seem intended for the judges and kings of Israel. Similar illustrations are not unfrequently found in ancient Bibles. "

Descending the great staircase we enter the great Hall, the most ancient of the buildings dating subsequent to the Reformation, the west wall being part of the old convent. This wall, the local antiquaries think, was rebuilt by Sir Edward North. The unfortunate Duke of Norfolk, it is *supposed*, lifted the roof of the hall higher, to make room for a new music-gallery. Its date, 1571, marks the time when he was released from the Tower on a kind of furlough, and employed himself here on such improvements as this. The carving is executed with extreme care and finish. A small side-gallery leads to the great staircase. The room is lighted by three large windows with some stained glass, and there is a lantern in the roof.

" In the windows are some curious fragments of stained glass. One pane contains the arms of the Lord Protector, Duke of Somerset, encirclech by the garter ; another contains a collection of pieces, the subject of which is rather ambiguous, the chief objects being a woman walking over a bridge, two horsemen galloping through the water underneath, a ship, the crown of Spain, the arms of Castile and Arragon, and the date, 1670. A third pane displays the arms of the founder, Sutton.

" The chimney-piece was an addition by Mr.

Sutton, and is of later date than any other part of the building. It is carved in stone, but is of grotesque design, consisting of imaginary scrolls in the style of the Rénaissance school. The arms of the founder, surmounted by helmet, mantlings, and crest, complete, are well executed ; as also are two small pieces of ordnance on each side, which are boldly yet accurately wrought. Beneath these, and in the centre above the space allotted to the stove, is an oval, upon which is carved a dragon, or some fabulous monster. It is now," adds Carthusian (1847), "very much mutilated.

"One thing yet remains to be spoken of, and that is the noble portrait of Mr. Sutton at the upper end of the hall. He is represented dressed in a black gown, sitting in an antique high-backed chair, and holding in his right hand the ground-plan of the Charterhouse. . . . . The room is now used as a dining-hall for the pensioners, and the banquet is held here on the ever-memorable 12th of December," Founder's Day.

A door on the right opens into the upper hall, a small, low room, adorned by a carved stone chimney-piece, with the founder's arms sculptured above. The windows are square-headed. It is traditionally supposed to be the former refectory of the lay brothers of the monastery. It was latterly used as a dining-hall for the foundation scholars. A massive door at one corner opens into the cloister.

A door in the Great Hall, under the music-gallery, opens into a stone passage, on the right of which were the apartments of the manciple. On the left there is an opening into the Master's Court, and in the centre are three doorways with depressed square-headed Tudor arches, the spandrils being filled with roses, foliage, and angels bearing shields.

The great kitchen boasts a fireplace, at which fifteen sirloins could be roasted at the same time. In one of the stones of the pavement there are brass rivets remaining, which once fastened down the monumental brass of some Carthusian brother.

Returning through the master's court and the entrance court, on our way to the court of the pensioners, we pass a gateway, older than the outer one already described. It has a four-centred arch, but no mouldings or drip-stone. The wall built over it for some height terminates in a horizontal parapet, supported by a plain corbel table. The rough unhewn stone of a wall to the right proves it, according to antiquaries, to have been part of the old monastic building. "The letters 'I. H.,' says Carthusian (1847), "with a cross of Calvary, which are worked into the wall, prove the ecclesiastical character of its former inmates. The letters 'I. H.,' worked out in red brick on the

wall, have been a matter of some discussion. Some have supposed them to be the two first letters of our Saviour's monogram, but, upon close examination, it will be found that there are no traces of the final S. The arch beneath, over which is the cross of Calvary, must have had its meaning. It has been suggested that it is the entrance to a burial crypt, and that the letters 'I. H.' are the initials of the unfortunate Prior Houghton, interred in the vault beneath. A doorway on the right opens into the Abbot's Court. This was called, at the period when Charterhouse was known as Howard House, by the name of the Kitchen Court. Subsequently it obtained the name of the Washhouse Court, and this was changed, some time since, for Poplar Court, on account of some poplar-trees which formerly grew there, but which so inconvenienced the buildings that they were removed a few years since. The name disappeared with them, and the court is now called by its former incorrect cognomen." This is the most solitary and the most ancient of all the Charterhouse courts. In one corner half an arch can be distinguished, and the square-headed windows are older than they seem.

The Preacher's Court, with its castellated and turreted modern buildings, was built in 1825, after the designs of Edward Blore, Esq. The preacher's residence is on the east side. One of the octangular turrets over the northern gateway of this court holds the bell, which rings regularly a quarter of an hour before the pensioners' meals, to call home the loiterers. Some of the poor brethren lodge on the west side. On the south and east sides runs a paved cloister, and at the south-east angle is the large west window of the governor's room, above which five shields are carved in stone. The northern gateway is a depressed Tudor arch, with spandrils filled with the Charterhouse arms.

The Pensioner's Court, also built in 1825, has three gateways, but no cloister or octangular tower. The one gateway opens into the stable-yard and servants' quarter, the second into the burial-ground, the third into the Scholars' Court. In this last, at the north-east angle, the head-master used to reside, while the matron occupied a house to the north, and the gown boys' butler sheltered himself cosily at the south-east corner lodge. The stones round the semicircular arch, on the east side, were thickly engraved with the names of scholars once on the foundation, and the date of their departure.

The foundation boys' school-rooms were called "Gown Boys," after their occupants, and consisted of a hall and a writing-school. The hall had an Elizabethan stone chimney-piece, and the ceiling was adorned with arabesque shields and scrolls. The scholars used to have all their meals but dinners here, and it was also a sitting-room for the "Uppers." The writing-school opposite, a square room, was part of the old school. The roof was upheld by wooden pillars, and ornamented with nine shields, charged with the armorial bearings. But this has all been pulled down.

Part of the cloister of the old monastery, which led to the fives-court of the Duke of Norfolk's palace, runs along the west side of the green, and above it is a terrace of old Norfolk House. This cloister formerly adjoined the monks' cells, as an ancient doorway still proves. The brick wall to the east bears the date 1571, the date of the music-gallery in the Great Hall, and the date of the duke's final imprisonment. The present cloister windows are mere square openings, and there seems to have formerly been a false flat roof. In the centre of the cloisters is an octagonal abutment, which has for generations been called by the boys "Middle Briars." The cloisters used to be the great resort of the football and hockey players, especially in bad weather. The Upper Green is three acres of grass-plot. The Under Green, formerly used by the "Unders," was bounded on the north by Wilderness Row, on the east by Goswell Street, on the south by the school and Upper Green, and on the west by the master's garden. Here there was a fountain, in a stone basin, in the centre of the lawn, which was divided by iron railings from the burial ground of the poor brethren.

In 1873 the greater part of the Charterhouse, including the school and grounds, was purchased by the Merchant Taylors' Company for £90,000, as a site for their school; and in 1874, on the completion of the new buildings, the boys were removed hither from the old Merchant Taylors' School in Suffolk Lane. The great school of the Charterhouse stood on a small hill which separated the two greens, and which was said to have been thrown up over the bodies of those buried during the plague in the reign of Edward. The head-master used to preside, at prayers, on a large seat, elevated on three steps, and regally surmounted by a canopy. There were five lesser thrones for the ushers and assistant-masters, with horseshoe seats before each, capable of seating sixteen boys. Six large windows, and a central octagonal lantern lit the room. At the east and west ends there were small retiring-rooms—little tusculums for masters and their classes. Behind the head-master's desk was another room. On the outer keystone of the arch the names of several of the head-masters were engraved—Crusins, 1719;

Hotchkis, 1720; Berdmore, 1755; Raine, 1778; Russell, 1803; Saunders, 1819.

On ground given by the governors of Charterhouse St. Thomas's Church and Schools were built, some years ago. The entrance to the school is in Goswell Street.

The Upper Green was the cricket-ground of the "Uppers." The gravel walk to the left was the site of the eastern cloisters. Two doorways of ancient cells still remain. Near one of them are two flat square stones, which tradition reports to have formed the foot of the coffin of a former inhabitant of the cell.

A door from the cloister on the right opens into a room called Brooke Hall, "named," says the author of "Chronicles of the Charterhouse," "after Mr. Robert Brooke, fourth master of the school, who was ejected for not taking the Solemn League and Covenant, but to whom, on the Restoration, this apartment belonged. Over the fireplace is an ancient portrait of a man reading, with the following motto inscribed on the sides :—

"And gladly would he learn, and gladly teach. 1626."

"This has occasioned many surmises and suppositions. Some suppose it to be a likeness of Brooke, while others assert that neither the date nor the apparent age of the figure by any means agrees with the account received of that gentleman, who, it appears, was but a young man when admitted usher, in 1626. The last conjecture is that the portrait was either that of Nicholas Grey, the first schoolmaster, who resigned his place in 1624, or of his brother, Robert Grey, who ceased to be master in 1626. This room was used as a dining-room for the officers of the house."

On the eastern wall of what was called the Upper Green, between two doorways, is, in white paint, a large figure of a crown, with the word "Crown" under it. It is the spot where the "Crown" Inn formerly stood, says Carthusian. Tradition states that this was painted by the first Lord Ellenborough, when he was a boy in the school, as a sign-post for the boys to halt at when they played at coaches; and finding it there perfect when he visited the place as a man, he expressed a wish that it might be kept renewed. In the south-west corner of the green was an old tree, cut down about thirty years ago, which was called "Hoop Tree," from a custom among the boys of throwing their hoops into the branches when they broke up for the holidays. Hoop-bowling was a great game at Charterhouse, up to about 1825 or 1830; and some boys attained such proficiency, that they could trundle five or six hoops, or even more, at one time. At the north-east corner of the Under Green, now built over, was the "Coach Tree," so called from the boys climbing into it at certain times of the day, to see the coaches pass up Goswell Street, between Islington and St. Martin's-le-Grand. The site of St. Thomas's Church, Charterhouse, was the ground where boys scholars on the foundation. An extra half-holiday is given at Charterhouse when a Carthusian obtains distinction at either of the universities. The gown-boys were prohibited going out during Lent. The chapel-bell rings at eight or nine at night, to warn the pensioners. When one of the old men dies, his comrades are informed of his departure

THOMAS SUTTON. *From an Engraving, by Virtue, of the Charterhouse Portrait.* (*See page* 383)

who quarrelled were accustomed to give each other pugilistic satisfaction.

In the south-east corner of the green was the "Tennis Court," really a "Fives-Court."

The school, which moved to Godalming, for sanitary and other reasons, in May, 1872, was divided into seven forms, inclusive of the "shell," or transition state between the third and fourth forms. The very young boys were called "Petties." The present number of boys is 500, of which 55 are

by one stroke less being given than on the preceding evening. The number of strokes usually given is eighty, corresponding to the number of the old gentlemen in the black cloaks.

The following description of Charterhouse discipline and customs, from 1842 to 1847, was kindly communicated to us by Arthur Locker, Esq.:—

"I was," says Mr. Locker, "at the Charterhouse from 1842 to 1847. At that time Dr. A. P.

Saunders was head-master (since Dean of Peterborough); Rev. Oliver Walford was second-master (since dead); Rev. H. W. Phillott and Rev. F. Poynder were assistant-masters; Rev. C. R. Dicken, the reader, read the daily prayers in the chapel, and also taught in the school. While I was there the numbers of the school varied from about 150 to 180. Of these 44 (and, at one time, by a special privilege, 45) were foundationers, or gown-boys, who were fed, educated, and partially

fag or be fagged, and very often, in consequence, great bullies. The lower school (all subject to fagging) were the shell, the third, second, first forms, and the petties. In our house we had four monitors, who exercised some of the duties of masters. They could cane boys for breach of rules, and could put their names down in the black book; three insertions during one week in that volume involved a flogging; and the floggings, administered with long apple-twigs, were very severe. These moni-

STREET FRONT OF THE FLEET PRISON.   (See page 404.)

clothed, by the institution. Each governor (the governors were the leading men of the country, cabinet ministers, archbishops, &c.) selected a boy in turn, as a vacancy occurred, and the eligible age was from ten till fourteen. Most of the gown-boys were either aristocratically connected, or possessed interest with the higher class. The remainder of the boys, whose parents paid for their education, lived respectively in the three boarding-houses of Messrs. Saunders, Walford, and Dicken, and were called Sanderites, "Verrites," and Dickenites. There were also about twenty day-scholars. The upper school consisted of the sixth and fifth forms, which had the privilege of fagging; then came the fourth form, a sort of neutral class, neither allowed to

tors, and some others of the big boys, had little slips of rooms for their own use, called 'studies,' and each proprietor of a study had a study-fag, who, besides keeping his books free from dust and in good order, made his coffee, toasted his roll, washed his hair-brushes, &c. Boys rather liked this special service, as it saved them from the indiscriminate fagging inflicted by strangers. The cricket-fagging was the worst. I have been kept stopping balls behind a wicket for a fellow practising for five hours at a stretch, and beaten on the back with a bat if I missed a ball. Fagging produced laziness and tyranny among the big boys, and lying and deception among the little ones. The monitors, by the way, had a special set of fags called 'basinites,' whose business it was to take care that the basins were filled, towels dried, and soap ready in the monitors' bedroom, for they washed up-stairs. We washed in a public room, fitted up with basins.' The dietary arrangements at Charterhouse were under the management of a jolly old red-faced gentleman named Tucker, who had formerly been in the army. He was called the 'Manciple.' The food was very good; and on Fridays (perhaps as a protest against Roman Catholicism) we fared especially well. Friday was styled 'Consolation Day,' and we had roast lamb and currant tart, or roast pork and apple tart, according to the season of the year. We *said* our lessons in a large building called the New School, in the centre of the two greens; but we learnt our lessons, and had for an in-door playing-place a writing-school of our own. Here, from eight till nine o'clock every evening, one of the masters kept 'banco'—that is to say, everybody was bound to be quiet for one hour, though they might read story-books, or do what they pleased. We were locked up at night in our bedrooms, the windows of which were further secured by iron bars. The doors were unfastened at seven o'clock, and school began at eight. Cricket was the chief game in the summer quarter; during the rest of the year we had football and hockey. Fives was also played in one of the courts, but tops and marbles were discountenanced, as savouring (heaven save the mark!) of private schools. As a rule, boys are very conventional and narrow-minded. We were kept quite apart from the eighty old pensioners, or 'codds,' as they were called, and only saw them on Sundays and saints' days in chapel. I remember two in whom we felt an interest—Mr. Moncrieff, the dramatist; and a Mr. Bayzand (or some such name), who had been a harlequin, but who at fourscore had grown a very decrepit, unwieldy man. The upper form boys were allowed the privilege of going out from Saturday afternoon till Sunday evening, at nine p.m., provided they received an invitation from parents or friends, which invitation had to be submitted for approval to the head-master. The lower forms were allowed the same privilege every alternate Saturday. At all other times we were strictly confined to our own part of the premises; and many a time have we, imprisoned behind those gloomy walls, longed for the liberty of Goswell Street, the houses of which overlooked our under green.

"The great festival of the year was the 12th December, held in memory of our benefactor, Thomas Sutton, when, after a service in the chapel, a Latin oration was delivered by the head gown-boy, then going to college, and a collection put into the trencher-cap by the visitors who came to hear him. A hundred pounds, or more, was often thus collected. After this the old Carthusians dined together, and spent the rest of the evening at the house of the master (Archdeacon Hale). The master was supreme over the whole establishment, both boys and pensioners: he must not at all be confounded with the *school*-master. When a boy left school, his name was engraved on the stone wall which faced the school buildings, with the date of the year of his departure."

"In former times," says Mr. Howard Staunton, "there was a curious custom in this school, termed 'pulling-in,' by which the lower boys manifested their opinion of the seniors in a rough but very intelligible fashion. One day in the year the fags, like the slaves in Rome, had freedom, and held a kind of saturnalia. On this privileged occasion they used to seize the upper boys, one by one, and drag them from the playground into the school-room, and, accordingly as the victim was popular or the reverse, he was either cheered and mildly treated, or was hooted, groaned at, and sometimes soundly cuffed. The day selected was Good Friday, and, although the practice was nominally forbidden, the officials, for many years, took no measures to prevent it. One ill-omened day, however, when the sport was at the best, the doctor was espied approaching the scene of battle. A general *sauve qui peut* ensued, and, in the hurry of flight, a meek and quiet lad (the Hon. Mr. Howard), who happened to be seated on some steps, was crushed so dreadfully that, to the grief of the whole school, he shortly after died. 'Pulling-in' was thenceforth sternly interdicted."

Before the retirement, in 1832, of Dr. Russell (who was appointed to the living of Bishopsgate, the number of the school fell off from about 400 boys to something about 100 or 80, consequently many of the junior masters were dismissed.

The poor brothers of the Charterhouse (a very interesting feature of Sutton's rather perverted charity) are now eighty in number. They receive £36 a year, have comfortable rooms rent free, and are required to wear, when in bounds, a long black cloak. They attend chapel twice a day, at half-past nine and six, and dine together in the Duke of Norfolk's fine old hall. The only special restriction over the old brothers is the need of being indoors every night at eleven, and they are fined a shilling for every non-attendance at chapel—a rule that secures, as might have been expected, the most Pharisaic punctuality at such ceremonials. This respectable brotherhood used to contain a good many of Wellington's old Peninsular officers, now and then a bankrupt country squire, and now and then —much out of place—came the old butler of one of the governors.

Thackeray has immortalised his old school, about which he writes so fondly, and with that air of thoughtful regret that so marks his sadder passages: "Mention," says the great novelist, in "The Newcomes," "has been made once or twice, in the course of this history, of the Grey Friars' School—where the colonel, and Clive, and I had been brought up—an ancient foundation of the time of James I., still subsisting in the heart of London city. The death-day of the founder of the place is still kept solemnly by the Cistercians. In their chapel, where assemble the boys of the school, and the fourscore old men of the hospital, the founder's tomb stands—a huge edifice, emblazoned with heraldic decorations and clumsy carved allegories. There is an old hall, a beautiful specimen of the architecture of James's time. An old hall? Many old halls, old staircases, old passages, old chambers decorated with old portraits, walking in the midst of which we walk, as it were, in the early seventeenth century. To others than Cistercians, Grey Friars is a dreary place, possibly. Nevertheless, the pupils educated there love to revisit it, and the oldest of us grow young again for an hour or two as we come back into those scenes of childhood.

"The custom of the school is, that on the 12th of December, the Founder's Day, the head gown-boy shall recite a Latin oration, in praise *Fundatoris Nostri*, and upon other subjects, and a goodly company of old Cistercians is generally brought together to attend this oration; after which we go to chapel, and hear a sermon; after which we adjourn to a great dinner, where old condisciples meet, old toasts are given, and speeches are made. Before marching from the oration-hall to chapel, the stewards of the day's dinner, according to old-fashioned rite, have wands put into their hands, walk to church at the head of the procession, and sit there in places of honour. The boys are already in their seats, with smug fresh faces, and shining white collars; the old black-gowned pensioners are on their benches, the chapel is lighted, and founder's tomb, with its grotesque carvings, monsters, heraldries, darkles and shines with the most wonderful shadows and lights. There he lies, Fundator Noster, in his ruff and gown, awaiting the Great Examination Day. We oldsters, be we ever so old, become boys again as we look at that familiar old tomb, and think how the seats are altered since we were here, and how the doctor— not the present doctor, the doctor of *our* time—

used to sit yonder, and his awful eye used to frighten us shuddering boys, on whom it lighted; and how the boy next us *would* kick our shins during service-time, and how the monitor would cane us afterwards because our shins were kicked. Yonder sit forty cherry-cheeked boys, thinking about home and holidays to-morrow. Yonder sit some threescore old gentlemen-pensioners of the hospital, listening to the prayers and the psalms. You hear them coughing feebly in the twilight—the old reverend blackgowns. Is Codd Ajax alive? you wonder. The Cistercian lads called these old gentlemen 'codds,' I know not wherefore—I know not wherefore—but is old Codd Ajax alive? I wonder; or Codd Soldier, or kind old Codd Gentleman, or has the grave closed over them? A plenty of candles light up this chapel, and this scene of age and youth, and early memories, and pompous death. How solemn the well-remembered prayers are, here uttered again in the place where in childhood we used to hear them! How beautiful and decorous the rite! How noble the ancient words of the supplications which the priest utters, and to which generations of fresh children, and troops of bygone seniors, have cried 'Amen' under those arches! The service for Founder's Day is a special one, one of the Psalms selected being the thirty-seventh, and we hear—'23. The steps of a good man are ordered by the Lord: and he delighteth in his way. 24. Though he fall, he shall not be utterly cast down: for the Lord upholdeth him with his hand. 25. I have been young, and now am old: yet have I not seen the righteous forsaken, nor his seed begging bread.' As we came to this verse I chanced to look up from my book towards the swarm of black-coated pensioners, and amongst them—amongst them—sat Thomas Newcome.

"His dear old head was bent down over his prayer-book; there was no mistaking him. He wore the black gown of the pensioners of the Hospital of Grey Friars. His order of the Bath was on his breast. He stood there amongst the poor brethren, uttering the responses to the psalm. The steps of this good man had been ordered hither by Heaven's decree: to this almshouse! Here it was ordained that a life all love, and kindness, and honour should end! I heard no more of prayers, and psalms, and sermon after that." * * * *

And who can forget the solemn picture of the colonel's death? "One afternoon," says Thackeray, "he asked for his little gown-boy, and the child was brought to him and sate by the bed with a very awe-stricken face; and then gathered courage, and tried to amuse him by telling him how it was a half-holiday, and they were having a cricket match with the St. Peter's boys in the green, and Grey Friars were in and winning. . . . At the usual evening hour, the chapel bell began to toll, and Thomas Newcome's hands, outside the bed, feebly beat time; and just as the last bell struck, a peculiar sweet smile shone over his face, and he lifted up his head a little, and quickly said, 'Adsum,' and fell back. It was the word we used at school when names were called, and lo! he, whose heart was as that of a little child, had answered to his name, and stood in the presence of the Master."

At the Poor Brothers' celebration was formerly sung the old Carthusian melody, with this quaint chorus:—

> "Then blessed be the memory
> Of good old *Thomas Sutton*,
> Who gave us lodging—learning,
> And he gave us beef and mutton."

Among the poor brothers of the Charterhouse who have here found a refuge the rough outer world denied, the most justly celebrated was Stephen Gray, Copley medallist of the Royal Society, and a humble and patient resident here in the early part of the eighteenth century. This remarkable and now almost forgotten discoverer formed the subject of a lecture lately delivered at Charterhouse by Dr. Benjamin Ward Richardson, F.R.S., from which we derive the following facts:—The first time that Mr. Gray was known anything about was in the year 1692, when he was, perhaps, about the age of forty, and was living at Canterbury, pursuing astronomical studies. In that year he was known to have made astronomical inquiries as to certain mock suns which he saw. He then, in 1696, turned his attention to microscopes, and made one by melting a rod of glass, which, when the end was in a molten state, dropped off and formed a round solid globe, which acted as a powerful magnifier. That, however, was not sufficiently powerful, so he made a more powerful one by having a hollow globe of glass filled with water, and with this he was enabled to discover animalculæ in the water. The same year witnessed a great improvement of his in the barometer. It had been invented some years before, but Mr. Gray hit upon an ingenious method of taking an accurate reading of the instrument. In 1699 the same gentleman observed again mock suns in the heavens, and a halo round the true sun, but did nothing more than record the fact. His next step in science was to obtain a meridian line, after which, in about a couple of years, spots in the sun attracted his attention: Mr. Gray was one of the first observers of that phenomenon, and in 1706 he re-

corded an eclipse of the sun. From that time to 1720, not much was heard of either him or his discoveries, but in the latter year a letter was sent by Prince George to the Charterhouse, requesting that he might be admitted. After his admission to the charity he remained without doing much for some time, but at length he recommenced his labour by sending a paper to the Royal Society, denominated "Some New Electrical Experiments," and some little time after that he became known to Dr. Gilbert, a man of great research. Dr. Gilbert made several experiments with the magnet, as to its power of attraction; he also discovered that amber when rubbed would lead a balance-needle, and in prosecuting his inquiries further, found out that sealing-wax, resin, and glass possessed the same qualities, but that they were different from the magnet in many other respects. He therefore named them after the Greek word for amber (*electron*), thus bringing into use the word electricity. That was one of the men who took notice of Mr. Gray and his experiments. About this period some experiments were made with reference to repulsion and attraction by Mr. Gray, which were followed up by Sir Isaac Newton, during which the great philosopher discovered that small pieces of gold leaf and paper placed in a box with a glass lid would fly up to the lid when it was briskly rubbed. Mr. Gray then discovered if parchment, goldbeaters' skin, and brown paper were heated, they would all attract feathers towards them. A fir rod, with an ivory ball attached to it and placed in a cork, and the tube in a charged glass rod, would also produce the same result. That showed to the ingenious mind of Mr. Gray that electricity could be transmitted from one substance to another. Mr. Gray having discovered that electricity could be so transmitted, was led to try packthread as a conductor. Packthread was accordingly employed, and found to act very well as such a medium when used in a vertical position, but when in a horizontal one it would not carry any spark at all. This discovery was made in a barn by Mr. Granville Wheler, at Otterden House, near Faversham. The cause of the failure was owing to the fact that the current passed off up to the ceiling. The line was then suspended at distances by means of pieces of silk thread, and when that was done the current passed through to the end of the line. As silk thread was easily broken copper wire was employed, but with no better result, and by that means the discovery was arrived at that there were some bodies which carried off the electric current, and others which concentrated it. After this later discovery the first electric line in the world was made on Mr. Wheler's ground, and a message through a packthread, and attached to a charged glass rod, was sent a distance of 870 yards from the grounds of Mr. Wheler up to his garret window. Mr. Gray having thus made one of the grandest discoveries in the world, followed up his researches, and found out that it was not necessary to have contact to pass an electrical current. That was called induction, and some short time afterwards, in 1732, the Royal Society awarded their gold medal; and in the same year the recipient of the gold medal further contributed to science by discovering that water could be made a conductor, and also that resin could be made to act as a good insulator—a grand discovery, for without insulators we could not make much use of the electric current. In 1735 Mr. Gray also succeeded in obtaining the electric spark, which he did by means of a charged glass rod brought into contact with an iron bar resting upon bands of silk. After this period nothing much was heard of him, and his time was fast drawing to a close. Before that time, however, he invented a machine which he called his planetarium. It was a round box filled with resin, and a metal ball in its centre, over this was suspended a pith pellet, and if the pellet gyrated in a circle the ball was in the centre, but if it were not it would move in an elliptic. By such a means as that he thought he could show a complete planetary system. He was, however, mistaken, for the twirling of the pith pellet round the globe of metal was no doubt caused by the pulsation of the blood through the fingers. As a further proof of Mr. Gray's intellect, when he obtained the first spark of electricity, he prophesied that electricity generated by a machine would become as powerful as the same force in nature. That, no doubt, will soon be the case, for sheep and other large animals have been instantaneously killed by a machine weighing fifteen hundredweight.

With all the vices that superstition and laziness could engender, there can never be a doubt among tolerant men that learning owes a deep debt to the much-abused tenants of monasteries. Many great Biblical works and ponderous dictionaries were the products of the indomitable patience of those ascetic workers. The Carthusian order had at least its share of these sturdy toilers, whose life's silent but faithful labour was often summed up in an old brown folio. Among the more celebrated of these patient men we find Theobald English (beginning of the fourteenth century), who wrote the lives of all holy men, from the Creation to his own time; Dr. Adam (about 1340), whose works are now in the Bodleian, wrote the " Life of Saint

Hugh, Bishop of Lincoln," treatises and works on Tribulation and on the Eucharist; John Olvey (1350) wrote a book on the miracles of the Virgin; Prior Rock, who died in 1470, left dialogues, epigrams, and poems behind him, in MS. ; Thomas Spencer (1529) produced commentaries on St. Paul's Epistles; John Batmore, or Batmanson, prior in the sixteenth century, wrote against Luther and Erasmus; Prior Chauncey, of Bruges, who succeeded Houghton, wrote a " History of the Emigration of the Carthusians," and " Passio Octodecim Cartusianorum."

The allowance to each pensioner was originally £26 12s., paid in quarterly instalments. The scholars of the foundation were not to exceed forty. The schoolmaster and usher were not allowed to take in their houses more than sixty other scholars, " unless they entertained another under-usher out of their own means, to be dieted and lodged in the hospital." The entire internal economy of the establishment is vested in the master ; the manciple, or house-steward, provides the diet of the hospital.

Several histories of this noble foundation have been written, notably by Bearcroft, Hearne, and Smythe ; and more recently in the " Chronicles of the Charterhouse," by a Carthusian, to which we are indebted for many of the particulars here given.

" It was anciently the custom of the Charterhouse scholars to perform a dramatic piece on " Founder's Day." It appears, however, that there were other epochs set apart for conviviality and merriment, such as the 5th of November, the anniversary of the deliverance of the kingdom from the Popish plot. A play is still extant, entitled " A Dramatic Piece, by the Charterhouse Scholars, in memory of the Powder Plot, performed at the Charterhouse, Nov. 6th, 1732." The scene is the Vatican, and the characters represented are the Pope, the devil (in the character of a pilgrim), and two Jesuits. The plot is by no means uninteresting, and some passages evince considerable tact and experience." An attempt has been made to connect this play with a dramatist, Elkanah Settle by name, who died a pensioner of Charterhouse in 1724.

" Dr. Young," says the author of the " Chronicles of the Charterhouse," " in his epistle to Mr. Pope, refers to Settle's last days in the following lines:—

' Poor Elkanah, all other changes past,
    For bread in Smithfield dragons hissed at last ;
    Spit streams of fire to make the butchers gape,
    And found his manners suited to his shape.' "

" Mr. Settle finally obtained admission into Charterhouse, and there, resting from his literary labours, died in obscurity in the year 1724. The similarity of sentiment which appears between Mr. Settle's works and the play performed by the Charterhouse scholars, gives rise to a supposition that the latter was the work of Settle himself. The active part which Mr. Settle took in the famous ceremony of Pope-burning in the year 1680, agrees strictly with the ridicule which is laid upon his Holiness, when made to 'run away in a fright' in the said play, and the date of his

commenced by Bishop Wilson, of translating the Scriptures into the Manx language; Joseph Addison; Richard Steele; John Wesley, the founder of Wesleyan Methodism; Sir William Blackstone Dr. John Jortin; Dr. Martin Benson, formerly Bishop of Gloucester; Monk, late Bishop of Gloucester, one of our best Greek scholars; Sir Simon Le Blanc, one of the late Judges of the King's Bench. There was a time when this school could claim as her sons the then Primate of England, Dr. Manners

COURTYARD IN THE FLEET PRISON　(See page 408.)

death was only a few years anterior to the said performance; there can be but little or no doubt that it is a composition of the fallen bard, who, it is said, 'had a numerous poetical issue, but shared the misfortune of several other gentlemen, to survive them all.'"

"The register of Charterhouse," says Mr. Staunton, in his "Great Schools of England," 1869, contains the names of numerous pupils afterwards illustrious in various departments of public life. Among these may be noted Richard Crashaw, the poet; Richard Lovelace; Dr. Isaac Barrow; Dr. John Davies, Master of Queen's College, Cambridge; Dr. Mark Hildersley, Bishop of Sodor and Man, who completed the arduous task,

Sutton; the Prime Minister of England, the Earl of Liverpool; and the Chief Justice of England, Lord Ellenborough. The Lord Chancellor of Ireland, Lord Manners; Basil Montagu; Baron Alderson; Sir Astley P. Cooper; Sir Cresswell Cresswell, and General Havelock; Lord Justice Turner, and the late Sir Henry Russell, Chief Justice of the Supreme Court of Indian Judicature; Sir C. Eastlake, P.R.A.; William Makepeace Thackeray, the great novelist, and John Leech, the well-known artist, are proud names for Charterhouse. Other famous Carthusians"—but it will be seen that death has already played havoc with this list—"are Bishop Thirlwall, of St. David's, the historian of Greece, and his eminent

INTERIOR OF THE FLEET PRISON—THE RACKET COURT. (See page 413.)

rival, George Grote ; Dr. Waddington, Dean of Durham, and his brother Horatio Waddington, Secretary for the Home Department; the Earl of Dalhousie ; the Right Hon. T. Milner Gibson, M.P. ; Sir J. D. Harding, late Queen's Advocate ; the late Archdeacon Churton ; the late Dean of Peterborough ; the Dean of Christchurch ; Sir Erskine Perry ; Sir Joseph Arnould, Judge of the Supreme Court of Bombay, and the Rev. Thomas Mozley ; W. G. Palgrave and F. T. Palgrave ; Sir H. Storks ; Sir Charles Trevelyan ; Sir G. Bowen, and others.

In the head-monitor's room was long preserved the iron bedstead on which died W. M. Thackeray, and outside the chapel are memorial tablets to Thackeray, Leech, and Havelock, erected by fellow Carthusians.

The collection of pictures in the Charterhouse, besides those already noticed, includes a portrait of William, Earl of Craven, who fought bravely beside Gustavus Adolphus. The earl is supposed to have married James's daughter, the widowed Queen of Bohemia ; he gave a name to Craven Street, Strand, and lived on the site of the Olympic Theatre. The picture is a full-length, in armour. The old soldier wields a general's truncheon, and behind him spreads a camp. There are also portraits of Bishops Robinson, Gibson, Morley, and others.

CHAPTER XLIX.

THE FLEET PRISON.

An Ancient Debtors' Prison—Grievous Abuses—Star Chamber Offenders in the Fleet—Prynne and Lilburne—James Howell, the Letter-writer —Howard, the Philanthropist, at the Fleet—The Evils of Farming the Fleet—The Cases of Jacob Mendez Solas and Captain Mackpheadris —A Parliamentary Inquiry into the State of the Fleet Prison—Hogarth's Picture on the Subject—The Poet Thomson's Eulogy of Mr. Oglethorpe—The Fleet Prison before and after it was Burnt in 1780—Code of Laws enforced in the Fleet—The Liberty of the "Rules"—The Gordon Rioters at the Fleet—Weddings in the Fleet—Scandalous Scenes—Mr. Pickwick's Sojourn in the Fleet—Famous Inmates of the Prison.

IT is difficult to carry the mind back and imagine this old London prison, carted away in 1846, a building of nearly seven centuries' existence ; yet so it was. Stow, to whom a century was a mere trifle, traces it back, in his grave, unpretending way (condensing a week's research in a line), as early as Richard I., who confirmed the custody of his house at Westminster, and his gaol of the Fleet at London, to Osbert, brother of William Long-shampe, Chancellor of England. King John, also, says the same writer, handed over the same important, and, as one might perhaps be allowed to think, somewhat incongruous trusts, to the Archdeacon of Wells. The Fleet is proved to have been a debtors' prison as early as 1290, but it does not figure largely in London chronicles. It was probably as disgraceful and loathsome as other prisons of those early days, the gaolers levying fees from the prisoners, and habeas corpus, that Magna Charta of the unfortunate, being as yet unknown.

The Fleet Prison was formerly held in conjunction with the Manor of Leveland, in Kent, and appears in a grant from Archbishop Lanfranc as part of the ancient possessions of the See of Canterbury, soon after the accession of William the Conqueror. That it was burnt by Wat Tyler's men is only another proof of the especial dislike of the mob to such institutions. In Queen Mary's time some of the Protestant martyrs were con- fined here. Bishop Hooper, for instance, was twice thrust in the Fleet, till the fire at Gloucester could be got ready to burn his opinions out of him. His bed there is described as "a little pad of straw, with a rotten covering."

Strype says that about the year 1586 (Elizabeth) the suffering prisoners of the Fleet petitioned the Lords of the Council on the matter of certain grievous abuses in the management of the prison —abuses that were, indeed, never thoroughly corrected. It was the "middleman" system that had led to many evils. The warden, wishing to earn his money without trouble, had let the prison to two deputies. These men being poor, and greedy for money, had established an iniquitous system of bribery and extortion, inflicting constant fines and payments, and cruelly punishing all refractory prisoners who ventured to rebel, or even to remonstrate, stopping their exercise, and forbidding them to see their friends. A commission was granted, but nothing satisfactory seems to have come from it, as we find, in 1593, another groan arising from the wretched prisoners of the Fleet, who preferred a bill to Parliament, reciting in twenty-eight articles, the misdemeanours and even murders of the obnoxious deputy-warden. "The warden's fees in the reign of Elizabeth," says Mr. Timbs, "were—An archbishop, duke, or duchess, for his commitment fee, and the first week's 'dyett,' £21 10s.; a lord, spiritual or temporal, £10 5s. 10d.; a knight, £5; an esquire, £3 6s. 8d.; and even 'a poor man in the wards, that hath *a part at the box*, to pay for his fee, having no dyett, 7s. 4d.' The warden's charge for licence to a prisoner 'to go abroad' was 20d. per diem."

The fruitless martyrdoms of Tudor times had not-convinced such narrow-minded bigots as Laud of the folly of attempting to convert adversaries by force. The Fleet became the special prison for Star Chamber offenders, including many dogged Puritan lampooners and many generous champions of liberty, and even bishops were crammed into the Fleet for unorthodox conduct. Two of the most historical of the theoretical culprits were Prynne and Lilburne. The former tough old lawyer, for simply denouncing actresses, with a supposed glance at the Queen of Charles I., was taken from the Fleet to the pillory, to have his nostrils slit and his ears cut off—a revenge for which the king paid dearly, and gained an inexorable and pitiless foe. Lilburne, "free-born John," as he was called by the Republicans, was one of the most extraordinary men the dens of the Fleet ever contained, or the Fleet irons ever cramped. For reprinting one of Prynne's violent books, honest John, who afterwards fought bravely in support of his opinions at Edgehill and elsewhere, was whipped at the cart's tail from the Fleet to the pillory at Westminster. Even at the pillory he threw seditious pamphlets to the populace, and when he was gagged, to prevent his indignant orations, he stamped, to express his indignation. That pleasant letter-writer, James Howell, was also a prisoner here, from 1643 to 1647, when his glasshouse schemes failed, and on his return from his business travels in Italy and Spain. In a letter to the Earl of B—— he describes being arrested by five men armed with " swords, pistols, and bills;" and he adds, in his usual cheery way, "as far as I see, I must be at dead anchor in this Fleet a long time, unless some gentle gale blow thence, to make me launch out."

After the abolition of Laud's despotical Star Chamber court, in 1641, the Fleet Prison was reserved for debtors only, and for contempt of the Courts of Chancery, Common Pleas, and Exchequer. The prison was burnt down in the Great Fire, when the prisoners were removed for a time to Caroone House, South Lambeth, the mansion of the Netherlands ambassador in the reigns of Elizabeth and James.

Howard, the philanthropist, visited the Fleet for the first time in April, 1774, and, in his "State of the Prisons in England and Wales," speaks of it five years later, as clean and free from offensive odours. The building was burnt by the rioters in 1780, but was immediately rebuilt on the old plan. The new gaol is thus described by Howard :—

" At the front," he says, " is a narrow court. At each end of the building there is a small projection, or wing. There are four floors—they call them galleries—besides the cellar floor, called 'Bartholomew Fair.' Each gallery consists of a passage in the middle the whole length of the prison, 66 yards; and rooms on each side of it about 14½ feet by 12½, and 9½ feet high; a chimney and window in every room. The passages are narrow (not 7 feet wide) and darkish, having only a window at each end. On the first floor, the hall-gallery, to which you ascend by eight steps, are a chapel, a tap-room, a coffee-room (made out of two rooms for debtors), a room for the turnkey, another for the watchman, and eighteen rooms for prisoners. Besides the coffee-room and tap-room, two of those eighteen rooms, and all the cellar-floor, except a lock-up room to confine the disorderly, and another room for the turnkey, were held by the tapster, John Cartwright, who bought the remainder of the lease at public auction in 1775. The cellar-floor is sixteen steps below the hall-gallery. It consists of the two rooms just now mentioned, the tapster's kitchen, his four large beer and wine cellars, and fifteen rooms for prisoners. These fifteen, and the two before mentioned on the hall-gallery, the tapster lets to prisoners for from 4s. to 8s. a week. On the second floor (that next above the hall-gallery) are twenty-five rooms for prisoners; on the next gallery, twenty-seven. One of them, fronting the staircase, is their committee-room. A room at one end is an infirmary; at the other end, in a large room over the chapel, is a dirty billiard-table, kept by the prisoner who sleeps in that room. On the highest storey are twenty-seven rooms. Some of these upper rooms—viz., those in the wings—are larger than the rest, being over the chapel, the tap-room, &c. All the rooms I have mentioned are for Master's Side debtors. The weekly rent of those not held by the tapster is 1s. 3d., unfurnished. They fall to the prisoners in succession ; thus, when a room becomes vacant, the first prisoner upon the list of such as have paid their entrance-fees takes possession of it. When the prison was built, the warder gave each prisoner his choice of a room, according to his seniority as prisoner. If all the rooms be occupied, a new comer must hire of some tenant a part of his room, or shift as he can. Prisoners are excluded from all right of succession to the rooms held by the tapster, and let at the high rents aforesaid. The apartments for Common Side debtors are only part of the right wing of the prison. Besides the cellar (which was intended for their kitchen, but is occupied with lumber, and shut up) there are four floors. On each floor is a room about twenty-four or twenty-five feet square, with a fireplace ; and on the sides, seven closets or cabins to sleep in. Such of these prisoners as swear in court, or before a commissioner, that they are not worth £5, and cannot subsist without charity, have the donations which are sent to the prison, the begging-box, and the grate. Of them there were at one of my visits sixteen, at some other times not so many."

In 1726, the evils of farming the Fleet having increased to a disgraceful and perfectly unbearable pitch, a Parliamentary investigation took place, and Huggins, the farmer, and Bambridge, a low, greedy fellow, who was his lessee, were tried for murder. The examination of the witnesses led to some ghastly disclosures, which Hogarth, who was present, immortalised in a picture which at once made him celebrated. The following extract from the governor's report discloses infamous cruelty :—

" Jacob Mendez Solas, a Portuguese, was, as far as it appeared to the committee, one of the first prisoners for debt that ever was loaded with irons at the Fleet. The said Bambridge one day called him into the gatehouse of the prison called the Lodge, where he caused him to be seized, fettered, and carried to Corbett's the spunging-house, and there kept for upwards of a week ; and when brought back into the prison, Bambridge caused him to be turned into the dungeon called the Strong-room of the Master's Side.

" The place is a vault, like those in which the dead are interred, and wherein the bodies of persons dying in the said prison are usually deposited, till the coroner's inquest hath passed upon them. It has no chimney nor fireplace, nor any light but what comes over the door, or through a hole of about eight inches square. It is neither paved nor boarded ; and the rough bricks appear both on the sides and top, being neither wainscoted nor plastered. What adds to the dampness and stench of the place is its being built over the common shore, and adjoining to the sink and dunghill, where all the nastiness of the prison is cast. In this miserable place the poor wretch was kept by the said Bambridge, manacled and shackled, for near two months. At length, on receiving five guineas from Mr. Kemp, a friend of Solas's, Bambridge released the prisoner from his cruel confinement. But though his chains were taken off, his terror still remained, and the unhappy man was prevailed upon by that terror not only to labour gratis for the said Bambridge, but to swear also at random

all that he hath required of him. And this committee themselves saw an instance of the deep impression his sufferings had made upon him ; for, on his surmising, from something said, that Bambridge was to return again as warden of the Fleet, he fainted, and the blood started out of his mouth and nose.

" Captain John Mackpheadris, who was bred a merchant, is another melancholy instance of the cruel use the said Bambridge hath made of his assumed authority. Mackpheadris was a considerable trader, and in a very flourishing condition, until the year 1720, when, being bound for large sums to the Crown, for a person afterwards ruined by the misfortunes of that year, he was undone. In June, 1727, he was prisoner in the Fleet, and although he had before paid his commitment-fee, the like fee was extorted from him a second time ; and he having furnished a room, Bambridge demanded an extravagant price for it, which he refused to pay, and urged that it was unlawful for the warden to demand extravagant rents, and offered to pay what was legally due. Notwithstanding which, the said Bambridge, assisted by the said James Barnes, and other accomplices, broke open his room and took away several things of great value, amongst others, the king's Extent in aid of the prisoner (which was to have been returned in a few days, in order to procure the debt to the Crown, and the prisoner's enlargement), which Bambridge still detains. Not content with this, Bambridge locked the prisoner out of his room, and forced him to lie in the open yard, called the ' Bare.' He sat quietly under his wrongs, and getting some poor materials, built a little hut, to protect himself as well as he could from the injuries of the weather. The said Bambridge, seeing his unconcernedness, said, '—— him ! he is easy ! I will put him into the Strong-room before to-morrow !' and ordered Barnes to pull down his little hut, which was done accordingly. The poor prisoner, being in an ill state of health, and the night rainy, was put to great distress. Some time after this he was (about eleven o'clock at night) assaulted by Bambridge, with several other persons, his accomplices, in a violent manner ; and Bambridge, though the prisoner was unarmed, attacked him with his sword, but by good fortune was prevented from killing him ; and several other prisoners coming out upon the noise, they carried Mackpheadris for safety into another gentleman's room ; soon after which Bambridge, coming with one Savage, and several others, broke open the door, and Bambridge strove with his sword to kill the prisoner, but he again got away, and hid himself in another room. Next morning the said Bambridge entered the prison with a detachment of soldiers, and ordered the prisoner to be dragged to the lodge, and ironed with great irons. On which he, desiring to know for what cause and by what authority he was to be so cruelly used, Bambridge replied, it was by his own authority, and, —— him, he would do it, and have his life. The prisoner desired he might be carried before a magistrate, that he might know his crime before he was punished; but Bambridge refused, and put irons upon his legs which were too little, so that in forcing them on his legs were like to have been broken, and the torture was impossible to be endured. Upon which the prisoner, complaining of the grievous pain and straitness of the irons, Bambridge answered, that he did it on purpose to torture him. On which the prisoner replying that by the law of England no man ought to be tortured, Bambridge declared that he would do it first and answer for it afterwards; and caused him to be dragged away to the dungeon, where he lay without a bed, loaded with irons so close riveted, that they kept him in continual torture, and mortified his legs. After long application his irons were changed, and a surgeon directed to dress his legs; but his lameness is not, nor can be, cured. He was kept in this miserable condition for three weeks, by which his sight is greatly prejudiced, and in danger of being lost.

"The prisoner, upon this usage, petitioned the judges; and after several meetings, and a full hearing, the judges reprimanded Mr. Huggins and Bambridge, and declared that a gaoler could not answer the ironing of a man before he was found guilty of a crime, but it being out of term, they could not give the prisoner any relief or satisfaction."

Notwithstanding the judges' remonstrance, Bambridge, cruel and greedy to the last, did not release the captain from his irons till he had wrung from him six guineas, and indicted him for an imaginary assault. But the case of Captain David Sinclair, an old officer of courage and honour, was even a worse one. Bambridge, who disliked his prisoner, had boasted to one of his turnkeys that he would have Sinclair's blood. Selecting the king's birthday, when he thought the captain would be warm with wine, he rushed into Sinclair's room with his escort, armed with musket and bayonet, struck him with his cane, and ordered the men to stab the poor wretch with their bayonets if he resisted being dragged down to the Strong-room. In that damp and dark dungeon Sinclair was confined, till he lost the use of his limbs and also his memory; and when near dying he was taken into a better room, where he was left four days without food. In the case of Mr. John Holder, a Spanish merchant, the prisoner died from an illness produced by horror at the miseries of the Common Side to which he had been consigned.

Bambridge is said to have been the first gaoler of the Fleet who put mere debtors in irons. The old method of punishing drunken and disorderly persons in this prison was the stocks; while those who escaped, or tried to escape, were either set in tubs at the prison gate, or locked in their rooms for several days. This cruel gaoler seems to have defied even habeas corpus, to have stolen charitable bequests, and bribed or frightened the lawyers who came to defend ill-used prisoners. In the case of Sir William Rich, a prisoner who was unable to pay up his arrears for lodging, Barnes, a turnkey, tried to burn him with a red-hot poker; while the warden threatened to fire at him, struck him with a stick, and slashed at him with a hanger. Rich was then loaded with heavy irons, thrown into the dungeon on the Master's Side, and kept there ten days for having, almost unconsciously, in the midst of these cruelties, wounded Bambridge with a shoemaker's knife. For an application to the Court of Common Pleas Sir William had to pay £14, the motion costing him £2 13s. 7d. In another case the prisoner paid, at his entrance into the Fleet, to judges' clerks, tipstaff, and warden, £45 16s.

Although the rascally Huggins and the wretch Bambridge escaped with a fright and a short imprisonment, there is no doubt this Parliamentary inquiry eventually led to reforms in this vilely-managed prison. A picture by Hogarth of the Fleet Prison Committee was that painter's first real step to popularity. Sir James Thornhill probably obtained his son-in-law permission to sketch the scene, of which Horace Walpole says :—

"The scene is the committee. On the table are the instruments of torture. A prisoner in rags, half-starved, appears before them. The poor man has a good countenance, that adds to the interest. On the other hand is the inhuman gaoler. It is the very figure that Salvator Rosa would have drawn for Iago in the moment of detection. Villainy, fear, and conscience are mixed in yellow and livid on his countenance. His lips are contracted by tremor, his face advances as eager to lie, his legs step back as thinking to make his escape. One hand is thrust precipitately into his bosom, the fingers of the other are catching uncertainly at his button-holes. If this was a portrait, it is the most striking that ever was drawn; if it was not, it is still finer."

The poet Thomson, in his "Seasons," finds an opportunity to eulogise Mr. Oglethorpe, whose generous hatred of cruelty led to the formation of the Fleet Committee. With his usual high-toned enthusiasm for what is good, the poet sings :—

mitted here, as at another public-house. The same may be seen in many other prisons where the gaoler keeps or lets the tap. Besides the inconvenience of this to prisoners, the frequenting a prison lessens the dread of being confined in one.

THE LAST REMAINS OF THE FLEET PRISON.

"And here can I forget the generous band
    Who, touch'd with human woe, redressive search'd
    Into the horrors of the gloomy jail,
    Unpitied and unheard, where Misery moans,
    Where Sickness pines, where Thirst and Hunger burn,
    And poor Misfortune feels the lash of vice?

Howard, the philanthropist, describes the Fleet as an ill-managed prison, even in 1776.

"The prisoners," he says, "play in the courtyard at skittles, mississippi, fives, tennis, &c. And not only the prisoners. I saw among them several butchers and others from the market, who are ad-

On Monday night there was a wine club; on Thursday night a beer club; each lasting usually till one or two in the morning. I need not say how much riot these occasion, and how the sober prisoners, and those that are sick, are annoyed by them. "Seeing the prison crowded with women and children, I procured an accurate list of them, and found that on (or about) the 6th April, 1776, there were on the Master's Side 213 prisoners, on the Common Side 30, total 243; their wives and children were 475."

The Fleet after the fire of 1780 was rebuilt on the old plan. The floors of the cellar, the hall, and the first storey were stone, and arched with brick. The tapster still had all the cellar-floor. He and several of the prisoners kept dogs. The billiard and mississippi tables were, however, put down, and the *little code* of laws (referred to by Howard), was abolished.

The "little code of laws," eighteen in number, enacted by the Master-Side debtors, and printed

before eight, and to light the lamps all over the house. No person was to throw out water, &c. anywhere but at the sinks in the yard. The crier might take of a stranger a penny for calling a prisoner to him, and of a complainant twopence for summoning a special committee. For blasphemy, swearing, riot, drunkenness, &c., the committee was to fine at discretion. For damaging a lamp the fine was a shilling. They were to take from a new comer, on the first Sunday, besides the two shillings,

A WEDDING IN THE FLEET. *From a Print of the Eighteenth Century.* (*See page* 410.)

by D. Jones, 1774, established a president, a secretary, and a committee, which was to be chosen every month, and was to consist of three members from each gallery. These were to meet in the committee-room every Thursday, and at other times when summoned by the crier, at command of the president, or of a majority of their own number. They were to raise contributions by assessment; to hear complaints, determine disputes, levy fines, and seize goods for payment. Their sense was to be deemed the sense of the whole house. The president or secretary was to hold the cash, the committee to dispose of it. Their scavenger was to wash the galleries once a week, to water and sweep them every morning

"garnish," to be spent in wine, one shilling and sixpence, to be appropriated to the use of the house. Common-side prisoners were to be confined to their own apartments, and not to associate with these law-makers.

"The liberty of the rules, and the 'day rules' of the Fleet, may be traced," says Mr. Timbs, "to the time of Richard II., when prisoners were allowed to go at large by bail, or with a 'baston' (tipstaff), for nights and days together. This licence was paid at eightpence per day, and twelvepence for his keeper that shall be with him. These were day rules. However, they were confirmed by a rule of court during the reign of James I. The rules wherein prisoners were allowed to lodge were enlarged in 1824, so as to include the churches of St. Bride's and St. Martin's, Ludgate; New Bridge Street, Blackfriars, to the Thames; Dorset Street and Salisbury Square; and part of Fleet Street, Ludgate Hill, and Ludgate Street, to the entrance of St. Paul's Churchyard, the Old Bailey, and the lanes, courts, &c., in the vicinity of the above; the extreme circumference of the liberty being about a mile and a half. Those requiring the rules had to provide sureties for their forthcoming and keeping within the boundaries, and to pay a per-centage on the amount of debts for which they were detained, which also entitled them to the liberty of the day rules, enabling them during term, or the sitting of the courts at Westminster, to go abroad during the day, to transact or arrange their affairs, &c. The Fleet and the Queen's Bench were the only prisons in the kingdom to which these privileges had for centuries been attached." For certain payments favoured prisoners were allowed to be long absent; Charles Dickens tells a story of one old resident, whose heaviest punishment was being locked out for the night.

The Fleet was one of the prisons burnt by the insane rioters of Lord George Gordon's mob, in 1780. The polite rioters sent a notice the night before that the work must be done, but delayed it some hours, at the request of their restricted friends. The papers of the time mention only one special occurrence during the fire, and that was the behaviour of a ringleader dressed like a chimney sweep, whom every one seems to have insisted on dubbing a nobleman in disguise; or if not himself a nobleman, says a writer in the *Gentleman's Magazine*, an agent, at least, entrusted with his purse, to enlist conspirators and promote sedition. This quasi-nobleman had, however, more of foolhardiness than cunning in his composition, for he perched himself upon the tiles of the market-house, over against the Fleet Prison, as a mark for the soldiers to shoot at; and as he was on the opposite side of the roof to that where they were posted, at every discharge he popped up his head and assailed them with tiles, till a ball passing through the roof lodged in his heart and tumbled him down. He had gold in his pockets, it is true, but he had no commission, nor was he any other than a pilfering thief, who had well lined his pockets in what to him was a fair way of trade.

In the seventeenth and early part of the eighteenth centuries couples desiring to be secretly married came to the Fleet and King's Bench prisons, where degraded clergymen could easily be found among the herd of debtors to perform the ceremony.

In Charles I.'s time a chapel in the Tower (in the White Tower) was a favourite place for clandestine marriages. On Archbishop Laud stopping these illegal practices, hurried lovers then betook themselves to one of two churches at the east end of London—St. James's, Duke's Place, or Trinity, in the Minories. A register of marriages preserved at the former church proves that in twenty-seven years from 1664 nearly 40,000 marriages were celebrated. The fee seems to have fluctuated between two crowns and a guinea.

The Fleet Chapel was used for debtors' marriages till 1686, when the incumbent of St. James's, Duke's Place, Aldgate, being suspended by the Commissioners for Ecclesiastical Causes, made it popular as a place for other secret marriages; and the chapel becoming the haunt of dangerous lookers-on, the degraded clergymen of the prison and neighbourhood began to celebrate secret marriages in rooms of adjoining taverns, or in private houses adjacent to Fleet Street, Ludgate Hill, and the Mint, keeping registers, to give an appearance of legality, and employing touts, to attract and bring in victims.

Mr. J. C. Jeaffreson, in his valuable work, "Brides and Bridals," has taken great pains with this subject of Fleet parsons, and has ransacked all possible books, old or new, for information about them.

"Scanty particulars," he says, "have been preserved of about forty persons who were keepers of marrying-houses. Some of these persons were turn-keys, or subordinate officials, in the Fleet Prison, like Bartholomew Bassett, who was clerk of the Fleet Chapel, and tenant, at the exorbitant rent of £100, of the Fleet cellars, where marriages were solemnised secretly. It was at Bassett's office, or private chapel, that Beau Fielding married his first wife, before he fixed his affections on the Duchess of Cleveland. A few of the forty negotiators in wedlock were women, who had come into possession of a register and marrying business by inheritance. Most of them, however, had in the first instance been simple innkeepers, supplying the public with adulterated liquors before they entered the matrimonial trade.

"Standing in the chief thoroughfares or side-alleys and by-yards of the Fleet quarter, their taverns had signs, some of which still pertain to hostelries of the locality. For instance: 'The Cock,' near Fleet Bridge, and 'The Rainbow' Coffee House, at the corner of Fleet Ditch, were famous marrying-houses, with signs honourably known at the present day to frequenters of Fleet Street taverns. The 'Cock and Acorn,' the 'Fighting Cocks,' the 'Shepherd and Goat,' the 'Golden Lion,' the 'Bishop Blaze,' the 'Two Lawyers,' the 'Wheatsheaf,' the 'Horseshoe and Magpie,' the 'King's Head,' the 'Lamb,' the 'Swan,' the 'Hoop and Bunch of Grapes,' were some of the taverns in or near Fleet Street and Fleet Market, provided with chaplains and chapels, or private rooms, in which marriages were solemnised on every day and night of the year. William Wyatt—brother of the notorious and very successful Fleet parson, Walter Wyatt—was landlord, first of a public-house in Sea Coal Lane, and afterwards of the 'New Market House,' Fleet Lane, in both of which houses he drove a great trade, and flourished under his stately brother's patronage. The 'Hand and Pen' was a sign which proved so attractive to the generality of spouses, that after it had brought success in trade to one house, competitors of the original 'Hand and Pen' public-house adopted it. Joshua Lilley's 'Hand and Pen' stood near Fleet Bridge; Matthias Wilson's 'Hand and Pen' looked out on the Fleet Ditch; John Burnford's 'Hand and Pen' kept open door at the foot of Ludgate Hill; and Mrs. Balls had her 'Hand and Pen' office and registry of marriages within sight of the other three establishments of the same name. When Ben the Bunter married fair Kitty of Kent Street, he went to the 'Hand and Pen,' and was fast bound to his damsel by a stout and florid clergyman, for the moderate fee of half-a-crown."

A collection by some enthusiastic collector on this subject exists at the British Museum; he has illustrated a small poem called "The Humours of the Fleet," with many sketches of the low prison life. The following quotations paint the Fleet parson, and the noisy touts who wrangled for each new arrival, in bold colours:—

" Scarce had the coach discharged its trusty fare,
But gaping crowds surround th' amorous pair ;
The busy plyers make a mighty stir,
And whispering cry, 'D'ye want the parson, sir ?
Pray step this way—just to the " Pen in Hand,"
The doctor's ready there at your command.'
'This way !' another cries. ' Sir, I declare,
The true and ancient register is here.'
The alarmèd parsons quickly hear the din,
And haste with soothing words to invite 'em in.
In this confusion, jostled to and fro,
The inamoured couple know not where to go,
Till slow advancing from the coach's side,
The experienced matron came (an artful guide);
She led the way without regarding either,
And the first parson spliced 'em both together.
  *   *   *   *   *   *
Where lead my wandering footsteps now ?—the Fleet
Presents her tattered sons in Luxury's cause ;
Here venerable *crape* and scarlet cheeks,
With nose of purple hue, high, eminent,
And squinting, leering looks, now strikes the eye.
B—s—p of H—, once in the precincts call'd,
Renown'd for making thoughtless contracts, here

He reigned in bloated majesty,
And passed in sottishness and smoke his time.
Revered by gin's adorers and the tribe
Who pass in brawls, lewd jests, and drink, their days ;
Sons of low growling riot and debauch.
Here cleric grave from Oxford ready stands,
Obsequious to conclude the Gordian knot,
Entwin'd beyond all dissolution sure ;
A regular this from Cambridge ; both alike
In artful stratagem to tye the noose,
While wo. .en, 'Do you want the parson ?' cry."

A writer (May 29, 1736) gives the following account of what he witnessed during a walk through the Fleet quarter:—" Gentlemen, having frequently heard of the many abominable practices of the Fleet, I had the curiosity, on Sunday, May 23rd, to take a view of the place as I was accidentally passing by. The first thing observed was one J. L., by trade a carpenter (whose brother, it is said, keeps the sign of the B. and G.), cursing and swearing, and raving in the streets, in the time of Divine service, with a mob of people about him, calling one of his fraternity (J. E.), a plyer for weddings, an informing rogue, for informing against one of their ministers for profane cursing and swearing, for which he paid three pounds odd money ; the hearing of which pleased me much, since I could find one in that notorious place which had some spark of grace left ; as was manifested by the dislike he showed to the person that was guilty of the profanation of God's sacred name. When the riot was dispersed, I walked about some small time, and saw a person exceedingly well dressed in a flowered morning gown, a band, hat, and wig, who appeared so clean that I took him for some worthy divine who might accidentally have come out of the country, and as accidentally be making the same remarks with myself; but upon inquiry, was surprised at being assured that he was one T. C., a watchmaker, who goes in a minister's dress, personating a clergyman, and taking upon him the name of 'Doctor,' to the scandal of the sacred function. He may be seen at any time at the 'Bull and Garter,' or the great 'Hand and Pen,' with these words written, 'The Old and True Register,' near the 'Rainbow' Coffee House. Please to give this a place in your paper, and you will not only oblige one of your constant readers, but may prevent many innocent persons from being ruined. I am, gentlemen, your humble servant, T. L."

The Rev. Alexander Keith, who had been reader at the Rolls Chapel, and afterwards incumbent of a Mayfair proprietary chapel, a great place for illegal marriages, on being suspended, excommunicated, and committed to Fleet Prison for contempt, in 1743, wrote a pamphlet to defend his conduct. The following extract gives some curious examples of the sort of reckless and shameless marriages that were contracted :—

"As I have married many thousands, and, consequently, have on those occasions seen the humour of the lower class of people, I have often asked the married pair how long they have been acquainted. They would reply, some more, some less, but the generality did not exceed the acquaintance of a week, some only of a day—half a day. . . . . Another inconveniency which will arise from this Act will be, that the expense of being married will be so great, that few of the lower class of people can afford it ; for I have often heard a Fleet parson say that many have come to be married when they have had but half-a-crown in their pockets, and sixpence to buy a pot of beer, and for which they have pawned some of their clothes. . . . . I remember, once upon a time, I was at a public-house at Radcliff, which was then full of sailors and their girls. There was fiddling, piping, jigging, and eating. At length one of the tars starts up and says, '—— me, Jack, I'll be married just now ; I will have my partner !' The joke took, and in less than two hours ten couple set out for the Fleet. I stayed their return. They returned in coaches, five women in each coach ; the tars, some running before, others riding on the coach-box, and others behind. The cavalcade being over, the couples went up into an upper room, where they concluded the evening with great jollity. The next time I went that way, I called on my landlord and asked him concerning this marriage adventure. He at first stared at me, but, recollecting, he said those things were so frequent, that he hardly took any notice of them. 'For,' added he, 'it is a common thing, when a fleet comes in, to have two or three hundred marriages in a week's time among the sailors.' . . . . If the present Act, in the form it now stands, should (which I am sure is impossible) be of any service to my country, I shall then have the satisfaction of having been the occasion of it, because the compilers thereof have done it with a pure design of suppressing my chapel, which makes me the most celebrated man in this kingdom, though not the greatest." (See Keith's "Observations on the Act for Preventing Clandestine Marriages.")

"One of these comparatively fortunate offenders against the canons," says Mr. Jeaffreson, whom we have before quoted, "was the stately Dr. Gaynam, who lived for many years in Bride Lane, and never walked down Fleet Street in his silk gown and bands without drawing attention to his commanding

figure, and handsome though significantly rubicund face. Nothing ever put the doctor out of humour or countenance. He was on several occasions required to bring one of his marriage registers to the Old Bailey, and give evidence in a trial for bigamy ; but no gentleman of the long robe ever disturbed the equanimity of the shameless ecclesiastic, who, smiling and bowing courteously to his questioner, answered, ' *Video meliora, deteriora sequor*,' when an advocate asked him, 'Are you not ashamed to come and own a clandestine marriage in the face of a court of justice ?' Even when Walter Chandler beat him with a stick, the doctor took his caning with well-bred composure. The popular nickname of the doctor declared him the bishop of an extremely hot diocese, but his manner and language were never deficient in coolness.

*   *   *   *   *

"Mr. John Mottram, who bore for his arms a chevron argent, charged, with three roses between three crosslets, or,' used to marry couples within the walls of the Fleet, not in the chapel of the prison, but 'in a room of the Fleet they called the Lord Mayor's Chapel, which was furnished with chairs, cushions, and proper conveniences.' It is recorded in the *Weekly Journal*, respecting this establishment for weddings, 'that a coalheaver was generally set to ply at the door, to recommend all couples that had a mind to be marry'd, to the prisoner, who would do it cheaper than anybody.' Mr. Mottram could afford to be moderate in his charges, for he transacted an enormous amount of business. From one of its registers, it appears that he married more than 2,200 couples in a single year. He was a very obliging gentleman, and never declined to put on a certificate of marriage the date that was most agreeable to the feelings of the bride. On the occasion of his trial at the Guildhall, in 1717, before Lord Chief Justice Parker, it appeared that this accommodating spirit had caused him to enrich certificates of his own penmanship with dates prior to the day of his own ordination. Convicted of solemnising marriages unlawfully, Mr. Mottram was fined £200 ; but this misadventure did not deter him from persevering in his practices."

Lando was another of these rascals. "Whoever thinks meanly," says the author of "Brides and Bridals," "of the Reverend John Lando, whilom Chaplain to His Majesty's ship *The Falkland*, holds an opinion at variance with that gentleman's estimate of himself ; for Mr. Lando used to inform the readers of newspaper advertisements that he was a 'gentleman,' who had 'gloriously distinguished himself in the defence of his king and country,' and that he was 'determined to have everything conducted with the utmost decency and regularity' at his place of business, 'the New Chapel, next to the china shop, near Fleet Bridge, London. His charge for officiating at a wedding, and providing the happy couple with a 'certificate and crown stamp,' was a guinea. He 'was a regular bred clergyman,' in spite of the calumnious insinuations of his rivals ; and he was 'above committing those little mean actions that some men impose on people.' In his zeal for the welfare of society, he taught young people Latin and French at his chapel three times a week."

But how can we leave this den of misery and infamy without reminding our readers that some years ago a respectable inhabitant of Goswell Street, through the disgraceful duplicity of a person named Bardell, a lodging-house keeper, and the shameful chicanery of two pettifogging lawyers named Dodson and Fogg, spent many months among the sordid population of the Fleet? Need we say that the stout and respectable gentleman we refer to was no other than the celebrated Mr. Pickwick? On no occasion has Mr. Charles Dickens sketched a part of London with more earnest and truthful care.

"These staircases," says Mr. Dickens, describing what first met Mr. Pickwick's eye when he arrived at the Fleet, "received light from sundry windows placed at some little distance above the floor, and looking into a gravelled area bounded by a high brick wall, with iron *chevaux-de-frise* at the top. This area, it appeared from Mr. Roker's statement, was the racket-ground ; and it further appeared, on the testimony of the same gentleman, that there was a smaller area, in that portion of the prison which was nearest Farringdon Street, denominated and called 'the Painted Ground,' from the fact of its walls having once displayed the semblances of various men-of-war in full sail, and other artistical effects, achieved in bygone times by some imprisoned draughtsman in his leisure hours.

*   *   *   *   *   *

"It was getting dark, that is to say, a few gas jets were kindled in this place, which was never light, by way of compliment to the evening, which had set in outside. As it was rather warm, some of the tenants of the numerous little rooms, which opened into the gallery on either hand, had set their doors ajar. Mr. Pickwick peeped into them as he passed along, with great curiosity and interest. Here, four or five great hulking fellows, just visible through a cloud of tobacco-smoke, were engaged in noisy and riotous conversation over

half-emptied pots of beer, or playing at all-fours with a very greasy pack of cards. In the adjoining room some solitary tenant might be seen, poring, by the light of a feeble tallow candle, over a bundle of soiled and tattered papers, yellow with dust, and dropping to pieces from age, writing, for the hundredth time, some lengthened statement of his grievances, for the perusal of some great man whose eyes it would never reach, or whose heart it would never touch. In a third, a man, with his wife and a whole crowd of children, might be seen making up a scanty bed on the ground, or upon a few chairs, for the younger ones to pass the night in. And in a fourth, and a fifth, and a sixth, and a seventh, the noise, and the beer, and the tobacco-smoke, and the cards, all came over again in greater force than before.

" In the galleries themselves, and more especially on the staircases, there lingered a great number of people, who came there, some because their rooms were empty and lonesome ; others because their rooms were full and hot ; the greater part because they were restless and uncomfortable, and not possessed of the secret of exactly knowing what to do with themselves. There were many classes of people here, from the labouring man in his fustian jacket, to the broken-down spendthrift in his shawl dressing-gown, most appropriately out at elbows ; but there was the same air about them all—a listless, jail-bird, careless swagger, a vagabondish, who's-afraid sort of bearing—which is wholly indescribable in words ; but which any man can understand in one moment if he wish, by just setting foot in the nearest debtor's prison, and looking at the very first group of people he sees there, with the same interest as Mr. Pickwick did.

*   *   *   *   *   *

" In this frame of mind he turned again into the coffee-room gallery, and walked slowly to and fro. The place was intolerably dirty, and the smell of tobacco-smoke perfectly suffocating. There was a perpetual slamming and banging of doors as the people went in and out, and the noise of their voices and footsteps echoed and re-echoed through the passages constantly. A young woman, with a child in her arms, who seemed scarcely able to crawl, from emaciation and misery, was walking up and down the passage in conversation with her husband, who had no other place to see her in. As they passed Mr. Pickwick, he could hear the female sob ; and once she burst into such a passion of grief, that she was compelled to lean against the wall for support, while the man took the child in his arms and tried to soothe her.

A chapter on the Fleet Prison would be incomplete without some notice of the more eminent persons who have been confined there. Among these unhappy illustrious, we may mention the young poet Earl of Surrey, who describes it as "a noisome place, with a pestilent atmosphere." Keys was sent here, for daring to marry Lady Mary Grey, sister of the ill-starred Lady Jane; Dr. Donne, the poet, when a private tutor, for secretly marrying the daughter of his patron, Sir George by country gentlemen in Addison's time, died in the Fleet Prison (1644–5). Sir Richard was sprung from a good old Kentish family, but had become security for an embarrassed father-in-law. Wycherly, the rake and wit, was a prisoner in the Fleet seven years, but it did not tame him much. Francis Sandford, author of a genealogical history of great research, died in the Fleet, in 1693. Penn, the Quaker founder of Pennsylvania, was living in the Rules of the Fleet, in 1707 (Queen Anne).

REMAINS OF OLD HOLBORN BRIDGE. *From a Sketch taken during the Alterations,* 1844. (See page 418.)

More, whom he had met at Lord Chancellor Ellesmere's; Nash, the unhappy poet and truculent satirist, for writing *The Isle of Dogs,* a libellous play; Sir Robert Killigrew (1613), for talking to Sir Thomas Overbury, at his prison-gate at the Tower, on returning from a visit to Sir Walter Raleigh, then also buried alive in the river-side fortress, by James I.; the Dowager Countess of Dorset (1610), for pressing into the Council Chamber, and importuning King James I. Those sturdy martyrs of liberty, Prynne and honest John Lilburne, we have already mentioned. Sir Richard Baker, who wrote the "Chronicle," so much read Penn was at this time in debt, from a vexatious lawsuit with the executors of a quondam steward. He died in 1718. That clever impostor, Richard Savage, to be safe from his raging creditors, took lodgings within the Liberties of the Fleet, his almost tired-out friends sending him an eleemosynary guinea every Monday. Parson Ford, a convivial dissolute parson, and a relative of Dr. Johnson, died in the Fleet, in 1731, and his ghost, it was firmly believed, appeared to a waiter, as he was going down to the cellar of the old "Hummums," in Covent Garden. Robert Lloyd, the schoolmaster friend of Churchill, died in the Fleet

HOLBORN VALLEY AND SNOW HILL PREVIOUS TO THE CONSTRUCTION OF THE VIADUCT. (*See page* 419.)

in 1764; here, too, died, in 1797, the celebrated Miss Cornelys, of Soho Square.

Among the secret marriages in the Fleet we should not forget Churchill the poet, and Edward Wortley Montague. In 1821 the Fleet register books (1686–1754) were purchased by Government, and deposited in the Registry Office of the Bishop of London. The site of the Fleet Prison is now occupied by the Congregational Memorial Hall and Library, a large Gothic edifice, built in the year 1872, of which we shall have more to say hereafter.

CHAPTER L.

THE FLEET RIVER AND FLEET DITCH.

Origin of the Name—Rise of the Fleet—Its Course—Early Impurity—The Holeburne —Antiquities found in the Fleet—How far Navigable for Ships—Early mention of it—Clearing of the Fleet Valley—A Deposit of Pins—The Old Bridges—Fleet Bridge—Holborn Bridge—Historical Associations—Discovery of the Arches of the Old Bridge—Thieves' Houses—Pope on the " Fleet "—The River arched over—Floods on the Fleet—Disaster in 1846—The Fleet under the Main Drainage System—Dangers of Exploring the Sewer—A Strange Denizen of the Ditch— Turnmill Street and the Thieves' Quarter—West Street—Chick Lane—The Old " Red Lion " known as " Jonathan Wild's House."

THE name of this ill-used stream, once fresh and fleet, now a mere sluggish and plague-breeding sewer, is traced by some to the Anglo-Saxon *fleotan*, "to float;" and by others, to the Saxon *fleot*, or *flod*, "a flood." The sources of the river Fleet were on the high lands of Hampstead and Highgate, and the chief of them rise near Caen Wood. The Fleet was fed by the Oldborne, which rose, says Stow, "where now the Bars do stand," and ran down to Old Borne Bridge, and into the River of Wells or Turnmill Brook. The Fleet was also fed by all the springs of Clerkenwell, such as Clerkenwell itself, Skinner's Well, Fogg's Well, Tod's Well, Loder's Well, Rad Well (near the Charterhouse), and the Horse Pool, at Smithfield.

"The principal spring of the Fleet," says Mr. Pinks, "rises in a secluded lane at the rear of Caen Wood, the seat of Lord Mansfield; another is on the left of a footpath leading thence to Highgate; and the tiny brooklet formed by its waters communicates by a small arch with a reservoir, the first of seven storage-ponds, on different levels, belonging to the Hampstead Water Company. Another of the spring-heads rises in the midst of Caen Wood. All three springs are diverted so as to fill the reservoirs above mentioned, a small stream carrying off the redundant water, which is very trifling, except in wet seasons. A fourth spring flows from the Vale of Health, at Hampstead, in a narrow channel, to another of the reservoirs, which are connected by means of large pipes passing from one to another. At a lower level the main stream meanders through the fields between Haverstock Hill and Kentish Town, in a wide, deep, and rugged channel, indicating that a considerable body of water must have originally flowed through it with a rapid current. The name of Kentish Town, which was formerly a mere country village, is supplied by tradition, which ascribes its origin to the place being situated on the bank of a stream (the river Fleet) which rose among the hills about Caen or Ken Wood, and which was formerly called Ken or Caen Ditch, hence Ken Ditch Town, the Town of Ken Ditch, or Kentish Town. But the correctness of this etymology has been questioned by at least one historian. The Fleet passes on through Kentish Town, its course there being much hidden, and, flowing in a south-east direction, it passes under the Regent's Canal to St. Pancras, where, until the year 1766, when it was arched over, it bore the name of Pancras Wash. Running at the foot of the gardens in the rear of the houses in the Old St. Pancras Road, it arrives at Battle Bridge, and so makes its entrance into Clerkenwell. Following the line of the Bagnigge Wells Road, its covered course nearly coincides with the parochial boundary in this direction. Passing in an artificial channel alongside the western boundary wall of the House of Correction, its course lies beneath the valley between Turnmill Street and Saffron Hill; thence, under Farringdon Street and Bridge Street, emptying itself into the Thames on the western side of Blackfriars Bridge." It was called "the River of Wells" as early as the days of William the Conqueror.

The Fleet seems early to have become impure, and hardly fit to drink, for, in 1290 (Edward I.), the prior of a Carmelite house in Whitefriars complained of the noxious exhalations, the miasma of which had killed many of the hooded brethren, and the corruption of which overpowered the odours of the incense. The Black Friars and the Bishop of Salisbury, whose palace was in Salisbury Court, Fleet Street, also signed the same doleful petition. Mr. Pinks, with whom we do not in this case altogether agree, thinks that the Fleet was called the Holeburne, or burne of the Hollow, above Holborn Bridge; and the Fleet, between Holborn Bridge and its embouchure. The Holeburne is distinctly mentioned in Domesday Book.

In the register of the Nunnery of St. Mary, Clerkenwell, of the time of Richard I. or John, the oldest cartulary extant, mention is made of a meadow near Holeburne, and of a ditch that led from Holeburne to the mill of the nuns. The garden of the Hospitallers of St. John of Jerusalem was also situated upon the Holeburne, thus perfectly proving, says an ingenious writer in the *Gentleman's Magazine* for 1856, that Holeburne was only another name for that venerable and injured stream, the Fleet, the southern part of it, the mere embouchure (between Holborn Bridge and the Thames), probably always maintaining the name of Fleet, or Flood. Stow is therefore incorrect in his description of the imaginary stream, the old Bourne.

The same acute writer, who signs himself "T. E. T.," shows, also, that the word "Flete," referring to a special limited place, is used in the ancient book of the Templars' lands (1185) now in the Record Office; and the word "Flete Hithe," in the ancient "Liber A, sive Pilosus;" while in the first of King John, the Templars received the grant of a place upon the Flete, near Castle Baynard, to enable them to construct a mill, which was removed in the reign of Edward I., on the complaint of Henry Lacy, Earl of Lincoln, that it had lessened the breadth and depth of water under *Holeburne* Bridge and Fleet Bridge into the Thames. The holes that gave the Saxon name to the Holeburne are still marked by the sites of Hockley-in-the-Hole and Black Mary's Hole, Bagnigge Wells, both already described by us in previous chapters. The overflowing part of the Fleet, near its foul mouth, probably gave the name to the stream, as the same cause led to the naming the Fleets of the Trent; and the site of Paris Bear Garden, Southwark, now the parish of Christchurch, Surrey, was anciently called Widefleet, from the overflowing of the trenches at high tides, which formed a large stagnant backwater to a river that, from man's neglect and idleness, has probably caused the death of more Londoners than have been slain in English battles since the Conquest.

But turning back to earlier times, let us dive far below the deepest Stygian blackness of the Fleet Sewer. To see the antiquities found in the Fleet, which really deserves a daring discoverer's attention nearly as much as the Tiber, let us follow Mr. Pinks into the vast rag and bone shop of relics which his loving and patient industry has catalogued so carefully. During the digging and widening of the Fleet Ditch, in 1676, there, at a depth of fifteen feet were found the stray rubbish, bones, and refuse of Roman London. The coins were of silver, copper, and brass, but none of gold. The silver was ring-money, of several sizes, the largest as big as a crown, the smallest about the size of a silver twopence, every one having a snip in the edge. At Holborn Bridge, thrown away by spoilers or dropped by thieves, were two brass Lares (about four inches high), one a Ceres, the other a Bacchus, both covered with a petrified crust, but the stream had washed much of the oxydizing matter from the coins, "thrown away on the approach of Boadicea," says the vivacious and imaginative Pennant, his mind, like a true antiquary, of course reverting to the one special crisis of interest in ancient London story. The excavators also discovered in the miserly river various British and Saxon antiquities of interest—arrowheads, broad spur rowels, keys, daggers, scales, seals, with Saxon names, ships' counters, with Saxon characters, and medals, crosses, and crucifixes, of a later date. In the bed of the Fleet, at Black Mary's Hole, near the end of Baker Street, a ship's anchor, it is said, was found some years ago; and a correspondent in the *Gentleman's Magazine* (1843) describes a small anchor, three feet ten inches long, found in the Fleet Ditch, as then in the collection of Mr. Walter Hawkins, F.S.A.

In 1856 there was exhibited at the British Archæological Association a globular iron padlock, so constructed that the whole shackle could be drawn out when the bolt was thrown back. This was found in the Fleet Ditch, near the bottom of Holborn Hill. In 1857 the same association exhibited a jug of hard-baked pottery (the upper part covered with mottled green glaze), of the sixteenth century, found in 1854, in the ditch, near Smithfield. In 1838 a beautiful hunting-knife, of the seventeenth century, was found in the same dirty repository of "unconsidered trifles." The ivory haft was wrought with a figure of Mercury, with winged petasus, hunting-horn and caduceus. The blade was of the time of George I. About 1862 two target bosses, of latten, of the time of Henry VIII., were dredged up. In 1862 Mr. Gunston exhibited, at the British Archæological meeting, a rude penknife of the fifteenth, and one of the sixteenth century, both Fleet relics; also the carved wooden haft of a dagger, and a little knife, the bone haft carved with a female bust that resembled Catherine de Medicis; also a knife-blade, with a motto, and a Roman sharpening steel.

Stow says that before 1307 ten or twelve ships used to go up the Fleet to Fleet Bridge, "with divers things and merchandizes, and some of these ships went under the bridge unto Holborn Bridge." A "Process of Recognition," in third folio of the ancient "Liber A, sive Pilosus," containing the ancient evidences of the Dean and Chapter of St. Paul's, mentions Fleet Hythe as in the possession of Henry the Woodmonger, a man, says Mr. Pinks, mentioned in the great "Roll of the Pipe" for the 31st of Henry I., and also in the "Registrum de Clerkenwell," as one of the earliest donors to the Clerkenwell nunnery. The process shows that ships and store-barges belonging to the Dean and Chapter of St. Paul's unshipped their lading at Fleet Hythe, and that the owners complained of a toll there exacted from them. The river was no doubt navigable, ages ago, much further than Holborn Bridge.

"In a parliament held at Carlisle, in the thirty-fifth year of Edward I. (1307), Henry Lacy, Earl of Lincoln, complained that in former times the course of water running under 'Holeburne' Bridge and Fleet Bridge, into the Thames, had been of such breadth and depth, that ten or twelve 'naves' (ships) 'were wont to come to Flete Bridge, and some of them to 'Holeburne' Bridge, yet that 'by the filth of the tanners and others, and by the raising of wharfs, and especially by a diversion of the water in the first year of King John (1200), by them of the New Temple, for their mills without Baynard's Castle, and by other impediments, the course was decayed, and ships could not enter as they were used.' On the petition of the earl, the constable of the Tower, with the mayor and sheriffs of London, were directed by writ to take with them certain 'honest and discreet men to inquire into the former state of the river, to leave nothing that might hurt or stop it,' and restore it to its original condition. The creek was cleansed, the mills removed, and other means taken for the preservation of the course; but it was not brought to its old depth and breadth, and therefore it was no longer termed a river but a brook, called Turnmill or Tremill Brook, because mills were erected on it. 'But still, as if by nature intended for a common sewer of London, it was soon choked with filth again.' The scouring of this muddy stream, which seems to have silted up about every thirty or forty years, was a continual expense to the City of London."

Several years ago, on making a great sewer, some piles of oak, apparently portions of a mill-dam, were found in the Fleet Ditch, thirteen feet below the surface of Ray Street, near Little Saffron Hill.

"In 1855," says Mr. Timbs, "the valley of the Fleet, from Coppice Row to Farringdon Street, was cleared of many old and decaying dwellings, many of a date anterior to the Fire of London. From Coppice Row a fine view of St. Paul's Cathedral was opened by the removal of these buildings. 'In making the excavation,' says a writer in the *Builder*, 'for the great sewer which now conveys from view the Fleet Ditch, at a depth of about thirteen feet below the surface in Ray Street, near the corner of Little Saffron Hill, the workmen came upon the pavement of an old street, consisting of very large blocks of ragstone of irregular shape. An examination of the paving-stones showed that the street had been well used. They are worn quite smooth by the footsteps and traffic of a past generation. Below the old street was found another phase of Old London. Thickly covered with slime were piles of oak, hard and black, which had seemingly been portions of a mill-dam. A few feet below were very old wooden water-pipes, nothing but the rough trunks of trees. The course of time, and the weight of matter above the old pavement, had pressed the gravel, clay, granite, portions of tiles, &c., into a hard and almost solid mass, and it was curious to observe that near the old surface were great numbers of pins. Whither have the pins gone? is a query which has puzzled many. The now hard concrete, stuck with these useful articles, almost like a pincushion, is a partial reply to the query. The thirteen feet of newer deposit would seem to have accumulated in two or three centuries. It is not unlikely that a portion of the rubbish from the City, after the Great Fire, was shot here.'"

About the year 1502 (Henry VII.), Lambert, in his "London," says that the intolerable Fleet Ditch was cleared, from Holborn to the Thames, and it became once more navigable for large barges, laden with fuel and fish. In 1560 Aggas, in his curious Map of London, marks two bridges over the Fleet—Holborne and Fleet Bridge. Holborne Bridge was situated about where Holborn Viaduct now crosses Farringdon Street; and the Fleet Bridge, says Mr. Pinks, an excellent authority, about the spot where the present Fleet Street and Ludgate Hill join, the circus between the two obelisks. Southward stood a dwelling-house, or warehouse, opposite the northern end of Bridewell, which reached to the Thames, and was situated on the western side of the Fleet. From the dwelling-house above mentioned as far as the Thames, the Fleet was open, Bridewell Bridge (afterwards built on its mouth) not being yet erected.

In Stow's "Survey" Fleet Bridge, without Lud

Gate, is described as a stone bridge, coped on both sides, with iron pikes, with stone lanthorns on the south side for winter evening travellers. Under this ran the River of Wells, *alias* Turnmill Brook, *alias* the Fleet Dyke, or Ditch. The bridge had been larger in old times, but was lessened as the water-course narrowed. It had either been built or repaired by John Wells, mayor in 1431 (Henry VI.), and on the coping Wells "imbraced by angels" is engraved, as on the Standard in Cheape, which he also built. This bridge melted away in the Great Fire, and its successor lasted till 1765, when it was removed, to widen Farringdon Street, and the Fleet was abandoned as incapable of improvement, and finally bricked over without any respectful funeral service. Strype, in 1720, describes Fleet Bridge as having sides breast high, and on them the City arms engraved. At Holborn Bridge the Canal, as it was then called, was fed by Turnmill Brook. The Bridewell and Fleet Bridges adjoining were ascended by steps. Between the six piers of Fleet Bridge were iron rails and banisters at both sides. The roadway was level with the street. There was a coffee-house (the "Rainbow") on the bridge in 1751. The older bridge was a stone bridge of one arch, with no stone parapet, but wooden rails and posts.

Prynne's "Records," folio, 1669, mention several old documents referring to the nuisances of the river of Fleet, and efforts to make it navigable "as formerly," to and under Holborn Bridge. Prynne also quotes from the record itself the interesting petition of the Commons of London (Edward I.), noted by Stow, complaining of the obstruction of the "Flete River," the corruption of the air it had engendered, and the hindrance of the former navigation as far as "Holeburne" Bridge. We have seen from the Earl of Lincoln's petition mentioned above that ten or twelve ships had been known to bring merchandise as far as the Fleet Bridge, and some of them to penetrate as far as Holeburne Bridge. The commission was issued to perfect the work, which was, however, stopped by the king's death. Prynne quietly urges the Government of Charles II., for the benefit of the health and trade of the City, to make the river navigable to Holborn Bridge or Clerkenwell.

In the celebrated "Liber Albus" or White Book of the City of London, compiled in 1419 (Henry V.), the street of "Flete Brigge" is mentioned, as is also the cleansing of "the Foss of the Flete." Amongst the City tolls the compiler notes : "Every cart that brings corn into the City for sale shall pay one halfpenny ; if it enters by way of Holburne or by the Flete, it shall pay one penny, the franchise excepted. . . . . The cart that brings nuts or cheese shall pay twopence ; and if it enters by the Flete, or by Holeburn, it shall pay twopence halfpenny."

In the "Calendar of State Papers" (Mary, 1553—1558), in connection with the reign of Queen Mary the Sanguinary, we find a note of certain conspirators against the queen meeting at Fleet Bridge, just as in the Rye House rebellion (1683) we meet with Monmouth, Sir Thomas Armstrong, and Lord Grey, going from the Fleet Ditch to Snow Hill, to arrange the Sunday-night rising, when at midnight, according to the traitor, Grey, the train-bands at the Royal Exchange were to be attacked, and the western City gates seized. At Fleet Bridge and Snow Hill the conspirators were to wait the onslaught of the king's guard. At Snow Hill there was to be a barricade thrown up, and mounted with three or four ships' cannon, while at Fleet Bridge there were to be several regular cannon, and a breastwork for musqueteers on each side of the bridge, while the houses on the east bank of the Fleet were to be lined with firelock-men, who were to fire from the windows as the royal troops approached the bridge. There were at least two taverns on Fleet Bridge at the Restoration. In Aggas' Map of London (1560, second year of Queen Elizabeth), Holborn Bridge has houses on the north side.

In 1670 (Charles II.), in rebuilding London, after the Great Fire, it was decreed that Holborn Bridge being too narrow for the traffic of London, the northern approach should be enlarged so that the "way and passage" might run in "a bevil line from a certain timber house on the north side thereof commonly called or known by the name or sign of the Cock," to the "Swan Inn." Wren, therefore, built the new bridge on the north side of Holborn Hill accordingly ; and the name of William Hooker, Lord Mayor in 1673–74, was cut on the stone coping of the east approach. In March, 1840, Sir William Tite, during the opening of a sewer at Holborn Hill, was lucky enough to be passing, and saw the southern face of the old bridge disinterred. The arch was about twenty feet span. The road from the east intersected the bridge obliquely, and out of the angle thus formed a stone corbel arose, to carry the parapet. The worthy mayor's name and the date were still visible. The width of the bridge was eleven feet six inches, says Mr. Crosby, who had spent many years collecting memorabilia of the Fleet valley. It had probably originally been twelve feet six inches. According to this best authority on the subject, Holborn Bridge consisted of four different bridges joined together at the sides, and two of these had been added, to widen the passage. The entrance of the old Swan Inn, with premises that covered an acre and a half, faced what is now Farringdon Street.

A writer in the *Times*, August 22nd, 1838, states as follows:—"The rear of the houses on Holborn

"To where Fleet-ditch with disemboguing streams
Rolls the large tribute of dead dogs to Thames,
The king of dykes! than whom no sluice of mud
With deeper sable blots the silver flood.
 'Here strip, my children! here at once leap in,
Here prove who best can dash thro' thick and thin,
And who the most in love of dirt excel,
Or dark dexterity of groping well.

THE FLEET DITCH NEAR WEST STREET. *From a Sketch taken in* 1844. (*See page* 425.)

Bridge has for many years been a receptacle for characters of the most daring and desperate condition. It was here in a brick tenement, now called by the Peachums and Lockets of the day 'Cromwell's House,' that murderous consultations were held, by the result of one of which the assassination of the unfortunate Mr. Steel was accomplished."

In the "Dunciad," Pope, lashing the poorer of his enemies, drives them headlong past Bridewell to the mud-pools of the Fleet—

Who flings most filth and wide pollutes around
The stream, be his the Weekly Journals bound;
A pig of lead to him who dives the best;
A peck of coals a-piece shall glad the rest.'
In naked majesty, Oldmixon stands,
And, Milo-like, surveys his arms and hands;
Then sighing, thus, 'And am I now threescore?
Ah, why, ye gods! should two and two make four?'
He said, and climb'd a stranded lighter's height,
Shot to the black abyss, and plung'd downright.
The Senior's judgment all the crowd admire,
Who but to sink the deeper, rose the higher.
 Next Smedley div'd; low circles dimpled o'er

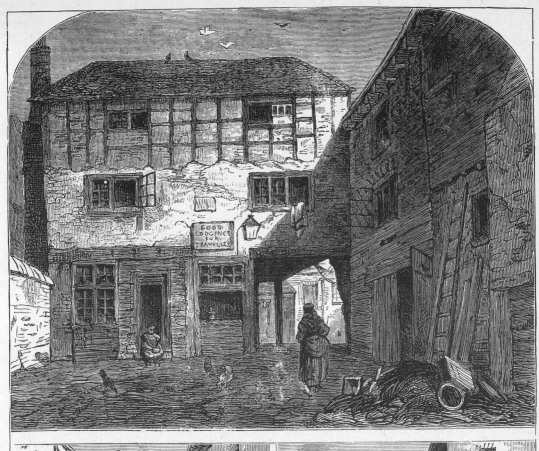

THE OLD "RED LION," FROM THE FRONT.

BACK OF THE "RED LION," FROM THE FLEET.   THE FLEET DITCH, FROM THE "RED LION."

From Sketches taken before the Demolition.   (*See page* 426.)

The quaking mud, that clos'd, and op'd no more.
All look, all sigh, and call on Smedley lost ;
Smedley, in vain, resounds thro' all the coast.
    Then * * essayed ; scarce vanish'd out of sight,
''o buoys up instant, and returns to light,
He bears no tokens of the sabler streams,
And mounts far off among the swans of Thames."

Gay again, in his "Trivia ; or, The Art of Walking the Streets of London," in his pleasant way sketches the same noisome place :—

" If where Fleet Ditch with muddy current flows
    You chance to roam ; where oyster-tubs in rows
Are ranged beside the posts ; there stay thy haste,
    And with the savoury fish indulge thy taste :
The damsel's knife the gaping shell commands,
    While the salt liquor streams between her hands."

Swift, too, with his coarse pen, giving a description of a city shower, revels in the congenial filth of the odorous locality :—

"Now from all parts the swelling kennels flow,
And bear their trophies with them as they go ;
Filths of all hues and odours seem to tell
What street they sail'd from by their sight and smell.
They, as each torrent drives, with rapid force,
From Smithfield to St. 'Pulchre's shape their course,
And in huge confluence join'd at Snow Hill ridge,
Fall from the conduit prone to Holborn Bridge ;
Sweepings from butchers' stalls, dung, guts, and blood,
Drown'd puppies, stinking sprats, all drench'd in mud,
Dead cats, and turnip-tops, come tumbling down the
    flood."

The Fleet seems always to have been a sort of dirty and troublesome child to the Corporation of London. In 1589 (Elizabeth) the Common Council collected a thousand marks (£666 13s. 4d.) to draw the springs of Hampstead Heath into one head, for the service of the City, and to scour down the Fleet; but the constant encroachment on the Fleet banks, and the rubbish and dirt thrown into the narrow channel, soon, says Stow, clogged it worse than ever. In 1606 (James I.) flood-gates were erected, to dam the water back when required; and in Cromwell's time (1652) the sewer was thoroughly cleansed, and many encroachments checked. · The ditch had now become impassable to boats, in consequence of the numerous pigsties on the banks, and the vast quantities of offal and garbage thrown in by the butchers.

Honest John Fuller, writing in 1662, remarks of the Fleet River, that it was so called "from its former fleetness, though now it creepeth slow enough, not so much for age as the injection of the City refuse wherewith it is obstructed." In an early play, one of the characters says, " I was just dead of a consumption, till the sweet smoke of Cheapside and the dear perfume of Fleet

Ditch made me a man again." In Sir Christopher Wren's design for the rebuilding of London, after the Great Fire of 1666, we find six bridges between the Thames and Clerkenwell, viz., Bridewell-dock Bridge, Wood-market, Bridge, Fleet Bridge—a bridge in the line of street from the proposed piazza in Fleet Street to Pye Corner, Smithfield—Holborn Bridge, and Cock Lane Bridge. But this design was not carried out.

After the Fire, by cleansing and enlarging of Fleet Ditch, coal-barges, &c., were enabled to come up as far as Holborn Bridge, where Turnmill Brook fell into the wider and equally sable flood. Wharves and store-houses were built on the Fleet side, but they did not prove successful. The channel had five feet of water at the lowest tide. The wharves were thirty feet broad, and had oak rails, to prevent passers-by at night falling in. Sir Thomas Fitch, the bricklayer who built the ditch, made a fortune by it, the cost being, as Ned Ward says, in his "London Spy," £74,000.

The first Bridewell Bridge over the Fleet, according to Stow, was of timber, through a breach in the City wall, opposite Bridewell. Hatton, in his "New View of London," 1708, describes Bridewell Bridge as of stone, and right against the back gate of the prison. It was ascended by fourteen steps, and was pulled down in 1765.

The bridge at the end of Fleet Lane, called the Middle Bridge, was of stone, and was, like Bridewell, ascended by fourteen steps ; the arch being high enough to admit of boats with merchandise to pass under it.

In 1733 (George II.) the Fleet, being so often tried and found guilty, underwent at last its final doom. The City of London petitioned the House of Commons for permission to cover it up out of sight, as all navigation had ceased, it had become impossible to cleanse it, and several persons had fallen in and been suffocated in the mud. A bill was accordingly passed, by virtue of which the fee-simple of the site of the premises on the line of the Fleet Ditch was vested in the Corporation for ever, on condition that proper drains were made, to receive the mud-choked stream. In 1735 two sewer-arches, ten feet high and six feet wide, were completed from Fleet Bridge to Holborn Bridge, and covered over, and the new Fleet Market erected on the site, in 1737. The work was only half done, after all ; for the noisome part, from the corner of Bridge Street to the Thames, still remained open, and was not arched over till the approaches to Blackfriars Bridge were completed, between 1760 and 1768, and even then one stubborn conservative kept a small, filthy dock still uncovered. In 1763, a drunken barber, from Bromley, in Kent, was found in Fleet Ditch, standing upright and frozen to death.

Floods of the Fleet were not uncommon, before it was boxed up. In 1679, after heavy rains, it broke down the back of several wholesale butcher-houses at Cow Cross, and carried off cattle, dead and alive. At Hockley-in-the-Hole barrels of ale, beer, and brandy floated down the black stream, and were treated by the rabble as fair flotsam. In 1768 the Hampstead Ponds overflowing after a severe storm, the Fleet channel grew into a torrent, and the roads and fields about Bagnigge Wells were overflowed. In the gardens of Bagnigge Wells the water was four feet deep. A man was nearly drowned, and several thousand pounds' damage was done in Coldbath Fields, Mutton Lane, and Peter Street and vicinity. Three oxen and several hogs were carried off and drowned. A Blackfriars boatman took his boat to Turnmill Street, and there plied, removing the inhabitants, who could not leave their houses for the rising flood. In 1809 a sudden thaw produced a flood, and the whole space between St. Pancras, Somers' Town, and the foot of the hill at Pentonville was soon under water; two cart-horses were drowned; and for several days persons received their provisions in at their windows, from carts sent round to convey them.

In 1846 a furious thunderstorm caused the Fleet Ditch to blow up. The rush from the drain at the second arch of Blackfriars Bridge drove a steamer against one of the piers, and damaged it. The overflow of the Fleet penetrated into the cellars on the west side of Farringdon Street, so that one draper alone had £3,000 worth of goods destroyed or damaged. In the lower part of Clerkenwell, where the sewer ran open, the effects of the flood were most severe, especially in the valley below Brook Hill and Vine Street. In Bull's Head Court, Peter Street, the water rose five feet, and swept away cattle and furniture. Three poor houses in Round Court, Brook Hill, were partly carried away. From Acton Place, Bagnigge Wells Road, to King's Cross the roads were impassable, and the kitchens inundated. One baker alone lost thirty-six sacks of flour. A few days after another storm produced a renewed flood, and two more houses fell in Round Court, Brook Hill. The introduction of the cholera into Clerkenwell Prison, in 1832, was attributed to the effluvia of the river Fleet, then open.

In 1855, the Fleet, as one of the metropolitan main sewers till then under the Commissioners of Sewers, became vested in the newly-created Metropolitan Board of Works. The gigantic main drainage system began with the great subterranean roads, the high, the low, and the mid level, which, intercepting all lesser sewers, carry their united floods to Barking Creek and Crossness Point. The high level runs from Hampstead to Bow; the mid-level from Kensal Green to Bow; the low level, from Cremorne to Abbey Mills on the marshes near Stratford. The mid-level main-drainage works were commenced in Clerkenwell in March, 1863, in Wilderness Row. From Goswell Street to Wilderness Row it was an open cutting, with the exception of a short tunnel under the Charterhouse grounds. The distance from Old Ford, Bow, to Kensal Green is 9 miles 2,650 feet, exclusive of 2½ miles of junctions. The sewer through Clerkenwell is 8 feet 9 inches in diameter. There were generally 400 or 500 men at work, with eleven steam-engines to pump water and draw earth.

" The Fleet Sewer," says Mr. Pinks, " the 'Cloaca Maxima' of our metropolis, receives the drainage of parts of Hampstead and Highgate, all Kentish Town, Camden Town, and Somers' Town, parts of Islington, Clerkenwell, and St. Sepulchre, and nearly all that part of the Holborn division of sewers south of the New Road, the total surface draining into it in the Holborn and Finsbury division being about 4,220 acres. In 1746 about 400 acres of this district were covered with houses. At present there are nearly 2,000 acres built upon, of necessity requiring a sewer of large capacity to carry off the refuse waters. The dimensions of the Fleet vary according to the locality : at its northern portion it is 6 feet 6 inches high, and 6 feet 6 inches wide ; at other parts it varies from 12 feet high and 12 in width, to 9 feet high by 10 feet wide ; then 8 feet 6 inches wide by 8 feet 3 inches high ; and before reaching the Thames the dimensions of this huge sewer are 14 feet wide by 10 feet 6 inches high, and at its mouth 18 feet by 12. The ordinary movement of the current from Bagnigge Wells is three miles an hour, but after heavy showers, when sometimes the water rises almost instantly five feet or more, the speed is greatly accelerated. The amount per day of sewage discharged by this monster sewer is on the average 1,741,775 cubic feet."

The dangers of exploring the Fleet Sewer have been described by Mr. Crosby, who made great collections for a history of the Fleet Valley :—" At near twelve o'clock on Tuesday night, the 28th July, 1840," says this gentleman, " the tide flowed in so fast from the Thames to Fleet Bridge, that myself and Bridgewater were obliged to fly. It reached the hip, and we got somewhat wet before arriving at Holborn Bridge, quite safe, but much exhausted in splashing through the water in our heavy boots.

"Fleet Bridge, Tuesday, July 28th, 1840.—As I could not depend upon the admeasurements, which at the beginning of the year I had taken in a hurried manner at Fleet Bridges, while bricklayers were placing in a brick bottom in place of the original one of alluvial soil, I determined to obtain them the first opportunity. This evening, therefore, at ten o'clock, I met Bridgewater (one of the workmen employed in constructing the new sewer from Holborn Bridge to Clerkenwell) by appointment at the hoard there. Water boots being in readiness, I lighted my lamps, and, assisted by the watchmen, King and Anon, we descended the ladder, and got into that branch of the sewer which joins Wren's Bridge at Holborn. We then walked carefully till we reached Fleet Bridge. I suspended my argand lamp on the breakwater of the sewer, and with my lanthorn light we proceeded towards the Thames. We got a considerable distance, during which the channel of the sewer twice turned to the right at a slight angle. The last portion we entered into was barrelled at the bottom, and the middle so full of holes, and the water so deep as we approached the Thames, that we thought it prudent to return to Fleet Bridge. Here I lighted up four candles, which, with my two lamps, enabled me to see the admeasurements I required. Bridgewater, who is a sober, steady, and good-tempered man, was of great use to me in so doing. I measured the heights with a fishing-rod, twelve feet in length, joined to my two measuring-rods, which, tied, gave me another rod of nine feet six inches. All went on well till about a quarter to twelve o'clock, when, to our surprise, we found the tide had suddenly come in to the depth of two feet and a half. No time was to be lost; but I had only one more admeasurement to make, viz., the width of the North Bridge. I managed this, and we then snatched up the basket, and, holding our lamps aloft, dashed up the sewer which we had to get up one half before out of danger. The air was close and made us faint. However, we got safe to Holborn Bridge with all our things, and the argand lamp did not blow out till we just reached it."

Mr. Archer, in his "Vestiges of Old London," 1851, says that by the opening at the Thames "many persons enter at low tide, armed with sticks to defend themselves from rats, as well as for the purpose 'of sounding on their perilous way' among the slimy shallows; and carrying a lanthern to light the dreary passage, they wander for miles under the crowded streets in search of such waifs as are carried there from above. A more dismal pursuit can

scarcely be conceived; so near to the great concourse of London streets that the rolling of the numerous vehicles incessantly thundering overhead, and even the voices of wayfarers, are heard, where, here and there, a grating admits a glimmer of the light of day; yet so utterly cut off from all communion with the busy world above, so lonely in the very heart of the great and populous city, that of the thousands who pass along, not one is even conscious of the proximity of the wretched wanderer creeping in noisome darkness and peril beneath his very feet. A source of momentary destruction ever lurking in these gloomy regions exists in the gases, which generate in their confined and putrefying atmosphere, and sometimes explode with a force sufficient to dislodge the very masonry; or which, taking light from the contact of the lantern, might envelope the miserable intruder in sudden flame. Many venturers have been struck down in such a dismal pilgrimage, to be heard of no more; may have fallen suddenly choked, sunk bodily in the treacherous slime, become a prey to swarms of voracious rats, or have been overwhelmed by a sudden increase of the polluted stream."

The polite Lord Chesterfield was asked by an enthusiastic Parisian whether London could show a river like the Seine. "Yes," replied his lordship, "we call it Fleet Ditch."

The following serves to show what nourishing contributions of refuse were made to the Fleet:— "A fatter boar was hardly ever seen," says the *Gentleman's Magazine* for 1836, "than one taken up this day (24th August, 1736) coming out of Fleet Ditch into the Thames. It proved to be a butcher's, near Smithfield Bars, who had missed him five months, all which time he had been in the common sewer, and was improved in price from ten shillings to two guineas."

Turnmill Street, pulled down in the Clerkenwell improvements of 1856-7, was undoubtedly for several centuries one of the most disreputable streets in all London. It is mentioned as Trylmyl Streate as early as the reign of Henry IV. It is marked in Aggas's map, and is noticed in a letter from Recorder Fleetwood to Burleigh in 1585 as a place for thieves' houses. The name was sometimes corrupted into Turnbull and Trunball Street. It seems to have been the very sink of the vice of London, and to have been frequented by highwaymen and rogues of every description. It is mentioned as an infamous resort by some half-dozen of the Elizabethan dramatists, more especially by Beaumont and Fletcher, Lodowick Barry, Marston, Middleton, Ben Jonson, Randolph, Webster, &c. Nor must we forget that it was of his wild and youthful feats in Turnbull Street that Justice Shallow brags of to Falstaff. Here the Pistols and Bardolphs of the time swaggered and cheated, and here the Tybalts of the day occasionally received their quietus from a subtle thrust.

"At the close of the last century," says Mr. Pinks, "a reward of £300 was offered by proclamation for the apprehension of one Bunworth, the leader of a desperate gang of thieves; yet none dared to attempt his capture, such was the weak state of the law. Once, with daring effrontery, 'on the approach of evening (to quote the *Newgate Calendar*), he and his gang ventured towards London, and having got as far as Turnmill Street, the keeper of the Clerkenwell Bridewell happening to see Bunworth, called to him, and said he wanted to speak with him. Bunworth hesitated, but the other assuring him that he intended no injury, and the thief being confident that his associates would not desert him, swore he did not regard the keeper, whom he advanced to meet with a pistol in his hand, the other miscreants walking on the opposite side of the street, armed with cutlasses and pistols. This singular spectacle attracted the attention of the populace. A considerable crowd soon gathered round them, on which Bunworth joined his companions, who thought their safest plan would be to retreat towards the fields; wherefore they kept together, and, facing the people, retired in a body, presenting their pistols, and swearing they would fire on any who should molest them.'

"This same Bunworth gave another proof of his audacity. Sitting down at the door of a public-house in Holborn, where he was well known, he called for a pint of beer and drank it, holding a pistol in his hand by way of protection. He then went off with the greatest apparent unconcern.

"The 'White Hart,' in Turnmill Street, opposite Cock Court, was formerly a noted house of call for footpads and highwaymen. It was long since pulled down."

"In 1740, Cave, the printer," says Mr. Pinks, "purchased a machine to spin wool or cotton into thread yarn, or worsted, consisting of one hundred spindles, and he had a mill erected to work it, on the course of Turnmill Brook. The patentee, Paul of Birmingham, undertook its management, but it was never brought into profitable order."

In 1416, a parchment-maker of Turnmill Street, says Stow, was drawn, hanged, and beheaded, for harbouring Sir John Oldcastle, the good Lord Cobham, the leader of the insurgent Lollards. The parchment-maker's head was spiked upon London Bridge. Lollard books were found in the house of the unfortunate man. In 1624 Dr. Thomas Worthington, one of the translators of the Douay Bible, and author of "The Anker of Christian Doctrine," lived in Turnmill Street.

In Faithorne's Map of London, 1658, the houses on the west side of Turnmill Street are represented as having gardens leading down to the Fleet, which is fenced on both sides. At the sign of the "Swan," on the west side of Turnmill Street, lived, in 1661, Giles Russell, a brewer, who left an estate in Hertfordshire for the education of three poor children of Clerkenwell parish in Christ's Hospital.

"The stream north of Fleet Bridge," says Mr. Pinks, "justified the epithet of Turnmill Brook till a comparatively recent period, as even in the present century it gave motion to flour and flatting mills at the back of Field Lane." In 1741 an advertisement in the *Daily Courant* announces a house to let in Bowling Alley, Turnmill Street, with a common sewer, with a good stream and current, "that will turn a mill to grind hair-powder or liquorish, and other things."

Among other infamous lurking-places of thieves pulled down for the Clerkenwell improvements of 1857, was the notorious West Street, formerly known by the innocent name of Chick Lane. Stow mentions it, in 1633, as near a timber bridge that crossed Turnmill Brook, near the end of Field Lane. In a flood in 1661, when casks swam down the streets, several hogs were washed out of their sties in Castle Inn Yard, Smithfield, and were carried down to Chick Lane.

There was a cruel murder committed in Chick Lane in 1758. Two women named Metyard killed a woman named Naylor, and then cut up the body, intending to throw the pieces down the gulley-hole in Chick Lane, but eventually left them in the mud which had collected before the grate of the sewer. The two women were convicted of the murder ten years after, and were both hung at Tyburn in 1768. At an inquest, in 1834, at the "Horseshoe and Magpie," Saffron Hill, on a man found dead in a low lodging-house in West Street, the landlady deposed that in her house there were eight beds in one room, and two or three persons in each bed.

Near Chick Lane was Cow Bridge, mentioned by Stow as north of Oldbourn Bridge, over the River of Wells. In the time of Elizabeth the ground from Cow Cross towards the river Fleet, and towards Ely House, was either entirely vacant, or occupied with gardens.

"Among the houses in West Street," says Mr. Pinks, "was one which was, at the time when it was demolished, supposed to have been built about three hundred years. It was once known as the 'Red Lion Tavern,' but for the century preceding its destruction it was used as a lodging-house, and was the resort of thieves, and the lowest grade of the frail sisterhood. It was numbered 3 in West Street, and was situate on the north-west side of the Fleet Ditch, a few houses from Saffron Hill, and at the eastern corner of Brewhouse Yard. It was sometimes called Jonathan Wild's House, and 'the Old House in West Street.' From its remarkable adaptation as a hiding-place, with its various means of escape, it was a curious habitation. Its dark closets, trap-doors, sliding panels, and secret recesses rendered it one of the most secure places for robbery and murder. It was here that a chimney-sweep named Jones, who escaped out of Newgate about three years before the destruction of the house, was so securely hidden for about six weeks, that, although it was repeatedly searched by the police, he was never discovered until his lair was divulged by one of its inmates, who, by incautiously observing that he knew whereabouts Jones was concealed, was taken up and remanded from time to time as an accessory to his escape, but who, at last, tired of prison fare and prison discipline, pointed out the place to obtain his own liberty. Jones was concealed by parting off a portion of a cellar with brickwork, well besmeared with soot and dirt, to prevent detection. This cell, or, more properly, den, was about four feet wide, by nine in depth; and during Jones's incarceration therein, he had food conveyed to him through a small aperture, by a brick or two being left out next the rafters. It was here that a sailor was robbed, and afterwards flung naked through one of the convenient apertures in the wall into the Fleet, for which crime two men and a woman

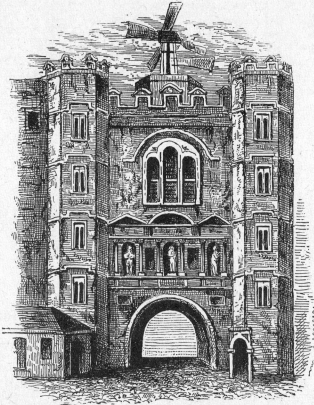

OLD NEWGATE. (*See page* 441.)

were transported. A skull, and several human bones, were found in the cellars. Numerous parties daily visited the premises, among whom were many of the police and county magistrates. It was said to have been the rendezvous, and often the hiding-place, of Jack Sheppard and Jerry Abershaw ; and the place looked as if many a foul deed had been there planned and decided on, the sewer or ditch receiving and floating away anything thrown into it. On one occasion the police had surrounded the house to take a thief, whom they knew to be there, but he made his escape in their actual presence. At another time an officer went into one of the rooms to apprehend a man, and saw him in bed. While at the door, calling to another to help him, he turned his head and saw the man getting under the bed. He did not take any notice of it, but when the other man came up, on looking under the bed, the man had vanished. After some search they discovered a trap-door through which one of them jumped, but he, breaking his leg in the fall, the fellow escaped. In this house was a place where a gang of coiners carried on their trade, and had also a private still. This place, like all the rest, had a communication with the sewer. In one of the garrets was a secret door, which led to the roof of the next house from which any offender could be in Saffron Hill in a few minutes. Amongst Mr. Crosby's drawings are a view of this old house, taken August 10, 1844 ; and an inner view of the cellar windows, taken August 19, 1844. The pulling down of this house was commenced on the first-mentioned date. It appears to have been left standing several years after some of the surrounding buildings had been removed." Three views of the old house taken shortly before its demolition are given on page 421.

CHAPTER LI.

NEWGATE STREET.

Christ Church, Newgate Street: As it was and as it is—Exorbitant Burial Fees—Richard Baxter—Dr. Trapp and Sir John Bosworth—The Steeple of Christ Church—The Spital Sermons—A small Giant and a very great Dwarf—The Adventures of Sir Jeffrey Hudson—Coleridge at the "Salutation and Cat"—The "Magpie and Stump"—Tom D'Urfey at the "Queen's Arms Tavern"—The College of Physicians in Warwick Lane—Some Famous Old Physicians—Dr. Radcliffe—The College of Physicians cruelly duped—Dr. Mead—Other Famous Physicians: Askew, Pitcairne, Sir Hans Sloane—A Poetical Doctor—Monsey and his Practical Dentistry—The Cauliflower Club: the President's Chair—The Bagnio in Bath Street—Cock Lane and the famous Ghost: Walpole: Dr. Johnson: the Imposture Detected: Scratching Fanny: Coffin—Old Inns in the Neighbourhood: the "Old Bell:" the "Oxford Arms"—Snow Hill and John Bunyan—Dobson.

IN 1244 four Grey Franciscan friars arrived in London from Italy, and by the assistance of the "Preaching Friars" of Holborn, obtained a temporary residence in Cornhill. They soon found patrons, John Ewin, a mercer, purchasing for them a vacant spot of ground in the parish of St. Nicholas Shambles (from a flesh-market held there), which he gave for the use of these friars; and William Joyner, Lord Mayor in 1239 (Henry III.), built the choir. Henry Wallis, a succeeding Lord Mayor, added the body of the church. A new and grander church was commenced in 1306 (Edward I.) at the joint expense of Queen Margaret, second wife of Edward I.; John of Brittany, Earl of Richmond; Gilbert de Clare, the Earl of Gloucester; and other pious and generous persons. This church, according to Stow, was consecrated in 1325, and is described as 300 feet long, 89 feet broad, and 64 feet 2 inches high. The chancel ceiling was painted, and the windows glowed with stained glass.

In connection with this church the illustrious Richard Whittington founded a library, in 1429, and furnished it with desks and settles for students. It is especially noted that one patient transcriber was paid 100 marks for copying the works of Nicholas de Lira.

At the dissolution, Henry VIII., who tore all he could from piety and poverty, used the church as a warehouse for French plunder. In 1546 the king gave the priory, church, library, chapter-house,

KING CHARLES'S PORTER AND DWARF.
From the old bas-relief. (*See page* 430.)

and cloisters, to the Mayor and Corporation of London. The magnificent tyrant, at the same time, gave the City the Hospital of St. Bartholomew the Little, and the parish churches of St. Ewin in Newgate Market and St. Nicholas in the Shambles, and directed that these two parishes, a part of St. Sepulchre's parish, situated within Newgate, and all the site of the late dissolved priory, should form one parish, and that the church of the priory should be the parish church, and be called "Christ Church within Newgate, founded by Henry VIII."

The church, swept away in the fiery flood of 1666, was rebuilt from Wren's design, in 1687, and was completed in the second year of Queen Anne. The patronage of Christ Church is vested in the Mayor and Commonalty of London, as governors of St. Bartholomew's Hospital. The parish of St. Leonard, Foster Lane, was united to that of Christ Church, and the Dean and Chapter of Westminster, patrons of St. Leonard's, therefore present alternately. By the original grant of Henry VIII. there *should* be five assistant readers. The present Christ Church, 114 feet long and 81 broad, is not more than half as large as the old church, the western plot of ground being turned into a burial-ground. The steeple is 153 feet high. The interior is lofty and spacious, with a wagon-headed ceiling and twelve clerestory windows, with the old pagan adornments of fat cherubim, tasteless scrolls, and coarse foliage. An ornamental band connects each

Corinthian column. A great theatrical gallery at the west end, piled up with a huge organ, is set apart, together with the side galleries, for the Bluecoat boys. The pulpit has carved panels representing, after a fashion, the four Evangelists and the Last Supper. The marble font is carved with fruit, flowers, and cherubim. The church was repaired, and what churchwardens are pleased to call beautified, in 1834, and again in 1862. The old burial fees in the happily bygone days of intra-mural interments were high enough at this church —£2 10s. for an inhabitant in the chancel; £5 for a stranger. While the lucky inhabitant paid £12 12s. for his tombstone, the poor stranger's friends had to lay down £21 for his.

On the north wall at the east end of the church is a brass tablet to the memory of Dame Mary Ramsey, who died in 1596,' and who established a free writing-school in Christ's Hospital. Here, where queens have rested and murderers mouldered, lies the great Nonconformist minister, Richard Baxter, on whose tomb no more fitting epitaph could be placed than the title of his own book, "The Saint's Rest." This excellent man, of Shropshire birth, in the earlier part of his life became master of a free-school at Dudley. In 1638 he took orders, having then no scruples about conformity, but soon after, some Non-conformist friends began to slowly influence his mind. He then began to distrust the surplice, objected to the cross in baptism, and found flaws in the Prayer Book and the Liturgy. In 1640 he was minister at Kidderminster; but when the civil wars broke out, and after Naseby, he became chaplain to Colonel Whalley's Puritan regiment, and was present at several sieges. The Cavaliers said he killed one of their party and stole his medal, a story which Baxter publicly denied. On his preaching against Cromwell he was sent for to Court, and told of the great things God had done for the Parliament. Baxter replied that the honest people of the land took their ancient monarchy to be a blessing, and not an evil, and humbly craved Cromwell's patience, that he might ask him how they had forfeited that blessing, and to whom that forfeiture was made. Cromwell replied, angrily, "There was no forfeiture; but God had changed it as pleased Him." A few days after, Cromwell sent to ask Baxter for his opinion on liberty of conscience, which Baxter gave him. On Charles's restoration, Baxter, who was a sect in himself, was appointed one of the king's chaplains, and was frequently with the godless monarch. He assisted as a commissioner at the Savoy Conference, and drew up a reformed liturgy. Lord Clarendon

offered this crochety but honest theologian the bishopric of Hereford, but he declined the appoint-ment, and went on preaching about London. For illegal preaching he was sent to gaol for six months, but eventually discharged before the expiration of that period. After the indulgence in 1672 he preached at Pinner's Hall, in Fetter Lane, in St. James's Market House, at a chapel he built himself in Oxenden Street, and in Southwark. In 1685 Baxter was taken before Lord Chief Justice Jefferies, for remarks on James II. in his "New Testament Paraphrase," and sent to prison, after much vulgar abuse from Jefferies, for two years, but in 1686 he was pardoned by King James. At Baxter's last disgraceful trial, that cruel bully, the Chief Justice Jefferies, told him that Oates was then standing in the pillory in New Palace Yard, and that if he (Baxter) was on the other side of the pillory at the same time, he (Jefferies) would say that two of the greatest rogues and rascals in the kingdom stood there. Like an avalanche of mud the foul words poured forth from this unjust judge. "Ay," said Jefferies, "this is your Presbyterian cant; truly called to be bishops; that is, himself and such rascals, called to be bishops of Kidder-minster, and other such places; bishops set apart by such factious, snivelling Presbyterians as him-self; a Kidderminster bishop, he means. Accord-ing to the saying of a late learned author, every parish shall maintain a tithe-pig metropolitan." Mr. Baxter beginning to speak again, says he to him, " Richard, Richard, dost thou think we will hear thee poison the court, &c.? Richard, thou art an old fellow—an old knave; thou hast written books enough to load a cart, every one as full of sedition (I might say, treason) as an egg is full of meat. Hadst thou been whipped out of thy writing-trade forty years ago it had been happy. Thou pre-tendest to be a preacher of the gospel of peace, and thou hast one foot in the grave; 'tis time for thee to begin to think what account thou intendest to give. But leave thee to thyself, and I see thoul't go on as thou hast begun; but, by the grace of God, I will look after thee. I know thou hast a mighty party, and I see a great many of the brother-hood in corners, waiting to see what will become of their mighty don, and a doctor of the party (looking to Dr. Bates) at your elbow; but, by the grace of Almighty God, I'll crush you all."

After this Baxter retired to a house in Charter-house Yard, where he assisted a Mr. Sylvester every Sunday morning, and preached a lecture every Thursday. He died in the year 1691. Baxter is said to have written more than 145 dis-tinct treatises. This somewhat hair-splitting man believed in election, but rejected the doctrine of reprobation. If any one improved the common grace given to all mankind, it was Baxter's belief that the improvement must be followed by special grace, which led one on to final acceptance and salvation. This was the half-way road between Calvinism and Arminianism.

On the east wall is a tablet to the memory of Dr. Trapp, who was vicar of the united parishes of Christ Church and St. Leonard, Foster Lane, for twenty-six years, and died in 1747. This learned translator and controversialist lived in Warwick Lane. Near the communion-table is a large monument to Sir John Bosworth, Chamberlain of the City, who died in 1749, and his wife, Dame Hester Bosworth; and also a plain tablet to Mr. John Stock, many years a painter at the Royal Dock-yard, and who died in 1781. He left £13,700 for charitable and philanthropic purposes. A marble monument, with a bust, records the Rev. Samuel Crowther, nearly thirty years incumbent of this church. He was a grandson of Richardson, the novelist, and was born in New Boswell Court. He was struck down with apoplexy while reading morning prayers. The inscription to his memory runs thus :—

"This monument is raised by his grateful parishioners and friends to the memory of the Reverend Samuel Crowther, M.A., formerly fellow of New College, Oxford, and nearly thirty years minister of these united parishes. He was born January 9, 1769, and died September 28, 1829. Gifted with many excellent endowments, he was enabled by grace to consecrate all to the service of his Divine Master. The zeal, perseverance, and fidelity with which, under much bodily infirmity, he laboured in this place till his last illness (borne nearly five years with exemplary resignation), his humble, disinterested, and catholic spirit, his suavity of manners, and sanctity of life, manifested a self-devotion to the cause of Christ, and the best interests of mankind, never to be forgotten by his flock ; to whom he endeared himself, not more in the able discharge of his public duties than in his assiduous and affectionate ministrations, as their private counsellor, comforter, and friend ; and among whom the young, the poor, and the afflicted were the especial objects of his solicitude. To the excellence of that gospel which he preached with a simple and persuasive eloquence, that gained every ear, his life has left a testimony, sealed in death, by which he yet speaks."

The ten tombs of alabaster and marble, and the 140 marble gravestones from this church, sold for £50 by the greedy goldsmith, Martin Bowes, we have already mentioned in our chapter on Christ's Hospital.

Among the more remarkable epitaphs is the following, on the tablet to the memory of the Rev. Joseph Trapp just referred to. It was written by Trapp himself :—

"Death, judgement, heaven and hell ! think, Christian,
　　think !
You stand on vast eternity's dread brink ;
Faith and repentance, piety and prayer,
Despise this world, the next be all your care ;
Thus, while my tomb the solemn silence breaks,
And to the eye this cold dumb marble speaks,
Tho' dead I preach : if e'er with ill success
Living, I strove the important truths to press,
Your precious, your immortal souls to save,
Hear me at least, oh, hear me from the grave !"

The steeple of Christ Church is thought by many very pleasing. "It rises," says Mr. Godwin, who in some respects condemns it, "as all Wren's towers *do* rise, and as all towers *should* rise, directly from the ground, giving to the mind of the beholder that assurance of stability which under other circumstances is wanting." There are small Grecian columns on each storey of the tower, and an elliptical pediment. The vases on the top of the peristyle were taken down some years ago. The basement storey of the tower is open on three sides, and forms a porch to the east chancel. The east end, which faces King Edward Street, is disfigured by two enormous buttresses. In a vault, discovered in 1790, near the church, is the well-preserved body of a man, supposed to be that of some Newgate malefactor.

The Spital sermons, says Mr. Trollope in 1834, in his book on Christ's Hospital, originated in an old custom, by which some learned person was appointed yearly by the Bishop of London to preach at St. Paul's Cross, on Good Friday, on the subject of "Christ's Passion." On the Monday, Tuesday, and Wednesday following, three other divines were appointed to uphold the doctrine of "The Resurrection," at the pulpit-cross in the Spital (Spitalfields). On the Sunday following, a fifth preached at Paul's Cross, and passed judgment upon the merits of those who had preceded him. At these sermons the Lord Mayor and aldermen attended, ladies also, on the Monday, forming part of the procession ; and, at the close of each day's solemnity, his lordship and the sheriffs gave a private dinner to such of their friends amongst the aldermen as attended the sermon. From this practice the civic festivities at Easter were at length extended to a magnificent scale. The children of Christ's Hospital took part in the above solemnities, so that, in 1594, when it became necessary to rebuild the pulpit-cross at the Spital, a gallery was erected also for their accommodation. In the great Rebellion the pulpit was destroyed, and the sermons were discontinued till the Restoration, after which the *three* Spital sermons, as they were still called, were revived at St. Bride's Church,

Fleet Street. They have since been reduced to two, and, from 1797, have been delivered at Christ Church, Newgate Street.

It was on their first appearance at the Spital that the children of Christ's Hospital wore the blue costume by which they have since been distinguished. "Instead of the subjects," continues Mr. Trollope, "which were wont to be discussed from the pulpit-cross of St. Mary Spital, discourses are now delivered commemorative of the objects of the five sister hospitals; and a report is read of the number of children maintained and educated, and of sick, disorderly, and lunatic persons for whom provision is made in each respectively. On each day the boys of Christ's Hospital, with the legend 'He is risen' attached to their left shoulders, form part of the civic procession, walking, on the first day, in the order of their schools, the king's boys bearing their nautical instruments, and, on the second, according to their several wards, headed by their nurses."

A curious old bas-relief, says Peter Cunningham (writing in 1849), not ill-cut, over the entrance to Bull's Head Court, preserves the memory of a small giant and a very great dwarf. The quaint effigies of the disproportioned couple represent William Evans, an enormous Welsh porter, at Whitehall, in the service of Charles I., and Sir Geoffrey, or Jeffrey Hudson, the vain but gallant dwarf immortalised by Scott, in "Peveril of the Peak." This bas-relief, Walpole thinks, was probably a shop-sign. Evans, a mammoth-like man, stood seven feet six inches high, while his choleric companion was only three feet nine inches. At a court masque at Whitehall, the porter drew Sir Jeffrey out of his pocket, to the amazement and amusement of all the ladies of that not too respectable court.

"Hudson's first appearance at Court," says Sir Walter, in a note to "Peveril of the Peak," "was his being presented, as mentioned in the text, in a pie, at an entertainment given by the Duke of Buckingham to Charles I. and Henrietta Maria. Upon the same occasion the duke presented the tenant of the pasty to the queen, who retained him as her page. When about eight years of age, he was but eighteen or twenty inches high, and he remained stationary at that stature till he was thirty years old, when he grew to the height of three feet nine inches, and there stopped." Being teased by a young gallant, named Crofts, who threatened to drown him with a syringe, Hudson called out his antagonist at Calais, and killed him with his first shot.

"This singular *lusus naturæ*," says Scott, "was trusted in some negotiations of consequence. He went to France, to fetch over a midwife to his mistress, Henrietta Maria. On his return he was taken by Dunkirk privateers, when he lost many valuable presents sent to the queen from France, and about £2,500 of his own. Sir William Davenant makes a real or supposed combat between the dwarf and a turkey-cock the subject of a poem called 'Jeffreidos.' The scene is laid at Dunkirk, where, as the satire concludes—

> 'Jeffrey strait was thrown when, faint and weak,
> The cruel fowl assaults him with his beak.
> A lady midwife now he there by chance
> Espied, that came along with him from France.
> "A heart brought up in war, that ne'er before
> This time could bow," he said, "doth now implore
> Thou, that *delivered* hast so many, be
> So kind of nature as deliver me."'

"In 1644 the dwarf attended his royal mistress to France. The Restoration recalled him, with other royalists, to England. But this poor being, who received, it would seem, hard measure both from nature and fortune, was not doomed to close his days in peace. Poor Jeffrey, upon some suspicion respecting the Popish Plot, was taken up in 1682, and confined in the Gatehouse Prison, Westminster, where he ended his life, in the sixty-third year of his age. Jeffrey Hudson has been immortalised by the brush of Vandyke, and his clothes are said to be preserved as articles of curiosity in Sir Hans Sloane's museum."

It was to the "Salutation and Cat" (odd combination of two incongruous signs), No. 17, Newgate Street, that Coleridge used to retreat, in his youthful fits of melancholy abstraction at college debts, bad health, impotency of will, and lost opportunities. This was about the time when, by a wild impulse, one day, at the corner of Chancery Lane, the young philosopher enlisted in the 15th Light Dragoons, under the odd north-country name of Comberbach. It was at the "Salutation and Cat" that Southey one day ferreted out the lost dreamer, the veritable Alnaschar of modern literature, and tried to rouse him from the trance of fear and half-insane idleness. The "Magpie and Stump," a very old inn on the north side of this street (where the old sign of the place was reverently preserved in the bar), has lately been pulled down.

At a convivial meeting at the "Queen's Arms Tavern" (No. 70), says Peter Cunningham, Tom D'Urfey obtained the suggestion of his merry but coarse miscellany, "Pills to purge Melancholy." This Court wit, a naturalised French Huguenot, seems to have been the gay, witty, careless Captain Morris of his day. People often spoke of seeing

King Charles II., at Whitehall, leaning on Tom's shoulder and humming over a song with him, and to have heard him at Kensington, singing his own gay songs, to amuse heavy Queen Anne. He was the author of thirty-one plays, which have not been forgotten by original dramatists of a later date. He became poor in his old age, and Addison saved him from poverty by a well-timed theatrical benefit.

In Warwick Lane, south side of Newgate Street, a College of Physicians was built by Wren, when the Great Fire had destroyed their house at Amen Corner, where Harvey had lectured on his great discovery of the circulation of the blood. The house, built on part of the mansion of the old Earl of Warwick, was begun in 1674, and opened in 1689. The special point of the college was the octagonal domed entrance-porch, forty feet in diameter, which was a *tour de force* of the ingenious architect. The interior above the porch was the lecture-room, light, lofty, and open to the roof. Garth, in "The Dispensary"—his pleasant satire against the apothecaries, thus sketched it—

> "Not far from that most celebrated place
> Where angry Justice shows her awful face,
> Where little villains must submit to fate,
> That great ones may enjoy the world in state,
> There stands a dome, majestic to the sight,
> And sumptuous arches bear its oval height;
> A golden globe, plac'd high with artful skill,
> Seems to the distant sight—a gilded pill."

The amphitheatre, afterwards degraded into a meat-market, is praised by Elmes for its convenient arrangement and its acoustic qualities. Nor could even the modern Goth despise the fine lofty hall, the magnificent staircase, the stucco-garlands of the dining-room, and the carved oak chimney-piece and gallery. On the north and south were the residences of the college officers, on the west the principal front, two-storeyed, the lower Ionic, the upper Corinthian. On the east was the octagon, with the gilt ball above, and below a statue of Sir John Cutler.

About this same Cutler an odd story is told, which is well worth repeating.

In 1675 (Charles II.) Sir John Cutler, a rich City man, and a notorious miser, related to Dr. Whistler, the president of the college, expressed a generous wish to contribute largely to the rebuilding of the house, and a committee was actually appointed to thank him for his kind intentions. Cutler gravely accepted the thanks, renewed his promises, and mentioned the parts of the building for which he intended to pay. In 1680 the college, grateful for favours yet to come, voted statues to the king and Cutler, and nine years afterwards borrowed money of Sir John, to discharge some builder's debts, the

college being now completed. This loan seems to have in some way changed Cutler's intentions, for in 1699 his executors brought a demand on the college for £7,000, including the promised sum, which had never been given, but had been set down as a debt. The indignant college threw down £2,000, which the imperturbable executors took as payment in full. The college at once erased the grateful inscription—

"Omnis Cutleri cedit labor Amphitheatro,"

which they had engraved on the pedestal of the miser's statue, and would no doubt have ground the statue down to powder, had they not been ashamed.

This Cutler was the same Volpone whom Pope mentions, in his "Moral Essay:"—

> "His grace's fate sage Cutler could foresee,
> And well (he thought) advised him, 'Live like me.
> As well his grace replied, 'Like you, Sir John?
> That I can do, when all I have is gone.'"

Cutler is ridiculed by Arbuthnot, in his "Scriblerus," where, in ridicule of one of Locke's philosophic opinions, he describes a pair of Cutler's cottons, which were darned so often by his maid, that they at last became silk. Cutler's funeral is said to have cost £7,000, and one of his daughters married the Earl of Radnor.

Some anecdotes of the old physicians who have paced up and down Warwick Lane seem almost indispensable to a sketch, however brief, of the old College of Physicians. Nor can we begin better than with the famous Dr. Radcliffe, the first preeminent physician that arose after the removal of the college to the building erected by Wren in Warwick Lane. Radcliffe, a man eager for money, and of rough Abernethy manners, had the cream of all the London practice, when he lived in Bow Street, next door to Sir Godfrey Kneller, the great painter. He was brusque even with kings. When called in to see King William, at Kensington, finding his legs dropsically swollen, he frankly said, 'I would not have your two legs, your Majesty, not for your three kingdoms;" and on another visit the Jacobite doctor boldly told the little Dutch hero—"Your juices are all vitiated, your whole mass of blood corrupted, and the nutriment for the most part turned to water; but," added the doctor, "if your Majesty will forbear making long visits to the Earl of Bradford" (where, to tell the truth, the king was wont to drink very hard), "I'll engage to make you live three or four years longer, but beyond that time no physic can protract your Majesty's existence."

On one occasion, when Radcliffe was sent for from the tavern (for he did not dislike wine) by

Queen Anne, he flatly refused to leave his bottle and the company. "Tell her Royal Highness," he bellowed, "that it's nothing but the vapours. She is as well as any woman breathing, only she won't believe it." With a fantastic wit worthy of Sydney Smith himself, he told a hypochondriacal lady who consulted him about a nervous singing in the head, to "curl her hair with a ballad;" and in his vexation at the fancies of female patients, he antici-

Spoonfuls of hot pudding were discharged on both sides, and at last handfuls were pelted at each other. The patient was seized with a hearty fit of laughter, the quinsy burst, and discharged its contents, and my master soon completed the cure."

Steele, in the *Tatler*, ridiculed the old doctor's love-making. Dr. Radcliffe was unlucky enough to be accused by the Whigs of killing Queen Mary, and by the Tories of causing the death of Queen Anne,

COLLEGE OF PHYSICIANS, WARWICK LANE. THE QUADRANGLE. (*See page* 431.)

pated female doctors, by proposing an Act of Parliament to entitle nurses alone to attend women.

"Dr. Radcliffe was once sent for," says the author of "The Gold-headed Cane," "into the country, to visit a gentleman ill of a quinsy. Finding that no external or internal application would be of service, he desired the lady of the house to order a hasty-pudding to be made. When it was done, his own servants were to bring it up; and while the pudding was preparing, he gave them his private instructions. In a short time it was set on the table, and in full view of the patient. 'Come, Jack and Dick,' said Radcliffe, 'eat as quickly as possible; you have had no breakfast this morning.' Both began with their spoons; but on Jack's dipping once only for Dick's twice, a quarrel arose.

by refusing to attend her in her last illness. He was himself dying at the time, and was unable to attend; but the clamour of the mob was so loud, accompanied even by threats of assassination, that they are said to have hastened the great physician's death, which took place just three months after the queen died.

Dr. Mead, the physician of George II., was, unlike Radcliffe, a polished and learned man, who succeeded to much of his predecessor's business, and occupied also his old house in Bloomsbury. He was the first doctor to encourage inoculation for the small-pox, and practised the Oriental system on six condemned criminals, with the consent of George I. He attended Pope, Sir Isaac Newton, and Bishop Burnet in their last illnesses. Mead is said to have gained nearly £6,000 a year, yet was so hospitable, that he did not leave more than £50,000. When not at his house in Great Ormond Street, Mead usually spent his evenings at "Batson's" Coffee House, and in the afternoon his apothecaries used to meet him at "Toms'," near

Dr. Askew, another of the great physicians of the Georgian era, lived in Queen Square, where he crammed his house with books, and entertained such men as Archbishop Markham, Sir William Jones, Dr. Farmer, "Demosthenes" Taylor, Dr. Parr, and Hogarth. The sale of Dr. Askew's

COCK LANE. (*See page* 435.)

Covent Garden, with written or verbal reports of cases for which he prescribed without seeing the patient, and took half-guinea fees. He died in 1754, and was buried in the Temple. As an instance of Mead's generosity the following story is told :—In 1723, when the celebrated Dr. Friend, a friend of Atterbury, was sent to the Tower, Mead kindly took his practice, and on his release by Sir Robert Walpole, presented the escaped Jacobite with the result, 5,000 guineas.

library, in York Street, Covent Garden (1755), occupied twenty days.

Dr. William Pitcairn, who resided in Warwick Court, Warwick Lane, was for several years president of the college. Dr. Baillie, another eminent physician here, was a nephew of the great John Hunter. Sir Hans Sloane was elected President of the College of Physicians in 1719. He was an Irishman by birth, and a Scotchman by descent, and had accompanied the Duke of Albemarle to

Jamaica as his physician. In 1727 he was created President of the Royal Society, on the death of Sir Isaac Newton, and became physician to George II. On his death, in 1753, his museum and library were purchased by the nation, and became the nucleus of the British Museum.

In this brief notice of early physicians we must not forget to include that very second-rate poet, Sir Richard Blackmore, son of a Wiltshire attorney. No poor poet was ever so ridiculed as this great man of Saddlers' Hall. Dryden and Pope both set him up in their Parnassian pillory; and of him Swift wrote—

"Sternhold himself he out-Sternholded."

Dryden called him—

"A pedant, canting preacher, and a quack."

In spite of this endless abuse of a well-meaning man, William III. knighted him, and Addison pronounced his ambitious poem, "The Creation," to be "one of the most useful and noble productions in our English verse."

Among the eccentric physicians who have paced up and down Warwick Lane, and passed across the shadow of the Golden Pill, was Monsey, a friend of Garrick, and physician to Chelsea College. Of this rough old cynic Mr. J. C. Jeaffreson, in his "Book about Doctors," tells the following capital stories :—

"Amongst the vagaries of this eccentric physician," says Mr. Jeaffreson, "was the way in which he extracted his own teeth. Round the tooth sentenced to be drawn he fastened securely a strong piece of catgut, to the opposite side of which he affixed a bullet. With this bullet, and a full measure of powder, a pistol was charged. On the trigger being pulled, the operation was performed effectually and speedily. The doctor could only rarely prevail upon his friends to permit him to remove their teeth by this original process. Once a gentleman who had agreed to try the novelty, and had even allowed the apparatus to be adjusted, at the last moment exclaimed, 'Stop, stop, I have changed my mind !' 'But I haven't, and you're a fool and a coward for your pains,' answered the doctor, pulling the trigger. In another instant, the tooth was extracted, much to the timid patient's delight and astonishment. . . . .

"Before setting out, on one occasion, for a journey to Norfolk, incredulous with regard to cash-boxes and bureaus, he hid a considerable quantity of gold and notes in the fireplace of his study, covering them up artistically with cinders and shavings. A month afterwards, returning (luckily a few days before he was expected), he found his old house-maid preparing to entertain a few friends at tea in her master's room. The hospitable domestic was on the point of lighting the fire, and had just applied a candle to the doctor's notes, when he entered the room, seized on a pail of water that chanced to be standing near, and, throwing its contents over the fuel and the old woman, extinguished the fire and her presence of mind at the same time. Some of the notes, as it was, were injured, and the Bank of England made objections to cashing them."

Monsey lived to extreme old age, dying in his Rooms in Chelsea College on the 26th of December, 1788, in his ninety-fifth year; "and his will," continues Mr. Jeaffreson, "was as remarkable as any other feature of his career. To a young lady mentioned in it, with the most lavish encomiums on her wit, taste, and elegance, was left an old battered snuff-box, not worth sixpence; and to another young lady, whom the testator says he intended to have enriched with a handsome legacy, he leaves the gratifying assurance that he changed his mind on finding her 'a pert, conceited minx.' After inveighing against bishops, deans, and chapters, he left an annuity to two clergymen who had resigned their preferment on account of the Athanasian doctrine. He directed that his body should not be insulted with any funeral ceremony, but should undergo dissection. After which, the 'remainder of my carcase' (to use his own words) 'may be put into a hole, or crammed into a box with holes, and thrown into the Thames.' In obedience to this part of the will, Mr. Forster, surgeon, of Union Court, Broad Street, dissected the body, and delivered a lecture on it to the medical students, in the theatre of Guy's Hospital. The bulk of the doctor's fortune, amounting to about £16,000, was left to his only daughter for life, and after her demise, by a complicated entail, to her *female* descendants."

As a physician, Dr. John C. Lettsom, who died in 1815, was a most fortunate man; for without any high reputation for professional acquirements, and with the exact reverse of a good preliminary education, he made a larger income than any other physician of the same time. After the erection of the new College of Physicians at Trafalgar Square, in 1825, the buildings here were gradually demolished; the last portion to disappear being the entrance-porch in Warwick Lane, which was pulled down shortly after the removal of Newgate Market.

That singular club, the Cauliflower, chiefly patronised by booksellers from Paternoster Row, was held at the "Three Jolly Pigeons" in Butcher Hall

Lane, now King Edward Street. "The Three Pigeons," says the anonymous author of Tavern Anecdotes (1825), "is situated in Butcher Hall Lane, bounded by Christ Church and Snow Hill on the west, St. Martin's-le-Grand and Cheapside on the east, by Newgate Street and Ivy Lane (where Dr. Johnson's club was held), and Paternoster Row on the south, and by Little Britain on the north. Of the last-mentioned, Washington Irving has given an admirable picture in his 'Sketch Book;' but as he has not given a portrait of the last resident bookseller of eminence in that ancient mart of bibliopolists, he has left us the pleasing task of performing an humble attempt in that way; but even we, who knew the character, are almost spared the trouble; for, could the old literary frequenters of Batson's and Will's Coffee-houses again appear in human shapes, with their large, wiry, white, curled wigs, coats without a collar, raised hair buttons, square pendicular cut in front, with immense long hanging sleeves, covering a delicate hand, further graced by fine ruffles; a long waistcoat, with angled-off flaps, descending to the centre of the thigh; the small-clothes slashed in front, and closed with three small buttons; with accurate and mathematically cut, square-toed, short-quartered shoes, with a large tongue, to prevent a small-sized square silver buckle hurting the instep, or soiling the fine silken hose, they would present an exact and faithful portrait of the late Edward Ballard standing at his shop, at the 'Globe,' over against the pump, in Little Britain. He was the last remaining bookseller of that school, if we except the late James Buckland, at the sign of the 'Buck,' in Paternoster Row, with one or two others, and put one in mind of Alexander Pope, in stature, size, dress, and appearance. The writer of this article recollects, when a boy, frequently calling at his shop, and purchasing various books, in a new and unbound state, when they were considered to be out of print, and some of them really scarce. This arose from the *obscurity* of the once celebrated Little Britain, and the great age of its last resident bookseller, who to the last retained some shares and copyrights (notwithstanding he and his brother had sold the most valuable to Lintot), in school and religious books; with the last remains of a stock, principally guarded and watched by an old faithful female servant."

The permanent secretary of the "Free and Easy Counsellors under the Cauliflower" was a worthy old fellow, Mr. Christopher Brown, an assistant of Mr. Thomas Longman, in Paternoster Row, who delighted in his quiet glass of Tabby's punch, a pipe, and a song, after the labours of the day.

This faithful old clerk had refused all offers of friends to set him up in independent business. Before the purchase of Mr. Evans's business the great firm of Longman was conducted by merely two principals and three assistants.

The large cauliflower painted on the ceiling of the club was intended to represent the cauliflower head on the gallon of porter, which was paid for by every member who sat under it at his initiation. The president's chair, a masterpiece of Chippendale's workmanship, was sold in 1874 at Christie and Manson's. The height is five feet less two inches; breadth in front, from twenty-five to twenty-seven inches. An exquisitely-carved cauliflower adorns the chair, extending from near the top of the chair downwards to the end of the root exactly one foot; while the spread-out leaves, including the flower, extend a foot across; so that it was literally true of whoever occupied the chair, that he sat "under the cauliflower." The sides and arms of the chair are adorned with leaves, and both legs and arms are fluted, the whole being carved out of solid dark Spanish mahogany. A footboard, serving the purpose of a slightly-raised platform for the use of the speaker, also of solid mahogany, is attached to the chair by hinges.

In Bath Street, Newgate Street, one of the first bagnios, or Turkish baths, was opened in 1679, as Aubrey carefully records. Strype calls it "a neat-contrived building, after the Turkish mode, seated in a large handsome yard, and at the upper end of Pincock Lane, which is indifferent well-built, and inhabited. This bagnio is much resorted unto for sweating, being found very good for aches, &c., and approved of by our physicians." A writer in the *Spectator*, No. 332, mentions the bagnio in Newgate Street, and one in Chancery Lane. Hatton, in 1708, describes it as a very spacious and commodious place for sweating, hot bathing, and cupping, and with a temperature of eighteen degrees of heat. The roof was of a cupola shape, and the walls set with Dutch tiles. The charge was four shillings a person, and there were special days for ladies. There were nine servants in attendance; and to prove the healthiness of the place, Hatton mentions that one servant had been in attendance for twenty-eight years, four days a week.

Cock Lane, an obscure turning between Newgate Street and West Smithfield, was, in 1762, the scene of a great imposture. The ghost supposed to have been heard rapping there in reply to questions, singularly resembled the familiar spirits of our modern mediums. The affair commenced in 1762, by Parsons, the officiating clerk of St. Sepulchre's, observing, at early prayer, a genteel couple standing in the aisle, and ordering them into a pew. On the service ending, the gentleman stopped to thank Parsons, and to ask him if he knew of a lodging in the neighbourhood. Parsons at once offered rooms in his own house, in Cock Lane, and they were accepted. The gentleman proved to be a widower of family from Norfolk, and the lady the sister of his deceased wife, with whom he privately lived, unable, from the severity of the ancient canon law, to marry her as they both wished. In his absence in the country, the lady, who went by the name of Miss Fanny, had Parson's daughter, a little artful girl about eleven years of age, to sleep with her. In the night the lady and the child were disturbed by extraordinary noises, which were at first attributed to a neighbouring shoemaker. Neighbours were called in to hear the sounds, which continued till the gentleman and lady removed to Clerkenwell, where the lady soon after died of small-pox. In January of the next year, according to Parsons, who, from a spirit of revenge against his late lodger, organised the whole fraud, the spiritualistic knockings and scratchings re-commenced. The child, from under whose bedstead these supposed supernatural sounds emanated, pretended to have fits, and Parsons began to interrogate the ghost, and was answered with affirmative and negative knocks. The ghost, under cross-examination, declared that it was the deceased lady lodger, who, according to Parsons, had been poisoned by a glass of purl, which had contained arsenic. Thousands of persons, of all ranks and stations, now crowded to Cock Lane, to hear the ghost, and the most ludicrous scenes took place with these poor gulls.

Even Horace Walpole was magnetically drawn to the clerk's house in Cock Lane. The clever fribble writes to Sir Horace Mann, January 29, 1762: "I am ashamed to tell you that we are again dipped into an egregious scene of folly. The reigning fashion is a ghost—a ghost, that would not pass muster in the paltriest convent in the Apennines. It only knocks and scratches; does not pretend to appear or to speak. The clergy give it their benediction; and all the world, whether believers or infidels, go to hear it. I, in which number you may guess, go to-morrow; for it is as much the mode to visit the ghost as the Prince of Mecklenburg, who is just arrived. I have not seen him yet, though I have left my name for him."

Again Walpole writes:—" I went to hear it, for it is not an apparition, but an audition. We set out from the opera, changed our clothes at Northumberland House, the Duke of York, Lady Northumberland, Lady Mary Coke, Lord Hertford, and I, all in one hackney-coach, and drove to the spot. It rained torrents; yet the lane was full of mob, and the house so full we could not get in. At last they discovered it was the Duke of York, and the company squeezed themselves into one another's pockets to make room for us. The house, which is borrowed, and to which the ghost has adjourned, is wretchedly small and miserable. When we opened the chamber, in which were fifty people, with no light, but one tallow candle at the end, we tumbled over the bed of the child to whom the ghost comes, and whom they are murdering by inches in such insufferable heat and stench. At the top of the room are ropes to dry clothes. I asked if we were to have rope-dancing between the acts. We heard nothing. They told us (as they would at a puppet-show) that it would not come that night till seven in the morning, that is, when there are only 'prentices and old women. We stayed, however, till half an hour after one. The Methodists have promised them contributions. Provisions are sent in like forage, and all the taverns and ale-houses in the neighbourhood make fortunes." (Walpole to George Montagu, Feb. 2nd, 1762.)

Of the descent into the vaults of St. John's, Clerkenwell, to hear the spirits rap on her coffin-lid, Johnson, who was present, writes:—"About ten at-night the gentlemen met in the chamber in which the girl, supposed to be disturbed by a spirit, had with proper caution been put to bed by several ladies. They sat rather more than an hour, and hearing nothing, went down-stairs, where they interrogated the father of the girl, who denied in the strongest terms any knowledge or belief of fraud. While they were inquiring and deliberating, they were summoned into the girl's chamber by some ladies who were near her bed, and who had heard knocks and scratches. When the gentlemen entered, the girl declared that she felt the spirit like a mouse upon her back, when the spirit was very solemnly required to manifest its existence by appearance, by impression on the hand or body of any present, or any other agency; but no evidence of any preternatural power was exhibited. The spirit was then very seriously advertised that the person to whom the promise was made of striking the coffin was then about to visit the vault, and that the performance of the promise was then claimed. The company at one o'clock went into the church, and the gentleman to whom the promise was made, went with another into the vault. The spirit was solemnly required to perform its promise, but nothing more than silence ensued. The person supposed to be accused by the spirit then went down with several others, but no effect was perceived. Upon their return, they examined the girl, but could draw no confession from her. Between two and three she desired and was permitted to go home with her father. It is therefore the opinion of the whole assembly, that the child has some art of making or counterfeiting a particular noise, and that there is no agency of any higher cause."

In the following account of a Cock Lane *séance*, a pamphleteer of the time says :—

"To have a proper idea of this scene, as it is now carried on, the reader is to conceive a very small room, with a bed in the middle ; the girl at the usual hour of going to bed, is undressed, and put in with proper solemnity. The spectators are next introduced, who sit looking at each other, suppressing laughter, and wait in silent expectation for the opening of the scene. As the ghost is a good deal offended at incredulity, the persons present are to conceal theirs, if they have any, as by this concealment they can only hope to gratify their curiosity ; for, if they show, either before or when the knocking is begun, a too prying, inquisitive, or ludicrous turn of thinking, the ghost continues usually silent, or, to use the expression of the house, 'Miss Fanny is angry.' The spectators, therefore, have nothing for it but to sit quiet and credulous, otherwise they must hear no ghost, which is no small disappointment to persons who have come for no other purpose.

"The girl, who knows, by some secret, when the ghost is to appear, sometimes apprizes the assistants of its intended visitation. It first begins to scratch, and then to answer questions, giving two knocks for a negative, but one for an affirmative. By this means it tells whether a watch, when held up, be white, blue, yellow, or black ; how many clergymen are in the room, though in this sometimes mistaken. It evidently distinguishes white men from negroes, with similar other marks of sagacity. However, it is sometimes mistaken in questions of a private nature, when it deigns to answer them. For instance, the ghost was ignorant where she had dined upon Mr. K——'s marriage ; how many of her relations were at church upon the same occasion ; but, particularly, she called her father John, instead of Thomas—a mistake, indeed, a little extraordinary in a ghost. But perhaps she was willing to verify the old proverb, that 'It is a wise child that knows its own father.' However, though sometimes right, and sometimes wrong, she pretty invariably persists in one story, namely, that she was poisoned, in a cup of purl, by red arsenic, a poison unheard of before, by Mr. K——, in her last illness, and that she heartily wishes him hanged.

"It is no easy matter to remark upon an evidence of this nature ; but it may not be unnecessary to observe, that the ghost, though fond of company, is particularly modest upon these occasions, an enemy to the light of a candle, and always most silent before those from whose rank and understanding she could most reasonably expect redress.

*   *   *   *   *

"This knocking and scratching was generally heard in a little room in which Mr. P——'s two children lay, the eldest of which was a girl about twelve or thirteen years old. The purport of this knocking was not thoroughly conceived till the eldest child pretended to see the actual ghost of the deceased lady mentioned above. When she had seen the ghost, a weak, ignorant publican also, who lived in the neighbourhood, asserted that he had seen it too, and Mr. P—— himself (the gentleman whom Mr. K—— had disobliged by suing for money) also saw the ghost about the same time. The girl saw it without hands, in a shroud ; the other two saw it with hands, all luminous and shining. There was one unlucky circumstance, however, in the apparition. Though it appeared to three several persons, and could knock, scratch, and flutter, yet its coming would have been to no manner of purpose had it not been kindly assisted by the persons thus haunted. It was impossible for a ghost that could not speak to make any discovery ; the people, therefore, to whom it appeared, kindly undertook to make the discovery themselves, and the ghost, by knocking, gave its assent to their method of wording the accusation."

The girl was at last, we are glad to say, detected. When the child was bound hand and foot in a hammock, the ghost, it was found, was always silent. One morning, when the child had been threatened with Newgate if she did not arouse the ghost, she was found to have concealed, under her stays, a small board, on which she produced the supernatural sounds. The bubble then burst.

The gentleman accused, remarks Mr. Pinks, "thought proper to vindicate his character in a legal way. On the 10th of July the father and mother of the child, one Mary Frazer, who acted as interpreter of the noises, a clergyman, and a tradesman, were tried at Guildhall, before Lord Mansfield, by a special jury, and convicted of conspiracy. Sentence was deferred for several months, in order to give the offenders an opportunity of making Mr. —— some compensation in the meantime. Accordingly, the clergyman and tradesman gave him several hundred pounds, and were thereupon dismissed with a reprimand. Parsons was sentenced to be placed three times in the pillory, at the end of Cock Lane, and then to be imprisoned for two years in the King's Bench gaol. Strange to relate, the rabble, who usually assembled in large numbers to witness and to assist in carrying out the former part of such a sentence, were

"While drawing the crypt of St. John's, Clerkenwell," says Mr. J. W. Archer, "in a narrow cloister on the north side, there being at that time coffins, fragments of shrouds, and human remains lying about in disorder, the sexton's boy pointed to one of the coffins, and said that it was 'Scratching

THE "GHOST'S" HOUSE IN COCK LANE. (*See page* 436.)

in this case moved with compassion for the victim of the strong arm of the law, and refrained from offering him, while thus exposed, any insult, either by word or deed, and a public subscription was afterwards raised for his benefit. Mrs. Parsons was sentenced to be imprisoned for one year, and Mary Frazer for six months, with hard labour. Miss Parsons, the agent of the mysterious noise, and who doubtless acted under her father's instructions, was twice married, and died in 1806."

Fanny.' This reminding me of the Cock Lane Ghost, I removed the lid of the coffin, which was loose, and saw the body of a woman, which had become adipocere. The face was perfect, handsome, oval, with an aquiline nose. Will not arsenic produce adipocere? She is said to have been poisoned, although the charge is understood to have been disproved. I inquired of one of the churchwardens of the time, Mr. Bird, who said the coffin had always been understood to contain the body of the woman whose spirit was said to have haunted the house in Cock Lane."

At the "King's Head," in Ivy Lane, Dr. Johnson established one of his earliest clubs for literary discussion. The chief members were the Rev. Dr. Salter, father of the Master of the Charterhouse; Mr. (afterwards Dr.) John Hawkesworth; Mr. Ryland, a merchant, a relation of Johnson's; Mr. John Payne, then a bookseller, afterwards chief accountant of the Bank; Mr. Samuel Dyer, a

when the stalls and sheds were removed from Butcher Hall Lane and the localities round the church of St. Nicholas Shambles.

Warwick Lane, Stow says, derived its name from an ancient house there, built by the Earls of Warwick. This messuage in Eldenese Lane (the old name) is on record in the 28th year of Henry VI. as occupied by Cicille, Duchess of Warwick. In the 36th year of Henry VI., when the greater estates of the realm were called to London,

THE SARACEN'S HEAD, SNOW HILL.　*From a Sketch taken during its Demolition.*　(*See page* 485.)

learned young man, intended for the dissenting ministry; Dr. William M'Ghie, a Scots physician; Dr. Edmund Barker, a young physician; Dr. Richard Bathurst, and Mr. (afterwards Sir John) Hawkins.

Newgate Market, now removed to the neighbourhood of Charterhouse, was originally a meal-market. "R. B.," in Strype, says that before the Great Fire there was a market-house here for meal, and a middle row of sheds, which had gradually been converted into houses for butchers, tripe-sellers, and the like. The country-people who brought provisions were forced to stand with their stalls in the open street, exposed to all the coaches, carts, horses, and cattle. The meat-market, says Peter Cunningham, had first become a centre of trade

Richard Nevill, the Earl of Warwick, justly named the "king-maker," came there, backed by six hundred sturdy vassals, all in red jackets embroidered with ragged staves before and behind. "At whose house," says Stow, "there were oftentimes six oxen eaten at a breakfast; and every tavern was full of his meat, for he that had any acquaintance at that house might have there so much of sodden and roast meat as he could prick and carry upon a long dagger." A little bas-relief of the famous Guy, Earl of Warwick, with the date 1668, is inserted in the wall of Newgate Street end of Warwick Lane.

The "Old Bell" Inn, on the east side of the lane, is the house where Archbishop Leighton died. According to Burnet, in his "History of His Own Times," "he (Archbishop Leighton) used often to say that if he were to choose a place to die in, it should be an inn; it looking like a pilgrim's going home, to whom this world was all as an inn, and who was weary of the noise and confusion in it. He added that the officious tenderness and care of friends was an entanglement to a dying man; and that the unconcerned attendance of those that could be procured in such a place would give less disturbance. And he obtained what he desired; for he died (1684) at the 'Bell' Inn, in Warwick Lane."

The "Oxford Arms" Inn, formerly on the west side of the street, is mentioned in a carrier's advertisement in the *London Gazette*, 1672–73. Edward Bartlet, an Oxford carrier, who had removed from the "Swan" at Holborn Bridge, started his coaches and wagons from thence three times a week. He also announced that he kept a hearse, to convey "a corps" to any part of England.

Snow Hill is called Snore Hill by Stow, and Sore Hill by Howell. At the time of the Great Fire it seems to have been known as Snore Hill and Snow Hill indifferently. By the time Gay wrote his antithetical line—

"When from Snow Hill black steepy torrents run,"

however, the latter name seems to have become fixed. It was always an awkward, roundabout road; and in 1802, when Skinner Street was built, it was superseded as the highway between Newgate Street and Holborn.

There is one event in its history, brief as it is, that deserves special remembrance. At the house of his friend, Mr. Strudwick, a grocer, at the sign of the "Star," Snow Hill, that brave old Christian, John Bunyan, died, in 1688. This extraordinary genius was the son of a tinker, at Elstow, near Bedford, and grew up a wild, dissolute youth, but seems to have received early strong religious impressions. He served in the Parliamentary army at the siege of Leicester, and the death of a comrade who took his post as a sentry produced a deep effect on his thoughtful mind. On returning to Elstow, Bunyan married a pious young woman, who seems to have led him to read and study religious books. At the age of twenty-five, after great spiritual struggles, Bunyan was admitted into church-fellowship with the Baptists, and baptised, probably near midnight, in a small stream near Bedford Bridge. His spiritual struggles still continued, he believed himself rejected, and the day of grace past; then came even doubts of the being of a God, and of the authority of the Scriptures. A terrible illness, threatening consumption, fol-

lowed this mental struggle, but with health came the calm of a serene faith, and he entered the ministry. A great trouble followed, to further purify this great soul. He lost his first wife; but a second wife proved equally good and faithful. It being a time of persecution, Bunyan was soon thrown into Bedford gaol, where he pined for twelve long years. There, with some sixty other innocent people, Bunyan preached and prayed incessantly, and wrote the first part of his immortal "Pilgrim's Progress."

Parting with his wife and children Bunyan himself describes as "pulling the flesh from his bones," and his heart was especially wrung by the possible hardships of his poor blind daughter, Mary. "Oh, the thought of the hardships my poor blind one might be under," he says, "would break my heart to pieces." Bunyan maintained himself in prison by making tagged laces, and the only books he had were the Bible and Foxe's "Book of Martyrs." "When God makes the bed," he says, in one of his works, "he must needs be easy that is cast thereon. A blessed pillow hath that man for his head, though to all beholders it is hard as a stone." The jug in which his broth was daily taken to the prison is still preserved as a relic, and his gold ring was discovered under the floor when the prison was demolished.

Bunyan was released in 1672, when 471 Quakers and twenty Baptists were also set free. He then obtained a licence to preach at a chapel in Bedford, and he also continued his trade as a brazier. In 1682 this good man published his second allegory, "The Holy War," and completed the last part of "The Pilgrim's Progress."

In spite of his consistent zeal, Bunyan was denounced by his enemies as a wizard, a Jesuit, and a highwayman. His popularity among his own people was, however, very great. When he preached in London some 3,000 people used to collect, so that he had almost to be pulled over their heads into the pulpit. His end was characteristic. He was returning home from a visit to Reading, where he had gone to reconcile an offended father to a prodigal son, when he was seized, at the house in Snow Hill, with a fatal fever. His departure must have been like that of the pilgrims he himself describes:—"Now I saw in my dream that by this time the pilgrims were got over the Enchanted Ground, and entering into the country of Beulah (Isa. lxii. 4—12; Cant. ii. 10—12), whose air was very sweet and pleasant; the way lying directly through it, they solaced themselves there for a season. Yea, here they heard continually the singing of birds, and saw every day the flowers appear in the earth, and heard the voice of the turtle in the land. In this country the sun shineth night and day; wherefore this was beyond the Valley of the Shadow of Death, and also out of the reach of Giant Despair, neither could they from this place so much as see Doubting Castle. Here they were within sight of the city they were going to; also here met them some of the inhabitants thereof; for in this land the shining ones commonly walked, because it was upon the borders of Heaven."

To Snow Hill also belongs an anecdote of Dobson, one of the most eminent of our early painters. Dobson, son of the master in the Alienation Office, was compelled by his father's extravagance to become an apprentice to a stationer and picture-dealer. He soon began to excel in copying Titian and Vandyke, and exhibited his copies in a window in Snow Hill. Vandyke himself, who lived in Blackfriars, not far off, passing one day, was so struck with Dobson's work, that he went in and inquired for the author. He found him at work in a poor garret, from which he soon rescued him. He shortly afterwards recommended him to King Charles, who took him into his service, and sat to him often for his portrait, and gave him the name of the English Tintoret. Dobson's style is dignified and thoughtful, and his colour delightful in tone. One of his finest portrait groups belongs to the Duke of Northumberland, and in the "Decollation of St. John," in the collection at Wilton, he is said to have introduced a portrait of Prince Rupert. The Civil Wars, and the indifference which the Puritans manifested to art, no doubt reduced Dobson to poverty, and he died poor and neglected, in St. Martin's Lane, in 1646.

CHAPTER LII.

NEWGATE.

The Fifth City Gate—Howard's Description of Newgate—The Gordon Riots—The Attack on Newgate—The Mad Quaker—Crabbe, the Poet—His Account of the Burning of Newgate—Dr. Johnson's Visit to the Ruins.

NEWGATE, which Stow classifies as the fifth principal gate in the City wall, was first built about the reign of Henry I. or Stephen, and was a prison for felons and trespassers at least as early as the reign of King John. It was erected when, St. Paul's being rebuilt, the old wards, from Aldgate to Ludgate, were stopped up by enclosures and building materials, and people had to work round deviously by Paternoster Row and the old Exchange to get to Ludgate.

In the year 1218 the king wrote to the Sheriffs of London, "commanding them to repair the gaol at Newgate, for the safe keeping of his prisoners, promising that the charges laid out should be allowed them upon their accompt in the Exchequer" (Stow). In 1241 some rich Jews (accused of imaginary crimes) were ordered to pay 20,000 marks, or be kept perpetual prisoners at Newgate and other prisons. In this same reign Henry sent the sheriffs to the Tower, and fined the City 3,000 marks, for allowing a convicted priest, who had killed a prior, a cousin of the queen, to escape from Newgate. Sir William Walworth in 1385 left money to relieve the prisoners in Newgate, and Whittington left money to rebuild the prison. In 1457 there was again a break-out from Newgate prison. Lord Egremond, Sir Thomas and Sir Richard Percy, committed to Newgate for a fray in the north country with the Earl of Salisbury's sons, in which fray many were maimed or slain, broke out of prison by night, and went to petition the king, the other prisoners, in the meantime, garrisoning the leads of Newgate, and defending it against all the sheriffs; till at last the citizens were called up to subdue and lay in irons the reckless rebels.

The gate was repaired in 1630–3, destroyed in the Great Fire, and rebuilt in a stronger and more convenient way, with a postern for foot passengers. On the east or City side of the old prison were three stone statues—Justice, Mercy, and Truth; and four on the west, or Holborn side—Liberty (with Whittington's cat at her feet), Peace, Plenty, and Concord. Four of these figures, which survived the Gordon riots, ornament part of the front of the present prison.

Howard, the philanthropist, writing in 1784, gives a favourable account of the Newgate of 1779.

"The cells," says Howard, "built in old Newgate, a few years since, for condemned malefactors, are still used for the same purpose. There are upon each of the three floors five, all vaulted, near 9 feet high to the crown. Those on the ground-floor measure full 9 feet by near 6 feet; the five on the first storey are a little larger (9½ feet by 6 feet), on account of the set-off in the wall; and the five uppermost still a little larger, for the same reason. In the upper part of each cell is a window, double grated, near 3 feet by 1½. The doors are 4 inches thick. The strong stone wall is lined all round each cell with planks, studded with broad-headed nails. In each cell is a barrack bedstead. I was told by those who attended them that criminals who had affected an air of boldness during their trial, and appeared quite unconcerned at the pronouncing sentence upon them, were struck with horror, and shed tears, when brought to these darksome, solitary abodes.

"The chapel is plain and neat. Below is the chaplain's seat, and three or four pews for the felons; that in the centre is for the condemned. On each side is a gallery: that for the women is towards their ward; in it is a pew for the keeper, whose presence may set a good example, and be otherwise useful. The other gallery, towards the debtors' ward, is for them. The stairs to each gallery are on the outside of the chapel. I attended there several times, and Mr. Villette read the prayers distinctly, and with propriety. The prisoners who were present seemed attentive; but we were disturbed by the noise in the court. Surely they who will not go to chapel, who are by far the greater number, should be locked up in their rooms during the time of divine service, and not suffered to hinder the edification of such as are better disposed.

"The chaplain, or ordinary, besides his salary, has a house in Newgate Street, clear of land-tax; Lady Barnadiston's legacy, £6 a year; an old legacy paid by the Governors of St. Bartholomew's Hospital, £10 a year; and lately had two freedoms yearly, which commonly sold for £25 each; and the City generally presented him, once in six months, with another freedom. Now he has not the freedoms, but his salary is augmented to £180, and the sheriffs pay him £3 12s. He engages, when chosen, to hold no other living.

"Debtors have, every Saturday, from the Chamber of London, eight stone of beef; fines, four stone; and, some years, felons, eight stone. Debtors have several legacies. I inquired for a list of them, and Mr. Akerman told me the table in Maitland's 'Survey' was authentic. The amount of it is £52 5s. 8d. a year. There are other donations mentioned by Maitland, amounting to sixty-four stone of beef, and five dozen of bread. . . . . .

"Here I cannot forbear mentioning a practice, which probably had its origin from the ancient mode of torture, though now it seems only a matter of form. When prisoners capitally convicted at the Old Bailey are brought up to receive sentence, and the judge asks, 'What have you to say why judgment of death and execution should not be awarded against you?' the executioner slips a whipcord noose about their thumbs. This custom ought to be abolished.

"At my visit, in 1779, the gaol was clean, and free from offensive scents. On the felons' side there were only three sick, in one of the upper wards. An infirmary was building, near the condemned cells. Of the 141 felons, &c., there were ninety-one convicts and fines who had only the prison allowance of a penny loaf a day. Mr. Akerman generously contributed towards their relief. In the felons' court the table of fees, painted on a board, was hung up.

"The gaol was burnt by the rioters in 1780, but is rebuilt on the same plan. The men's quadrangle is now divided into three courts. In the first court are those who pay 3s. 6d. a week for a bed; in the next, the poorer felons; and in the other, *now*, the women. Under the chapel are cells for the refractory. Two rooms, adjoining to the condemned cells, are built for an infirmary, in one of which, at my last visit, there were sixteen sick. Of the 291 prisoners in 1782, 225 were men and 66 women. Upwards of 100 of them were transports, 89 fines, 21 under sentence of death, and the remainder lay for trial. Some of the condemned had been long sick and languishing in their cells."

From the Old Bailey Session Papers for June, 1780, we gather a very vivid and picturesque notion of the destruction of Newgate during the Gordon riots. The mob came pouring down Holborn, between six and seven o'clock, on the evening of the 6th of June. There were three flags carried by the ringleaders—the first of green silk, with a Protestant motto; the second, dirty blue, with a red cross; the third, a flag of the Protestant Union. A sailor named Jackson had hoisted the second flag in Palace Yard, when Justice Hyde had launched a party of horse upon the people; and when the rabble had sacked the justice's house in St. Martin's Street, Jackson shouted, "Newgate, a-hoy!" and led the people on to the Old Bailey. Mr. Akerman, a friend of Boswell, and one of the keepers of Newgate, had had intimation of the danger two hours before, when a friend of one of the prisoners called upon him just as he was packing up his plate for removal, told him "he should be the one hung presently," and cursed him. Exactly at seven, one of the rioters knocked at Mr. Akerman's door, which had been already barred, bolted, and chained. A maid-servant had just put up the shutters, when the glass over the hall-door was dashed into her face. The ringleader who knocked was better dressed than the rest, and wore a dark brown coat and round hat. The man knocked three times, and rang three times; then, finding no one came, ran down the steps, "made his obeisance to the mob," pointed to the door, then retired. The mob was perfectly organised, and led by about thirty men walking three abreast. Thirty men carried iron crowbars, mattocks, and chisels, and after them followed "an innumerable company," armed with bludgeons and the spokes of cart-wheels. The band instantly divided into three parts—one set went to work at Mr. Akerman's door with the mattocks, a second went to the debtors' door, and a third to the felons'. A shower of bludgeons instantly demolished the windows of the keeper's house; and while these sticks were still falling in showers, two men, one of them a mad Quaker, the son of a rich corn-factor, who wore a mariner's jacket, came forward with a scaffold-pole, and drove it like a battering-ram against the parlour shutters. A lad in a sailor's jacket then got on a man's shoulders, and jammed in the half-broken shutters with furious blows of his bullet-head. A chimney-sweeper's boy then scrambled in, cheered by the mob, and after him the mad Quaker. A moment more, and the Quaker appeared at the first-floor window, flinging out pictures into the street. Presently, the second parlour window gave way, the house-door was forced, and the furniture and broken chattels in the street were set in a blaze. All this time a circle of men, better dressed than the rest, stood in the Old Bailey, exciting and encouraging the rioters. The leader of these sympathisers was a negro servant, named Benjamin Bowsey, afterwards hung for his share in the riot. One of the leaders in this attack was a mad waiter from the St. Alban's Tavern, named Thomas Haycock. He was very prominent, and he swore that there should not be a prison standing in London on the morrow, and that the Bishop of London's house and the Duke of Norfolk's should come down that night. "They were well supported, he shouted to the mob," for there were six or seven noblemen and members of Parliament on their side. This man helped to break up a bureau, and collected sticks to burn down the doors of Akerman's house. While Akerman's house was still burning, the servants escaping over the roofs, and Akerman's neighbours were down among the mob, entreating them to spare the houses of innocent persons, a waiter, named Francis Mockford, who wore a hat with a blue cockade in it, went up to the prison-gate and held up the main key, and shouted to the turnkeys, "D—— you, here is the key of Newgate; open the door!" Mockford, who was eventually sentenced to death for this riot, afterwards took the prison keys, and flung them over Westminster Bridge. George Sims, a tripeman in St. James's Market, always forward in street quarrels, then went up to the great gate in the Old Bailey with some others, and swore desperately that "he would have the gates down—curse him, he would have the gates down!" Then the storm broke; the mob rushed on the gate with the sledge-hammers and pickaxes they had stolen from coachmakers, blacksmiths, and braziers in Drury Lane and Long Acre, and plied them with untiring fury. The tripeman, who carried a bludgeon, urged them on; and the servant of Akerman, having known the man for several years, called to him through the hatch, "Very well, George the tripeman; I shall mark you in particular!" Then John Glover, a black, a servant of a Mr. Phillips, a barrister in Lincoln's Inn, who was standing on the steps leading to the felons' gate (the main gate), dressed in a rough short jacket, and a round hat trimmed with dirty silver lace, thumped at the door with a gun-barrel, which he afterwards tried to thrust through the grating into the faces of the turnkeys, while another split the door with a hatchet. The mob, finding they could not force the stones out round the hatch, then piled Akerman's shattered furniture, and placing it against the gates set the heap on fire.

Several times the gate caught fire, and as often the turnkeys inside pushed down the burning furniture with broomsticks, which they pushed through the hatch, and kept swilling the gates with water, in order to cool them, and to keep the lead that soldered the hinges from melting and giving way. But all their efforts were in vain; for the flames, now spreading fast from Akerman's house, gradually burnt in to the fore-lodge and chapel, and set the different wards one after the other on fire. Crabbe the poet, who was there as a spectator, describes seeing the prisoners come up out of the dark cells with their heavy irons, and looking pale and scared. Some of them were carried off on horseback, their irons still on, in triumph by the mob, who then went and burnt down the Fleet. At the trial of Richard Hyde, the poor mad Quaker, who had been one of the first to scramble through Mr. Akerman's windows, the most conclusive proofs were brought forward of the prisoner's insanity. A grocer in Bishopsgate Street, with whom he had lodged, deposed to his burning a Bible, and to his thrashing him. One day at the "Doctor

Butler's Head," in Coleman Street, the crazed fellow had come in, and pretended to cast the nativities of persons drinking there. He also prophesied how long each of them would live. On hearing this evidence, the prisoner broke out: "Well, and they might live three hundred years, if they knew how to live; but they gorge themselves like aldermen. Callipash and callipee kills half the people." It was also shown that, the night after the burning of Newgate, the prisoner came to a poor woman's

Crabbe, who, having failed as a surgeon and apothecary down at Aldborough, his native place, had just come up to London to earn his bread as a poet, and being on the brink of starvation, was about to apply to Burke for patronage and bread. Rambling in a purposeless way about London to while away the miserable time, the young poet happened to reach the Old Bailey just as the ragged rioters set it on fire to warm their Protestantism. Suddenly, at a turning out of Ludgate Hill, on his

DOOR OF NEWGATE.

house in Bedford Court, Covent Garden, and he then wore an old grey great-coat and a flapped hat, painted blue. As the paint was wet, the woman asked him to let her dry it. He replied, "No, you are a fool; my hat is *blue*" (the Protestant colour); "it is the colour of the heavens. I would not have it dried for the world." When the woman brought him a pint of beer, he drank once, and then pushed it angrily on one side. He then said, "I have tasted it once, I must taste it three times; it is against the heavens to drink only once out of a pot." Doctor Munro, the physician who attended George III. in his madness, deposed to the insanity both of the prisoner's father and the prisoner. He was sent to a mad-house.

way back to his lodgings at a hairdresser's shop near the Exchange, a scene of terror and horror broke red upon the view of the mild young Suffolk apothecary. The new prison, Crabbe says, in his "Journal" kept for the perusal of his Myra (June 8th), was a very large, strong, and beautiful building, having two wings besides Mr. Akerman's house, and strong intermediate works and other adjuncts. Akerman had four rioters in custody, and these rascals the mob demanded. He begged he might send to the sheriff, but this was not permitted. "How he escaped, or where he is gone, I know not; but just at the time I speak of, they set fire to his house, broke in, and threw every piece of furniture they could find into the street.

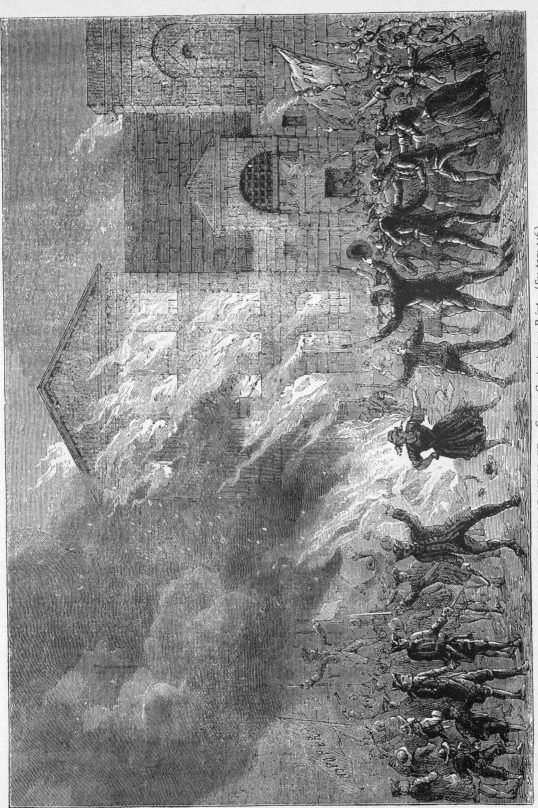

BURNING OF NEWGATE. *From a Contemporary Print.* (*See page 446.*)

firing them also in an instant. The engines came" (they were mere squirts in those days), "but were only suffered to preserve the private houses near the prison." This was about half-past seven. "As I was standing near the spot, there approached another body of men—I suppose five hundred—and Lord George Gordon in a coach drawn by the mob, towards Alderman Bull's, bowing as he passed along. He is a lively-looking young man in appearance, and nothing more, though just now the reigning hero. By eight o'clock Akerman's house was in flames. I went close to it, and never saw anything so dreadful. The prison was, as I said, a remarkably strong building; but, determined to force it, they broke the gates with crows and other instruments, and climbed up the outside of the cell part, which joins the two great wings of the building, where the felons were confined; and I stood where I plainly saw their operations. They broke the roof, tore away the rafters, and having got ladders they descended. Not Orpheus himself had more courage or better luck. Flames all around them, and a body of soldiers expected, they defied and laughed at all opposition. The prisoners escaped. I stood and saw about twelve women and eight men ascend from their confinement to the open air, and they were conducted through the street in their chains. Three of these were to be hanged on Friday" (Newgate was burnt on the Tuesday). "You have no conception of the frenzy of the multitude. This being done, and Akerman's house now a mere shell of brickwork, they kept a store of flame there for other purposes. It became red-hot, and the doors and windows appeared like the entrance to so many volcanoes. With some difficulty they then fired the debtors' prison, broke the doors, and they, too, all made their escape. Tired of the scene, I went home, and returned again at eleven o'clock at night. I met large bodies of horse and foot soldiers, coming to guard the Bank, and some houses of Roman Catholics near it. Newgate was at this time open to all; any one might get in, and, what was never the case before, any one might get out. I did both, for the people were now chiefly lookers-on. The mischief was done, and the doers of it gone to another part of the town" (to Bloomsbury Square, to burn Lord Mansfield's house). "But I must not omit what struck me most: about ten or twelve of the mob getting to the top of the debtors' prison, whilst it was burning, to halloo, they appeared rolled in black smoke mixed with sudden bursts of fire—like Milton's infernals, who were as familiar with flame as with each other."

On the Wednesday, the day after the fire, a big carelessly-dressed man worked his way to the ruins from Bolt Court, Fleet Street. The burly man's name was Doctor Samuel Johnson, and he wrote to Mrs. Thrale and her husband a brief account of what had happened since the Friday before. On that day Lord George Gordon and the mob went to Westminster, and that night the rioters burnt the Catholic chapel in Duke Street, Lincoln's Inn Fields. On Monday they gutted Sir George Saville's house in Leicester Square; on Tuesday pulled down the house of Sir John Fielding, the blind magistrate and the novelist's half-brother, in Bow Street; and the same night burnt Newgate, Lord Mansfield's house in Bloomsbury, and a Catholic chapel in Moorfields. On Wednesday they burnt the Fleet and the King's Bench, and attacked the Bank of England, but were driven off by a party of constables headed by John Wilkes.

"On Wednesday," says the doctor, to come to what he actually saw himself, "I walked with Doctor Scott, to look at Newgate, and found it in ruins, with the fire yet glowing. As I went by, the Protestants were plundering the Sessions House at the Old Bailey. There were not, I believe, a hundred; but they did their work at leisure, in full security, without sentinels, without trepidation, as men lawfully employed in full day. Such is the cowardice of a commercial place. On Wednesday they broke open the Fleet, and the King's Bench, and the Marshalsea, and Wood Street Compter, and Clerkenwell Bridewell, and released all the prisoners. At night they set fire to the Fleet, and to the King's Bench, and I don't know how many other places; and one might see the glare of conflagration fill the sky from many parts. The sight was dreadful. Some people were threatened. Mr. Strahan advised me to take care of myself. . . . . . . Several chapels have been destroyed, and several inoffensive Papists have been plundered; but the high sport was to burn the gaols. This was a good rabble trick. The debtors and the criminals were all set at liberty; but of the criminals, as has always happened, many are already re-taken, and two pirates have surrendered themselves, and it is expected that they will be pardoned." Then follows a fine touch of irony : "Jack" (Wilkes), "who was always zealous for order and decency, declares that if he be trusted with power, he will not leave a rioter alive. There is, however, now no longer any need of heroism or bloodshed; no blue ribbon" (the badge of the rioters) "is any longer worn." As for Thrale, his brewery escaped pretty well. The men gave away a cask or two of beer to the mob, and when the rioters came on a second and more importunate visit, the soldiers received them.

CHAPTER LIII.

NEWGATE (continued).

Methodist Preachers in Newgate—Silas Told—The Surgeons' Crew—Dr. Dodd, the Popular Preacher—His Forgery—Governor Wall at Goree flogs a Soldier to Death—His Last Moments—Murder of Mr. Steele—Execution of the Cato Street Conspirators—Fauntleroy, the Banker —The Murder of the Italian Boy—Greenacre—Müller—Courvoisier—His Execution—Mrs. Brownrigg—Mr. Akerman and the Fire in Newgate—Mrs. Fry's Good Work in Newgate—Escapes from Newgate—Jack Sheppard—A Good Sermon on a Bad Text—Sanitary Condition of Newgate—Effect upon the Prisoners.

IN the year 1744 Silas Told, a worthy Wesleyan, deeply touched by a sermon preached by Wesley on the text, "I was sick and in prison, and ye visited me not" (Matt. xxv. 43), began to exert himself among the prisoners at Newgate, and has left a graphic and simple-hearted account of his labours among them; and from this book we obtain many curious glimpses of prison life at that period. The first persons Told visited were ten malefactors, then under sentence of death. "The report having been made," says Told, "and the dead-warrant coming down, eight of the ten were ordered for execution. The other two were respited; nor did either of those two appear to have any the least regard or concern for their deathless souls; therefore I trust they were spared for a good purpose, that they might have time for repentance and amendment of life.

"The day arrived whereon the other eight malefactors were to die. Sarah Peters and myself were early at the cell, in order to render them all the spiritual service that was within our power. The keeper having received directions on the over-night to lock them all up in one cell, that they might pour out their souls together in fervent solemn prayer to Almighty God, they paid very circumspect attention thereto, and a happy night it proved to each of them; so that when they were led down from their cell, they appeared like giants refreshed with wine, nor was the fear of death apparent in any of their countenances. We then went up to the chapel, when my companion and myself conversed with them in the press-yard room. Upon being called out to have their irons taken off, Lancaster was the first. While they were disburthening his legs thereof, the sheriff being present, Lancaster looked up to heaven with a pleasant smile, and said, 'Glory be to God for the first moment of my entrance into this place! For before I came hither my heart was as hard as my cell wall, and my soul was as black as hell. But, oh, I am now washed, clearly washed, from all my sins, and by one o'clock shall be with Jesus in Paradise!' And with many strong and forcible expressions he exhorted the innumerable spectators to flee from the wrath to come. This caused the sheriff to shed tears, and ask Mr. Lancaster if he was really in

earnest, being so greatly affected with his lively and animated spirit. As their irons were taken off they were remanded back to the press-yard room; but, by some accident, they were a long time getting off the last man's fetters. When they were gotten off, Lancaster, beholding him at a short distance, clapped his hands together, and joyfully proclaimed, 'Here comes another of our little flock!' A gentleman present said, with an apparent sympathising spirit, 'I think it is too great a flock upon such an occasion.' Lancaster, with the greatest fluency of speech, and with an aspiring voice, said, 'Oh, no; it is not too great a flock for the shepherd Jesus; there is room enough in heaven for us all.' When he exhorted the populace to forsake their sins, he particularly endeavoured to press on them to come to the Throne of Grace immediately, and without fear, assuring them that they would find Him a gracious and merciful God, to forgive them, as He had forgiven him. At length they were ordered into the cart, and I was prevailed upon to go with them. When we were in the cart, I addressed myself to each of these separately."

Told's account of the execution of these men shows clearly how lawless and savage were the mobs which gathered at Tyburn. "When we came to the fatal tree Lancaster lifted up his eyes thereto, and said, 'Blessed be God,' then prayed extemporary in a very excellent manner, and the others behaved with great discretion. John Lancaster had no friend who could procure for his body a proper interment; so that, when they had hung the usual space of time, and were cut down, the surgeon's mob secured the body of Lancaster, and carried it over to Paddington. There was a very crowded concourse, among whom were numberless gin and gingerbread vendors, accompanied by pickpockets and even less respectable characters, of almost every denomination in London; in short, the whole scene resembled a principal fair, rather than an awful execution. Now, when the mob was nearly dispersed, and there remained only a few bystanders, with an old woman who sold gin, a remarkable occurrence took place, and operated to the following effect:—

"A company of eight sailors, with truncheons in their hands, having come to see the execution, looked up to the gallows with an angry countenance, the bodies having been cut down some minutes previous to their arrival. The old woman before named, who sold gin, observing these tars to grow violent, by reason of their disappointment, mildly accosted them and said, 'Gentlemen, I suppose you want the man that the surgeons have got?' 'Aye,' replied the sailors; 'where is he?' The poor affrighted woman gave them to understand that the surgeons' crew had carried him over to Paddington, and she pointed out to them the direct road thereto. They hastened away, and as they entered the town, inquiry was made by them where the surgeons' mob was to be discovered, and receiving the information they wanted, they went and demanded the body of John Lancaster. When the sailors had obtained the body, two of them cast it on their shoulders, and carried him round by Islington. They being tired out with its pressure, two others laid themselves under the weight of the body, and carried it from thence to Shoreditch. Then two more carried it from Shoreditch to Coverley's Fields. At length, after they were all rendered completely weary, and unable to carry it any farther, the sequel of their project, and their ultimate contrivance to rid themselves of the body was an unanimous consent to lay it on the step of the first door they came to. They did so, and then went their way. This gave birth to a great riot in the neighbourhood, which brought an old woman, who lived in the house, down-stairs. When she saw the corpse lie at the step of the door, she proclaimed, with an agitated spirit, 'Lord, here is my son, John Lancaster!' This being spread abroad, came to the knowledge of the Methodists, who made a collection, and got him a shroud and a good strong coffin. I was soon informed of this event, which was peculiarly singular, as the seamen had no knowledge of the body, nor to whom he belonged when living. My second wife went with me to see him, previous to the burial; but neither of us could perceive the least alteration in his visage or features, or any appearance of violence on any part of his body. A pleasant smile appeared in his countenance, and he lay as in a sweet sleep."

Told gives a terrible picture of the state of Newgate about 1744—the felons swearing and cursing at the preacher, and the ordinary himself guarding the prison doors on Sunday morning, to obstruct Told's entrance. Told, however, zealous in the cause, persevered, and soon formed a society of about forty of the debtors, who formed his Sunday congregation. The ordinary, however, soon contrived to shut out Told from this part of the prison

also. He therefore betook himself almost entirely to the graver malefactors. His account of some of these unhappy men is extremely interesting. During his visits to Newgate six men of good family were lying there, sentenced to death for highway robbery. Of these, one was the son of an Irish divine, two others were men of fortune, and a fourth was a naval officer, to whom a daughter of the Duke of Hamilton was engaged to be married. After an election dinner, at Chelmsford, these men, for fun, had sallied out and robbed a farmer in the highway. The king was unwilling to pardon any of the party; but at the incessant importunities of Lady Elizabeth Hamilton, at last consented to reprieve her lover, but only at the gallows' foot. He fainted when the halter was removed, and was instantly lifted into the carriage, where Lady Betty awaited him. Six weeks after, to Told's vexation, he found the reprieved man gambling with a fraudulent bankrupt, who shortly afterwards was himself executed at Tyburn. Told's next visit was to Mary Edmonson, a poor girl hung at Kennington Common for murdering her aunt at Rotherhithe. The girl was entirely innocent, and the real murderer, a relation, who was a foot-soldier, came up into the cart to salute her before she was turned off. Some time after, this man riding in a post-chaise past the gallows at Kennington, said to a friend, "There is the place where my kinswoman was hung wrongfully. I should have gone in her room." The rascal was soon after found guilty of highway robbery, and cast for death, but reprieved by the judge, who did not wish to draw attention to the scandal of an innocent person having been sent to the gallows. Silas Told says that at the execution of Mary Edmonson he walked by the cart, urging her to prayer, holding the bridle of the sheriff's horse, in spite of a most cruel and violent mob. Told also mentions attending Harris, the "Flying Highwayman," to the gallows, a man who, the very morning of his execution, was so violent in the chapel that the ordinary ran for his life. Just beyond Hatton Garden, after some exhortations of honest Told, the indomitable ruffian, at his request, shut his eyes, hung back his head on the side-rail of the cart, and after ten minutes' meditation burst into tears, and, clapping his hands together, cried, "Now I know that the Lord Jesus has forgiven me all my sins, and I have nothing to do but to die." He then burst into a loud extemporary prayer, and continued happy to the last, but still denying that he ever "flew" a turnpike-gate in his life. Another case mentioned by Told does not give us a very enlarged view of the tender mercies of the time. A poor man, Anderson, entirely destitute, was sentenced to death for taking sixpence from two washerwomen in Hoxton Fields. The man had served with credit on board a man-of-war, and his own parish had petitioned on his behalf. The Privy Council, however, insisted on confounding him with one of the same name, a celebrated highwayman of the day, and to Tyburn he went.

In 1770, when Mr. Akerman, one of the keepers, appeared before a Committee of the House of Commons, Newgate appears to have been a sink of filth and a den of iniquity. It was over-crowded, ill-disciplined, badly ventilated, and ill-supplied with water. The prisoners died in great numbers; and as Mr. Akerman, a good and trusty official, stated, two whole sets of gaol-officers had been cut off by gaol distemper since he had been in office; and in the spring of 1750 the gaol was so terribly infectious, that the contagion was carried into the Old Bailey court, and two of the judges, the Lord Mayor, and several of the jury, more than sixty in all, died in consequence. A huge ventilator was then erected, but this alarmed the whole neighbourhood, and the residents complained, with bitter outcries, that the poisonous air was drawn from the prison cells, to destroy all who lived near.

One of the earliest anecdotes of Newgate is to be found in a letter to the Duke of Shrewsbury, dated August 10, 1699. "All the talk of the town," says the writer, "is about a tragical piece of gallantry at Newgate. I don't doubt but what your grace has heard of a bastard son of Sir George Norton, who was under sentence of death for killing a dancing-master in the streets. The Lords Justices reprieved him, till they heard from the judge that no exception was to be taken at the verdict. It being signified to the young man, on Tuesday last in the afternoon, that he was to die the next day, his aunt, who was sister to his mother, brought two doses of opium, and they took it between them. The ordinary came soon after to perform his functions; but before he had done, he found so great alterations in both persons that it was no hard matter to find out the cause of it. The aunt frankly declared she could not survive her nephew, her life being wrapped up in his; and he declared that the law having put a period to his life, he thought it no offence to choose the way he would go out of the world. The keeper sent for his apothecary to apply remedies, who brought two vomits. The young man refused to take it, till they threatened to force it down by instruments. He told them, since he hoped the business was done, he would make him-

self and them easy, and swallowed the potion, and his aunt did the like. The remedy worked upon her, and set her a-vomiting, but had no effect on Mr. Norton, so that he dozed away gradually, and by eight that evening was grown senseless, though he did not expire till nine next morning. He was fully resolved upon the business, for he had likewise a charged pistol hid in the room. The aunt was carried to a neighbouring house, and has a guard upon her. They say she is like to recover; if she does, it will be hard if she suffer for such a transport of affection."

Among the many guilty and unhappy criminals who have sat in Newgate and counted the moments that lay between them and death, one of the most unhappy must have been that once popular preacher, Dr. Dodd, who was hung for forgery in 1777. Dodd was the son of a clergyman who was vicar of Bourne, in Lincolnshire. On leaving Cambridge he married imprudently, and became a small poet, and compiler of the "Beauties of Shakespeare," a work still reprinted. He then renounced literature, entered the Church, and in 1758 was appointed preacher to the Magdalen Hospital, where Horace Walpole describes his flowery sermons, which set all the ladies of fashion sobbing. Gross flattery of Dr. Squire, Bishop of St. David's, procured him, in 1763, the prebendaryship of Brecon. Soon after this the grateful bishop introduced Dodd to the Earl of Chesterfield, as a tutor to his son, and about the same time Dodd was appointed one of the king's chaplains, and in 1766 took his degree of LL.D. at Cambridge. He now dabbled in lotteries, and, having won a £1,000 prize, erected a chapel near Buckingham Palace, and also bought a share in Charlotte Chapel, Bloomsbury. Overwhelmed with debt, Dodd brought out several religious works, with the hope of winning patrons by his fulsome dedications. In 1773 he was appointed chaplain to the young Lord Chesterfield, the hopeless cub to whom the celebrated "Letters" were addressed. The rich living of St. George's, Hanover Square, just then falling vacant, Dodd was unwise enough to write an anonymous letter to Lady Apsley, wife of the Lord Chancellor, offering £3,000 for the appointment. The letter was traced to its source, and handed to the king, and the writer's name was ordered immediately to be struck out of the list of chaplains. Foote, always cruel in his fun, introduced Dodd into one of his Haymarket pieces as Dr. Simony. Dodd promised an explanation, but it never came. He retired for a time to Geneva, and the society of Lord Chesterfield, till the storm blew over.

Though enjoying an income of £800 a year,

Dodd, entangled by press of debts, one fatal day, signed the name of Lord Chesterfield, his old pupil, to a bond for £4,200. The signature disowned, Dodd, who then lived in Argyle Street, was apprehended. He at once repaid part of the money, and gave a judgment on his goods for the remainder. The prosecutors were reluctant to pro-

In Newgate this vain and shallow man acted the martyr, and wrote a book called "Thoughts in Prison," and believed in the possibility of a reprieve, though the king was inflexible, because in a recent case of forgery (that of Daniel and Robert Perreau, wine merchants), the sentence had been carried out. "If Dr. Dodd is pardoned,"

THE CONDEMNED CELL IN NEWGATE.

ceed; and Lord Chesterfield, it is said, placed the forgery in Dodd's hands, as he stood near a fire, in hopes that he would destroy it; but Dodd wanted promptitude and presence of mind, and soon after the Lord Mayor compelled the prosecution. He was tried and found guilty. Dr. Johnson, on being applied to, wrote the speech delivered by Dodd before his sentence. He also composed several petitions for him, and a sermon which Dr. Dodd delivered to his fellow-prisoners shortly before his execution.

the king said, "then the Perreaus were murdered."

The friends of Dodd were zealous to the last. Dr. Johnson told Boswell that £1,000 were ready for any gaoler who would let him escape. A wax image of him had also been made, to be left in his bed, but the scheme, somehow or other, miscarried. Anthony Morris Storer, writing to George Selwyn, who had a passion for executions, thus describes Dodd's behaviour at Tyburn :—

"The doctor, to all appearance, was rendered

THE OLD SESSIONS' HOUSE IN THE OLD BAILEY IN 1750. (See page 462.)

perfectly stupid from despair. His hat was flapped all round, and pulled over his eyes, which were never directed to any object around, nor even raised, except now and then lifted up in the course of his prayers. He came in a coach, and a very heavy shower of rain fell just upon his entering the cart, and another just at his putting on his night-cap.

"He was a considerable time in praying, which some people standing about seemed rather tired with; they rather wished for some more interesting part of the tragedy. The wind, which was high, blew off his hat, which rather embarrassed him, and discovered to us his countenance, which we could scarcely see before. His hat, however, was soon restored to him, and he went on with his prayers. There were two clergymen attending him, one of whom seemed very much affected; the other, I suppose, was the ordinary of Newgate, as he was perfectly indifferent and unfeeling in everything that he said and did.

"The executioner took both the hat and wig off at the same time. Why he put on his wig again I do not know, but he did, and the doctor took off his wig a second time, and then tied on a nightcap which did not fit him; but whether he stretched that, or took another, I could not perceive. He then put on his nightcap himself, and upon his taking it, he certainly had a smile on his countenance. Very soon afterwards there was an end of all his hopes and fears on this side the grave. He never moved from the place he first took in the cart; seemed absorbed in despair, and utterly dejected without any other signs of animation but in praying."

There is a tradition that the hangman had been bribed to place the knot of the rope in a particular manner under Dodd's ear, and also that when cut down, the body was driven off to a house in Goodge Street, where Pott, the celebrated surgeon, endeavoured to restore animation. But the crowd had been great, and the delay too long; nevertheless, it was believed by many at the time that Dodd was really resuscitated and sent abroad. His wife, who regarded him with great affection, died some years after, in poverty.

In 1802 Governor Wall was hung at Newgate, for the murder of Benjamin Armstrong, a soldier, who had been under his command at Goree, in Africa. The high rank of Wall, and the long period that had elapsed since the crime had been committed, excited great interest in his fate. He had been Governor of Goree in 1782, and was disliked by both officers and men, for his severe and unforgiving disposition. The day before he returned to England, worn out with the climate,

twenty or thirty men of the African corps came to petition the governor with regard to certain money stopped from their pay. The spokesman at the head of these soldiers was the unfortunate Benjamin Armstrong, who was extremely respectful in his manner, and paid the governor every deference. Wall, whose temper was no doubt aggravated by illness, instantly ordered Armstrong and his companions back to the barracks, and threatened them with punishment. The men obeyed, and quietly retired. Soon after his dinner-hour, Wall ran out of his rooms, and beat a man who appeared to be drunk, and snatching a bayonet from the sentry, struck him with it, and ordered both men under arrest. Eager for revenge on the "mutinous rascals," as he called them, Wall then ordered the long-roll to be beat, and parade called. Three hundred men, without firearms, were formed into a circle, two deep, in the midst of which stood the drummers, and the governor and his staff. A gun-carriage was then dragged up, and Benjamin Armstrong was called from the ranks. Five or six black slaves then lashed the unfortunate soldier to the rings of the gun-carriage, and Armstrong was ordered 800 lashes. With unusual cruelty, the governor ordered the slaves to use, not the cat-o'-nine-tails, but long lashings of rope, nearly an inch in circumference. Every twenty-five lashes a fresh slave was called up to continue the punishment, and the governor encouraged the slaves by shouting "Lay on, you black beasts, or I'll lay on you. Cut him to the heart; cut his liver out At the end of this ferocity, Armstrong, with his back beaten black, was led to the hospital, saying he should certainly die. The rope had bruised, not cut the flesh, yet the injuries were only the more dangerous. Five days after the governor left Goree Armstrong died.

In 1784 Wall was arrested at Bath, but managed to escape from the king's messengers, at the "Brown Bear," Reading, and escaped to France, where he changed his name. Many years later Wall rashly returned to England, and in 1801 wrote to Lord Pelham, Secretary of State, announcing his readiness to submit to a trial. He was tried in 1802. He pleaded that Armstrong was the ringleader of an open mutiny. A prisoner had been released, he himself had been threatened with a bayonet, and the soldiers had threatened to break open the stores. He denied that he had ever blown men from cannon. It was clear from the evidence that the grossest cruelty had been used, and Wall was at once found guilty, and sentence of death passed.

In that curious and amusing work, "A Book for a Rainy Day," Mr. J. T. Smith, formerly keeper of the Print Room in the British Museum. says:—

"Solomon, a pencil dealer, assured me that he could procure me a sight of the governor, if I would only accompany him in the evening to Hatton Garden, and smoke a pipe with Dr. Ford, the ordinary of Newgate, with whom he said he was particularly intimate. Away we trudged, and upon entering the club-room of a public-house, we found the said doctor most pompously seated in a superb masonic chair, under a stately crimson canopy, placed between the windows. The room was clouded with smoke whiffed to the ceiling, which gave me a better idea of what I had heard of the Black Hole of Calcutta than any place I had seen. There were present at least a hundred associates of every denomination. Of this number, my Jew, being a favoured man, was admitted to a whispering audience with the doctor, which soon produced my introduction to him."

Sunrise, the next morning, found Mr. Smith waiting by appointment for his new friend, Dr. Ford, at Newgate ; and this is how he describes the end of Governor Wall :—

"As we crossed the press-yard a cock crew, and the solitary clanking of a restless chain was dreadfully horrible. The prisoners had not risen. Upon our entering a cold stone room, a most sickly stench of green twigs, with which an old round-shouldered, goggle-eyed man was endeavouring to kindle a fire, annoyed me almost as much as the canaster fumigation of the doctor's Hatton Garden friends.

"The prisoner entered. He was death's counterfeit, tall, shrivelled, and pale ; and his soul shot so piercingly through the port-holes of his head, that the first glance of him nearly terrified me. I said in my heart, putting my pencil in my pocket, 'God forbid that I should disturb thy last moments !' His hands were clasped, and he was truly penitent. After the yeoman had requested him to stand up, he 'pinioned him,' as the Newgate phrase is, and tied the cord with so little feeling, that the governor, who had not given the wretch the accustomed fee, observed, 'You have tied me very tight,' upon which Dr. Ford ordered him to slacken the cord, which he did, but not without muttering. 'Thank you, sir,' said the governor to the doctor, 'it is of little moment.' He then observed to the attendant, who had brought in an immense iron shovelful of coals to throw on the fire, 'Ay, in one hour that will be a blazing fire;' then, turning to the doctor, questioned him, 'Do tell me, sir : I am informed I shall go down with great force ; is that so ?' After the construction and action of the machine had been explained, the doctor questioned the governor as to what kind of men he had at

Goree. 'Sir,' he answered, 'they sent me the very riff-raff.' The poor soul then joined the doctor in prayer ; and never did I witness more contrition at any condemned sermon than he then evinced."

Directly the execution was over, Mr. Smith left Newgate, where the hangman was selling the rope that had hung Governor Wall for a shilling an inch, and in Newgate Street a starved old man was selling another identical rope, at the ridiculously low price of only sixpence an inch ; while at the north-east corner of Warwick Lane a woman known as "Rosy Emma," reputed wife of the yeoman of the halter, was selling a third identical noose to the Epping buttermen, who had come that morning to Newgate Market.

The execution, in the year 1807, of two men, named Haggerty and Holloway, for the murder in November, 1802, of Mr. Steel, a lavender-merchant in the Strand, led to a frightful catastrophe. The body of the murdered man was found in a gravel-pit between Hounslow and Staines, the head crushed in by the blow of a bludgeon. Nothing could be discovered of the offenders till the beginning of 1807, when Hanfield, a convict at Portsmouth, confessed that he had helped in the murder, and disclosed the names of his two accomplices. One of these men, Haggerty, was a marine on board the *Shannon* frigate, then lying in at Deal ; the other, Holloway, a thief, was then lying in Clerkenwell Prison. The informer's story was this :—The robbery had been planned at the "Black Horse and Turk's Head," Dyot Street, Bloomsbury, whence the three men had started together to Hounslow Heath. The doomed man came at the time expected, and they knocked him down. While they were searching him a night-coach appeared, and Mr. Steele struggled to get across the road. Holloway then called out, "I'll silence the beggar," and killed him with two furious blows of a bludgeon. The evidence of this man was much doubted at the time. He had been a hackney-coachman, and a thief, and had deserted from several regiments ; and it was proved that he had been heard to say, that rather than bear seven years at the hulks, he would hang as many men as were killed at the battle of Copenhagen. In the court, the two men, who were found guilty, pleaded their innocence, and the last act of Holloway, in the press-yard, was to fall on his knees, and declare before God that he was innocent. Haggerty also protested his innocence, but without going on his knees. On the day of execution some 80,000 people assembled. Even before the prisoners appeared, several women were trampled to death. At the end of Green Arbour

Court, a pieman and his basket being upset, many persons fell and perished. One poor woman, feeling herself lost, threw an infant at her breast to a bystander, who passed it on and on, till it was placed safely under a cart. In one part of the crowd seven persons died from suffocation alone. A cart, overladen with spectators, broke down, and many of those who were in it were trampled to death. Nothing could be so horrible as this fighting crowd, mad with rage and fear. Till the gallows was removed, and the marshals and constables cleared the street, nothing could be done for the sufferers. Twenty-eight persons were killed and nearly seventy injured in this brutal struggle.

The execution of the Cato Street conspirators before Newgate, on Monday, May 1, 1820, was one of the most ghastly scenes ever witnessed by a London mob. Thistlewood, the leader of this conspiracy, had been in the Marines. His companions were James Ings, a butcher; Richard Tidd, a bootmaker; William Davidson, a cabinet-maker; John T. Brunt, and others. They had agreed to take advantage of a dinner at the Earl of Harrowby's, in Grosvenor Square, to which all the cabinet ministers had been invited, to break in and murder them all. Ings had resolved that the heads of Lords Castlereagh and Sidmouth should be cut off and put in two bags provided for the purpose; and he particularly wished to preserve the right hand of Lord Castlereagh as a valuable curiosity. The cannon in Gray's Inn Lane and the Artillery Ground were to be captured, the Mansion House taken, the Bank sacked, the barracks fired, and a Provisional Government established. Pikes and guns had been collected, and hand-grenades made. The conspirators were discovered in a loft in Cato Street, Edgware Road. Smithers, about the first police-officer who entered, was run through with a sword by Thistlewood, and a desperate struggle then ensued. At this moment Captain Fitzclarence (son of the Duke of Clarence) arrived, with a party of the Coldstream Guards, and captured nine of the conspirators. Thistlewood was taken the next day, at a house in Little Moorfields.

At the trial eleven of the conspirators were sentenced to death, but six of these were afterwards respited. Thistlewood, Ings, Brunt, Tidd, and Davidson were executed. The Government had shown the utmost anxiety to prevent a riot or a rescue. Life Guards were stationed in the Old Bailey, Newgate Street, and Ludgate Hill, and one hundred artillerymen and six pieces of artillery were placed in the centre of Blackfriars Bridge. The scaffold was lined with black cloth, and near

the drop were five plain coffins, and a block for the decapitation of the criminals. Thistlewood was the first to ascend the scaffold. He was collected and calm, and bowed twice to the crowd. When Mr. Cotton exhorted him to pray, and asked him if he repented of his crime, he exclaimed, several times, "No, not at all!" and was also heard to say, "I shall soon know the last grand secret." Tidd ran up the steps, and bowed on all sides. There was a slight cheering when he appeared, in which he made a faint attempt to join. Ings seemed mad with excitement. He moved his head to and fro, cried "Huzza!" three times, and commenced singing, "Oh, give me death or liberty!" There was partial cheering. He exclaimed, from time to time, "Here we go, my lads! You see the last remains of James Ings. Remember, I die the enemy of tyranny, and would sooner die in chains than live in slavery." When the chaplain exhorted him, the reckless ruffian said, with a coarse laugh, "I am not afraid to go before God or man." Then he shouted to the silent executioner, "Now, old man, finish me tidy. Pull the halter a little tighter: it might slip." He then waved a handkerchief three times, and said he hoped the chaplain would give him a good character. Davidson, a man of colour, who had just received the sacrament, prayed with great fervency, and expressed penitence for his crimes. All he said was, "God bless you all! Good-bye!" and after the Lord's Prayer, he exclaimed, "God save the king!"

Brunt, the last who came out, requested some bystander to get him some snuff out of his pocket, as his hands were tied. He took it with great coolness, and said he wondered where the gaoler would put him, but he supposed it would be somewhere where he should sleep well. He would make a present of his body to King George the Fourth.

Thistlewood, just before he was turned off, said in a low tone to a person under the scaffold, "I have now but a few moments to live, and I hope the world will think that I have at least been sincere in my endeavours." At the last moment, Tidd cried out to Ings, "How are you, my hearty?"

At a signal given by the Rev. Mr. Cotton the platform fell. At the very instant Ings was observed to join Davidson in prayer. Half an hour after, a "resurrection-man," who received a fee of twenty guineas, disguised in a rough jacket and trousers, and a mask on his face, appeared with an amputating-knife, and severed Thistlewood's head from his body. The hangman's man then held up the head by the hair, and exclaimed three times,

"This is the head of Arthur Thistlewood, a traitor." The same ceremony was then performed with skill on Tidd, Ings, Davidson, and Brunt. The mob loudly hissed, and there was a deep groan from the crowd, and shrieks from the women, when Thistlewood's head was removed. When the conspirators appeared on the scaffold, the troops were ordered as close as possible to the scene of execution; but no disorder took place. Five of the remaining conspirators were transported for life.

The execution of Fauntleroy, the great banker, of 6, Berners Street, took place at Newgate, in 1824. It was supposed that this man, by forged powers of attorney, had disposed of about £400,000 worth of Bank of England stock; the Bank, however, prosecuted for only £170,000 worth. Such was Fauntleroy's audacity, that it is said he would sometimes forge the name of a man with whom he was conversing, and then send it, still wet, into the clerks' room, to show that it had just been written by his visitor. Singularly enough, a tin box was found in his possession, with a list of the greater part of his frauds, and this formal statement at the bottom of all:—"In order to keep up the credit of our house, I have forged powers of attorney for the above sums and parties, and sold out to the amount here stated, and without the knowledge of my partners. I kept up the payments of the dividends, but made no entries of such payments in our books. *The Bank began first to refuse to discount our acceptances, and destroy the credit of our house. The Bank shall smart for it.*" It was known that Fauntleroy was an epicure and a voluptuary, but his hospitality had won many friends, and no one doubted his honour. He attributed his losses to building speculations. He denied embezzling one shilling. Sixteen respectable witnesses vouched for his honour and integrity. The crowd at his execution, on the 30th of November, was unprecedented. Every window and house-roof near Newgate was crowded with well-dressed men. Nothing had been seen like the mob since Thistlewood and his gang were decapitated. When the sheriffs entered the banker's cell, at a quarter before eight, he lifted his eyes sadly, bowed, but said nothing. The felon was still a gentleman. He was dressed in a black coat and trousers, with silk stockings, and dress shoes. He was perfectly calm and composed. The terrible procession formed quickly. Two friends gave him their arms, and he followed the sheriffs and the Rev. Mr. Cotton, the ordinary of Newgate. The moment he appeared every hat was taken off. Two minutes more, and his body swayed in the thick November air.

Only two other executions for forgery ever took place in England; and in 1837 the capital punishment for that crime was abolished. The late Mr. Charles Dickens used to relate an anecdote of the last moments of Fauntleroy. His elegant dinners had always been enriched by some remarkable and matchless curaçoa. Three of his boon companions had a parting interview with him in the condemned cell. They were about to retire, when the most impressive of the three stepped back, and said, "Fauntleroy, you stand on the verge of the grave. Remember the text, my dear man, that 'we brought nothing into this world, and it is certain we can take nothing out.' Have you any objection, therefore, to tell me now, as a friend, where you got that curaçoa?"

It was long rumoured in London, of course absurdly, that Fauntleroy, by means of his vast wealth and acquaintance, had bribed the hangman to slip a silver tube down his throat, which saved his life. More resolute people declared he had escaped to America, and had actually been seen in Paris. So legends, even in our own days, spring up and take root.

The murder of a poor Italian boy, by a body-snatcher named Bishop, and another scoundrel called Williams, excited the utmost horror and alarm in London, in the year 1831. Upwards of 30,000 persons assembled to witness their execution, on the 5th of December, at Newgate. These men had decoyed the poor boy to a hovel in Nova Scotia Gardens, Bethnal Green, and had then drugged him with rum and laudanum, and drowned him in a well. At King's College they had asked twelve guineas for the body, and Bishop owned to having sold from 500 to 1,000 bodies, and to two other murders. The "Fortune of War" public-house, in Giltspur Street, seems to have been the rendezvous of these monsters. A great many persons were maimed and bruised at these executions, and the moment the murderers were turned off, the barriers between the gallows and Ludgate Hill were simultaneously broken asunder and torn up by the crowd.

In 1837 the execution of James Greenacre lent an additional horror to Newgate. This man had murdered Hannah Brown, a woman to whom he had been engaged to be married, and had then cut the body in pieces, and hidden portions of it in various parts of London, the trunk being placed in a sack, and concealed behind some flagstones, near the "Pine Apple" toll-bar, Edgware Road. He confessed at last that Hannah Brown had deceived him, by pretending to have property, and that one night, when she called at his lodgings, in Carpenters' Buildings, Lambeth, she laughed at her trick. In a rage at this, he struck her with a silk-roller a blow which proved mortal, and he then formed the resolution of cutting up and concealing the body.

The night of the execution of this wretch, hundreds of persons slept on the steps of the prison and of St. Sepulchre's Church, and boys remained all night clinging to the lamp-posts. The crowds in the streets spent the night in ribald jokes and drunken scuffles. Greenacre, when he passed to the gallows, was totally unmanned. He could not

commanding a sight of the drop were filled with spectators, who paid for places, at prices ranging from five or seven shillings to a couple of guineas a head. In some instances a first-floor was let for £12. The visitors (not always of the lower description) spent the night playing at cards and singing choruses. To one of the exhortations to confession from those who visited him, Müller turned away, with the remark, "Man has no power to forgive sins, and there is no use in confessing them to him." As he approached the gallows he looked

CATO STREET. *From a View published in 1820.* (*See page 454.*)

articulate the responses to the ordinary, and was obliged to be supported, or he would have fallen. His last words, with a look of contempt at the yelling and hissing crowd, were, "Don't leave me long in the concourse."

Another of the celebrated executions at Newgate was that of Franz Müller, a young German tailor, in 1864. This man, in order, it is supposed, to obtain money to get to America, murdered a Mr. Briggs, in a carriage on the North London Railway, between Bow station and Hackney Wick. The murdered man's hat, watch, and chain had been seen in the possession of the murderer, who had fled to New York. Müller denied his guilt to the last. The night before the execution there was a most disgraceful scene round Newgate. The houses

up at the chain with perfect self-possession. The final conversation with the German minister of the Lutheran Church in Alie Street, Goodman's Fields, was to the following effect :—

Dr. Cappel : Müller, in a few moments you will stand before God. I ask you again, and for the last time, are you guilty, or not guilty?

Müller : Not guilty.

Dr. Cappel : You are not guilty?

Müller : God knows what I have done.

Dr. Cappel : God knows what you have done. Does He also know that you have committed this crime?

Müller : Yes, I have done it.

Dr. Cappel was actually leaning forward and listening when the drop fell. The Germans of London had exerted themselves warmly to obtain a reprieve for Müller, and even the King of Prussia telegraphed to the Queen to request her intervention to save Müller's life.

The execution of François Benjamin Courvoisier, a Swiss valet, found guilty of the murder of his master, Lord William Russell, took place at Newgate in 1840. Lord William, who was in his seventy-

down, saying, "Some person has been robbing; for God's sake go and see where his lordship is!" They went into the room, and found Lord William on his bed murdered, and his head nearly severed from his body. When the policeman came, and asked Courvoisier to assist him, he fell back in a

MRS. BROWNRIGG.   *From the Original Print.*   (*See page* 458.)

third year, lived alone in his house, in Norfolk Street, Park Lane, his establishment consisting of two women-servants and Courvoisier, a Swiss valet. On the morning of the murder the housemaid, rising as usual, found the papers in her master's writing-room scattered about, and in the hall an opera-glass, a cloak, and some other articles of dress wrapped up, as if ready to be carried off. She instantly went up-stairs and called Courvoisier, who was almost dressed, and he at once ran

chair, and said, "This is a shocking job. I shall lose my place, and lose my character." The premises having been searched, two bank-notes for £10 and £5, supposed to have been taken from Lord Russell's box, and several rings, were found concealed behind the skirting-board of the butler's pantry. Suspicion at once fell on Courvoisier; and on being tried and found guilty, he confessed the murder. He said that, disliking his place, he stole some plate, and had subsequently resolved to rob the house. Then before midnight his master found him in the dining-room, and suspected him of theft. On Lord William's return to his room, the thought of murder first entered Courvoisier's mind. His character was gone, and he said he thought the only way to cover his fault was the murder of his master. He went into the dining-room, and took a carving-knife from the side-board. He then went up-stairs and opened his master's bed-room door. There was a rushlight burning, and Lord William was asleep. Courvoisier accomplished the murder, the old man never speaking a word, and only moving his arm a little. Courvoisier then opened a Russia leather case, took several things, and also a £10 note, which he hid behind the skirting-board. After he had committed this foul murder, Courvoisier went to bed, as usual, having first made marks on the outer door, as if there had been thieves there. The execution of Courvoisier took place on the 6th of July, 1840. His constant exclamation in prison had been, "O God! how could I have committed so dreadful a crime? It was madness. When I think of it I can't believe it." He also confessed that he had contemplated self-destruction. Upwards of 20,000 persons had gathered to witness the murderer's end. Several hundreds had waited all night at the debtors' door of the Old Bailey, and high fees had been paid for windows, and even the roofs of the houses opposite Newgate were crowded. There was a sprinkling of women and boys in the crowd, and a distinguishable number of men-servants. As the bell began to toll, at five minutes to eight o'clock, the vast multitude uncovered, and at two minutes after the hour Courvoisier ascended the steps leading to the drop, followed by the executioner and the ordinary of the prison. A few yells were uttered, but the mass of the spectators were silent. Courvoisier's step was steady and collected, his face pale, but calm and unmoved. When on the drop he waved his bound hands up and down two or three times, and this was the only visible symptom of emotion. When the noose was adjusted, he lifted up his hands to his breast, as if in fervent prayer. He died without any violent struggle, his raised hands gradually sinking. His counsel, Mr. C. Phillips, was afterwards much blamed for trying to prove the police guilty of conspiracy, to obtain the large reward, when, as it was said, Courvoisier had already confessed to him his guilt; but the confession of Courvoisier was really of a much later date.

There is still an old print extant (of which we give a copy on page 457), representing that cruel old hag, Mrs. Elizabeth Brownrigg, in the condemned cell at Newgate. This celebrated murderess, who was nearly torn to pieces by the mob, on her way to Tyburn, was a parish midwife, living in Flower-de-Luce Court, Fetter Lane. Her cruelties to her apprentices we have before related.

Of the cruelties of the old press-yard we have a terrible instance, in the case of Edward Burnworth, in 1726. This man, a most daring highwayman and murderer, having refused to plead, was loaded with boards and weights. He continued an hour and three minutes, with a mass of metal upon him weighing three hundred, three quarters, and two pounds. He then prayed he might be put to the bar again, which the court granted, and he was arraigned, and pleaded "not guilty." He was, however, found guilty, and received sentence of death.

There is an interesting story of Mr. Akerman, one of the old governors of Newgate, with whom Boswell contracted a friendship. On one occasion, says Boswell, a fire broke out in Newgate. The prisoners were turbulent and in much alarm. Mr. Akerman, addressing them, told them there was no fear, for the fire was not in the stone prison; and that if they would be quiet, he then promised to come in among them, and lead them to a further end of the building; offering, in addition, not to leave them till they were reassured, and gave him leave. To this generous proposal they agreed. Mr. Akerman then, having first made them fall back from the gate, lest they should be tempted to break out, went in, closed the gate, and, with the determined resolution of an ancient Roman, ordered the outer turnkey upon no account to unbar the gate, even though the prisoners should break their word (which he trusted they would not), and by force bring him to order it. "Never mind me," said he, "should that happen." The prisoners then peaceably followed him though passages of which he had the keys, to a part of the gaol the farthest from the fire. Having, by this judicious conduct, says Boswell, fully satisfied them that there was no immediate risk, if any at all, he then addressed them: "Gentlemen, you are now convinced that I told you true. I have no doubt that the engines will soon extinguish this fire. If they should not, a sufficient guard will come, and you shall be all taken out and lodged in the compters. I assure you, upon my word and honour, that I have not a farthing insured. I have left my house that I might take care of you. I will keep my promise, and stay with you, if you insist upon it; but if you will allow me to go out and look after my family and property, I shall be obliged to you." Struck with his courage, truthfulness, and honourable sense of duty, the felons shouted: "Master Akerman, you have done bravely. It was very kind of you. By all means go and take care of your own concerns." He did so accordingly; and they remained, and were all preserved. Dr. Johnson said of this man, whom Wellington would have esteemed: "Sir, he who has long had constantly in view the worst of mankind, and is yet eminent for the humanity of his disposition, must have had it originally in a high degree, and continued to cultivate it very carefully."

Great good was effected in Newgate by the Ladies' Prison Visiting Association, which commenced its labours among the female prisoners of Newgate in 1817. The Quakers had originated the movement, and it soon produced its effects. Mrs. Fry was the indefatigable leader of these philanthropists. The female prisoners in Newgate, before the good work began, were idle, abandoned, riotous, and drunken. There was no attempt at general inspection; the only distinction was between the tried and the untried. They slept promiscuously in large companies. Frequent communication was allowed them, through an iron grating, with visitors of both sexes, many of them more degraded and desperate than themselves. The good effected was rapid and palpable. The worst women became quiet, orderly, and industrious; the whole of them grew neater and cleaner; many learned to read; others sat for hours knitting with the ladies who visited Newgate. Two of the committee, if possible, visited the prison daily, and observed the cases of the individual prisoners. The prisoners' patchwork, spinning, and knitting were sold for them, and, if possible, part of their earnings was put by, to accumulate for their benefit when they returned to the outer world. Schools were started for the children and the grown-up women. The governesses were chosen from the most intelligent, steady, and persevering of the prisoners. A careful system of supervision was also established. Over every twelve or thirteen women a matron was placed, who was answerable for their work, and kept an account of their conduct. A ward woman attended to the cleanliness of the wards. A yard woman maintained good order in the yard, and the sick room was ruled by a nurse and an assistant. These managers were all prisoners, selected from their orderly and respectable habits, and these situations became the best badge for good conduct. The female prisoners assembled every day in the committee-room, to hear the Bible read, or a prayer delivered, by the matron or one of the visitors. The women, on being dismissed, says Mr. J. J. Gurney, returned to their several employments, with perfect order and obedience. The women grew very honest among

themselves. In no less than 100,000 manufactured articles of work not one article was stolen. The best proof of amelioration was the fact of the great decrease of re-commitments between 1817 and 1819. Many of the women kept under supervision by the committee preserved good characters as servants, or earned an honest livelihood at home. Several of the women, on discharge, received small loans, to help them on, and these loans they repaid by most punctual weekly instalments. At the end of 1817, Sir T. F. Buxton obtained a return of the re-commitments on the male side of Newgate, and it appeared that out of 203 men 47 of those convicted had been confined there before within the two previous years. The returns on the female side, since the Ladies' Association had reformed the prison, were not more, as compared with the male side, than as 4 to 47. It had at one time been as 3 to 5. Can anything more be said to prove what a great good women may effect, who look upon female prisoners not as brute beasts, to be punished and despised, but as souls, to be won back and reclaimed? They softened these women's hearts, and tenderly restored them to humanity. The object of justice, in their eyes, was to reform, not merely to punish. Hence the kind look did more than the lash—the soft word than the hard fetter. The good work has, since those days, been carried further, and there is still much to do.

The first memorable escape from Newgate was that of Jack Sheppard, a thievish young London carpenter, in 1724. This hero of modern thieves (mischievously immortalised by Mr. Harrison Ainsworth) had been condemned to death with a rogue named Blueskin, for stealing cloth from a Mr. Kneebone, a draper in the Strand, to whom Sheppard had formerly been apprenticed. The whole story of his adventures shows the loose discipline of Newgate at the time. Considering the lad was a practical carpenter and locksmith, and probably bribed the gaolers heavily, we see no great miracles in his escapes, which only needed cleverness, knowledge of wood and iron work, and steady perseverance. On the first occasion Jack, during an interview with two female friends in the lodge at Newgate, broke a spike off the hatch, and, by the assistance of the two women, being slim and flexible, was pulled through the opening, and so escaped. Retaken at Finchley, the angry turnkeys gripped the young thief with handcuffs, loaded him with heavy irons (such as are still fastened above the side doors of the prison), and chained him to a stout staple in the floor of a strong room called "The Castle." There people of all ranks came to see him, and all gave money to the young lion of the hour, but extreme care was taken that no sympathisers should pass him a chisel or a file. Jack was, however, eager for notoriety, and resolute to baffle the turnkeys. He chose a quiet afternoon, when most of the keepers were away with their amiable charges at the Old Bailey Sessions. With a small nail he had found he loosened his chain from the floor-staple, then slipped his small thievish hands through his handcuffs, and tied up his fetters as high as he could with his garters. With a piece of his broken chain he worked out of the chimney a transverse iron bar that stopped his upward progress. The keepers smoked and drank, and left Jack alone with mischief. Once on the airy roof, Jack, quick at breaking out of prisons, now tried his hand at breaking in, for, to force a way to the chapel, Jack broke into the Red Room, over the Castle, having found a large nail, with which he could work wonders. The Red Room door had not been unbolted for seven long years. Jack forced off the lock in seven short minutes, and got into a passage leading to the chapel. To force a strong bolt here, he broke a hole through the wall, and, with an iron spike from the chapel door, opened a way between the chapel and the lower leads. Three more doors flew open before him; over a wall, and he was on the upper leads. At this crisis, requiring a blanket, to tear up and make a rope for his descent, he had the courage to go back for it, all the way to his cell, and then, making a tough rope, he fastened it with the chapel spike, and let himself down on the leads of a turner, who lived adjoining the prison. Slipping in at a garret window, he stole softly down stairs, and let himself out (a woman who heard his irons clink thought it was the cat). Passing the watch-house of St. Sepulchre, he went up Gray's Inn Lane, and hid himself in a cow-house, near Tottenham Court. The next day he bribed a shoemaker to procure him a smith's hammer and a punch, and rid himself of his irons, the last souvenirs of Newgate. A few nights after, this incorrigible scamp broke into a pawnbroker's shop in Drury Lane, stole a sword and some coats, snuff-boxes, rings, and watches, and rigged himself out in black, with ruffled shirt, diamond ring, silver-hilted sword, gold watch, and other suitable garnishings. Two nights afterwards, getting drunk with his mother near his old haunts, the young thief was seized and thrown again into Newgate, no more to escape. Sir James Thornhill painted his portrait in prison, and, after an unsuccessful plot to rescue him at Turnstile, he was hung at Tyburn. An opera and a farce were founded upon his adventures, and a preacher in the City is said to have thus spiritualised his career:—

"Now, my beloved, what a melancholy consideration it is, that men should show so much regard for the preservation of a poor, perishing body, that can remain at most but a few years, and at the same time be so unaccountably negligent of a precious soul, which must continue to the ages of eternity! Oh, what care, what pains, what diligence, and what contrivances are made use of for, and laid out upon, these frail and tottering tabernacles of clay, when, alas! the nobler part of us is allowed so very small a share of our concern, that we scarce will give ourselves the trouble of bestowing a thought upon it.

"We have a remarkable instance of this in a notorious malefactor, well known by the name of Jack Sheppard. What amazing difficulties has he overcome! what astonishing things has he performed, for the sake of a stinking, miserable carcase, hardly worth hanging! How dexterously did he pick the padlock of his chain with a crooked nail! How manfully burst his fetters asunder, climb up the chimney, wrench out an iron bar, break his way through a stone wall, and make the strong door of a dark entry fly before him, till he got upon the leads of the prison! And then, fixing a blanket to the wall with a spike, how intrepidly did he descend to the top of the turner's house, and how cautiously pass down the stairs, and make his escape at the street-door!

"Oh, that ye were all like Jack Sheppard! Mistake me not, my brethren; I don't mean in a carnal, but a spiritual sense; for I purpose to spiritualise these things. What a shame it would be, if we should not think it worth our while to take as much pains, and employ as many deep thoughts, to save our souls, as he has done to preserve his body! Let me exhort you, then, to open the locks of your hearts with the nail of repentance; burst asunder the fetters of your beloved lusts; mount the chimney of hope, take from thence the bar of good resolution; break through the stone wall of despair, and all the strongholds in the dark entry of the valley of the shadow of death; raise yourselves to the leads of divine meditation; fix the blanket of faith with the spike of the Church; let yourselves down to the turner's house of resignation, and descend the stairs of humility. So shall you come to the door of deliverance from the prison of iniquity, and escape the clutches of that old executioner, the devil, who 'goeth about like a roaring lion, seeking whom he may devour.'"

The condition of things in ancient Newgate was deplorable. When the contagious fever broke out·

there were no less than 800 prisoners crowded within the walls. It was not till 1810 that, through the exertions of Sir Richard Phillips, a Committee of the Common Council passed a resolution for building a new prison for debtors, and in 1815 the debtors were transferred from Newgate to the Giltspur Street Compter. In a Parliamentary Report of 1814, the following statement appeared of the way in which the chaplain's duties were performed :— " Beyond his attendance at chapel, and on those who are sentenced to death Dr. Ford feels but few duties to be attached to his office. He knows nothing of the state of morals in the prison; he never sees any of the prisoners in private. Though fourteen boys and girls from nine to thirteen years old were in Newgate in April last, he does not consider attention to them a point of his duty. He never knows that any have been sick till he gets a warning to attend their funeral ; and does not go to the infirmary, for it is not in his instructions." The prisoners were allowed to drink and gamble, and their amusement was the repeating stories of past villany and debauchery. " I scruple not to affirm," says Howard, " that half the robberies committed in and around London are planned in the prisons by that dreadful assemblage of criminals, and the number of idle people who visit them." Those who refused to associate with the criminals were submitted to mock trial, in which the oldest thief acted as judge, with a towel, tied in knots on each side of his head, for a wig ; and he had officers to put his sentences into execution. " Garnish," " footing," or " chummage," was demanded of all new prisoners. " Pay, or strip," was the order ; and the prisoner without

money had to part with some of his clothes, to contribute towards the expense of a revel, the older prisoners adding something to the " garnish" paid by the new comer. The practice of the prisoners cooking their own food had not been long discontinued in 1818.

Even in 1836 the Inspector of Prisons found fault with the system within the prison. The prisoners were allowed to amuse themselves with gambling, card-playing, and draughts ; sometimes they obtained, by stealth, says a writer in Knight's " London," the luxury of tobacco, and a newspaper. Sometimes they could get drunk. Instruments to facilitate prison-breaking were found in the prison. Combs and towels were not provided, and the supply of soap was insufficient. In their Report of 1843, the inspectors say, " It has been our painful duty, again and again, to point attention to the serious evils resulting from gaol association, and consequent necessary contamination in this prison. The importance of this prison, in this point of view, is very great. As the great metropolitan prison for the untried, it is here that those most skilled in crime of every form, those whom the temptations, the excesses, and the experience of this great city have led through a course of crime to the highest skill in the arts of depredation, and the lowest degradation of infamy, meet together with those who are new to such courses, and who are only too ready to learn how they may pursue the career they have just entered upon with most security from detection and punishment, and with greater success and indulgence." Since the passing of the Prisons' Regulation Act, Newgate has been under the control of the Government.

CHAPTER LIV.

THE OLD BAILEY.

Origin of the Name—The Old Sessions House—Constitution of the Court in Strype's Time—The Modern Central Criminal Court—Number of Persons tried here annually—Old Bailey Holidays—Speedy Justice—A Thief's Defence—The Interior of the Old Court—Celebrated Criminals tried here—Trial of the Regicides—Trial of Lord William Russell—The Press-yard—The Black Sessions of 1750—Sprigs of Rue in Court—Old Bailey Dinners—The Gallows in the Old Bailey—The Cart and the New Drop—Execution Statistics—Execution Customs—Memorable Executions—A Dreadful Catastrophe—The Pillory in the Old Bailey—The Surgeons' Hall—A Fatal Experiment—The Dissection of Lord Ferrers—Goldsmith as a Rejected Candidate—Famous Inhabitants—The Little Old Bailey—Sydney House—Green Arbour Court and Breakneck Steps—Goldsmith's Garret—A Region of Washerwomen—Percy's Visit to Goldsmith.

THERE is some dispute as to the origin of the name "Old Bailey," for while some think it implies the Ballium, or outer space beyond the wall, Maitland refers it to Bail Hill, an eminence where the bail, or bailiff, lived and held his court. Stow thinks the street was called from some old court held there, as, in the year 1356, the tenement and

ground upon Houndsditch, between Ludgate on the south and Newgate on the north, was appointed to John Cambridge, fishmonger and Chamberlain of London, " whereby," he says, " it seems that the Chamberlains of London have there kept their courts as now they do by the Guildhall ; and to this day the mayor and justices of this City kept their sessions in a part thereof now called the Sessions Hall, both for the City of London and Shire of Middlesex."

Strype describes the Old Sessions House as a fair and stately building, very commodious, and with large galleries on both sides for spectators, "the court-room," he remarks, "being advanced by stone steps from the ground, with rails and

destroyed in the "No Popery" Riots of 1780, but was rebuilt and enlarged in 1809 by the addition of the site of the old Surgeons' Hall.

The old constitution of this court for malefactors is given by "R. B.," in Strype (v. 384). "It," he says, "is called the King's Commission on the Peace of Oyer and Terminer, and Gaol Delivery of Newgate, for the City of London and County

THE CHAPEL IN NEWGATE. (*See page* 442.)

banisters, enclosed from the yard before it; and the bail-dock, which fronts the court where the prisoners are kept until brought to their trials, is also inclosed. Over the court-room is a stately dining-room, sustained by ten stone pillars, and over it a platform, headed with rails and banisters. There be five lodging-rooms, and other conveniences, on either side the court. It standeth backwards, so it hath no front toward the street; only the gateway leadeth into the yard before the house, which is spacious. It cost above £6,000 the building." A Court-house was erected here in 1773. It was

of Middlesex, which court is held at Justice Hall, in the Old Bailey, commonly called the Sessions House, and generally eight times, or oftener, every year. The judges are the Lord Mayor, the Recorder, and others of his Majesty's Justices of the Peace of the City of London, the two Sheriffs of London being always present; and oftentimes the judges (being always in these commissions) come, and sit to give their assistance. The jurors, for all matters committed in London, are citizens of London, . . . and the jurors for crimes and misdemeanors committed in Middlesex, are freeholders of the said county."

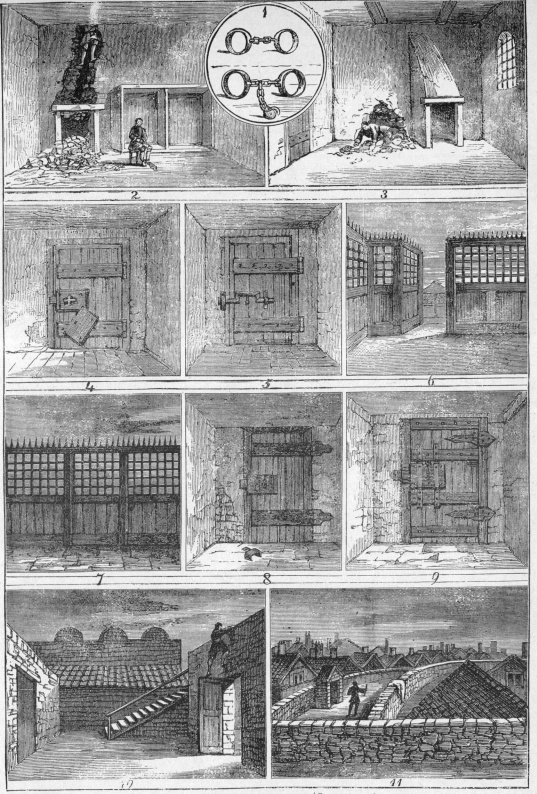

JACK SHEPPARD'S ESCAPES. (*See page* 459.)

1. Handcuffs and Feetlocks, and Padlock to Ground.   2. Cell over the Castle, Jack Sheppard fastened to the floor. Climbing up the Chimney, where he found a bar of iron.   3. Red Room over the Castle, into which he got out of the Chimney.   4. Door of the Red Room, the lock of which he put back.   5. Door of the Entry between the Red Room and the Chapel.   6 Door going into the Chapel, which he burst open.   7. Door going out of the Chapel towards the Leads.   8. Door with a Spring Lock, which he opened.   9. Door over the same Passage.   10. The Lower Leads.   11. The Higher Leads, the walls of which he got over, and descended by the staircase off the roof of a turner's house into the street.

Under the general title, "The Central Criminal Court," are joined both what are called the Old Court and the New. The former deals with the more weighty cases—those of deepest dye—and has echoed, without doubt, to more tales of the romance of crime than any other building in the kingdom.

"The judges of the Central Criminal Court," says Mr. Timbs (1868), "are the Lord Mayor (who opens the court), the Sheriffs, the Lord Chancellor (such is the order of the Act), the Judges, the Aldermen, Recorder, Common Serjeant of London, Judge of the Sheriff's Court, or City Commissioner, and any others whom the Crown may appoint as assistants. Of these the Recorder and Common Serjeant are in reality the presiding judges; a judge of the law only assisting when unusual points of the law are involved, or when conviction affects the life of the prisoner. Here are tried crimes of every kind, from treason to the pettiest larceny, and even offences committed on the high seas. The jurisdiction comprises the whole of the metropolis as now defined; with the remainder of Middlesex; the parishes of Richmond and Mortlake, in Surrey; and great part of Essex."

The court is regulated by Act of Parliament 4 and 5 Will. IV., c. 36.

As to the number of persons who are brought here into public notice, Mr. Sheriff Laurie, writing to the *Times* of November 28th, 1845, says, " I find upon investigation that upwards of two thousand persons annually are placed at the bar of the Old Bailey for trial. About one-third are acquitted, one-third are first offences, and the remaining portion have been convicted of felony before."

Trials are going on at the Old Bailey almost all the year round. Frequent, however, as they are, there are occasional pauses. Justice, it has been said, must nod sometimes, and therefore it is as well to provide for fitting repose elsewhere than on the judgment-seat. The sittings of the Central Criminal Court are held monthly, but as the whole of the month is not occupied in the trial of the prisoners on the calendar, the spare time forms a vacation, and such are the only vacations at the Old Bailey. In consequence of these frequent sittings, trials are often conducted and prisoners rewarded according to their merits, with surprising swiftness. A criminal may be guilty of theft in the morning, be apprehended before night, be committed by a magistrate the next day, and the day after that be tried, convicted, and sentenced at the Old Bailey—a speedy administration of justice, which must be highly gratifying to all concerned.

"The usual defence of a thief, especially at the Old Bailey," says Fielding, writing of the increase of robbers, "is an *alibi*. To prove this by perjury is a common act of Newgate friendship; and there seldom is any difficulty in procuring such witnesses. I remember a felon, within this twelvemonth, to have been proved to be in Ireland at the time when the robbery was sworn to have been done in London, and acquitted; but he was scarce gone from the bar, when the witness was himself arrested for a robbery committed in London, at that very time when he swore both he and his friend were in Dublin; for which robbery I think he was tried and executed."

The interior of the Old Court, which, naturally enough, from every point of view is more interesting than that of the New one, has been described in a lively manner by a writer in Knight's "Cyclopædia of London" (1851). "Passing," he says, "through a door in the wall which encloses the area between Newgate and the courts, we find a flight of steps on our right, leading up into the Old Court. This is used chiefly for prosecutors and witnesses. Farther on in the area, another flight of steps leads to a long passage into a corridor at the back of the court, with two doors opening into the latter, by one of which the judges and sheriffs reach the bench, and by the other, the barristers their place in the centre at the bottom. Both doors also lead to seats reserved for visitors. We enter, pause, and look round. The first sentiment is one of disappointment. The great and moral power and pre-eminence of the court makes one, however idly and unconsciously, anticipate a grander physical exhibition. What does meet our gaze is no more than a square hall of sufficient length, and breadth, and height, lighted up by three large square windows on the opposite wall, showing the top of the gloomy walls of Newgate, having on the left a gallery close to the ceiling, with projecting boxes, and on the right, the bench, extending the whole length of the wall, with desks at intervals for the use of the judges, whilst in the body of the court are, first, a dock for the prisoners below the gallery, with stairs descending to the covered passage by which prisoners are conveyed to and from the prison; then, just in advance of the left-hand corner of the dock, the circular witness-box, and in a similarly relative position to the witness-box, the jury-box, below the windows of the court, an arrangement that enables the jury to see clearly and without turning, the faces of the witnesses and of the prisoners; that enables the witness to identify the prisoner; and lastly, that enables the judges on the bench, and the counsel in the centre of the court below, to keep jury, witnesses, and prisoners all at once within the same, or nearly the same, line of view. We need only add to these features of the place the formidable row of law-books which occupies the centre of the green-baized table, around which are the counsel, reminding us of the passage in the 'Beggars' Opera'—

'The charge is prepared, the lawyers are met,
The judges all ranged, a terrible show ;'

the double line of reporters occupying the two seats below us ; the sheriff in attendance for the day, looking so spruce in his court suit, stepping noiselessly in and out ; and lastly the goodly personage in the blue and furred robes and gold chain, who sits in the centre on the chief seat, with the gilded sword of justice suspended over his head against the crimson-lined wall. Some abstruse document, apparently, just now engages his attention, for he appears utterly absorbed in it, bending over his desk. 'It must surely be the Lord Chancellor come to try some great case,' thinks many an innocent spectator ; but he rises, and we perceive it is only an ex-mayor reading the newspaper of the day. But we forgot : Hazlitt said that a City apprentice who did not esteem the Lord Mayor the greatest man in the world, would come some day to be hanged ; and here everybody apparently is of the same opinion. 'Who, then, is the judge?' one naturally asks ; when, looking more attentively, we perceive for the first time, beyond the representative of civic majesty, which thus asserts its rights, some one writing, taking frequent but brief glances at the prisoners or the witnesses, but never turning his head in any other direction, speaking to no one on the bench, unspoken to. That is a judge of the land, quietly doing the whole business of the court." The court formerly sat at the early hour of 7 a.m.

In 1841, both the Old Court and the New Court were ventilated, upon Dr. Reid's plan, from chambers beneath the floors, filled with air filtered from an apartment outside the building, the air being drawn into them by an enormous discharge upon the highest part of the edifice, or propelled into them by a fanner. From the entire building the vitiated air is received in a large chamber in the roof of the Old Court, whence it is discharged by a gigantic iron cowl, fifteen feet in diameter, weighing two tons, and the point of the arrow of the guiding vane weighing 150 pounds. The subterranean air-tunnels pass through a portion of the old City wall.

It was at the Old Bailey, in 1727, that Richard Savage, the dissolute poet, for whom Dr. Johnson seems to have felt an affection, was tried. The poet was out, one night, drinking and rioting with two gentlemen named Merchant and Gregory, when they agreed to turn in at "Robinson's" Coffee House, near Charing Cross. Merchant, demanding a room in a bullying way, was told there was a fire ready-made in the next partition, where the company were about to leave. The three men at once rushed in, and placed themselves between the fire and the persons who were there, and kicked down a table. A fight ensued, and Savage ran a Mr. James Sinclair through the body. He also wounded a servant-girl who tried to hold him, and broke his way out of the house. He was taken, however, in a back court, where some soldiers had come to his assistance. The next morning the three revellers were carried before the justices, who sent them to the Gate House, and on the death of Mr. Sinclair they were removed to Newgate. They were not, however, chained, and were placed apart from the vulgar herd in the press-yard. It was proved that the fatal stab was given by Savage, and he was consequently found guilty of murder. It is said that his supposed mother, the Countess of Macclesfield, did all she could to bring Savage to the gallows ; but the Countess of Hertford, Lord Tyrconnel, and Mrs. Oldfield, the actress, obtained for him at last the king's pardon.

Among other celebrated criminals who have been tried at the Old Bailey and Central Criminal Courts, may be briefly mentioned the following :— Major Strangways, the assassin, in 1659 ; Colonel Turner and his family, for burglary in Lime Street, 1663 ; Green, Berry, and Hill, for the murder of Sir Edmundbury Godfrey, 1678 ; Count Koningsmark and three others for the assassination of Mr. Thynne, 1681 ; Rowland Walters and others, for the murder of Sir Charles Pym, Bart., 1688 ; Harrison, for the murder of Dr. Clenche, 1692 ; Beau Fielding, for bigamy, 1706 ; Richard Thornhill, Esq., for killing Sir Cholmeley Deering in a duel, 1711 ; the Marquis di Paleotti, for the murder of his servant in Lisle Street, 1718 ; Major Oneby, for killing in a duel, 1718 and 1726 ; Jonathan Wild, the thief-taker, 1725 ; the infamous Colonel Charteris, 1730 ; Elizabeth Canning, an inexplicable mystery, 1753 ; Baretti, for stabbing, 1769 ; the two Perraus, for forgery, 1776 ; the Rev. Mr. Hackman, for shooting Miss Reay, 1779 ; Ryland, the engraver, for forgery, 1783 ; Barrington, the pickpocket, 1790 ; Renwick Williams, for stabbing, 1790 ; Theodore Gardelle, for murder, 1790 ; Hadfield, for shooting at George III., 1800 ; Captain Macnamara, for killing Colonel Montgomery in a duel, 1803 ; Aslett, the Bank clerk, for forgery on the Bank to the extent of £320,000.

1803 ; Holloway and Haggerty, for murder, 1807 ; Bellingham, the assassin of Mr. Spencer Percival, 1812 ; Cashman, the sailor, for riot on Snow Hill (where he was hanged), 1817 ; Richard Carlile, for blasphemy, 1819 and 1831 ; St. John Long, the counter-irritation surgeon, for manslaughter, 1830 and 1831 ; Bishop and Williams, for murder by " burking," 1831 ; Greenacre, for murder, 1837 ; G. Oxford, for shooting at the Queen, 1840 ; Francis, for an attempt to shoot the Queen, 1842 ; McNaughten, who shot Mr. Drummond in mistake for Sir Robert Peel, 1843 ; the Mannings, for murder, 1849 ; Palmer, the Rugeley poisoner, 1856 ; Franz Müller, for murder, and seven pirates, convicted of murder on the high seas, 1864 ; the Wainwrights, for murder, and the Fenians, Michael Barrett and others, 1868 ; Bidwell and others, for forgery on the Bank of England, 1873 ; five Greek sailors, for mutiny on board the *Flowery Land*, 1876 ; the detectives, Meiklejohn and others, for bribery, 1877 ; and the West of England Bank Directors, 1880.

But besides those criminals, notorious for their evil deeds, the Old Bailey has disposed of another class, some of them distinguished by their noble principles, and famed for their patriotism. Here were tried, in 1660, after the Restoration, those of the judges of Charles I. who were still alive, and, relying on the promised bill of indemnity, had remained in England ; and twenty three years later Algernon Sidney and Lord William Russell, two household names in connection with English freedom.

The trial of the regicides commenced on the 9th of October, 1660, before a court of thirty-four commissioners, of whom some were old royalists ; others, such as Manchester, Say, Annesley, and Hollis, had been all members of the Long Parliament ; and with these sat Monk, Montague, and Cooper, the associates of Cromwell, who, one would think, from motives of delicacy, would have withheld from the tribunal. The prisoners were twenty-nine in number, and included Sir Hardress Waller, Major-General Harrison, Colonel Carew, Cook, Hugh Peters, Scott, Harry Marten, and Scroop, among other scarcely less noticeable names. Waller was first called ; he pleaded guilty, and thus escaped the scaffold. Harrison's turn came next. Animated by a fervid spirit of enthusiasm, perfectly free from all alloy of worldly motives, he spoke boldly in his defence. " Maybe I might be a little mistaken," said he, " but I did it all according to the best of my understanding, desiring to make the revealed will of God in His Holy Scriptures as a guide to me. I humbly conceive that what was done was done in the name of the Parliament of England—that what was done was done by their power and authority ; and I do humbly conceive it is my duty to offer unto you in the beginning, that this court, or any court below the High Court of Parliament, hath no jurisdiction of their actions." His boldness could not save him ; he was sentenced to death, and retired saying he had no reason to be ashamed of the cause in which he had been engaged. Colonel Carew's frame of mind was in tune with that of Harrison, and he also was condemned to death. Harry Marten began a most ingenious and persevering defence by taking exception to the indictment. He declared he was not even mentioned in it ! It certainly included a name, Henry Marten, but that was not his—his was *Harry* Marten. This was overruled, and the trial proceeded. The Solicitor-General having said, " I am sorry to see in you so little repentance," Marten replied, " My lord, if it were possible for that blood to be in the body again, and every drop that was shed in the late wars, I could wish it with all my heart ; but, my lord, I hope it is lawful to offer in my defence that which, when I did it, I thought I might do. My lord, there was a House of Commons as I understood it : perhaps your lordship thinks it was not a House of Commons, but it was then the supreme authority of England ; it was so reputed both at home and abroad." He then went on to plead that the statute of Henry VIII. exempted from high treason any one acting under a king *de facto*, though he should not be a king *de jure*. No arguments would move the Old Bailey judge and jury of that day. Marten also was condemned. As for the other prisoners, all of them were found guilty, but those who had surrendered themselves voluntarily were, with one exception, that of Scroop, respited. Ten were executed. All, it has been remarked, died with the constancy of martyrs, and it is to be observed that not a single man of those who had a share in the death of the late king seems to have voluntarily repented of the deed.

It was at the trial of the regicides that the ridiculous story was first given in evidence by a soldier, who declared that when Harry Marten and Cromwell signed the death-warrant of the king, they wiped their pens on each other's faces.

The trial of Lord William Russell for his alleged connection with the Rye House Plot commenced at the Old Bailey on the 13th of July, 1683. He was charged with conspiring the death of the king, and consulting how to levy war against him. As was the case in the trial of the regicides, there is no doubt that the jury was packed by the sheriffs. Lord Russell desired the postponement of the trial till the afternoon, on account of an error in the list of the jury, and of the non-arrival of some witnesses from the country. The Attorney-General, Sir Robert Sawyer, corruptly assuming his guilt as already proven, answered harshly, "You would not have given the king an hour's notice for saving his life; the trial must proceed." Desiring to take notes of the evidence, the prisoner asked if he might have assistance. "Yes, a servant," said Sir Robert D. Pemberton, Chief Justice of the Common Pleas, who presided, adding, "any of your servants shall assist you in writing anything you please for you." "My lord," was the answer, "my wife is here to do it." No wonder that a thrill ran through the crowd of spectators when they saw the daughter of the excellent and popular Lord Southampton thus bravely aiding her husband in his defence! The incident was not likely to be forgotten, and both painters and poets have long delighted to dwell on the image

"Of that sweet saint who sat by Russell's side."

Every one knows how the trial ended, and how the unfortunate but noble-minded Russell was, on the 21st of July, executed in Lincoln's Inn Fields.

The Press-Yard at the Old Bailey still, by its name, commemorates one of the cruelties of our old statute-book. In all cases where a criminal refused to plead at the bar, in order to preserve his property from being forfeited to the Crown, the *peine forte et dure* was used. The most celebrated case of the application of this torture was in 1659, when Major Strangways endured it, to save his estate. He and his elder sister had shared a farm peacefully enough, till the sister married a lawyer named Fussell, whom Strangways disliked. He had been, indeed, heard to say that if ever his sister married Fussell, he would be the death of him in his study, or elsewhere. One day Fussell was shot at his lodgings in London, and suspicion fell on Strangways, who consented to the ordeal of touch. At his trial Strangways refused to plead. He wished to bestow his estate on his best friends, and he hoped to escape the ignominy of the gibbet. Lord Chief Justice Glynn then passed the sentence, "That he be put into a mean house, stopped from any light, and be laid upon his back, with his body bare; that his arms be stretched forth with a cord, the one to one side, the other to the other side of the prison, and in like manner his legs be used; and that upon his body be laid as much iron and stone as he can bear, and more. The first day he shall have three morsels of barley bread, and the next he shall drink thrice of the water in the next channel to the prison door, but of no spring or fountain water; and this shall be his punishment till he die."

On the Monday following Strangways was clothed in white from top to toe, and wearing a mourning cloak (for indeed it was his own funeral to which he was going). His friends placed themselves at the corner of the press, and when he gave the word, put on the weights. This was done till he uttered the words, "Lord Jesus, receive my soul," but the weight being too light to produce instant death, those present stood on the board, as a ghastly and last act of friendship. The poor fellow bore this some eight or ten minutes.

After the almost entire abolition of this cruel practice, it was the custom to force the prisoners to plead, if possible, by screwing the thumb with whipcord, a sort of buccaneer form of cruelty. In 1721, Mary Andrews was tortured thus. The first three whipcords broke, but she gave way with the fourth. The same year (for the press was still partially continued) the cord was tried first on a criminal named Nathaniel Hawes, who then was pressed under a weight of 250 pounds, and he consented to plead. According to one writer on the subject, the cord torture was last used about 1734.

A tragic episode in the history of the administration of justice in the Old Bailey was the invasion of the court by the gaol-fever during the sessions of May, 1750. The gaol-fever raged so violently in the neighbouring prison that the effluvia, entering the court, caused the death of the Judge of the Common Pleas, Sir Thomas Abney, Baron Clark, Pennant the historian's "respected kinsman," Sir Samuel Pennant, Lord Mayor, and several members of the Bar and of the jury.

The occasion of this misadventure, and a few particulars concerning it, have been recorded for the benefit of posterity. A Captain Clarke was being tried for killing a Captain Turner, and the court was unusually crowded. About one hundred prisoners were tried, and they were kept all day cooped up in two small rooms 14 feet by 11 feet each way, and only 7 feet high. It was remarked that the Lord Chief Justice and the Recorder, who sat on the Lord Mayor's right hand, caught, while the rest of the bench, on the left, escaped, the infection. This was attributed to the draught, that carried the infected air in that direction. Every precaution was afterwards taken, says Pennant, to keep the court airy; but as several of these fatal accidents had already happened in the kingdom, it was rather surprising "that the neglect of the salutary precautions was continued till the time of this awakening call." The disease again proved fatal to several in 1772.

Upon the first outbreak of the gaol-fever the custom arose of placing rue in front of the dock of the Old Bailey to prevent infection: so it is stated in Lawrence's "Life of Fielding" (1855). At the trial of Manning and his wife for murder, it will be remembered that at the conclusion of a speech by one of the counsel, Mrs. Manning gathered some of "the sprigs of rue placed on the dock," and threw them vehemently over the wigged heads of the "learned" gentlemen.

Over the court-room is a dining-room, where the

and varied with the season, though marrow-puddings always formed a part of it; the second never varied, and consisted exclusively of beef-steaks. The custom was to serve two dinners (exact duplicates) a day, the first at three o'clock, the second at five. As the judges relieved each other it was impracticable for them to partake of both; but the aldermen often did so, and the chaplain, whose duty it was to preside at the lower end of the table, was never absent from his post. This invaluable public servant persevered from a

FRONT OF NEWGATE FROM THE OLD BAILEY.

judges were till recently in the habit of dining when the court was over—a practice commemorated by a well-known line—

"And wretches hang that jurymen may dine."

"If we are not misinformed," says an amusing writer in the *Quarterly Review* for 1836, "the fiat has gone forth already against one class of City dinners, which was altogether peculiar of its kind. We allude to the dinner given by the sheriffs during the Old Bailey sittings to the judges and aldermen in attendance, the Recorder, Common Serjeant, City pleaders, and occasionally a few members of the Bar. The first course was rather miscellaneous,

sheer sense of duty, till he had acquired the habit of eating two dinners a day, and practised it for nearly ten years without any perceptible injury to his health. We had the pleasure of witnessing his performances at one of the five o'clock dinners, and can assert with confidence, that the vigour of his attack on the beef-steaks was wholly unimpaired by the effective execution a friend assured us he had done on them two hours before. The occasion to which we allude was so remarkable for other reasons, that we have the most distinct recollection of the circumstances. It was the first trial of the late St. John Long for rubbing a young lady into her grave. The presiding judges were Mr. Justice Park and Mr. Baron Garrow, who retired to dinner about five, having first desired the jury, amongst whom there was a difference of opinion, to be locked up. The dinner proceeded merrily, the beef-steaks were renewed again and again, and received the solemn sanction of judicial approbation repeatedly. Mr. Adolphus told some of his best stories, and the chaplain was on the point of being challenged for a song, when the court-keeper appeared with a face of consternation, to announce that the jury, after being very noisy for an hour or so, had sunk into a dull, dead lull, which, to the experienced in such

he deemed a reasonable hour—namely, about ten—and then informing the jury that, if they were not agreed, they must be locked up without fire or candle until a reasonable hour (about nine) on the Monday, by which time he trusted they would be unanimous. The effect of such an intimation was not put to the test, for Mr. St. John Long was found guilty about nine. We are sorry to be obliged to add that the worthy chaplain's digestion has at length proved unequal to the double burthen imposed upon it; but the Court of Aldermen, considering him a martyr to their cause, have very

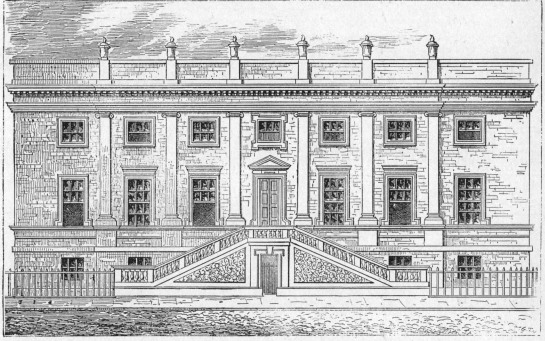

SURGEON'S HALL, OLD BAILEY, 1800. (*See page* 471.)

matters, augurs the longest period of deliberation which the heads, or rather stomachs, of the jury can endure. The trial had, unfortunately, taken place upon a Saturday, and it became a serious question in what manner the refractory jurymen were to be dealt with. Mr. Baron Garrow proposed waiting till within a few minutes of twelve, and then discharging them. Mr. Justice Park, the senior judge, and a warm admirer of the times when refractory juries were carried round the country in a cart, would hear of no expedient of the kind. He said a judge was not bound to wait beyond a reasonable hour at night, nor to attend before a reasonable hour in the morning; that Sunday was a *dies non* in law, and that a verdict must be delivered in the presence of the judge. He consequently declared his intention of waiting till what

properly agreed to grant him an adequate pension for his services."

In 1807-8 the dinners for three sessions, nineteen days, cost Sheriff Phillips and his colleague £35 per day—£665; 145 dozen of wine was consumed at these dinners, costing an additional £450. These dinners were discontinued about 1877.

And now we take leave of the Central Criminal Court, according to Garth, in his "Dispensary,"

> " ——That most celebrated place,
> Where angry Justice shows her awful face;
> Where little villains must submit to fate,
> That great ones may enjoy the world in state."

The Old Bailey—that part of the street opposite to Newgate—became the scene of public executions in 1783, on the 9th of December in which year the first culprit suffered here the extreme penalty of the law. Before that time the public executions ordinarily took place at Tyburn. The gallows of the Old Bailey was built with three cross-beams for as many rows of victims, and between February and December, 1785, ninety-six persons suffered by the "new drop," an ingenious invention which took the place of the cart. On but one occasion the old mode of execution was revived; a triangular gallows was set up in the road, opposite Green Arbour Court, and the cart was drawn from under the criminal's feet.

The front of Newgate continued to be the place of execution in London from 1783 to 1868, when an Act was passed directing executions to take place within the walls of prisons. This Act was the result of a commission on capital punishments, appointed in 1864, which, in their report issued in 1865, recommended, amongst other things, that executions should not be public. The number of executions throughout the country has been gradually decreasing for many years, as our laws have become less severe. In 1820 there were forty-three executions in London; in 1825, seventeen; in 1830, six; in 1835, none; in 1836, none; in 1837, two; in 1838, none; in 1839, two; in 1840, one; in 1842, two; in 1843, none; in 1844, one; in 1845, three; in 1846, two; and from 1847 to the present time the average has not exceeded two per annum. What a contrast to the old times when the law of the gallows and the scaffold kept our forefathers in order! In the reign of Henry VIII. —thirty-eight years—it is said that no fewer than 72,000 criminals were executed in England!

It used to be occasionally the usage to execute the criminal near the scene of his guilt. Those who were punished capitally for the riots of 1780 suffered in those parts of the town in which their crimes were committed; and in 1790 two incendiaries were hanged in Aldersgate Street, at the eastern end of Long Lane, opposite the site of the house to which they had set fire. "Since that period," Mr. Timbs observes, "there have been few executions in London except in front of Newgate. The last deviation from the regular course was in the case of the sailor Cashman, who was hung in 1817, in Skinner Street, opposite the house of Mr. Beckwith, the gunsmith, which he had plundered."

About 1786 was witnessed in the Old Bailey the end of an old practice: the body of the criminal just executed was burned for the last time. A woman was the sufferer in this case. She was hung on a low gibbet, and on life being extinct, fagots were heaped around her and over her head, fire was set to the pile, and the corpse was burned to ashes.

The memorable executions at the Old Bailey include those of Mrs. Phepoe, for murder, December 11, 1797; Holloway and Haggerty, February 23rd, 1807; Bellingham, May 18th, 1812; Joseph Hunton (Quaker), December 8th, 1828; Bishop and Williams, December 5, 1831; John Pegsworth, March 7th, 1837; James Greenacre, May 2, 1837; besides several others already mentioned by us as having undergone trial at the adjoining court of justice.

A dreadful accident took place here at the execution of Holloway and Haggerty, on the 23rd of February, 1807, for the murder of Mr. Steele, on Hounslow Heath, in 1802. Twenty-eight persons were crushed to death. We have already alluded to the circumstances, and to our previous notice the following account of the catastrophe, by a writer in the *Annual Register*, must be regarded as supplementary:—"On the north side of the Old Bailey, the multitude to see the execution was so immensely great that, in their movements, they were not inaptly compared to the flow and reflow of the waves of the sea, when in troubled motion. In the centre of this vast concourse of people was placed a cart, in which persons were accommodated with standing-places to see the culprits; but, it is supposed from the circumstance of too many being admitted into it, the axle-tree gave way, and by the concussion many persons were killed. Unhappily, the mischief did not stop here. A temporary chasm in the crowd being thus made by the fall of the cart, many persons rushed forward to get upon the body of it, which formed a kind of platform, from which they thought they could get a commanding view over the heads of the persons in front. All those who, from choice or necessity, were nearest to the cart, strove to get upon it; and in their eagerness drove those in front headforemost among the crowd beneath, by whom they were trampled under foot, without the power of relieving them. The latter in turn were in like manner assailed, and shared the same fate. This dreadful scene continued for some time. The shrieks of the dying men, women, and children were terrific beyond description, and could only be equalled by the horror of the event." The most affecting scene of distress was seen at Green Arbour Court, nearly opposite the Debtors' Door.

Offenders frequently stood in the pillory in the Old Bailey, and there, no doubt, were often, as was customary, stoned by the mob, and pelted with rotten eggs, and other equally offensive missiles. The pillory generally consisted of a wooden frame, erected on a scaffolding, with holes and folding boards for the admission of the head and hands of him whom it was desired to render thus publicly infamous. Rushworth says that it was invented for the special benefit of mountebanks and quacks, "who having gotten upon banks and forms to abuse the people, were exalted in the same kind," but it seems to have been freely used for cheats of all description. Bakers for making bread of light weight, and "dairymen for selling mingled butter," were in the olden time "sharply corrected" upon it. So also were fraudulent corn, coal, and cattle dealers, cutters of purses, sellers of sham gold rings, keepers of infamous houses, forgers of letters, bonds, and deeds, counterfeits of papal bulls, users of unstamped measures, and forestallers of the markets. But just as the Old Bailey Court witnessed occasionally the persecution of the innocent, so the pillory had at one time other heroes than cheats, thieves, scandalmongers, and perjurers. "Thanks to Archbishop Laud, and Star Chamber tyrants," says the late Dr. Robert Chambers, "it figured so conspicuously in the political and polemical disputes which heralded the downfall of the monarchy, as to justify a writer of our own time in saying, 'Noble hearts had been tried and tempered in it; daily had been elevated in it mental independence, manly self-reliance, robust, athletic endurance. All from within that has undying worth it had but more plainly exposed to public gaze from without.'" Many a courageous and outspoken thinker will occur to every reader of English history as having been set on this scaffold of infamy, to the lasting disgrace of narrow-minded tyranny.

The last who stood in the pillory of London was Peter James Bossy, tried for perjury, and sentenced to transportation for seven years. Previous to being transported he was to be kept for six months in Newgate, and to stand for one hour in the pillory in the Old Bailey. The pillory part of the sentence was executed on the 24th of June, 1830.

An Act of the British Parliament, dated June 30, 1837, put an end to the use of the pillory in the United Kingdom. In 1815 it had been abolished as a punishment except for perjury.

The Surgeons' Hall stood in the Old Bailey, on the site of the New Sessions House, till 1809. Pennant, in his "London," remarks, in connection with the old Court of Justice, that the erection of the Surgeons' Hall in its neighbourhood was an exceedingly convenient circumstance. "By a sort of second sight," he says, "the Surgeons' Theatre was built near this court of conviction and Newgate, the concluding stage of the lives forfeited to the justice of their country, several years

before the fatal tree was removed from Tyburn to its present site. It is a handsome building, ornamented with Ionic pilasters, and with a double flight of steps to the first floor. Beneath is a door for the admission of the bodies of murderers and other felons, who, noxious in their lives, make a sort of reparation to their fellow-creatures by becoming useful after death."

The bodies of murderers, after execution, were dissected in the Surgeons' Theatre, according to an Act passed in 1752, and which was only repealed in the reign of William IV. A curious experiment was performed here, in the beginning of the century, on the body of one Foster, who was executed for the murder of his wife. It was "lately," says a writer in the *Annual Register* for 1803, "subjected to the galvanic process, by Mr. Aldini (a nephew of Galvani), in presence of Mr. Keate, Mr. Carpue, and several other professional gentlemen. On the first application of the process to the face, the jaw of the deceased criminal began to quiver, and the adjoining muscles were horribly contorted, and one eye actually opened. In a subsequent course of the experiment, the right hand was raised and clenched, and the legs and thighs were set in motion; and it appeared to all the bystanders that the wretched man was on the point of being restored to life! The object of these experiments was to show the excitability of the human frame when animal electricity is duly applied; and the possibility of its being efficaciously used in cases of drowning, suffocation, or apoplexy, by reviving the action of the lungs, and thereby rekindling the expiring spark of vitality." But the most curious part of the proceedings remains to be told. According to Mr. J. Saunders, in Knight's "London," 1842, when the right arm was raised, as mentioned above, it struck one of the officers of the institution, who died that very afternoon of the shock.

In April, 1760, Laurence Earl Ferrers was tried before the House of Lords, for the murder of his steward. He was found guilty, and sentenced "to be hanged by the neck till he was dead; after which his body was to be delivered to Surgeons' Hall, to be dissected and anatomised." At the latter part of the sentence, we are told, his lordship cried out, "God forbid!" but, soon recollecting himself, added, "God's will be done!" On Monday, the 5th of May, he was hanged at Tyburn, and the body was conveyed, with some state, in his own landau and six, to the Surgeons' Hall, in the Old Bailey, to undergo the remainder of the sentence. A print of the time shows the corpse as it lay here.

It was at this hall that Goldsmith presented himself in a new suit—not paid for—to be examined as to his qualifications for being a surgeon's mate, on the 21st of December, 1758. "The beadle called my name," says Roderick Random, when he found himself in a similiar condition at that place of torture, "with a voice that made me tremble as much as if it had been the sound of the last trumpet. However, there was no remedy: I was conducted into a large hall, where I saw about a dozen of grim faces sitting at a long table, one of whom bade me come forward in such an imperious tone, that I was actually for a minute or two bereft of my senses."

"Whether the same process," says Mr. John Forster, "conducted through a like memorable scene, bereft poor Goldsmith altogether of his, cannot now be ascertained. All that is known is told in a dry extract from the books of the College of Surgeons : 'At a Court of Examiners, held at the Theatre, 21st December, 1758, present'—the names are not given, but there is a long list of the candidates who passed, in the midst of which these occur : 'James Bernard, mate to an hospital. Oliver Goldsmith, not qualified for ditto.'

"A harder sentence," continues Goldsmith's biographer, "a more cruel doom than this, at the time, must have seemed, even the Old Bailey has not often been witness to; yet, far from blaming that worthy court of examiners, should we not rather feel that much praise is due to them? That they did their duty in rejecting the short, thick, dull, ungainly, over-anxious, over-dressed, simple-looking Irishman who presented himself that memorable day, can hardly, I think, be doubted; but unconsciously they also did a great deal more. They found him not qualified to be a surgeon's mate, but left him qualified to heal the wounds and abridge the sufferings of all the world. They found him querulous with adversity, given up to irresolute fears, too much blinded with failures and sorrows to see the divine uses to which they tended still; and from all this their sternly just and awful decision drove him resolutely back. While the door of the Surgeons' Hall was shut upon him that day, the gate of the beautiful mountain was slowly opening."

At what used to be No. 68 of the Old Bailey, "the second door south of Ship Court," lived Jonathan Wild, the famous thief-taker, who had a very intimate acquaintance with the Sessions House.

A description of the Old Bailey would be decidedly incomplete were we to omit giving a sketch of the career of this noted inhabitant. Almost every great man arrives at eminence by zeal and energy, devoted to some particular calling; and it may be worth our pains to look for a little at that

which Jonathan made peculiarly his own. His occupation was the restoration of stolen goods, carried on from about the year 1712, through a secret confederacy with all the regular thieves, burglars, and highwaymen of the metropolis, whose depredations he prompted and directed. An Act of Parliament, passed in 1717, tended rather to check the display of his peculiar talents. By this Act persons convicted of receiving or buying goods, knowing them to be stolen, were made liable to transportation for fourteen years; and by another clause, with a particular view to Wild's proceedings, a heavy punishment was awarded to all who trafficked in such goods and divided the money with felons. Wild's ingenuity and audacity, however, long enabled him to elude this new law. He was one of the cleverest of rogues, and it has been well said, in one sense, merited the name of "great," bestowed upon him by Fielding, in whose history of him, although the incidents are fictitious, there is no exaggeration of his talents or courage, any more than of his unscrupulousness and want of all moral principle. The plan upon which he conducted his extensive business operations was this. When thieves made prizes of any sort, they delivered them up to him, instead of carrying them to the pawnbroker, and Wild restored the goods to the owners, for a consideration, by which means large sums were raised, and the thieves remained secure from detection. To manage this, he would apply to persons who had been robbed, and pretend to be greatly concerned at their misfortunes, adding that some suspected goods had been stopped by a friend of his, a broker, who would be willing to give them up; and he did not fail to throw out a hint that the broker merited some reward for his disinterested conduct and his trouble, and to exact a promise that no disagreeable consequences should follow on account of the broker's having omitted to secure the thieves as well as the property. The person whose goods had been carried off was generally not unwilling by this means to save himself the trouble and expense of a prosecution, and the money paid was usually sufficient to remunerate the "broker," as well as his agent.

At last, after he had amassed a considerable sum, he adopted another and a safer plan. He opened an office, to which great numbers resorted, in the hope of obtaining the restitution of their property. His light was by no means hid under a bushel, and he kept it burning with the greatest credit and profit to himself. Let us suppose some one to have had goods stolen of a considerable value. He calls upon Mr. Wild, at his office, and pays half-a-crown for advice. Wild enters his name and address in his books, inquires particularly about the robbery, and sounds his client as to the reward he will give in the event of the restitution being made. "If you call again," he says, "I hope I shall be able to give you some agreeable information." He calls again. Wild says that he has heard about the goods, but the agent he has employed tells him that the robbers pretend that by pawning them they can raise more money than the amount of the reward. Would it not, he suggests, be a good plan to increase the reward? The client consents, and retires. He calls the third time. He has the goods placed in his hands: he pays the reward over to Jonathan, and there is the end of the transaction.

In the course of this business it will readily be perceived that Wild became possessed of the secrets of every notorious thief about London. All the highwaymen, shoplifters, and housebreakers knew that they were under the necessity of complying with whatever he thought fit to demand. Should they oppose his inclination, they were certain, ere long, to be placed within reach of the clutches of justice, and be sacrificed to the injured laws of their country. Wild led two lives, so to speak; one amongst ruffians, and the other as a man of consequence, with laced clothes and a sword, before the public eye; and the latter life was as unlike the former as any two lives could well be.

He professed, in public, to be the most zealous of thief-takers; and to ordinary observation his life and strength seemed devoted to the pursuit and apprehension of felons. At his trial—for his trial came at last—he had a printed paper handed to the jury, entitled, "A List of Persons discovered, apprehended, and convicted of several robberies on the highway, and also for burglary and housebreaking, and also for returning from transportation, by Jonathan Wild;" and it contained the names of thirty-five robbers, twenty-two housebreakers, and ten returned convicts, whom he had been instrumental in getting hanged. This statement was probably true enough. In the records of the trials at the Old Bailey, for many years before it came to his own turn, he repeatedly appeared, figuring in the witness-box, and giving evidence for the prosecution, and in many cases he seems to have taken a leading part in the apprehension of the prisoner.

In carrying on his trade of blood, Wild, of course, was occasionally turned upon by his betrayed and desperate victim. But, when this happened, his brazen-faced effrontery carried everything before it. In a trial, for example, of three unfortunate wretches indicted for several robberies in January, 1723, he gave the following account of his proceedings:—"Some coming (I suppose from the prosecutors) to me about the robbery, I made it my business to search after the prisoners, for I had heard that they used to rob about Hampstead; and I went about it the more willingly, because I had heard they had threatened to shoot me through the head. I offered £10 a head for any person who would discover them; upon which a woman came and told me that the prisoners had been with her husband, to entice him to turn out with them; and if I would promise he should come and go safely he would give me some intelligence. I gave her my promise; and her husband came accordingly, and told me that Levee and Blake, two of the party, were at that time cleaning their pistols at a house in Fetter Lane. I went thither and seized them both." The husband of the woman, it appears, had really taken part in one of the robberies, though he now came forward to convict his associates, having been, no doubt, all along in league with Wild; and Blake (better known to fame as Blueskin) also figured as king's evidence on this occasion, and frankly admitted that he had been out with the prisoners. The three unlucky characters in the dock, while their comrades thus figured in a freer and more pleasant situation, "all," says the account of the trial, vehemently "exclaimed against Jonathan Wild;" but they were found guilty, and had the pleasure of swinging in company on Tyburn-tree a few days afterwards.

But, in all fairness to Jonathan, it must be said that he did not, till the last moment, desert his friends, and that he only sacrificed them for the general good of the concern, and from a bold and comprehensive view of the true policy of trade. Blueskin's turn to be tried, convicted, and hanged, came about a couple of years after the affair just mentioned. Wild was to have been a witness against him; but a day or two before the trial, when he went to pay a visit to his intended victim, Blueskin drew out a clasp-knife, and, in a twinkling, fell upon Jonathan, and cut his throat. The blade was too blunt, however, and the thief-taker received no lasting damage. When the verdict was given, Blueskin addressed the court, and told them of an exceedingly kindly promise his late partner had made him. "On Wednesday last, Jonathan Wild said to Simon Jacobs (another prisoner soon after transported), 'I believe you will not bring £40 this time; I wish Joe (meaning me) was in your case; but I'll do my endeavour to bring you off as a single felon'" (crimes punishable only by transportation, whipping, imprisonment, &c., were denominated single felonies). "And then, turning to me, he said, 'I believe you must die; *I'll send you a good book or two, and provide you a coffin, and you shall not be anatomised!'."*

The reward of £40, it has been explained, which Wild could not manage to make Jacobs bring "this time," was part of a system established by various Acts of Parliament, which assigned

"That for many years past he had been a confederate with great numbers of highwaymen, pick pockets, housebreakers, shoplifters, and other thieves;" and the eleventh and last, that it appeared "he had often sold human blood by procuring false evidence to swear persons into facts

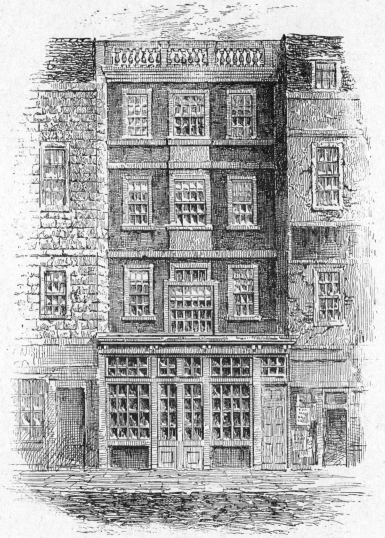

JONATHAN WILD'S HOUSE. (*See page* 472.)

certain money payments to be made to persons apprehending and prosecuting to conviction highway robbers, coiners, and other delinquents.

We come now to the end of Wild's career. He was committed to Newgate on the 15th of February, 1725, on a charge of having assisted a criminal in his escape from prison. In the course of a few days he moved to be either admitted to bail or discharged, but a warrant of detainer was produced against him in court, the first of several articles of information affixed to the warrant being,

of which they were not guilty." On Saturday, the 15th of May, he was brought to trial on two separate indictments. The jury found him guilty, and he was sentenced to be executed at Tyburn on Monday, the 24th of May, 1725. On the morning of the execution the wretched man swallowed a dose of poison, but it failed to end his life, and in a state of half-insensibility he was placed in the cart that was to convey him to the gallows. On the way he was pelted by the populace with stones and dirt, and, altogether, this arch-villain made rather a pitiable exit from this world. At the foot of the gallows he remained so long drowsy in the cart, that the mob called out to the hangman that they would knock him on the head if the hanging was not at once proceeded with.

from them. The body of this infamous fellow was secretly buried.

Jonathan Wild's skeleton, says Mr. Timbs, in 1868, was some years since in the possession of a surgeon at Windsor. And a relic of him was

JONATHAN WILD IN THE CART. *From a Contemporary Print.* (*See page* 474.)

The amiable Jonathan had five wives. His eldest son, soon after his father's execution, sold himself for a servant to the plantations. A skull claiming to be the great thief-taker's was exhibited, some years ago, in St. Giles's, but as it was not fractured in several places, it was probably spurious. Wild boasted in prison of the numerous robbers he had captured, and the wounds he had received

judged of suffici nt interest to be exhibited to the Society of Antiquaries in 1866. It was a musketoon given by Jonathan Wild to Blueskin, which had fallen into the hands of the well-known magistrate, Sir John Fielding, and by him had been given to his half-brother, Henry Fielding.

In 1841 a curious letter was found in the Town Clerk's Office of the City of London, from Jonathan

Wild, asking for remuneration for services he had rendered to the cause of justice. In the same letter, written in 1723, he also prayed the Lord Mayor and the Court of Aldermen "to be pleased to admit him into the freedom of this honourable City," in consideration of his valuable services. There is a record that Jonathan Wild's petition was read by the Court of Aldermen, but we do not find evidence that the coveted freedom was awarded to him. Wild's house was long distinguished by the sign of the head of Charles I.

In the Old Bailey stood Sydney House, occupied, in the time of Pennant, by a coachmaker. Once it was the proud mansion of the Sydneys. They occupied it till their removal to Leicester House, at the north-east corner of Leicester Square.

The names of several eminent persons—altogether independent of the "Old Bailey Sessions House"—occur to us as we perambulate this interesting locality. William Camden, the "nourrice of antiquitie," was born in the Old Bailey, in 1550. His father was a paper-stainer here. In Ship Court, on the west side, Hogarth's father, Richard Hogarth, kept a school. He seems to have come early from the North of England, and was employed in London as a teacher and as a corrector of the press. He was a man of some learning; and Chalmers, writing in 1814, mentions that a dictionary in Latin and English, which he compiled for the use of schools, was then extant in manuscript. At No. 67, at the corner of Ship Court, William Hone, in 1817, gave to the world his three celebrated political parodies on the Catechism, the Litany, and the Creed, for which he was three times tried at Guildhall, and acquitted.

Peter Bales, the celebrated penman of the time of Queen Elizabeth, kept a writing-school, in 1590, at the upper end of the Old Bailey, and published his "Writing Schoolmaster" here. In a writing competition he once won a golden pen, of the value of £20, and in addition had the "arms of caligraphy—viz., azure, a pen or—given him as a prize." This clever writer had a steady hand, and wrote with such minuteness, that, remarks D'Israeli, in his "Curiosities of Literature," he astonished the eyes of beholders, by showing them what they could not see. In the Harleian MSS. (530) we have a narrative of "a rare piece of work brought to pass by Peter Bales, an Englishman, and a clerk of the Chancery," which seems, by the description, to have been the whole Bible "in an English walnut no bigger than a hen's egg. The nut," the account goes on to say," holdeth the book. There are as many leaves in his little book as the great Bible; and he hath written as much in one of his little leaves as in a great leaf of the Bible." It is added that this wonderfully unreadable volume was "seen by thousands."

Prynne's "Histrio-Mastix, the Player's Scourge," was printed "for Michael Sparke, and sold at the 'Blue Bible,' in Green Arbour, in Little Old Bailey, 1633." This Little Old Bailey was a kind of Middle Row in the Old Bailey. It has long been removed.

One of the courts leading out of the Old Bailey was Green Arbour Court, which ran from the upper end of the street into Seacoal Lane. Here were the famous Breakneck Steps referred to by Ward in his "London Spy," when he speaks of "returning down-stairs with as much care and caution of tumbling head foremost as he that goes down Green Arbour Court steps in the middle of winter." This court, now destroyed, was specially interesting as the residence of Oliver Goldsmith, about 1758, a time when the poet was making shift to exist. As to his sojourn here we shall take the liberty of quoting a graphic passage from Mr. John Forster, one of the best of Goldsmith's numerous biographers.

"With part of the money," he says, "received from Hamilton"—the proprietor of the *Critical Review*, to which the poet was at this time contributing—"he moved into fresh lodgings; took unrivalled possession of a fresh garret, on a first floor. The house was No. 12, Green Arbour Court, Fleet Street, between the Old Bailey and the site of Fleet Market; and stood in the right-hand corner of the court, as the wayfarer approached it from Farringdon Street by the appropriate access of 'Breakneck Steps.' Green Arbour Court is now gone for ever; and of its miserable wretchedness, for a little time replaced by the more decent comforts of a stable, not a vestige remains. The houses, crumbling and tumbling in Goldsmith's day, were fairly rotted down some nineteen years since" (Mr. Forster is writing in 1854), "and it became necessary, for safety sake, to remove what time had spared. But Mr. Washington Irving saw them first, and with reverence had described them for Goldsmith's sake. Through alleys, courts, and blind passages; traversing Fleet Market, and thence turning along a narrow street to the bottom of a long steep flight of stone steps, he made good his toilsome way up into Green Arbour Court. He found it a small square of tall and miserable houses, the very intestines of which seemed turned inside out, to judge from the old garments and frippery that fluttered from every window. 'It appeared,' he says, in his 'Tales of a Traveller,' 'to be a region of washerwomen, and lines were stretched about the little square, on which clothes were dangling to dry.' The disputed right to a wash-tub was going on when he entered ; heads in mob-caps were protruded from every window ; and the loud clatter of vulgar tongues was assisted by the shrill pipe of swarming children, nestled and cradled in every procreant chamber of the hive. The whole scene, in short, was one of whose un-changed resemblance to the scenes of former days I have since found curious corroboration in a magazine engraving of the place nigh half a cen-tury old.* Here were the tall faded houses, with heads out of window at every storey ; the dirty neglected children ; the bawling slipshod women ; in one corner, clothes hanging to dry, and in another the cure of smoky chimneys announced. Without question, the same squalid squalling colony as it then was, it had been in Goldsmith's time. He would compromise with the children for occasional cessation of their noise, by occa-sional cakes or sweetmeats, or by a tune upon his flute, for which all the court assembled ; he would talk pleasantly with the poorest of his neighbours,

and was long recollected to have greatly enjoyed the talk of a working watchmaker in the court. Every night he would risk his neck at those steep stone stairs ; every day—for his clothes had become too ragged to submit to daylight scrutiny—he would keep within his dirty, naked, unfurnished room, with its single wooden chair and window bench. And that was Goldsmith's home."

It was in this lodging that the poet received a visit from Percy, then busily engaged in collecting material for his famous " Reliques of English Poetry." The grave church dignitary discovered Goldsmith in his wretched room busily writing. There being but one chair it was, out of civility, offered to the visitor, and Goldsmith was himself obliged to sit in the window. Whilst the two were sitting talking together—Percy relates in his memoir—some one was heard to rap gently at the door, and being desired to come in, a poor ragged little girl of very decent behaviour entered, who, dropping a curtsey, said, " My mamma sends her compliments, and begs the favour of you to lend her a pot-full of coals."

CHAPTER LV.

ST. SEPULCHRE'S AND ITS NEIGHBOURHOOD.

The Early History of St. Sepulchre's—Its Destruction in 1666—The Exterior and Interior—The Early Popularity of the Church—Interments here—Roger Ascham, the Author of the " Schoolmaster"—Captain John Smith, and his Romantic Adventures—Saved by an Indian Girl—St. Sepulchre's Churchyard—Accommodation for a Murderess—The Martyr Rogers—An Odd Circumstance—Good Company for the Dead—A Leap from the Tower—A Warning Bell and a Last Admonition—Nosegays for the Condemned—The Route to the Gallows-tree—The Deeds of the Charitable—The " Saracen's Head "—Description by Dickens—Giltspur Street—Giltspur Street Compter—A Disreputable Condition—Pie Corner—Hosier Lane—A Spurious Relic—The Conduit on Snow Hill—A Ladies' Charity School—Turnagain Lane—Poor Betty !—A Schoolmistress Censured—Skinner Street—Unpropitious Fortune—William Godwin—An Original Married Life.

MANY interesting associations—principally, how-ever, connected with the annals of crime and the execution of the laws of England—belong to the Church of St. Sepulchre, or St. 'Pulchre. This sacred edifice—anciently known as St. Sepulchre's in the Bailey, or by Chamberlain Gate (now New-gate)—stands at the eastern end of the Holborn Viaduct, at the corner of Giltspur Street, and between Smithfield and the Old Bailey. The genuine materials for its early history are scanty enough. It was probably founded about the com-mencement of the twelfth century, but of the exact date and circumstances of its origin there is no record whatever. Its name is derived from the Holy Sepulchre of our Saviour at Jerusalem, to the memory of which it was first dedicated.

The earliest authentic notice of the church, ac-cording to Maitland, is of the year 1178, at which date it was given by Roger, Bishop of Sarum, to the Prior and Canons of St. Bartholomew. These held the right of advowson until the dissolution of monasteries by Henry VIII., and from that time until 1610 it remained in the hands of the Crown. James I., however, then granted " the rectory and its appurtenances, with the advowson of the vicarage," to Francis Phillips and others. The next stage in its history is that the rectory was purchased by the parishioners, to be held in fee-farm of the Crown, and the advowson was obtained by the President and Fellows of St. John's College, Oxford.

The church was rebuilt about the middle of the fifteenth century, when one of the Popham family, who had been Chancellor of Normandy and Trea-surer of the King's Household, with distinguished

---

* See the frontispiece to vol. xliii. of the *European Magazine*, reproduced on p. 480.

liberality erected a handsome chapel on the south side of the choir, and the very beautiful porch still remaining at the south-west corner of the building. "His image," Stowe says, "fair graven in stone, was fixed over the said porch."

The dreadful fire of 1666 almost destroyed St. Sepulchre's, but the parishioners set energetically to work, and it was "rebuilt and beautified both within and without." The general reparation was under the direction of Sir Christopher Wren, and nothing but the walls of the old building, and these not entirely, were suffered to remain. The work was done rapidly, and the whole was completed within four years.

"The tower," says Mr. Godwin, "retained its original aspect, and the body of the church, after its restoration, presented a series of windows between buttresses, with pointed heads filled with tracery, crowned by a string-course and battlements. In this form it remained till the year 1790, when it appears the whole fabric was found to be in a state of great decay, and it was resolved to repair it throughout. Accordingly, the walls of the church were cased with Portland stone, and all the windows were taken out, and replaced by others with plain semi-circular heads, . . . certainly agreeing but badly with the tower and porch of the building, but according with the then prevailing spirit of economy. The battlements, too, were taken down, and a plain stone parapet was substituted, so that at this time (with the exception of the roof, which was wagon-headed, and presented on the outside an unsightly swell, visible above the parapet) the church assumed its present appearance." The ungainly roof was removed, and an entirely new one erected, about 1836.

At each corner of the tower—"one of the most ancient," says the author of "Londinium Redivivum," "in the outline of the circuit of London" —there are spires, and on the spires there are weathercocks. These have been made use of by Howell to point a moral : "Unreasonable people," says he, "are as hard to reconcile as the vanes of St. Sepulchre's tower, which never look all four upon one point of the heavens." Nothing can be said with certainty as to the date of the tower, but it is not without the bounds of probability that it formed part of the original building. The belfry is reached by a small winding staircase, in the south-west angle, and a similar staircase in an opposite angle leads to the summit. The spires at the corners, and some of the tower windows, underwent several alterations about 1873, and in 1878-9 the remainder of the church was thoroughly restored externally, in its original Perpendicular style of

architecture, so that it may now be said to bear perhaps a stronger resemblance to its original type than any other "restored" church in London. During these alterations much of the ancient workmanship, which had long been hidden, was brought to light.

The chief entrance to St. Sepulchre's is by a porch of singular beauty, projecting from the south side of the tower, at the western end of the church. The groining of the ceiling of this porch, it has been pointed out, takes an almost unique form ; the ribs are carved in bold relief, and the bosses at the intersections represent angels' heads, shields heraldically emblazoned, roses, &c., in great variety. Over the porch is a parvise, and above this another chamber which may have been originally used by the officials of the church.

Coming now to the interior of the church, we find it divided into three aisles, by two ranges of Tuscan columns. The aisles are of unequal widths, that in the centre being the widest, that to the south the narrowest. Semi-circular arches connect the columns on either side, springing directly from their capitals, without the interposition of an entablature, and support a large dental cornice, extending round the church. The ceiling of the middle aisle is divided into seven compartments, by horizontal bands, the middle compartment being formed into a small dome. A handsome Perpendicular screen extends across the church, near the western end.

The aisles have groined ceilings, ornamented at the angles with doves, &c. Over each of the aisles there was formerly a gallery, very clumsily introduced, which dated from the time when the church was built by Wren, and extended the whole length, excepting at the chancel. The front of the gallery, which was of oak, is described by Mr. Godwin as carved into scrolls, branches, &c., and in the centre panel, on either side, with the initials "C. R.," enriched with carvings of laurel. These galleries were removed when the church was restored in 1878-9, and the old-fashioned pews were superseded by open benches.

The central window, at the east end of the church, is semicircular-headed, and beneath it is a large Corinthian altar-piece of oak, displaying columns, entablatures, &c., elaborately carved and gilded.

The organ, said to be the oldest and one of the finest in London, was built in 1677, and has been greatly enlarged. Its reed-stops (hautboy, clarinet, &c.) are supposed to be unrivalled. In Newcourt's time the church was taken notice of as "remarkable for possessing an exceedingly fine organ, and the playing is thought so beautiful, that large congregations are attracted, though some of the parishioners object to the mode of performing divine service."

The organ is now on the north side of the church, in a large apartment known as "St. Stephen's Chapel." This building evidently formed a somewhat important part of the old church, and was probably appropriated to the votaries of the saint whose name it bears.

Between the exterior and the interior of the church there is little harmony. "For example," says Mr. Godwin, "the columns which form the south aisle face, in some instances, the centre of the large windows which occur in the external wall of the church, and in others the centre of the piers, indifferently." This discordance may likely enough have arisen from the fact that when the church was rebuilt, or rather restored, after the Great Fire, the works were done without much attention from Christopher Wren.

St. Sepulchre's appears to have enjoyed considerable popularity from the earliest period of its history, if one is to judge from the various sums left by well-disposed persons for the support of certain fraternities founded in the church—namely, those of St. Katherine, St. Michael, St. Anne, and Our Lady—and by others, for the maintenance of chantry priests to celebrate masses at stated intervals for the good of their souls. One of the fraternities just named—that of St. Katherine—originated, according to Stow, in the devotion of some poor persons in the parish, and was in honour of the conception of the Virgin Mary. They met in the church on the day of the Conception, and there heard the mass of the day, and made their offering, and provided a certain chaplain daily to celebrate divine service, and to set up wax lights before the image belonging to the fraternity, on all festival days.

The most famous of all who have been interred in St. Sepulchre's is Robert Ascham, the author of the "Schoolmaster," and the instructor of Queen Elizabeth in Greek and Latin. This learned old worthy was born in 1515, near Northallerton, in Yorkshire. He was educated at Cambridge University, and in time rose to be the university orator, being notably zealous in promoting what was then a novelty in England—the study of the Greek language. To divert himself after the fatigue of severe study, he used to devote himself to archery. This drew down upon him the censure of the all-work-and-no-play school; and in defence of himself, Ascham, in 1545, published "Toxophilus," a treatise on his favourite sport. This book is even yet well worthy of perusal, for its

enthusiasm, and for its curious descriptions of the personal appearance and manners of the principal persons whom the author had seen and conversed with. Henry VIII. rewarded him with a pension of £10 per annum, a considerable sum in those days. In 1548, Ascham, on the death of William Grindall, who had been his pupil, was appointed instructor in the learned languages to Lady Elizabeth, afterwards the good Queen Bess. At the end of two years he had some dispute with, or took a disgust at, Lady Elizabeth's attendants, resigned his situation, and returned to his college. Soon after this he was employed as secretary to the English ambassador at the court of Charles V. of Germany, and remained abroad till the death of Edward VI. During his absence he had been appointed Latin secretary to King Edward. Strangely enough, though Queen Mary and her ministers were Catholics, and Ascham a Protestant, he was retained in his office of Latin secretary, his pension was increased to £20, and he was allowed to retain his fellowship and his situation as university orator. In 1554 he married a lady of good family, by whom he had a considerable fortune, and of whom, in writing to a friend, he gives, as might perhaps be expected, an excellent character. On the accession of Queen Elizabeth, in 1558, she required his services, not only as Latin secretary, but as her instructor in Greek, and he resided at Court during the remainder of his life. During the last few days of his life he had been endeavouring to complete a Latin poem which he intended to present to the queen on the New Year's Day of 1569. He died two days before 1568 ran out, and was interred, according to his own directions, in the most private manner, in St. Sepulchre's Church, his funeral sermon being preached by Dr. Andrew Nowell, Dean of St. Paul's. He was universally lamented; and even the queen herself not only showed great concern, but was pleased to say that she would rather have lost ten thousand pounds than her tutor Ascham, which, from that somewhat close-handed sovereign, was truly an expression of high regard.

Ascham, like most men, had his little weaknesses. He had too great a propensity to dice and cock-fighting. Bishop Nicholson would try to convince us that this is an unfounded calumny, but, as the fact is mentioned by Camden, and other contemporary writers, it seems impossible to deny it. He died, from all accounts, in indifferent circumstances. "Whether," says Dr. Johnson, referring to this, "Ascham was poor by his own fault, or the fault of others, cannot now be decided; but it is certain that many have been rich with less merit. His philological learning would have gained him honour in any country; and among us it may justly call for that reverence which all nations owe to those who first rouse them from ignorance, short time, and with small pains, recover a sufficient habilitie to understand, write, and speak Latin: by Roger Ascham, ann. 1570. At London, printed by John Daye, dwelling over Aldersgate," a person,

GOLDSMITH'S HOUSE, GREEN ARBOUR COURT, ABOUT 1800. (*See page* 477.)

and kindle among them the light of literature." His most valuable work, "The Schoolmaster," was published by his widow. The nature of this celebrated performance may be gathered from the title : "The Schoolmaster; or a plain and perfite way of teaching children to understand, write, and speak the Latin tongue. . . . And commodious also for all such as have forgot the Latin tongue, and would by themselves, without a schoolmaster, in

by the way, already mentioned by us a few chapters back (see page 208), as having printed several noted works of the sixteenth century.

Dr. Johnson remarks that the instruction recommended in "The Schoolmaster" is perhaps the best ever given for the study of languages.

Here also lies buried Captain John Smith, a conspicuous soldier of fortune, whose romantic adventures and daring exploits have rarely been surpassed. He died on the 21st of June, 1631. This valiant captain was born at Willoughby, in the county of Lincoln, and helped by his doings to enliven the reigns of Elizabeth and James I. He had a share in the wars of Hungary in 1602, and in three single combats overcame three Turks, and cut off their heads. For this, and other equally brave deeds, Sigismund, Duke of Transylvania, gave him his picture set in gold, with a

and the saving of his life by the Indian girl Pocahontas, a story of adventure that charms as often as it is told. Bancroft, the historian of the United States, relates how, during the early settlement of Virginia, Smith left the infant colony on an exploring expedition, and not only ascended the river Chickahominy, but struck into the interior. His companions disobeyed his instructions, and being surprised by the Indians, were put to death.

ST. SEPULCHRE'S CHURCH IN 1737. *From a View by Toms.* (*See page* 478.)

pension of three hundred ducats; and allowed him to bear "three Turks' heads proper" as his shield of arms. He afterwards went to America, where he had the misfortune to fall into the hands of the Indians. He escaped from them, however, at last, and resumed his brilliant career by hazarding his life in naval engagements with pirates and Spanish men-of-war. The most important act of his life was the share he had in civilising the natives of New England, and reducing that province to obedience to Great Britain. In connection with his tomb in St. Sepulchre's, he is mentioned by Stow, in his "Survey," as "some time Governor of Virginia and Admiral of New England."

Certainly the most interesting events of his chequered career were his capture by the Indians,

Smith preserved his own life by calmness and self-possession. Displaying a pocket-compass, he amused the savages by an explanation of its power, and increased their admiration of his superior genius by imparting to them some vague conceptions of the form of the earth, and the nature of the planetary system. To the Indians, who retained him as their prisoner, his captivity was a more strange event than anything of which the traditions of their tribes preserved the memory. He was allowed to send a letter to the fort at Jamestown, and the wonder of the savages grew, for he seemed by some magic to endow the paper with the gift of intelligence. It was evident that their captive was a being of a high order, and then the question arose. Was his nature beneficent, or was he to be dreaded as a dangerous enemy? Their minds were bewildered, and the decision of his fate was referred to the chief Powhatan, and before Powhatan Smith was brought. "The fears of the feeble aborigines," says Bancroft, "were about to prevail, and his immediate death, already repeatedly threatened and repeatedly delayed, would have been inevitable, but for the timely intercession of Pocahontas, a girl twelve years old, the daughter of Powhatan, whose confiding fondness Smith had easily won, and who firmly clung to his neck, as his head was bowed down to receive the stroke of the tomahawks. His fearlessness, and her entreaties, persuaded the council to spare the agreeable stranger, who could make hatchets for her father, and rattles and strings of beads for herself, the favourite child. The barbarians, whose decision had long been held in suspense by the mysterious awe which Smith had inspired, now resolved to receive him as a friend, and to make him a partner of their councils. They tempted him to join their bands, and lend assistance in an attack upon the white men at Jamestown; and when his decision of character succeeded in changing the current of their thoughts, they dismissed him with mutual promises of friendship and benevolence. Thus the captivity of Smith did itself become a benefit to the colony; for he had not only observed with care the country between the James and the Potomac, and had gained some knowledge of the language and manners of the natives, but he now established a peaceful intercourse between the English and the tribes of Powhatan."

On the monument erected to Smith in St. Sepulchre's Church, the following quaint lines were formerly inscribed :—

"Here lies one conquered that hath conquered kings,
  Subdued large territories, and done things
  Which to the world impossible would seem,
  But that the truth is held in more esteem.
  Shall I report his former service done,
  In honour of his God, and Christendom?
  How that he did divide, from pagans three,
  Their heads and lives, types of his chivalry ? —
  For which great service, in that climate done,
  Brave Sigismundus, King of Hungarion,
  Did give him, as a coat of arms, to wear
  These conquered heads, got by his sword and spear.
  Or shall I tell of his adventures since
  Done in Virginia, that large continent ?
  How that he subdued kings unto his yoke,
  And made those heathens flee, as wind doth smoke ;
  And made their land, being so large a station,
  An habitation for our Christian nation,
  Where God is glorified, their wants supplied ;
  Which else for necessaries must have died.
  But what avail his conquests, now he lies
  Interred in earth, a prey to worms and flies ?

Oh! may his soul in sweet Elysium sleep,
  Until the Keeper, that all souls doth keep,
  Return to judgment ; and that after thence
  With angels he may have his recompense."

Sir Robert Peake, the engraver, also found a last resting-place here. He is known as the master of William Faithorne—the famous English engraver of the seventeenth century—and governor of Basing House for the king during the Civil War under Charles I. He died in 1667. Here also was interred the body of Dr. Bell, grandfather of the originator of a well-known system of education.

"The churchyard of St. Sepulchre's," we learn from Maitland, "at one time extended so far into the street on the south side of the church, as to render the passage-way dangerously narrow. In 1760 the churchyard was, in consequence, levelled, and thrown open to the public. But this led to much inconvenience, and it was re-enclosed in 1802."

Sarah Malcolm, the murderess, was buried in the churchyard of St. Sepulchre's in 1733. This cold-hearted and keen-eyed monster in human form has had her story told by us already. The parishioners seem, on this occasion, to have had no such scruples as had been exhibited by their predecessors a hundred and fifty years previous at the burial of Awfield, a traitor. We shall see presently that in those more remote days they were desirous of having at least respectable company for their deceased relatives and friends in the churchyard.

"For a long period," says Mr. Godwin (1838), "the church was surrounded by low mean buildings, by which its general appearance was hidden ; but these having been cleared away, and the neighbourhood made considerably more open, St. Sepulchre's now forms a somewhat pleasing object, notwithstanding that the tower and a part of the porch are so entirely dissimilar in style to the remainder of the building." And since Godwin's writing the surroundings of the church have been so improved that very few buildings in the metropolis stand more prominently before the public eye.

In the roll of Protestant martyrs who suffered at the stake for their religious principles, a vicar of St. Sepulchre's, the Reverend John Rogers, occupies a conspicuous place. He was the first who was burned in the reign of Queen Mary. This eminent person had at one time been chaplain to the English merchants at Antwerp, and while residing in that city had aided Tindal and Coverdale in their great work of translating the Bible. He married a German lady of good position, by whom he had a large family, and was enabled, by means of her relations, to reside in peace and safety in Germany. It appeared to be his duty, however, to return to England, and there publicly profess and advocate his religious convictions, even at the risk of death. He crossed the sea ; he took his place in the pulpit at St. Paul's Cross ; he preached a fearless and animated sermon, reminding his astonished audience of the " pure and wholesome doctrine " which had been promulgated from that pulpit in the days of the good King Edward, and solemnly warning them against the " pestilent idolatry and superstition of these new times." It was his last sermon. He was apprehended, tried, condemned, and burned at Smithfield. We described, when speaking of Smithfield, the manner in which he met his fate.

Connected with the life of John Rogers an odd circumstance is quoted in the " Churches of London." It is stated that when the bishops had resolved to put to death Joan Bocher, a friend came to Rogers and earnestly entreated his influence that the poor woman's life might be spared, and other means taken to prevent the spread of her heterodox doctrines. Rogers, however, contended that she should be executed ; and his friend then begged him to choose some other kind of death, which should be more agreeable to the gentleness and mercy prescribed in the gospel. " No," replied Rogers, " burning alive is not a cruel death, but easy enough." His friend hearing these words, expressive of so little regard for the sufferings of a fellow-creature, answered him with great vehemence, at the same time striking Rogers' hand, " Well, it may perhaps so happen that you yourself shall have your hands full of this mild burning." There is no record of Rogers among the papers belonging to St. Sepulchre's, but this may easily be accounted for by the fact that at the Great Fire of 1666 nearly all the registers and archives were destroyed.

A noteworthy incident in the history of St. Sepulchre's was connected with the execution, in 1585, of Awfield, for " sparcinge abrood certen lewed, sedicious, and traytorous bookes." " When he was executed," says Fleetwood, the Recorder, in a letter to Lord Burleigh, July 7th of that year, " his body was brought unto St. Pulcher's to be buryed, but the parishioners would not suffer a traytor's corpse to be laid in the earth where their parents, wives, children, kindred, masters, and old neighbours did rest ; and so his carcass was returned to the burial-ground near Tyburn, and there I leave it."

Another event in the history of the church is a tale of suicide. On the 10th of April, 1600, a man named William Dorrington threw himself from the roof of the tower, leaving there a prayer for forgiveness.

We come now to speak of the connection of St. Sepulchre's with the neighbouring prison of Newgate. Being the nearest church to the prison, that connection naturally was intimate. Its clock served to give the time to the hangman when there was an execution in the Old Bailey, and many a poor wretch's last moments must it have regulated.

On the right-hand side of the altar a board with a list of charitable donations and gifts used to contain the following item :—" 1605. Mr. Robert Dowe gave, for ringing the greatest bell in this church on the day the condemned prisoners are executed, and for other services, for ever, concerning such condemned prisoners, for which services the sexton is paid £1 6s. 8d.—£50.

It was formerly the practice for the clerk or bellman of St. Sepulchre's to go under Newgate, on the night preceding the execution of a criminal, ring his bell, and repeat the following wholesome advice :—

> " All you that in the condemned hold do lie,
> Prepare you, for to-morrow you shall die ;
> Watch all, and pray, the hour is drawing near
> That you before the Almighty must appear ;
> Examine well yourselves, in time repent,
> That you may not to eternal flames be sent.
> And when St. Sepulchre's bell to-morrow tolls,
> The Lord above have mercy on your souls.
> > Past twelve o'clock !"

This practice is explained by a passage in Munday's edition of Stow, in which it is told that a Mr. John Dowe, citizen and merchant taylor of London, gave £50 to the parish church of St. Sepulchre's, under the following conditions :—After the several sessions of London, on the night before the execution of such as were condemned to death, the clerk of the church was to go in the night-time, and also early in the morning, to the window of the prison in which they were lying. He was there to ring " certain tolls with a hand-bell" appointed for the purpose, and was afterwards, in a most Christian manner, to put them in mind of their present condition and approaching end, and to exhort them to be prepared, as they ought to be, to die. When they were in the cart, and brought before the walls of the church, the clerk was to stand there ready with the same bell, and, after certain tolls, rehearse a prayer, desiring all the people there present to pray for the unfortunate criminals. The beadle, also, of Merchant Taylors' Hall was allowed an " honest stipend " to see that this ceremony was regularly performed.

The affecting admonition—" affectingly good," Pennant calls it—addressed to the prisoners in

Newgate, on the night before execution, ran as follows :—

    " You prisoners that are within,
      Who, for wickedness and sin,

after many mercies shown you, are now appointed to die to-morrow in the forenoon; give ear and understand that, to-morrow morning, the greatest bell of St. Sepulchre's shall toll for you, in form and manner of a passing-bell, as used to be tolled for those that are at the point of death ; to the end that all godly people, hearing that bell, and knowing it is for your going to your deaths, may be stirred up heartily to pray to God to bestow his grace and mercy upon you, whilst you live. I beseech you, for Jesus Christ's sake, to keep this night in watching and prayer, to the salvation of your own souls while there is yet time and place for mercy ; as knowing to-morrow you must appear before the judgment-seat of your Creator, there to give an account of all things done in this life, and to suffer eternal torments for your sins committed against Him, unless, upon your hearty and unfeigned repentance, you find mercy through the merits, death, and passion of your only Mediator and Advocate, Jesus Christ, who now sits at the right hand of God, to make intercession for as many of you as penitently return to Him."

And the following was the admonition to condemned criminals, as they were passing by St. Sepulchre's Church wall to execution :—" All good people, pray heartily unto God for these poor sinners, who are now going to their death, for whom this great bell doth toll.

"You that are condemned to die, repent with lamentable tears ; ask mercy of the Lord, for the salvation of your own souls, through the merits, death, and passion of Jesus Christ, who now sits at the right hand of God, to make intercession for as many of you as penitently return unto Him.

    " Lord have mercy upon you ;
      Christ have mercy upon you.
    Lord have mercy upon you ;
      Christ have mercy upon you."

The charitable Mr. Dowe, who took such interest in the last moments of the occupants of the condemned cell, was buried in the church of St. Botolph, Aldgate.

Another curious custom observed at St. Sepulchre's was the presentation of a nosegay to every criminal on his way to execution at Tyburn. No doubt the practice had its origin in some kindly feeling for the poor unfortunates who were so soon to bid farewell to all the beauties of earth. One of the last who received a nosegay from the steps of St. Sepulchre's was "Sixteen-string Jack," *alias*

John Rann, who was hanged, in 1774, for robbing the Rev. Dr. Bell of his watch and eighteen pence in money, in Gunnersbury Lane, on the road to Brentford. Sixteen-string Jack wore the flowers in his button-hole as he rode dolefully to the gallows. This was witnessed by John Thomas Smith, who thus describes the scene in his admirable anecdotebook, " Nollekens and his Times :"—" I remember well, when I was in my eighth year, Mr. Nollekens calling at my father's house, in Great Portland Street, and taking us to Oxford Street, to see the notorious Jack Rann, commonly called Sixteenstring Jack, go to Tyburn to be hanged. . . . The criminal was dressed in a pea-green coat, with an immense nosegay in the button-hole, which had been presented to him at St. Sepulchre's steps ; and his nankeen small-clothes, we were told, were tied at each knee with sixteen strings. After he had passed, and Mr. Nollekens was leading me home by the hand, I recollect his stooping down to me and observing, in a low tone of voice, 'Tom, now, my little man, if my father-in-law, Mr. Justice Welch, had been high constable, we could have walked by the side of the cart all the way to Tyburn.'"

When criminals were conveyed from Newgate to Tyburn, the cart passed up Giltspur Street, and through Smithfield, to Cow Lane. Skinner Street had not then been built, and the Crooked Lane which turned down by St. Sepulchre's, as well as Ozier Lane, did not afford sufficient width to admit of the cavalcade passing by either of them, with convenience, to Holborn Hill, or "the Heavy Hill," as it used to be called. The procession seems at no time to have had much of the solemn element about it. "The heroes of the day were often," says a popular writer, "on good terms with the mob, and jokes were exchanged between the men who were going to be hanged and the men who deserved to be."

"On St. Paul's Day," says Mr. Timbs (1868), " service is performed in St. Sepulchre's, in accordance with the will of Mr. Paul Jervis, who, in 1717, devised certain land in trust that a sermon should be preached in the church upon every Paul's Day upon the excellence of the liturgy of the Church of England ; the preacher to receive 40s. for such sermon. Various sums are also bequeathed to the curate, the clerk, the treasurer, and masters of the parochial schools. To the poor of the parish he bequeathed 20s. a-piece to ten of the poorest householders within that part of the parish of St. Sepulchre commonly called Smithfield quarter, £4 to the treasurer of St. Bartholomew's Hospital, and 6s. 8d. yearly to the clerk, who shall attend to receive the same. The residue of the yearly rents and profits is to be distributed unto and amongst such poor people of the parish of St. Sepulchre's, London, who shall attend the service and sermon. At the close of the service the vestry-clerk reads aloud an extract from the will, and then proceeds to the distribution of the money. In the evening the vicar, churchwardens, and common councilmen of the precinct dine together."

In 1749, a Mr. Drinkwater made a praiseworthy bequest. He left the parish of St. Sepulchre £500 to be lent in sums of £25 to industrious young tradesmen. No interest was to be charged, and the money was to be lent for four years.

Next to St. Sepulchre's, on Snow Hill, used to stand the famous old inn of the "Saracen's Head." It was only swept away within the last few years by the ruthless army of City improvers: a view of it in course of demolition is given on page 439. It was one of the oldest of the London inns which bore the "Saracen's Head" for a sign. One of Dick Tarlton's jests makes mention of the "Saracen's Head" without Newgate, and Stow, describing this neighbourhood, speaks particularly of "a fair large inn for receipt of travellers" that "hath to sign the 'Saracen's Head.'" The courtyard had, to the last, many of the characteristics of an old English inn; there were galleries all round leading to the bedrooms, and a spacious gateway through which the dusty mail-coaches used to rumble, the tired passengers creeping forth "thanking their stars in having escaped the highwaymen and the holes and sloughs of the road." Into that court-yard how many have come on their first arrival in London with hearts beating high with hope, some of whom have risen to be aldermen and sit in state as lord mayor, whilst others have gone the way of the idle apprentice and come to a sad end at Tyburn! It was at this inn that Nicholas Nickleby and his uncle waited upon the Yorkshire school-master Squeers, of Dotheboys Hall. Mr. Dickens describes the tavern as it existed in the last days of mail-coaching, when it was a most important place for arrivals and departures in London :—

"Next to the jail, and by consequence near to Smithfield also, and the Compter and the bustle and noise of the City, and just on that particular part of Snow Hill where omnibus horses going eastwards seriously think of falling down on purpose, and where horses in hackney cabriolets going westwards not unfrequently fall by accident, is the coach-yard of the 'Saracen's Head' inn, its portals guarded by two Saracens' heads and shoulders, which it was once the pride and glory of the choice

spirits of this metropolis to pull down at night, but which have for some time remained in undisturbed tranquillity, possibly because this species of humour is now confined to St. James's parish, where door-knockers are preferred as being more portable, and bell-wires esteemed as convenient tooth-picks. Whether this be the reason or not, there they are, frowning upon you from each side of the gateway; and the inn itself, garnished with another Saracen's head, frowns upon you from the top of the yard; while from the door of the hind-boot of all the red coaches that are standing therein, there glares a small Saracen's head with a twin expression to the large Saracen's head below, so that the general appearance of the pile is of the Saracenic order."

To explain the use of the Saracen's head as an inn sign various reasons have been given. "When our countrymen," says Selden, "came home from fighting with the Saracens and were beaten by them, they pictured them with huge, big, terrible faces (as you still see the 'Saracen's Head' is), when in truth they were like other men. But this they did to save their own credit." Or the sign may have been adopted by those who had visited the Holy Land either as pilgrims or to fight the Saracens. Others, again, hold that it was first set up in compliment to the mother of Thomas à Becket, who was the daughter of a Saracen. How-ever this may be, it is certain that the use of the sign in former days was very general.

Running past the east end of St. Sepulchre's, from Newgate into West Smithfield, is Giltspur Street, anciently called Knightrider Street. This interest-ing thoroughfare derives its name from the knights with their gilt spurs having been accustomed to ride this way to the jousts and tournaments which in days of old were held in Smithfield.

In this street was Giltspur Street Compter, a debtors' prison and house of correction appertain-ing to the sheriffs of London and Middlesex. It stood over against St. Sepulchre's Church, and was removed hither from the east side of Wood Street, Cheapside, in 1791. At the time of its removal it was used as a place of imprisonment for debtors, but the yearly increasing demands upon the con-tracted space caused that department to be given up, and City debtors were sent to Whitecross Street. The architect was Dance, to whom we are also indebted for the grim pile of Newgate. The Compter was a dirty and appropriately convict-looking edifice. It was pulled down in 1855. Mr. Hepworth Dixon gave an interesting account of this City House of Correction, not long before its demo-lition, in his "London Prisons" (1850). "Enter-ing," he says, "at the door facing St. Sepulchre's, the visitor suddenly finds himself in a low dark passage, leading into the offices of the gaol, and branching off into other passages, darker, closer, more replete with noxious smells, than even those of Newgate. This is the fitting prelude to what follows. The prison, it must be noticed, is divided on Christ's Hospital. Curious it is to consider how thin a wall divides these widely-separate worlds! And sorrowful it is to think what a difference of destiny awaits the children—destiny inexorable, though often unearned in either case—who, on the one side of it or the other, receive an elee-

PORCH OF ST. SEPULCHRE'S CHURCH. (See page 478.)

into two principal divisions, the House of Correction and the Compter. The front in Giltspur Street, and the side nearest to Newgate Street, is called the Compter. In its wards are placed detenues of various kinds—remands, committals from the police-courts, and generally persons waiting for trial, and consequently still unconvicted. The other department, the House of Correction, occupies the back portion of the premises, abutting mosynary education! The collegian and the criminal! Who shall say how much mere accident—circumstances over which the child has little power—determines to a life of usefulness or mischief? From the yards of Giltspur Street prison almost the only objects visible, outside of the gaol itself, are the towers of Christ's Hospital; the only sounds audible, the shouts of the scholars at their play. The balls of the hospital boys often fall within the yards of the prison. Whether these sights and sounds ever cause the criminal to pause and reflect upon the courses of his life, we will not say, but the stranger visiting the place will be very apt to think for him. . . .

"In the department of the prison called the House of Correction, minor offenders within the City of London are imprisoned. No transports are sent hither, nor is any person whose sentence is above three years in length." This able writer

A large section of the prison used to be devoted to female delinquents, but lately it was almost entirely given up to male offenders.

"The House of Correction, and the Compter portion of the establishment," says Mr. Dixon, "are kept quite distinct, but it would be difficult to award the palm of empire in their respective facilities for demoralisation. We think the Compter rather the worse of the two. You are shown into a room, about the size of an apartment in an ordinary

GILTSPUR STREET COMPTER, 1840. (*See page* 485.)

then goes on to tell of the many crying evils connected with the institution—the want of air, the over-crowded state of the rooms, the absence of proper cellular accommodation, and the vicious intercourse carried on amongst the prisoners. The entire gaol, when he wrote, contained only thirty-six separate sleeping-rooms. Now by the highest prison calculation—and this, be it noted, proceeds on the assumption that *three* persons can sleep in small, miserable, unventilated cells, which are built for only *one*, and are too confined for that, being only about one-half the size of the *model cell* for one at Pentonville—it was capable of accommodating only 203 prisoners, yet by the returns issued at Michaelmas, 1850, it contained 246!

dwelling-house, which will be found crowded with from thirty to forty persons, young and old, and in their ordinary costume; the low thief in his filth and rags, and the member of the swell-mob with his bright buttons, flash finery, and false jewels. Here you notice the boy who has just been guilty of his first offence, and committed for trial, learning with a greedy mind a thousand criminal arts, and listening with the precocious instinct of guilty passions to stories and conversations the most depraved and disgusting. You regard him with a mixture of pity and loathing, for he knows that the eyes of *his peers* are upon him, and he stares at you with a familiar impudence, and exhibits a devil-may-care countenance, such as is only to be met with in the juvenile offender. Here, too, may be seen the young clerk, taken up on suspicion—perhaps innocent—who avoids you with a shy look of pain and uneasiness : what a hell must this prison be to him ! How frightful it is to think of a person really untainted with crime, compelled to herd for ten or twenty days with these abandoned wretches !

"On the other, the House of Correction side of the gaol, similar rooms will be found, full of prisoners communicating with each other, laughing and shouting without hindrance. All this is so little in accordance with existing notions of prison discipline, that one is continually fancying these disgraceful scenes cannot be in the capital of England, and in the year of grace 1850. Very few of the prisoners attend school or receive any instruction ; neither is any kind of employment afforded them, except oakum-picking, and the still more disgusting labour of the treadmill. When at work, an officer is in attendance to prevent disorderly conduct ; but his presence is of no avail as a protection to the less depraved. Conversation still goes on ; and every facility is afforded for making acquaintances, and for mutual contamination."

After having long been branded by intelligent inspectors as a disgrace to the metropolis, Giltspur Street Compter was condemned, closed in 1854, and subsequently taken down.

Nearly opposite what used to be the site of the Compter, and adjoining Cock Lane, is the spot called Pie Corner, near which terminated the Great Fire of 1666. The fire commenced at Pudding Lane, it will be remembered, so it was singularly appropriate that it should terminate at Pie Corner. Under the date of 4th September, 1666, Pepys, in his "Diary," records that "W. Hewer this day went to see how his mother did, and comes home late, telling us how he hath been forced to remove her to Islington, her house in Pye Corner being burned ; so that the fire is got so far that way." The figure of a fat naked boy stands over a public house at the corner of the lane ; it used to have the following warning inscription attached :—" This boy is in memory put up of the late fire of London, occasioned by the sin of gluttony, 1666." According to Stow, Pie Corner derived its name from the sign of a well-frequented hostelry, which anciently stood on the spot. Strype makes honourable mention of Pie Corner, as "noted chiefly for cooks' shops and pigs dressed there during Bartholomew Fair." Our old writers have many references—and not all, by the way, in the best taste—to its cook-stalls and dressed pork. Shadwell, for instance, in the *Woman Captain* (1680) speaks of "meat dressed

at Pie Corner by greasy scullions ;" and Ben Jonson writes in the *Alchemist* (1612)—

"I shall put you in mind, sir, at Pie Corner,
　　Taking your meal of steam in from cooks' stalls."

And in "The Great Boobee" ("Roxburgh Ballads"):

"Next day I through Pie Corner passed ;
　　The roast meat on the stall
　　Invited me to take a taste ;
　　My money was but small."

But Pie Corner seems to have been noted for more than eatables. A ballad from Tom D'Urfey's "Pills to Purge Melancholy," describing Bartholomew Fair, eleven years before the Fire of London, says :—

"At Pie-Corner end, mark well my good friend,
　　'Tis a very fine dirty place ;
　　Where there's more arrows and bows. . . .
　　Than was handled at Chivy Chase."

We have already given a view of Pie Corner in our chapter on Smithfield, page 361.

Hosier Lane, running from Cow Lane to Smithfield, and almost parallel to Cock Lane, is described by "R. B.," in Strype, as a place not over-well built or inhabited. The houses were all old timber erections. Some of these—those standing at the south corner of the lane—were in the beginning of this century depicted by Mr. J. T. Smith, in his "Ancient Topography of London." He describes them as probably of the reign of James I. The rooms were small, with low, unornamented ceilings; the timber, oak, profusely used ; the gables were plain, and the walls lath and plaster. They were taken down in 1809.

In the corner house, in Mr. Smith's time, there was a barber whose name was Catchpole ; at least, so it was written over the door. He was rather an odd fellow, and possessed, according to his own account, a famous relic of antiquity. He would gravely show his customers a short-bladed instrument, as the identical dagger with which Walworth killed Wat Tyler.

Hosier Lane, like Pie Corner, used to be a great resort during the time of Bartholomew Fair, "all the houses," it is said in Strype, "generally being made public for tippling."

We return now from our excursion to the north of St. Sepulchre's, and continue our rambles to the west, and before speaking of what is, let us refer to what has been.

Turnagain Lane is not far from this. "Near unto this Seacoal Lane," remarks Stow, "in the turning towards Holborn Conduit, is Turnagain Lane, or rather, as in a record of the 5th of Edward III., Windagain Lane for that it goeth down west to Fleet Dyke, from whence men must turn again the same way they came, but there it stopped." There used to be a proverb, "He must take him a house in Turnagain Lane."

A conduit formerly stood on Snow Hill, a little below the church. It is described as a building with four equal sides, ornamented with four columns and pediment, surmounted by a pyramid, on which stood a lamb—a rebus on the name of Lamb, from whose conduit in Red Lion Street the water came. There had been a conduit there, however, before Lamb's day, which was towards the close of the sixteenth century.

At No. 37, King Street, Snow Hill, there used to be a ladies' charity school, which was established in 1702, and remained in the parish 145 years. Dr. Johnson and Mrs. Thrale were subscribers to this school, and Johnson drew from it his story of Betty Broom, in "The Idler." The world of domestic service, in Betty's days, seems to have been pretty much as now. Betty was a poor girl, bred in the country at a charity-school, maintained by the contributions of wealthy neighbours. The patronesses visited the school from time to time, to see how the pupils got on, and everything went well, till "at last, the chief of the subscribers having passed a winter in London, came down full of an opinion new and strange to the whole country. She held it little less than criminal to teach poor girls to read and write. They who are born to poverty, she said, are born to ignorance, and will work the harder the less they know. She told her friends that London was in confusion by the insolence of servants; that scarcely a girl could be got for *all-work*, since education had made such numbers of fine ladies, that nobody would now accept a lower title than that of a waiting-maid, or something that might qualify her to wear laced shoes and long ruffles, and to sit at work in the parlour window. But she was resolved, for her part, to spoil no more girls. Those who were to live by their hands should neither read nor write out of her pocket. The world was bad enough already, and she would have no part in making it worse.

"She was for a long time warmly opposed; but she persevered in her notions, and withdrew her subscription. Few listen, without a desire of conviction, to those who advise them to spare their money. Her example and her arguments gained ground daily; and in less than a year the whole parish was convinced that the nation would be ruined if the children of the poor were taught to read and write." So the school was dissolved, and Betty with the rest was turned adrift into the wide and cold world; and her adventures there any one may read in "The Idler" for himself.

There is an entry in the school minutes of 1763, to the effect that the ladies of the committee censured the schoolmistress for listening to the story of the Cock Lane ghost, and "desired her to keep her belief in the article to herself."

Skinner Street—now one of the names of the past—which ran by the south side of St. Sepulchre's, and formed the connecting link between Newgate Street and Holborn, received its name from Alderman Skinner, through whose exertions, about 1802, it was principally built. The following account of Skinner Street is from the picturesque pen of Mr. William Harvey (" Aleph"), whose long familiarity with the places he describes renders doubly valuable his many contributions to the history of London scenes and people :—"As a building speculation," he says, writing in 1863, "it was a failure. When the buildings were ready for occupation, tall and substantial as they really were, the high rents frightened intending shopkeepers. Tenants were not to be had ; and in order to get over the money difficulty, a lottery, sanctioned by Parliament, was commenced. Lotteries were then common tricks of finance, and nobody wondered at the new venture ; but even the most desperate fortune-hunters were slow to invest their capital, and the tickets hung sadly on hand. The day for the drawing was postponed several times, and when it came, there was little or no excitement on the subject, and whoever rejoiced in becoming a house-owner on such easy terms, the original projectors and builders were understood to have suffered considerably. The winners found the property in a very unfinished condition. Few of the dwellings were habitable, and as funds were often wanting, a majority of the houses remained empty, and the shops unopened. After two or three years things began to improve ; the vast many-storeyed house which then covered the site of Commercial Place was converted into a warehousing depôt; a capital house opposite the 'Saracen's Head' was taken by a hosier of the name of Theobald, who, opening his shop with the determination of selling the best hosiery, and nothing else, was able to convince the citizens that his hose was first-rate, and, desiring only a living profit, succeeded, after thirty years of unwearied industry, in accumulating a large fortune. Theobald was possessed of literary tastes, and at the sale of Sir Walter Scott's manuscripts was a liberal purchaser. He also collected a library of exceedingly choice books, and when aristocratic customers purchased stockings of him, was soon able to interest them in matters of far higher interest. . .

"The most remarkable shop—but it was on the left-hand side, at a corner house—was that established for the sale of children's books. It boasted an immense extent of window-front, extending from the entrance into Snow Hill, and towards Fleet Market. Many a time have I lingered with loving eyes over those fascinating story-books, so rich in gaily-coloured prints; such careful editions of the marvellous old histories, 'Puss in Boots,' 'Cock Robin,' 'Cinderella,' and the like. Fortunately the front was kept low, so as exactly to suit the capacity of a childish admirer. . . . . But Skinner Street did not prosper much, and never could compete with even the dullest portions of Holborn. I have spoken of some reputable shops; but you know the proverb, 'One swallow will not make a summer,' and it was a declining neighbourhood almost before it could be called new. In 1810 the commercial depôt, which had been erected at a cost of £25,000, and was the chief prize in the lottery, was destroyed by fire, never to be rebuilt—a heavy blow and discouragement to Skinner Street, from which it never rallied. Perhaps the periodical hanging-days exercised an unfavourable influence, collecting, as they frequently did, all the thieves and vagabonds of London. I never sympathised with Pepys or Charles Fox in their passion for public executions, and made it a point to avoid those ghastly sights; but early of a Monday morning, when I had just reached the end of Giltspur Street, a miserable wretch had just been turned off from the platform of the debtors' door, and I was made the unwilling witness of his last struggles. That scene haunted me for months, and I often used to ask myself, 'Who that could help it would live in Skinner Street?' The next unpropitious event in these parts was the unexpected closing of the child's library. What could it mean? Such a well-to-do establishment shut up? Yes, the whole army of shutters looked blankly on the inquirer, and forbade even a single glance at 'Sinbad' or 'Robinson Crusoe.' It would soon be re-opened, we naturally thought; but the shutters never came down again. The whole house was deserted; not even a messenger in bankruptcy, or an ancient Charley, was found to regard the playful double knocks of the neighbouring juveniles. Gradually the glass of all the windows got broken in, a heavy cloud of black dust, solidifying into inches thick, gathered on sills and doors and brickwork, till the whole frontage grew as gloomy as Giant Despair's Castle. Not long after, the adjoining houses shared the same fate, and they remained from year to year without the slightest sign of life—absolute scarecrows, darkening with their uncomfortable shadows the busy streets. Within half a mile, in Stamford Street, Blackfriars,

there are (1863) seven houses in a similar predicament—window-glass demolished, doors cracked from top to bottom, spiders' webs hanging from every projecting sill or parapet. What can it mean? The loss in the article of rents alone must be over £1,000 annually. If the real owners are at feud with imaginary owners, surely the property might be rendered valuable, and the proceeds invested. Even the lawyers can derive no profit from such hopeless abandonment. I am told the whole mischief arose out of a Chancery suit. Can it be the famous 'Jarndyce v. Jarndyce' case? And have all the heirs starved each other out? If so, what hinders our lady the Queen from taking possession? Any change would be an improvement, for these dead houses make the streets they cumber as dispiriting and comfortless as graveyards. Busy fancy will sometimes people them, and fill the dreary rooms with strange guests. Do the victims of guilt congregate in these dark dens? Do wretches 'unfriended by the world or the world's law,' seek refuge in these deserted nooks, mourning in the silence of despair over their former lives, and anticipating the future in unappeasable agony? Such things have been—the silence and desolation of these doomed dwellings make them the more suitable for such tenants." These houses belonged to the same eccentric old woman who owned those which formerly stood in Stamford Street, Blackfriars Road.

In front of No. 58, the sailor Cashman was hung in 1817, as already mentioned, for plundering a gunsmith's shop there. William Godwin, the author of "Caleb Williams," kept a bookseller's shop for several years in Skinner Street, at No. 41, and published school-books in the name of Edward Baldwin. On the wall there was a stone carving of Æsop reciting one of his fables to children.

The most noteworthy event of the life of Godwin was his marriage with the celebrated Mary Wollstonecraft, authoress of a " Vindication of the Rights of Women," whose congenial mind, in politics and morals, he ardently admired. Godwin's account of the way in which they got on together is worth reading :—" Ours," he writes, " was not an idle happiness, a paradise of selfish and transitory pleasures. It is, perhaps, scarcely necessary to mention, that influenced by ideas I had long entertained, I engaged an apartment about twenty doors from our house, in the Polygon, Somers Town, which I designed for the purpose of my study and literary occupations. Trifles, however, will be interesting to some readers, when they relate to the last period of the life of such a person as Mary. I will add, therefore, that we were both of us of opinion, that it was possible for two persons to be too uniformly in each other's society. Influenced by that opinion, it was my practice to repair to the apartment I have mentioned as soon as I rose, and frequently not to make my appearance in the Polygon till the hour of dinner. We agreed in condemning the notion, prevalent in many situations in life, that a man and his wife cannot visit in mixed society but in company with each other, and we rather sought occasions of deviating from than of complying with this rule. By this means, though, for the most part, we spent the latter half of each day in one another's society, yet we were in no danger of satiety. We seemed to combine, in a considerable degree, the novelty and lively sensation of a visit with the more delicious and heartfelt pleasure of a domestic life."

This philosophic union, to Godwin's inexpressible affliction, did not last more than eighteen months, at the end of which time Mrs. Godwin died, leaving an only daughter, who in the course of time became the second wife of the poet Shelley, and was the author of the wild and extraordinary tale of " Frankenstein."

CHAPTER LVI.

THE METROPOLITAN MEAT MARKET.

History of the Metropolitan Meat Market—Newgate Market and its Inconvenience—The Meat Market described—The Ceremony of Opening—A Roaring Trade—The Metropolitan Poultry Market—London Trade in Poultry and Game—French Geese and Irish Geese—Packed in Ice—Plover's Eggs for the Queen.

BEFORE the establishment of a central meat and poultry market in Smithfield, London was behind every city of Europe in respect of public markets. For seven centuries, dating from 1150, Smithfield has been used as a market for live stock. Latterly, the dirt and crowd, and the rushes of horned beasts, had become intolerable, and after much opposition from vested interests, an Act of Parliament was passed in 1852, under the provisions of which a new and convenient cattle-market was constructed by the Corporation out to the quiet north, in Copenhagen Fields, once the resort of Cockney lovers, Cockney duellists, and Cockney agitators.

"At the opening of the Meat Market by the Prince Consort, in 1855," says the *Times* of November 25, 1868, "Smithfield became waste ground. The arrangements at Copenhagen Fields are about as good for their purpose as any that could have been desired; but since the time the market there was laid out there have been very great changes in respect of the supply of animal food for the population of the metropolis. Then most of the beasts and sheep converted into meat for sale in the shops of London butchers were brought to London alive and slaughtered by the retailers. With the development of our railway system, and the additions to the great main lines by extensions which brought them into the business parts of the metropolis, the dead meat traffic from the provinces exhibited year by year a heavier tonnage. But the Cattle Plague, and the consequent restrictions to the removal from one county to another of live stock which might communicate or become infected with the disease, brought about something like a revolution in our food supply; and at the present time not less than about 100,000 tons of dead meat are brought into the London market from all parts of the country. The centre to which all this immense quantity of meat has hitherto been consigned is Newgate Market. Here has been conducted an enormous wholesale trade between the salesmen, to whom the country dealers, nearly 300 in number, consign their meat, and retail butchers scattered all over London and its suburbs who do not slaughter for themselves. In addition, Newgate Market has been from time immemorial the principal retail meat market—a circumstance which may be attributed to the fact that it has the reputation of being cheaper than all others by 1d. or 2d. in the pound. Now, in modern London, it would be difficult to find any site more inconvenient for such a double trade than that of Newgate Market. The whole business has had to be done within the very limited space of which Paternoster Row, Ivy Lane, Newgate Street, and the Old Bailey are the boundaries. Last Christmas week 800 tons of meat were brought to London for the Newgate Market by the Great Eastern, the Great Northern, and the Midland railways. This, and the consignments by all the other lines, had to be conveyed to the market from the railway stations in wagons and vans. These vehicles, and the butchers' carts, completely block up Giltspur Street, Newgate Street, and the Old Bailey on several days in the week, Mondays and Fridays especially."

Through the filthy lanes and alleys no one could

PART OF THE CHARTERHOUSE

PART OF St ANDREWS PARISH

PART OF FARRINGDON

FARRINGDON WARD *without* *with its Division into* PARISHES *according to a New SURVEY.*

WITHIN

Smithfield Bars

SMITH FIELD

Bartholome

Snow Hill

FLEET MARKET

Holbourn Hill

HATTON GARDEN

Ely House

Holbourn

Fleet Bridge

Popinjoy Alley

The Fleet

FLEET STREET

Dorset St

Serjeants Inn Exchequer Court

Temple Walks

White Fryer

Hare Ct

Brick Ct

Essex Ct

High Holborn

Chancery Lane

LINCOLN'S INN

Gray's Inn

Fetter

THE RIVER THAMES

MAP OF FARRINGDON WARD WITHOUT, 1750. (*See page 496.*)

PART OF St CLEMENTS

pass without being either butted with the dripping end of a quarter of beef, or smeared by the greasy carcase of a newly-slain sheep. In many of the narrow lanes there was hardly room for two persons to pass abreast. Nevertheless, till the extension of the railway system, there was a difficulty in constructing a meat market worthy of London, from the size of the great city. A good meat market must be open to access from all quarters. Some

mentary powers enabled the committee to raise a sum of £235,000 for the purchase of property, and £200,000 for the erection of buildings. The Markets Improvement Committee concluded their contract with Messrs. Browne and Robinson for a sum within the estimated amount of £200,000. The chief element of the design was that the basement storey of the market was to be a "through" railway-station, with communication not only from

THE METROPOLITAN MEAT MARKET. (*See page* 494.)

years ago, when beef and mutton were far dearer in outlying shops than in Newgate Market itself, the inconvenient position, and the difficulty of reaching it compelled persons of moderate means to be taxed elsewhere, rather than face the dirt and bustle of Newgate. The Corporation, therefore, at last resolved on providing a new market in Smithfield, in order to utilise a waste, and develop the meat trade throughout the kingdom.

In 1860 the Corporation obtained an Act for erecting market buildings on the site of Smithfield, and the following year procured another, giving them power to abolish Newgate Market. The Markets Improvement Committee then took the matter in hand, and Mr. Horace Jones, the City architect, prepared a fitting design. Their parlia-

all parts of the country, but also with all the suburban lines.

The tremendous excavations soon began on a Roman scale of grandeur. About 3,500,000 loads of earth, weighing about 172,000 tons, had to be loosened and removed. Twenty-one main girders, of Titanic strength, were carried across the entire width of the excavation, 240 feet, on wrought-iron stanchions. On these main girders cross girders were laid, 2 feet 6 inches deep, and 7 feet 6 inches apart. Between the latter brick arches were turned, and concrete and asphalte were set in stone, to form a roof for the railway, and a bedding for the wood pavement of the building.

In these foundations were five miles of iron girding, carried on no fewer than 180 wrought-iron stanchions, while substantial retaining walls rose all around.

The first stone of this well-planned market was laid on the 5th of June, 1867, by Mr. Lowman Taylor, the chairman of the committee; and in the following year the work was completed. The market is a huge parallelogram, 631 feet long and 246 feet wide, and covers three and a half acres. It is not over-beautiful, but then its necessities were peculiar and imperative. The style would probably be called Italian, but it resembles more the Renaissance of France, that style which mediæval-ists shudder at, but which is more elastic in the architect's hands than the Gothic. The prevailing feature of the style is a series of arcaded recesses between Doric pilasters, fluted on the upper two triads, and elevated on pedestals. The entablature is returned and ornamented over the pilasters, with vase-like finials. The external wall is 32 feet high. Between the Portland stone pilasters are recesses of red brickwork. The semi-circular heads of the arches are filled in with rich iron scrolls, which let in the light and air freely.

The keystones of the arches are richly carved, especially those over the twelve side entrances. Under the iron openings are windows, with stone sills, trusses, architraves, and cornices. At the angles of the building rise four handsome towers of Portland stone. The lower storey of each octagonal tower is a square, with double pilasters at the corners, and a carved pediment on each face. Above this height the towers are octagonal. The square and the octagonal portions are joined by the huge couchant stone griffins of the City arms. On each side of the octagon are windows, with carved friezes. The dome of each tower is pierced on four sides by dormer windows, and above is a lantern, surrounded by an ornamental railing. The finest *coup d'œil* of the building, archi-tectural critics think, is the double façade of the public roadway which runs across the market, and divides it into equal parts. The roadway is 50 feet wide between the double piers, which carry a richly-moulded elliptical arch and cast-iron pediment, and over each double pier is an em-blematic figure in Portland stone, representing one of the four principal cities of the United Kingdom. At the south front London and Edinburgh stand confessed, and on the north are Dublin and Liver-pool. The sides of the outer roadway are shut off from the market by an elaborate open iron-work screen, 14 feet high, and at the intersection of the central avenue, east and west, the market is closed by ornamented iron gates, with iron span-drils and semi-circular heads, similar to those in the

arcade. Towards the north a gate gives access, by a double staircase, to the railway department below. The gates at the east and west entrances (the chief) are 25 feet high, and 19 feet wide, and each pair weighs 15 tons. They are formed of wrought ironwork, elaborately scrolled. The central avenue, a large inner street, is 27 feet wide, and has six side avenues. The shops are ranged on either side of this great thoroughfare. There is one bay at the east end of the market for game and poultry, but no fish or vegetables can be sold. The shops are of cast-iron, with light columns and lattice girders, and which, by brackets, serve to carry the rails and meat-hooks. There are about 162 shops in the market, each about 36 feet by 15 feet, and behind every shop is an enclosed counting-house, with private apartments overhead. To secure light and air the Mansard roof has been used. The broad glass louvres of this system let in the air and keep out the sun; the result is that the interior of the building is generally ten degrees cooler than the temperature in the shade outside. There are twelve hydrants on the floor-level. It was planned that when the meat which arrived by rail reached the depôt underneath the market, it should be raised to the level of the floorway by powerful hydraulic lifts. The Metropolitan, the Midland, the London, Chatham, and Dover, and the Great Western Railways have direct communi-cation with the depôt. The passenger trains of the Metropolitan, Great Northern, Midland, and Chatham and Dover Companies rush through every two minutes, and the Great Western Com-pany has an extensive receiving-store there. It was thought that if it were deemed desirable there would be no difficulty in making a passenger station right under the market.

For the ceremony of opening, in November, 1868, a raised daïs was erected in the eastern nave, and the public roadway dividing the market was fitted up as a magnificent banqueting-room. On both sides and at either end streamed rich scarlet draperies, and within the gate there were paintings and ornaments in white and gold-work. The tem-porary entrance was at the end of the eastern avenue. Opposite it was a scarlet sideboard, glowing with gold plate, and crowned with a trophy of lances. A table for the Lord Mayor and chief guests was placed in front of the sideboard, and twenty-four other tables, on which there were flowers and fruit, and covers for 1,200 people, ran in a transverse direction from the Lord Mayor's seat. Over the entrance was an orchestra for the band of the Grenadier Guards, led by that enthusiast of good time, Mr. Dan Godfrey. Jets of gas were carried along the elliptical roof girders, in simple lines, and in arches over the screen of open iron-work that shuts off the market from the roadway. Three thousand yards of gas-piping fed a number of candelabra and a centre star-light. There were four carvers, in Guildhall dignity, who, mounted on high pedestals, carved barons of beef and boars' heads. The Lord Mayor's footmen shone in gold lace, and the City trumpeter and toastmaster also dignified the feast by their attendance. The cere-mony of opening the market was simple enough. The Lord Mayor arrived in state from the Mansion House, and was received by Mr. H. Lowman Taylor and the Markets Improvement Committee, at the east end of the building, and conducted to the daïs, where his lordship received a number of pro-vincial mayors, members of Parliament, &c. The speakers at the banquet congratulated each other on the rapidity with which the market had been built, and hoped it would bring tolls to the Cor-poration, cheap meat to the people, and fair profits to the salesmen. Mr. Lowman Taylor considered the old market well replaced by the new building, with its ample thoroughfares, and trusted that the new rents and tolls would bring the Corporation exchequer a fair return for the £200,000 which the new building had cost. It was designed to supply 3,000,000 with food.

"The interior of the market," says a writer at the time of the opening, "has been of necessity even more subservient to the purposes of the building than the exterior. One of the leading features in the arrangements is that for securing light without sunshine, and free ventilation without exposure to rain. During the excessive heat of last summer the effect was tested by thermometers placed in various parts of the building, and the result found to be highly satisfactory. The upper parts of the roof all over the building are of wood, and communicate with other portions of the fabric, which are also of wood. In the event of fire it would probably spread with terrific rapidity through the building. The wooden portions of the roof have also the effect of throwing the avenues somewhat into shade. The shops are arranged on each side of the side avenues which cross the market from north to south, and intersect the central avenue. The latter is 27 feet wide, and the six side avenues 18 feet wide each. The backs of the shops are closed in, but at the sides are screened by light ironwork to ensure ventilation. The floor of the market is paved with blocks. Twelve hydrants, always at high pressure, will supply ample means of washing out the market avenues and stalls, and could be used in case of fire."

This great market has proved a decided success. An official report, issued in 1874, shows that the total amount of toll paid for all descriptions of produce brought into the market had risen from £14,220 3s. 6½d. in 1869 to £16,818 10s. 10½d. in 1873. The total receipts for both tolls and rentals were £76,325 6s. 7d. in 1880, as against £74,460 10s. 1d. during 1879. There has all along been a large demand for accommodation; so much so, indeed, that whenever there is a vacant shop, it is besieged by twenty or thirty tradesmen, eager to become tenants, and a place in the market is considered quite a prize amongst salesmen.

It was some time since resolved to erect a new market immediately west of the Meat Market, to be devoted to the poultry, game, and cognate trades. This market is now completed, and in 1879 the foundation-stone of a new Fruit and Vegetable Market was laid at the corner of Farringdon Road and Charterhouse Street. The area of this market is about 60,000 feet, and the cost of the land, with the buildings to be erected thereon, will be about £30,000.

The Poultry Market is, as regards architecture, in harmony with the Meat Market, and that it is as successful as regards trade can hardly be doubted. The traffic in London in poultry and game possesses many features of interest, and a few facts respecting the business done at Smithfield in these luxuries of the table may be worth noting. The following newspaper account may be rescued, on account of its merits, from that oblivion which so generally attends most of the ephemeral productions of the press :—" The 'foreign' branch of the poultry and game business is the most curious. The greater part of the eat-able ornithology of Smithfield, in this department, is derived from Ireland and France. The Belgian pig, as an eatable subject, has lately been beating his Irish brother, and it may be made another subject for an Irish grievance that the French goose has of late years become a formidable rival of his fellow-geese from the Emerald Isle. Formerly there was a prejudice against French geese ; the trade would not look at them, and the public would not eat them. But gastronomical prejudices are short-lived. Whether it is due to the soothing influence of sage and onions or to the quality of the noble bird itself, it is certain now that the French goose is very popular on this side of the Channel, for the poulterers say that they sell large numbers of them at good prices. Indeed, so successful is the French goose, that large numbers of his race are imported into England in an attenu-ated condition during the summer, and are sent into the country to be fattened for the London market at Michaelmas. But remoter lands than France supply us with birds for the table. We get an abundance of prairie hens and canvas-back ducks from the United States. These are frozen by machinery on the other side of the Atlantic, packed in barrels, and brought over in capital condition. From Norway we receive ptarmigan, black-cock, and that eatable eagle, the capercailzie. They are sent over in the winter, frozen naturally, in cases containing from eighty to a hundred each, being shipped at Christiansund, landed at Hull, and brought up to town by rail. Holland is good enough to send us, sometimes by forty or fifty baskets of two hundred each in one steamer, her delicious wild ducks, and those curious little birds called ruffs and rees, which are about the size of godwits, and the male of which has most wonderful plumage, with a pretty crown of grey feathers on his head, given him to make him look handsome at courting time. But our most curious importation is the quail from Egypt, which feeds us to this day, as it fed the Israelites in the desert, and is brought over alive, in consignments of from thirty to fifty thousand. These birds are shipped at Alexandria, and are sent to Marseilles in charge of a native attendant to minister to their bodily wants.

Thence they are 'railed' across France in cages, lodged for a time in Smithfield, and then dispersed to all parts of the kingdom. So carefully are they transported, that not more than seven per cent. of them perish by the way. From birds it is a natural transition to eggs, and there is an enormous market for plovers' eggs at Smithfield. They come chiefly from Holland — the home produce being very small—and they are received during the spring and summer from March to June. The first plovers' eggs of the season invariably go to the Queen's poulterer, for Her Majesty's table, and fetch from seven to ten shillings apiece.

"Besides all this foreign produce, there is, of course, an immense home trade, and of the English poultry, which comes principally from Surrey, Devonshire, Lincolnshire, and Suffolk, much might be said. No wonder the poulterers are getting crowded out of their small corner of Smithfield Market, and are eager for a market of their own where they will have some scope for the development of their business. The trade generally is favourable to removal, and it is likely to act as a severe drain on Leadenhall, if not to shut it up altogether, although it is said there is a knot of very conservative poulterers who vow that they will never desert the old place, come what may."

CHAPTER LVII.

FARRINGDON STREET, HOLBORN VIADUCT, AND ST. ANDREW'S CHURCH.

Farringdon Without—A Notorious Alderman—Farringdon Within—Farringdon Street—Fleet Market—Farringdon Market—Watercress Sellers— On a November Morning—The Congregational Memorial Hall—Holborn Viaduct described—The City Temple—Opening of the Viaduct by the Queen—St. Andrew's, Holborn—Its Interior—Its Exterior—Emery the Comedian—The Persecuting Lord Chancellor Wriothesley— Sacheverel : a Pugnacious Divine—The Registers of St. Andrew's—Marriages cried by the Bellman—Edward Coke's Marriage—Coke catches a Tartar—Colonel and Mrs. Hutchinson's Marriage—A Courtship worth reading—Christening of Richard Savage - The Unfortunate Chatterton—Henry Neele, the Poet—Webster, the Dramatist, and his White Devil—A Funeral Dirge—Tomkins, the Conspirator—Strutt, and "Sports and Pastimes"—"Wicked Will" Whiston—A Queen's Faults—Hacket, afterwards Bishop of Lichfield and Coventry—A Surprise for Dissenters—Stillingfleet : A Controversial Divine—Looking People in the Face—The Rev. Charles Barton—An Agreeable Surprise—St. George the Martyr, Queen Square, and St. Andrew's—St. Andrew's Grammar School.

IT is convenient here to devote a paragraph to the general subject of the ward—that of Farringdon Without—in which we now find ourselves. "The whole great Ward of Farindon," says Stow, "both intra and extra (*i.e.*, within and without the walls), took name of W. Farindon, goldsmith, alderman of that ward, and one of the sheriffs of London in the year 1281, the 9th of Edward I. He purchased the aldermanry of this ward." Farringdon Without is by far the largest of all the twenty-six wards of London. Its general boundaries are—on the north, Holborn and Smithfield ; on the south, the Thames, between Blackfriars Bridge and the Temple Stairs ; on the east, New

Bridge Street and the Old Bailey ; and on the west, Temple Bar and Chancery Lane. The notorious John Wilkes was chosen alderman of this ward on the 27th of January, 1769, "while yet," says Walpole, "a criminal of State and a prisoner." He was at this time immensely popular with a large party in the City of London, and the election established that connection with the metropolis which was afterwards so profitable to him. This violent politician seems to have exercised a powerful fascination over those he met, by his wit, happy temperament, and tact, and no doubt much of his success with the clear-headed mercantile community of London arose from this. Lord Mansfield, who had no reason to like him, was once heard to remark, " that he was the pleasantest companion, the politest gentleman, and the best scholar he ever knew." He excited great admiration by his fertility in expedients. " If," said one who knew him, " he were stripped and thrown over Westminster Bridge one day, you would meet him the next in Pall Mall, dressed in the height of fashion, and with money in his pocket."

Farringdon Without has been famous for its banking connections. The founders of the three rich banking-houses in Fleet Street—the Childs, the Hoares, and the Goslings—filled at various periods the office of alderman of this ward.

The companion ward of Farringdon Within, out of which we passed when we left speaking of Christ's Hospital, has for its general boundaries, on the north, Christ's Hospital (in the hall of which the wardmotes are held), and part of Cheapside ; on the south, the Thames ; on the east, Cheapside ; and on the west, New Bridge Street.

Farringdon Street, which runs from Bridge Street northward to the line of Holborn, is constructed over the celebrated Fleet Ditch. In this street stood Fleet Market. To understand the history of this market the reader must recall what we said when speaking of the Mansion House, that it was erected on the site of the old Stocks Market (*see* Vol. I., p. 436). When that happened, about 1737, and Fleet Ditch was arched over, the business of the Stocks Market was transferred to the ground above the ditch, now called, as we have mentioned, Farringdon Street. Such was the origin of Fleet Market. It was opened for the sale of meat, fish, and vegetables on the 30th of September, 1737 ; but it did not complete a century of existence here.

In 1829 it was found necessary to widen the thoroughfare from Holborn to Blackfriars Bridge ; so Fleet Market was removed from Farringdon Street, and Farringdon Market, in the immediate vicinity, but off the line of the street, was opened in its stead. This comparatively neglected mart covers a site of an acre and a half of ground, and was built by William Montague, the City architect. It has Stonecutter Street for its southern boundary. The cost of the site and buildings was about £280,000. The following description of the market is of the date of its being opened for business, on the 20th of November, 1829 :—" It forms a handsome and elevated quadrangle, of 232 feet by 150 feet. The purchase of the ground, and the buildings which stood thereon, is estimated in round numbers at £200,000 ; the building of the market, including paviours' accounts, &c., is stated at £80,000. The avenue under which are the shops

of the dealers, and which extends round three sides of the building, is 25 feet high, to what are technically termed the tie-beams, with ventilators ranged at equal distances. . . . In the centre of the roof of the principal avenue a turret and clock have been placed. . . . The chief entrance to the market is by two gates, for wagons, &c., in Stonecutter Street, which has been made double its former width, and two smaller ones for footpassengers ; besides these, on each side of the quadrangle, massive oak doors are to be thrown open, from morning till the close of public business."

But careful building and liberal outlay seemed only thrown away. At a meeting of the Court of Common Council, held on the 29th of June, 1874, to consider the advisability of reconstructing the market, it was stated that the receipts during the last five years had only averaged £225. No wonder, then, that the court exhibited very little inclination to expend more money on a site which, exceedingly valuable as it would prove for other purposes, seems little suited for that of a market.

" Many persons," says a recent writer, " are of opinion that it is desirable to maintain the old Farringdon Market. In fact, the Corporation lately invited designs for its improvement, and have actually awarded prizes for the best. There can be no doubt that Farringdon Market, as it stands, is in a very bad position. It is quite behind the times in the matter of accommodation, and the gradients by which access to it is gained are so steep that accidents to carts and horses not unfrequently happen. It may be open to improvement by the alteration of the levels as proposed, but the latest disposition of the Corporation appears to be to leave the old market to its fate, and build a new one west of that now in process of construction at Smithfield, a course which certainly would have many advantages. As regards the existing market, it may be said to do a fairish middle-class trade. Its produce, however, is very humble, and rarely rises above the rank of the modest onion, the plebeian cabbage, the barely respectable cauliflower, the homely apple, and other unpretending fruits and vegetables. Pineapples and hot-house grapes are unknown to its dingy sheds, and, as a sorrowing tradesman remarked, ' We never see such things as pears at 5s. a dozen !' The market for vegetables, in fact, is supplied chiefly from the gardens in the immediate vicinity of London, say within a ten or twelve miles' radius, while the fruit comes almost exclusively from Kent. The more important supplies, from distant parts of the country, go to Covent

Garden and the Borough. It is supposed that a better class trade would be done at Smithfield, but this is a disputed point.

"In one commodity Farringdon does a great business. It is *the* market, *par excellence*, for water-cresses. Of these there are about a score of vendors in the market, and sometimes as much as twenty tons a week are brought up for sale. The general market opens at four a.m., but the retailers

market value of a shilling. The price ranges from twelve to eighteen hands; but the buyer is always careful to see that he or she gets proper measure, calculated in a rough-and-ready sort of fashion, and one often hears the admonition, 'Don't pinch your hand, governor.'"

A visit to Farringdon Market in early morning, Mr. Henry Mayhew holds, is the proper way to form an estimate of the fortitude, courage, and

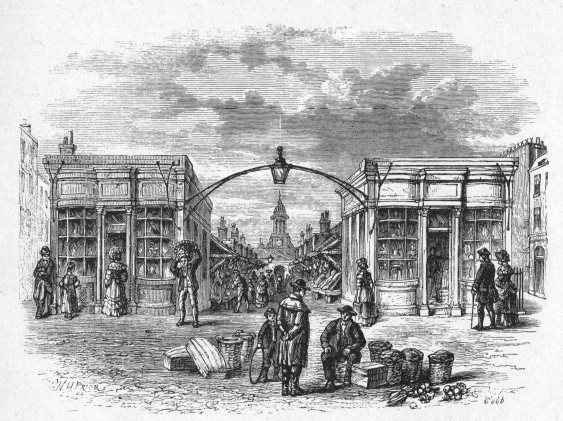

FLEET MARKET, ABOUT 1800. *From a Drawing in Mr. Gardner's Collection.* (*See page* 497.)

of the watercress are allowed to enter an hour earlier, and they flock thither—men, women, boys, and girls—by hundreds at a time. The 'water-creases' are brought in hampers, and in smaller baskets, called pads and flats. The toll for a hamper is twopence, and for a pad or flat one penny. The pleasant vegetable is sold by the 'end,' the 'middle,' and the 'side' of the basket— those in the middle, as they are, of course, fresher than the rest, fetching the best price. The value of a hamper of watercresses is sometimes as high as twenty shillings, and as low as five, that of a pad or flat being half as much. But the most popular way of buying watercresses is 'by the hand;' that is, the salesman sells as many handfuls—of his *own* hand, of course—as may be equivalent to the

perseverance of the poor. These watercress sellers are members of a class so poverty-stricken that their extreme want alone would almost justify them in taking to thieving, yet they can be trusted to pay the few pence they owe, even though hunger should pinch them for it. As Douglas Jerrold has truly said, "there is goodness, like wild honey, hived in strange nooks and corners of the earth." It must require no little energy of conscience on the part of the lads to make them resist the temp-tations around them, and refuse the cunning advice of the young thieves they meet at their cheap lodging-houses. Yet they prefer the early rising, the walk to market with naked feet over the cold stones, and the chance of earning a few pence by a day of honest labour, to all the comparative ease

FIELD LANE ABOUT 1840. (*See page* 542.)

of a career of fraud. "The heroism of the un-known poor," adds Mr. Mayhew, "is a thing to set even the dullest marvelling, and in no place in all London is the virtue of the humblest—both young and old—so conspicuous as amongst the watercress buyers at Farringdon Market."

Mr. Mayhew visited it one November morning. The poor, he says, were there, in every style of rags, laying in the necessary stock for their trade. "As the morning twilight drew on, the paved court was crowded with customers. The sheds and shops at the end of the market grew every moment more distinct, and a railway van, laden with carrots, came rumbling into the yard. The pigeons, too, began to fly into the sheds, or walk about the paving-stones, and the gas-man came round with his ladder to turn out the lamps. Then every one was pushing about, the children crying as their naked feet were trodden upon, and the women hurrying off with their baskets or shawls filled with cresses, and the bunch of rushes in their hands. In one corner of the market, busily tying up their bunches, were three or four girls, seated on the stones, with their legs curled up under them, and the ground near them was green with the leaves they had thrown away. A saleswoman, seeing me looking at the group, said, 'Ah, you should come here of a summer's morning, and then you'd see 'em, sitting tying up, young and old, upwards of a hundred poor things, as thick as crows in a ploughed field.'"

On the east side of Farringdon Street, and on a part of the site of the old Fleet Prison, stands the Congregational Memorial Hall and Library, a handsome new building, the foundation-stone of which was laid on the 10th of May, 1872. This hall has been erected by the Congregationalists of England and Wales, in commemoration of the ejection from their charges, two hundred years ago—it was on the 24th of August, 1662—of more than two thousand ministers of the Church of England, because they could not conscientiously subscribe to the Act of Uniformity. The ground purchased in Farringdon Street consisted of 9,000 feet of freehold land, with 84 feet frontage to the main road, and 32 feet to old Fleet Lane, and having a depth of about 100 feet. It cost £28,000. The design for the memorial building, prepared by Mr. Tarring, comprised a hall capable of holding 1,200 to 1,500 people; a library, with accommoda-tion for 300; a board-room, and twenty-five other offices, which it was calculated would be amply sufficient for all the societies connected with the denomination in London.

We come now to speak of one of the greatest and most successful works ever undertaken in the city of London — the Holborn Valley improve-ments, an undertaking which will ever be quoted as a notable example of the energy and public spirit of our time. We have already spoken of the incon-venience and disagreeableness of the approach to the City from the west by Holborn. To avoid the dangerous descent of Holborn Hill, it was at last resolved to construct a viaduct and high-level bridge over Farringdon Street, and so to supplant Skinner Street, and form a spacious and pleasant thoroughfare connecting the City with that great Mediterranean of western traffic, Holborn and Oxford Street. This was done after long consulta-tion, the consideration of many different schemes, and many attempts, not always successful, to recon-cile conflicting interests. The works were com-menced in May, 1863, and if it was more than six years before the valley was bridged over, and the viaduct opened to the public, we must consider the gigantic nature of the undertaking, and the delays in effecting the demolition of the old struc-tures and roadway, embarrassed, too, by much litigation. The cost of the improvements con-siderably exceeded two millions.

The scheme was originally calculated to cost about £1,500,000, the Corporation recouping themselves to the extent of from £600,000 or £700,000, by the sale of building land on the sides of the new viaduct. It was resolved to re-move the whole of the houses and shops on the south side of Skinner Street, Snow Hill, from the Old Bailey to Farringdon Street, and thence to the summit of Holborn Hill, while all the houses on the northern side were to be removed, enormous sums being paid in compensation—in one case alone about £30,000 being awarded.

The central object of this scheme was a stately and substantial viaduct across the Holborn Valley, between Hatton Garden and the western end of Newgate Street. A new street was also to open from opposite Hatton Garden, and pass by the back of St. Andrew's Church, to Shoe Lane, which was to be widened as far as Stonecutter Street. Thence another new line of street, fifty feet wide, and with easy gradients, was to be formed at the east end of Fleet Street, near its junction with Farringdon Street. The viaduct across Holborn Hill was to be eighty feet wide, and was to com-mence at the west end of Newgate Street.

"The impression left upon the mind after a first walk from Holborn to Newgate Street, along the Viaduct, is," says a writer in the *Builder*, "that of a wide and level thoroughfare raised above the old pavement, and of a spacious bridge crossing the busy line of Farringdon Street below. The improvement is so grand and yet so simple, and the direction taken by the new road is so obviously the easiest and the best, that difficulties of construction and engineering details are in a manner lost sight of, and it is not until the work concealed from the eye is dived into, that the true nature of the undertaking is understood. To know what has been accomplished, and to appreciate it rightly, the observer must leave the upper level, and penetrate the interior; to comprehend his subject, he must do as all patient learners do—commence at the foundation.

"The problem that the engineer had to work out appears at first sight a simple one. The postulates were a bridge crossing the great artery of Farringdon Street, and a level causeway on either side from Holborn to Newgate Street. Then came considerations of detail that soon assumed a complex and difficult shape. Sewers, and gas, and water-pipes had to be carried, levels to be regarded, and connection with lateral thoroughfares had to be maintained. Then arose questions of modes of construction. Obviously, a solid embankment was not possible, and an open arcade would be a waste of valuable space. So the design gradually shaped itself into what may be briefly and accurately described as a plan consisting of two lateral passages, one on either side supporting the pavement, and cross arches, forming vaults between, and carrying the carriage roadway above.

"As the great depth of the Holborn Valley caused the viaduct to be of considerable height at its point of crossing Farringdon Street, the engineer took advantage of this to subdivide his vaulted passages into storeys, and these accordingly are one, two, or three, as the dip of the level permits. First is appropriated a space for areas and vaulted cellars of the houses, and then against these is at top a subway, in which are the gas, water, and telegraph pipes; then a passage, and below these a vaulted chamber constructed with damp-proof courses through its walls, and of considerable depth, at the bottom of which, resting on a concrete bed, is the sewer. . .

" The height of these subways is 11 feet 6 inches, and their width 7 feet. They are constructed of brick-work, excepting where carried over the London, Chatham, and Dover Railway, at which point they are of tubular form, and are constructed of iron. . .

"The subways contain ventilating shafts, which are connected with trapped gullies in the roadway above; also with the pedestals of the lamp-posts, perforated for the purpose, and with flues expressly directed to be left in party-walls of buildings; all these contrivances being made for the carrying off gases that may escape, especially from leakage from the gas-mains. Provision is made for the easy ingress of workmen and materials, and the subways are lighted by means of gratings filled with globules of thick glass."

The great ornamental feature of the Viaduct is the bridge across Farringdon Street. Unfortunately for the effect, it is a skew-bridge—that is, it crosses the street obliquely—but the design is rich and striking. It is a cast-iron girder-bridge, in three spans, divided by the six granite piers which carry the girders. These piers are massive hexagonal shafts of polished red granite, resting on bases of black granite, and having capitals of grey granite with bronze leaves, the outer piers being, however, carried above the railing on the parapet of the bridge, and terminating in pedestals, on which are placed colossal bronze statues. These statues represent Commerce and Agriculture on the south, and Science and Fine Art on the north side. The iron palisading consists of circular panels united by scrolls, and bearing emblazonings of civic crests and devices, with the City arms on a larger scale. At the four corners of the bridge, and forming an intrinsic part of the design, are lofty houses, of ornate Renaissance character, within which are carried flights of steps, giving means of communication to pedestrians between the level of the Viaduct and that of Farringdon Street. The fronts of these houses are adorned with the statues of four civic worthies of the olden time. On the north are Sir Hugh Middleton (born 1555, died 1631) and Sir William Walworth (Mayor 1374 and 1380); and on the south are Henry Fitz-Aylwin (Mayor 1189 to 1212) and Sir Thomas Gresham (born 1519, died 1579).

On the south side of the Viaduct are the Viaduct Hotel, the station of the London, Chatham, and Dover Railway, and the new Congregational City Temple, erected by the congregation of Dr. Joseph Parker. The latter is in a light Italian style of architecture. The chapel has its floor on a level with the roadway of the Viaduct, and is seated for 2,500 persons. Underneath it are spacious school and class-rooms, entering from Shoe Lane. Dr. Parker's congregation used to meet in the old chapel in the Poultry, but that building was found too small; it was therefore sold, and the present one was erected, at a cost of £60,000, including the price (£25,000) paid for the site.

The length of the Viaduct from Newgate Street to Holborn is about 1,400 feet, and the width between the building-line 80 feet, affording space for a 50-feet carriage-way in the centre, and two pavements, each 15 feet wide, at either side. The surface of the carriage-way is paved with cubes of granite 9 inches by 3 inches, and the side pavements are laid with York flags, with perforated gratings to light the subways.

During the demolition of the old streets and houses, for the purpose of clearing the ground for the Viaduct, nothing of any special value or interest was brought to light. The most noteworthy incidents, says a writer in the *Builder*, of April 24th, 1869, were "the frequent discovery of all sorts of concealed passages for escape, and nooks for hiding plunder in the villainous old houses of Field Lane and its unsavoury neighbourhood, the removal of which alone should cause the Holborn Valley Improvement to be considered a blessing to this part of London. In carrying the new road through St. Andrew's Churchyard, a large slice of the ground was required, and this compelled the removal of a great number of human remains; between 11,000 and 12,000 were therefore decorously transferred to the City Cemetery at Ilford."

The opening of Holborn Viaduct by the Queen took place on the 6th of November, 1869, the same day as that on which Her Majesty opened the new bridge over the Thames at Blackfriars. The ceremony was an imposing one, and excited uncommon interest and enthusiasm amongst all classes in the metropolis. The day fortunately was bright and fair, and, leaving out of account a momentary interruption of its sunshine, was as good as could have been looked for in November. Blackfriars Bridge having been opened, and a loyal address from the Corporation of London having previously been presented, the combined royal and civic processions passed up Farringdon Street amidst an immense assemblage of people, the roadway in the middle being kept clear by soldiers and policemen. The Queen's carriage stopped for a moment before the Viaduct Bridge, that Her Majesty might observe the structure from below. She then passed under it, and turned up Charterhouse Street into Smithfield, which she traversed on the west side of the Meat Market. Her attention was particularly directed to the market-building, which was gorgeously decorated with flags and streamers. From West Smithfield the procession turned into Giltspur Street, and soon the neighbourhood re-echoed with the cheering of the Bluecoat boys, who, to the number of 750, were assembled in their playground, to give their sovereign a loyal welcome. Under St. Sepulchre's Church were ranged several hundreds of the boys and girls of the parish and charity schools; and what with their shrill acclamations, and those of the Bluecoat boys opposite, the effect is said to have been startling.

"Here was the east end of the Holborn Valley Viaduct, close to Newgate Prison and St. Sepulchre's Church. Two colossal plaster statues, one bearing the palm of Victory, the other the olive-branch of Peace, were set up at the entrance, and numerous banners helped the general effect. Along the level approach to the Viaduct, which was from end to end strewn with yellow sand, seats were placed under cover, and in well-arranged blocks, for the guests of the Corporation. Above these streamed in the fresh breeze bannerets of the dagger and St. George's Cross on a white ground, from days immemorial the arms of the City of London; and the masts to which they were attached were painted and gilt. The pavilion, which had seats for 600 spectators, was constructed of red and white striped canvas at the sides, but of gold-coloured hangings, with devices in colour at the end, and with curtains of maroon to keep out the draughts. The royal arms, in rich gilding, surmounted the main entrance, supported on each hand by the City arms above the side divisions. Four female figures, bearing golden baskets of fruit, were placed against the gilt divisions of the pavilion; and between each couple of fruit-bearers was a large statue, chosen from the best works in the possession of the Crystal Palace Company." In the centre of the pavilion the roadway was narrowed, so that the daïs might be carried close to the royal carriage, and at this point were assembled as a deputation to receive Her Majesty, Mr. Deputy Fry, the chairman of the Improvement Committee, Alderman Carter, Sir Benjamin Phillips, and several members of the Common Council.

The visitors accommodated in the reserved places all rose as they heard the welcome of the boys and children at Christ's Hospital and St. Sepulchre's, and then took up the cheering. The procession slowly passed along the viaduct. More than once it came to a stop as the carriage of the Lord Mayor or an alderman halted at the platform in the pavilion, and its occupants alighted. When Her Majesty reached the platform and the carriage halted, the Lord Mayor presented Mr. Deputy Fry and Mr. Haywood, the engineer of the viaduct. Mr. Fry then handed to the Queen a volume elaborately bound in cream-coloured morocco, relieved with gold, and ornamented with the Royal arms of England, in mosaic of leather and gold; and Her Majesty declared the viaduct open for public traffic. The Lord Mayor and the other civic dignitaries then took leave of Her Majesty and returned to their carriages, and the procession again got under weigh. But it broke up immediately on passing through the gates of the temporary barrier, and the Lord Mayor and his company turned towards the City, whilst Her Majesty drove quickly up Holborn, and so by Oxford Street to Paddington Station, from whence she returned by special train to Windsor.

No sooner was this gigantic undertaking completed, and the viaduct open for traffic, than an alarm was raised—cracks had appeared in some of the great polished granite pillars which supported the bridge over Farringdon Street. A lively newspaper correspondence was the result, and many wise things were said on both sides; but the pillars have borne heavy traffic and all the changes of temperature since then without any perceptible extension of the flaw, and the safety of the work is no longer, if it ever was seriously, in doubt.

The present church of St. Andrew's, Holborn, was erected by Wren, in 1686, on the site of the old church, in the Ward of Farringdon Without. Let us begin by speaking of the history of the old building. The exact date of its foundation is uncertain, but in 1297 we find it given by one Gladerinus to the Dean and Chapter of St. Paul's; it being stipulated at the same time that the church should be held of them by the Abbot and Convent of Bermondsey. The monasteries being dissolved in the reign of Henry VIII., the right of presentation devolved to the Crown, and the king made it over to Thomas Lord Wriothesley, afterwards Lord Chancellor and Earl of Southampton, who died July 30th, 1550, and was buried in St. Andrew's. At a later date the right of presentation became vested in the Duke of Buccleuch. The first vicar mentioned by Newcourt goes under the name of Richard de Tadeclowe; he was appointed before the year 1322, and among those who succeeded him in the old church were Thomas de Cottingham, in 1343, keeper of the Great Seal, and Gilbert Worthington, in 1443.

As to the appearance of the original building, we learn from the will of Gilbert Worthington, printed by Strype, that there were four altars in it, if not more. The steeple was commenced in 1446, but from some cause or other it was not finished till 1468. During the interval the north and south aisles were rebuilt. At the general clearance of the Reformation St. Andrew's fared no better than its neighbours: in the first year of Edward VI. most of the altars and statues were removed, and in that year and in the beginning of the reign of Elizabeth the numerous monumental brasses of this church were converted into current coin of the realm.

When the Great Fire ravaged the City, this church escaped; but being in a hopelessly ruinous condition it was taken down, with the exception of the tower, about ten years after that event, and a new building was in course of time erected in accordance with designs furnished by the great architect, Sir Christopher Wren.

The interior of this new church consisted of a nave, two aisles, and chancel; and has been praised by many writers for its magnificence and beauty. Mr. Godwin, however, remarks that "an alteration in taste, as regards architectural productions, has been produced. The value of simplicity and breadth of parts, in opposition to minute divisions and elaborate ornament, has been admitted; and therefore, although it may be regarded as a large and commodious church—a good specimen of the style in which it is built, and as a construction well executed—it will not again obtain the unconditional praise which was formerly bestowed upon it.

"Pillars," adds Mr. Godwin, describing the church interior as it appeared when he wrote, in 1839, "cased with wainscot, support a gallery on either side; and at the west end, and from the top of the gallery-front, rise diminutive Corinthian columns bearing small blocks intended to represent an entablature, reminding one of the columns with the two chapiters or capitals, called Jachin and Boaz, mentioned in the description of Solomon's Temple. A wagon-headed ceiling of large span, in panels, supported on these blocks, and adorned with festoons of flowers and fruit, covers the body of the church. The ceiling of the aisles is groined, and opens into the wagon-headed ceiling, forming an arch between each of the columns. At the west end of the church there is a second gallery, at a great height from the ground, which is appropriated to the children of the Sunday schools. On the wall behind it were formerly some large paintings, but these have been obliterated.

"The chancel is somewhat richly adorned with paintings, gilding, and stained glass; and the walls are covered with wainscot, which is veined to imitate Sienna marble, as high as the ceiling. Above the carved altar-piece is a large Palladian window in two storeys, containing in stained glass a representation of the Last Supper, and of the Ascension, executed by Price of York, in 1718. The colours are for the most part brilliant; but as a work of art, the window is not deserving of commendation. On either side of it are two large paintings (apparently in fresco) of St. Andrew and St. Peter, and two smaller panels representing the Holy Family and the infant St. John. In the ceiling of the chancel is introduced a glazed light, whereon is painted the dove. There are two other windows at the east end of the church which are filled with stained glass, namely, one in the north aisle containing the royal arms, and those of the donor, inscribed: ' 1687. Ex dono .Thomæ Hodgson de Bramwill in Agro Eboracen. Militis ;' and another, at the end of the south aisle, representing the arms of John Thavie, Esq., who, in the year 1348, ' left a considerable estate towards the support of this fabric for ever.' "

Towards the close of 1872, St. Andrew's under-

In addition to these alterations, the church was re-decorated. The nave ceiling and groined ceilings of the galleries were painted in panels of a tempered turquoise blue as a ground-colour, with margins in stone and vellum, the enrichments being in white. The blue grounds were filled with a classic diaper, in self-colouring and white, the walls being a neutral of silver grey. The shafts of columns were finished in Indian red. The chancel

THE WEST END OF ST. ANDREW'S, 1837.

went a most thorough restoration, and was re-opened for public worship on Sunday, the 13th of October of that year. The ancient tower, which used to be separated from the nave of the church by a screen-wall, with a gallery in front, was thrown open to the nave by the removal of the wall and gallery.

A ritual chancel was formed at the east end, the floor-level of which was raised two feet above the floor-line of the nave, and choir-stalis were arranged north and south of the same. The old high-backed square pewing was removed, and in its place new low oak seating was substituted. The old windows were done away with, and new iron ones took their place, glazed with tinted cathedral glass.

ceiling was treated in the same manner as that of the nave, with this exception, that the enrichments to the panels were gilded.

A new organ was also constructed. It spans over the Gothic arch, and rests upon the galleries on either side.

The church contains a carved oak pulpit, and a sculptured marble font, displaying four cherubim. The whole length of the building is stated as 105 feet, the breadth 63 feet, and the height 43 feet.

The old organ of St. Andrew's, made by Harris, was celebrated as being part of the discarded instrument in the contest for superiority between Father Schmydt and Harris, at the Temple Church. This contest has been described by us at page 145

Vol. I. When Dr. Sacheverell entered upon the living of St. Andrew's, he found that the organ, not having been paid for, had, from its erection in 1699, been shut up; he therefore had a collection made among his parishioners, raised the amount, and paid for the instrument.

There are no remarkable features to be pointed out in connection with the exterior of the church. It is divided into two storeys, and terminates with that the basement is there considerably elevated above the houses."

Among the tablets in the church is one mentioned by Godwin as affixed to the north wall, and inscribed to Mr. John Emery, the famous comedian, who died on the 25th of July, 1822. It bears the following couplet :—

> " Each part he shone in, but excelled in none
> So well as husband, father, friend, and son."

INTERIOR OF ST. ANDREW'S CHURCH. (*See page* 504.)

a cornice and balustrade. "The old Gothic tower," says Mr. Godwin, "notwithstanding it was re-cased and adorned with vanes and pine-apples at the four corners, is still to be detected by the large buttresses left standing at the angles, and the small pointed windows remaining in the lower storey. The windows in the belfry are singularly confused and ugly." The height of the tower is reported to be 110 feet; there are 188 steps from the bottom of it to the top.

St. Andrews, says Mr. Godwin, is one of the best-placed churches in London, "for as the west end is nearly at the summit of Holborn Hill, the foundation was necessarily continued throughout on this level, to the east end in Shoe Lane; so

Emery was born at Sunderland, on the 22nd of December, 1777, and was educated at Ecclesfield, in the West Riding of Yorkshire; and it was there doubtless that he acquired that knowledge of the Yorkshire dialect which obtained for him so much celebrity. His first appearance on the stage was at Brighton, in "Crazy" ("Peeping Tom"). He was excellent in his representation of the stupid dolt, and the arch, unsophisticated child of nature. "His *forte*," says Talfourd, "lay in showing the might of human passion and affection, not only unaided by circumstance, but attended by everything which could tend to associate them with the ludicrous or the vulgar. The parts in which he displayed this prodigious power were as far as possible removed from the elegant and romantic, and his own stout frame and broad iron countenance did not give him any extrinsic aid to refine or exalt them. But in spite of all these obstacles, the energy of passion or the strength of agony was triumphant. Every muscle was strained to bursting, and every fibre informed with sense and feeling; every quiver of the lip, and involuntary action of the hands, spoke the might of that emotion which he was more than counterfeiting; and all little provincialisms, all traits of vulgarity, were forgotten in wonder and sympathy. . . . His 'Tyke' was the grandest specimen of the rude sublime; his 'Giles,' in the *Miller's Man*, was almost as intense, and the whole conception of a loftier cast."

A fiery zealot of the days of English history lies buried here—Thomas Wriothesley, Lord Chancellor in the latter part of the reign of Henry VIII. This influential statesman was no wiser than his generation in respect to persecution. "Not content with seeing the amiable Anne Askew put to the torture," says Pennant, "for no other crime than difference in faith, he flung off his gown, degraded the Chancellor into the Bourreau, and with his own hands gave force to the rack. He was created Earl of Southampton just before the coronation of Edward VI., but obstinately adhering to the old religion, he was dismissed from his post, and confined to Southampton House, where he died in 1550."

One of the congenial tasks Wriothesley had to perform during the reign of Henry VIII., was to impeach and arrest the queen, Catherine Parr, for her supposed heterodoxy. When he arrived, however, to take her into custody, the king had made friends again with his sixth and last wife, and the chancellor was dismissed, his Majesty calling him knave, an arrant knave, a fool, a beast, and such-like complimentary names. It was the influence of Wriothesley which chiefly led to the execution of the Earl of Surrey, and the attainder of the Duke of Norfolk, in 1547. He was one of the executors of Henry VIII., and an opponent of the Protector Somerset.

Another of those buried in this church was Henry Sacheverel, who died in 1724. He was laid in the chancel, where there is an inscription on the pavement to his memory. It may well be left to another occasion to tell the story of this divine, and of the two famous sermons which he preached at Derby and at St. Paul's, with the object of exciting alarm for the safety of the Church, and creating hostility against the Dissenters. Being impeached in the House of Commons, in the year

1710, he was sentenced to be suspended from preaching for three years. But this prosecution established the popularity of the preacher; and the very month that his suspension terminated, he was appointed to the valuable rectory of St. Andrew's, Holborn. Like many who owe their popularity to circumstances, rather than to any merit of their own, Sacheverel dropped, in Holborn, into comparative obscurity, and nothing worthy of note is told of him, but that his quarrels with his parishioners were by no means unfrequent—just as one might have expected from so pugnacious a character. He had the good luck, during his latter days, to inherit a considerable fortune.

There is much of interest connected with the registers of St. Andrew's. Some of the books are dated as far back as 1558, the first year of Queen Elizabeth's reign. One of the volumes, containing entries from 1653 to 1658, is wholly occupied with proclamations of marriage during the interregnum, when they were published in the market-place. For example: "An agreement and intent of marriage between John Law and Ffrances Riley, both servants to the Lady Brooke, of this parish, was published three several markett-days in Newgate Markett; and in three several weeks, that is to say, &c." In various parts of this book the church is spoken of as the "Public Meeting-place, commonly called St. Andrew's, Holborn."

The extract quoted above from the register is an illustration of a curious chapter in the history of marriage customs and laws in England. By a statute of August, 1653, the betrothed couple were allowed to choose whether they would be "asked" in church or chapel on three several Sundays, or cried in the open market on three consecutive market-days, at the town nearest their ordinary place of worship. This was the assertion with a vengeance of the civil nature of the marriage contract. If the lovers chose the latter method, their proposed union was in most cases proclaimed by the bellman, though the kind offices of that official were not legally required for making the announcement. "In the absence of conclusive evidence on the matter," says Mr. J. C. Jeaffreson, the historian of "Brides and Bridals," "I have no doubt that the street banns of our forefathers, in Cromwell's England, were rarely proclaimed by clergymen. On the other hand it is certain that the bellman was, in many places, regularly employed to cry aloud for impediments to the wedding of precise lovers."

The parish register contains two interesting entries of marriage, the first of which is that of Edward Coke, "the Queen's Attorney-General," and "my Lady Elizabeth Hatton," in 1598. This lady was the relict of Sir William Hatton, and the daughter of the celebrated Thomas Lord Burleigh, afterwards Earl of Exeter. She became Coke's second wife, his first having been a lady of the ancient and highly-connected family of the Pastons, by whom he had the large sum (for those days) of £30,000. By the widow of Sir William he also obtained a considerable addition to his property; but his marriage with her is only another example to be added to the list of the unfortunate matrimonial alliances of distinguished men. The celebration of the ceremony involved both parties in some difficulty. There had been, the same year, a great deal of notice taken of irregular marriages, and Archbishop Whitgift had intimated to the bishops of his province that all who offended in point of time, place, or form were to be prosecuted with the utmost rigour of the law. Coke, however, seems to have presumed on his own and the lady's position, or on his acquaintance, if not friendship, with the prelate, and he disregarded the statute, and was married in a private house, without even having had the banns published or a licence obtained. But this act of contumacy was not passed over. Coke, the newly-married lady, the minister who officiated, Lord Burleigh, and several other persons, were prosecuted in the ecclesiastical court; but upon their submission by their proxies, the whole affair ended in smoke; they were absolved from excommunication, and the penalties consequent upon it, because, says the record, they had offended not out of contumacy, but through ignorance of the law in that point. It strikes one, at this distance of time, that the suit may have been commenced merely for the sake of public example.

Lady Elizabeth Hatton proved a Tartar. When, many years afterwards, Sir Edward Coke proposed a marriage between his younger daughter by Lady Hatton and Sir John Villiers, she raised a tempest, and resenting her husband's attempt to dispose of the daughter without asking her consent, carried the young lady off, and lodged her at Sir Edmund Withipole's, near Oatlands. Sir Edward complained to the Privy Council, and then went with his sons to Oatlands and captured his daughter, a proceeding which induced Lady Hatton to complain to the Privy Council in her turn. Much confusion followed, but at last the marriage of the young couple actually did take place. Then the ill-will between the old people broke out again, and many letters are still in existence, showing a great deal of heat and resentment in both parties. At one time Sir Edward publicly accused his wife of having purloined his plate, and substituted counterfeited

alkumy in its place, with intent to defraud him; but she had quite as good to say about him. In about four years their reconciliation seems to have been effected, and that by no less a mediator than James I., but they never enjoyed anything like domestic happiness.

The other entry of marriage is that of Colonel Hutchinson and Lucy Apsley, in 1638. And here, by way of contrast to the last, we have one of the most touching instances of womanly affection that ever was set down in writing. Mrs. Hutchinson is best known by her "Memoirs" of the life of her husband, a charming volume of biography. The account given by her of the courtship which led up to the ceremony before the altar of St. Andrew's is a narrative which all should read, and which all will enjoy.

Mr. Hutchinson fell in love with the lady before seeing her. He had been invited to go to Richmond by his music-master, a man who stood high in his profession, and had been warned by a friend to take heed of the place, for it was so fatal to love, that never any young disengaged person went thither who returned again free. He determined, however, to run the risk, and went. The musician's house was a lively one, frequented by much good company, including gentlemen and ladies connected with the court, and many of the king's musicians.

There happened to be boarded there, for the practice of the lute, and till the return of her mother, a younger daughter of Sir Allen Apsley, late Lieutenant of the Tower. The mother had gone into Wiltshire to complete a treaty, in which some progress had been made, about the marriage of her elder daughter. "This young girl," says Mrs. Hutchinson, "that was left in the house with Mr. Hutchinson, was a very child, her elder sister being at that time scarcely past it, but a child of such pleasantness and vivacity of spirit, and ingenuity in the quality she practised, that Mr. Hutchinson took pleasure in hearing her practise, and would fall in a discourse with her. She having the keys of her mother's house, some half a mile distant, would sometimes ask Mr. Hutchinson, when she went over, to walk along with her.

"One day, when he was there, looking upon an odd by-shelf in her sister's closet, he found a few Latin books. Asking whose they were, he was told they were her elder sister's, whereupon, inquiring more after her, he began first to be sorry she was gone before he had seen her, and gone upon such an account that he was not likely to see her. Then he grew to love to hear mention of her, and the other gentlewomen who had been her companions used to talk much to him of her, telling him how reserved and studious she was, and other things which they esteemed no advantage ; but it so much inflamed Mr. Hutchinson's desire of seeing her, that he began to wonder at himself that his heart, which had ever had such an indifferency for the most excellent of womenkind, should have so strong impulses towards a stranger he never saw ; and certainly it was of the Lord (though he perceived it not), who had ordained him, through so many providences, to be yoked with her in whom he found so much satisfaction." Her praises continued to be daily sounded in his ears ; but at last news arrived which led all the company present one day at table to conclude that Miss Lucy—or " Mrs." Lucy, as young ladies used to be called then—was really married. Mr. Hutchinson immediately turned pale as ashes, and had to retire from table to conceal his agitation.

But it proved a false alarm, and some little time after she made her appearance, and the lover, who had fallen in love with a shadow, met the reality. " His heart, being prepossessed with his own fancy, was not free to discern how little there was in her to answer so great an expectation. She was not ugly, in a careless riding habit ; she had a melancholy negligence both of herself and others, as if she neither affected to please others, nor took notice of anything before her ; yet in spite of all her indifferency, she was surprised with some unusual liking in her soul when she saw this gentleman, who had hair, eyes, shape, and countenance enough to beget love in any one at the first, and these set off with a graceful and generous mien, which promised an extraordinary person ; he was at that time, and indeed always, very neatly habited, for he wore good and rich clothes, and had variety of them, and had them well suited, and every way answerable ; in that little thing showing both good judgment and great generosity, he equally becoming them and they him, which he wore with such unaffectedness and such neatness, as do not often meet in one. Although he had but an evening sight of her he had so long desired, and that at disadvantage enough for her, yet the prevailing sympathy of his soul made him think all his pains well paid ; and this first did whet his desire to a second sight, which he had by accident the next day, and, to his joy, found she was wholly disengaged from that treaty which he so much feared had been accomplished ; he found withal, that though she was modest, she was accostable, and willing to entertain his acquaintance. This soon passed into a mutual friendship between them, and though she innocently thought nothing of love,

yet was she glad to have acquired such a friend, who had wisdom and virtue enough to be trusted with her councils, for she was then much perplexed in mind. Her mother and friends had a great desire she should marry, and were displeased that she refused many offers which they thought advantageous enough ; she was obedient, loath to displease them, but more herself, in marrying such as she could find no inclination to."

It was not long before friendship on her part passed into love ; but of their mutual affection in its full height Mrs. Hutchinson limits herself to saying this, "There never was a passion more ardent and less idolatrous ; he loved her better than his life, with inexpressible tenderness and kindness ; had a most high obliging esteem of her, yet still considered honour, religion, and duty above her, nor ever suffered the intrusion of such a dotage as should blind him from marking her imperfections ; these he looked upon with such an indulgent eye as did not abate his love and esteem of her, while it augmented his care to blot out all those spots which might make her appear less worthy of that respect he paid her ; and thus, indeed, he soon made her more equal to him than he found her ; for she was a very faithful mirror, reflecting truly, though but dimly, his own glories upon him, so long as he was present. But she, that was nothing before his inspection gave her a fair figure, when he was removed, was only filled with a dark mist, and never could again take in any delightful object, nor return any shining representation. The greatest excellency she had was the power of apprehending, and the virtue of loving his ; so, as his shadow, she waited on him everywhere, till he was taken into that region of light that admits of none, and then she vanished into nothing."

Unfortunately, the very day the friends on both sides met to conclude the marriage, she fell ill of the small-pox. "First her life was almost in desperate hazard, and then the disease, for the present, made her the most deformed person that could be seen for a great while after she recovered. Yet Mr. Hutchinson was nothing troubled at it, but married her as soon as she was able to quit the chamber, when the priest and all that saw her were affrighted to look on her ; but God recompensed his justice and constancy by restoring her, though she was longer than ordinary before she recovered, as well as before. . . . On the third day of July, 1638, he was married to Mrs. Lucy Apsley, the second daughter of Sir Allan Apsley, late lieutenant of the Tower of London, at St. Andrew's Church, in Holborn." The newly-married couple lived for some time afterwards in this neighbourhood.

Their subsequent career need only be glanced at. In 1642 Mr. Hutchinson became a lieutenant-colonel in the parliamentary army, and in 1643 was appointed governor of Nottingham Castle. He took an active part in the struggles of the civil war, and in the government of the days of the Commonwealth, and proved himself honest and earnest in his endeavours to serve the interests of the Parliament. He was an uncompromising republican, brave, high-minded, and unaffectedly pious. At the Restoration he was discharged from Parliament, and from all offices of state for ever. In October, 1663, he was arrested, imprisoned at Newark, thence carried to the Tower, and in the next year removed to Sandown Castle, where he fell ill and died on the 11th of September, 1664. His noble wife was refused permission to share his confinement.

Richard Savage, the poet, son of the unnatural Countess of Macclesfield, was, according to Dr. Johnson, christened in this church by the direction of Lord Rivers, his reputed father, in 1697-8.

In the register of burials of St. Andrew's parish, under the date August 28, 1770, appears the following entry :—"William Chatterton, Brooks Street ;" to which has been added, probably by an after incumbent, "the poet," signed "J. Mill." The addition is perfectly correct, although the poet's Christian name was Thomas, not William, and this slight memorial is the only record in the church of the end of a short chapter in the annals of genius. We shall have more to say on the subject of this unfortunate bard, as well as on the equally melancholy career of Richard Savage, when we come shortly to speak of Brooke Street, Holborn, and its neighbourhood.

In the churchyard of St. Andrew's, Holborn, lie the remains of another poet, Henry Neele, author, among other works, of the " Romance of English History." He was born in the Strand, on the 29th of January, 1798, and early in life was apprenticed to a solicitor. During his clerkship—namely, in 1817—he made his first appearance as an author before the public, and from that time continued to publish occasionally, until 1828, on the 8th of February of which year, in a fit of insanity, incipient, it is true, but encouraged by excessive reading, he unhappily destroyed himself. Against the west wall of the churchyard is a gravestone commemorative of his father, and bearing an epitaph written by Henry Neele. On the same stone, together with the names of several others of the family, is the record of the poet's own pre-

mature death. The epitaph written by him is as follows :—

"Good night, good night, sweet spirit ! Thou hast cast
　Thy bonds of clay away from thee at last ;
　Broke the vile earthly fetters, which alone
　Held thee at distance from thy Maker's throne.
　But, oh ! those fetters to th' immortal mind
　Were links of love to those thou'st left behind.
　For thee we mourn not ; as the apostle prest
　His dungeon pillow, till the angel guest
　Drew nigh ; and when the light that round him shone
　Beamed on the pris'ner, his bands were gone :
　So wert thou captive to disease and pain,
　Till death, the brightest of th' angelic train,
　Poured heaven's own radiance, by divine decree,
　Around thy suffering soul, and it was free."

St. Andrew's has been called "the poet's church," from the sons of song who have in some way or other been connected with it. We have named three already, and have here to speak of a fourth. John Webster, the dramatist, is said to have been parish clerk in St. Andrew's, but there is, unfortunately, no confirmation of this in the register. The clerkship, however, being in the gift of the rector, the vestry register could afford no direct evidence on the subject. Webster has, to us, an obscure personal history, but by those who love an old play he will ever be remembered as the author of the *White Devil* and the *Duchess of Malfy*—two performances, says Hazlitt, which upon the whole, perhaps, come the nearest to Shakespeare of anything we have on record. Charles Lamb had a great admiration of our parish clerk's *White Devil*. " I never saw anything," he writes, "like the funeral dirge in this play for the death of Marcello, except the ditty which reminds Ferdinand of his drowned father in the *Tempest*. As that is of the water, watery, so this is of the earth, earthy. Both have that intensity of feeling which seems to resolve itself into the element which it contemplates." Let us, while we have the chance, repeat, in honour to the memory of Webster, the exquisite lines alluded to by Lamb :—

"Call for the robin redbreast, and the wren,
　Since o'er shady groves they hover,
　And with leaves and flowers do cover
　The friendless bodies of unburied men.
　Call unto his funeral dole
　The ant, the fieldmouse, and the mole,
　To rear him hillocks that shall keep him warm,
　And (when gay tombs are robbed) sustain no harm ;
　But keep the wolf far thence, that's foe to men,
　For with his nails he'll dig them up again."

The *Duchess of Malfy*, Webster's second great play, " is not," remarks the critical Hazlitt, " in my judgment, quite so spirited or effectual a performance as the *White Devil*. But it is distinguished by the same kind of beauties, clad in the same terrors.

I do not know but the occasional gleams of passion are even profounder and more Shakesperian; but the story is more laboured, and the horror is accumulated to an overwhelming and insupportable height."

In the church register there is also entered the burial of Nathaniel Tomkins, executed for his share in Waller's plot. Tomkins was Waller's brother-in-law. The plot for which he suffered is

Tomkins and Challoner were hanged, the one in Holborn, and the other in Cornhill, both within sight of their own dwelling-houses; Blinkhorne, Hassell, White, and Waller were, by the mercy of Parliament and the Lord-General Essex, reprieved, and eventually saved. Waller, the chief of them, was detained in the Tower, but, about a year after, upon payment of £10,000, was pardoned 'and released to go travel abroad.'"

ST. ANDREW'S CHURCH, FROM SNOW HILL, IN 1850. (*See page* 505.)

one of the noted conspiracies of history. Waller, the poet, in conjunction with Tomkins, Challoner, Blinkhorne, and a few others, had undertaken to seize the persons of the leading members of the House of Commons, and to deliver up the City of London to Charles, who had sent in a commission of array very secretly, by means of the Lady Aubigny, whose husband had fallen at Edgehill. "A servant of Tomkins overheard the conversation of the conspirators, and revealed what he knew to Pym, who presently seized their chief and brought him to trial, where he confessed everything with amazing alacrity, and crawled in the dust, in the hope of saving his life. The jury of Guildhall found a verdict of guilty against all the prisoners.

Another burial we must notice is that, in 1802, of Joseph Strutt, the author of "Sports and Pastimes of the People of England," and several other works of an antiquarian character. Strutt was born at Springfield, in Essex, on the 27th of October, 1749, and was educated as an artist. In 1770 he became a student at the Royal Academy, and was successful in winning both the gold and silver medals there. He served an apprenticeship to the unfortunate Ryland, and when his term expired, began to unite literary labours of an antiquarian character with those of his artistic profession. In 1773 he published his first book, "The Regal and Ecclesiastical Antiquities of England," and subsequently a "Complete View of the Manners and

Others would Swell with Pride, if thus cares'd
But he bears humble Thoughts within his Breast

Without Concern he from his Coach alights,
To Stand a Tryal which its Hearers frights.

The College with alacrity receiv'd
Her Son return'd for whom accus'd She greiv'd

St. Asaphs Bishop, for his Flocks Instruction
Allows Him Institution and Induction

From hence the Church's Restoration rose;
And made Discovery of her Secret Foes.

The Derby Sheriff doth of him request,
That his Assize Discourse may be imprest.

The D__r and his Friends in Consultation,
How to reply to Commons. Accusation

Into the Church the Sheriff introduces.
The D__r who laments its Foes Abuses.

At Banbury the Courtious Corporation,
Salutes him who returns the Salutation.

"SACHEVERELL" CARDS.
(Selected from a Pack illustrating the Reign of Queen Anne.)

Customs, Arms, Habits, &c., of the Inhabitants of England;" a "Chronicle of England" (a "heavy book," Chalmers says); a "Dictionary of Engravers;" "The Sports and Pastimes of the People of England;" "Queen Hoo Hall, a Romance," and several other works. He died on the 16th of October, 1802, in Charles Street, Hatton Garden. His biographer sums up his character in these words:—"The calamities incident to man were indeed his portion on this earth, and these greatly augmented by unkindnesses where he least deserved to have met with them. He was charitable without ostentation; a sincere friend, without intentional guile; a dutiful son; a faithful and affectionate husband; a good father; a worthy man; and, above all, it is humbly hoped, a sincere Christian. His natural talents were great, but little cultivated by early education. The numerous works which he gave to the world as an author and as an artist, prove that he employed his time to the best advantage."

That celebrated preacher, William Whiston, once made himself rather troublesome in connection with this church. He constantly attended and partook of the communion. On his principles becoming known he was warned by Sacheverell to forbear partaking of the sacrament. "Wicked Will" Whiston, however, persisted, and at last the rector fairly turned him out. Whiston aired his grievances in print, and then shifted his camp into another parish. Pennant says that on the occasion of his ejection from the church, he had taken it into his head to disturb Dr. Sacheverell while he was in the pulpit, giving utterance to some doctrine contrary to the opinion of that heterodox divine. His lawyer, who had no liking for Dr. Sacheverell, tried to induce Whiston to prosecute the doctor for the insult, and offered to take the business in hand without fees; but this Whiston refused, replying, "If I should give my consent, I should show myself to be as foolish and passionate as Sacheverell himself."

Whiston was born in 1667, and died in 1752. During his life he had many ups and downs, and seems to have been long tossed to and fro on a sea of religious doubt and metaphysical uncertainty. Towards the close of his career he distinguished himself by an abortive attempt to discover the longitude, and by his opinions on the Millennium and the restoration of the Jews. He was a favourite with Queen Caroline, who presented him with £50 every year from the time she became queen, which pension was continued for some time after her death. We get a glimpse of the queen and the eccentric divine in the following anecdote

told by Whiston's son. The queen, who liked Whiston's free conversation, once asked him what people in general said of her. He replied that they justly esteemed her as a lady of great abilities, a patron of learned men, and a kind friend to the poor. "But," says she, "no one is without faults, pray what are mine?" Mr. Whiston begged to be excused speaking on that subject, but she insisting, he said her majesty did not behave with proper reverence at church. She replied, the king would persist in talking with her. He said, a greater than kings was there only to be regarded. She acknowledged the truth of this, and confessed her fault. "Pray," said she, "tell me what is my next?" He answered, "When your majesty has amended of that fault I will tell you of your next;" and so it ended.

But we must not be carried away, by recollection of such tales, to forget St. Andrew's. Hacket, who afterwards became a bishop, was rector here for several years. This divine was born near Exeter House in the Strand, on the 1st of September, 1592, and was educated at Trinity College, Cambridge. He took orders in the year 1618, and we find him passing through various stages of advancement till in 1623 he landed in the post of chaplain to James I., with whom he became a favourite preacher. In 1624, upon the recommendation of the Lord Keeper, Dr. Williams, he was made rector of St. Andrew's, Holborn. His patron also procured him, in the course of the same year, the rectory of Cheam, in Surrey, telling him that he intended Holborn for wealth and Cheam for health.

During the time of the Civil War he was in danger, through his allegiance to the unpopular party, of getting into trouble. "One Sunday," says Cunningham, "whilst he was reading the Common Prayer in St. Andrew's, a soldier of the Earl of Essex came, clapped a pistol to his breast, and commanded him to read no farther. Not at all terrified, Hacket said he would do what became a divine, and he might do what became a soldier. He was permitted to proceed."

At the Restoration he was made Bishop of Lichfield and Coventry, and set a noble example by exhibiting a degree of munificence worthy of his station. He expended £20,000 in repairing his cathedral, and was, besides, a liberal benefactor to the college of which he had been a member. He was the author of the Life of Archbishop Williams, a quaint and learned work, half made up of quotations, like Burton's "Anatomy of Melancholy."

As for his character, he is described as having

been exemplary in behaviour, cheerful in conversation, hospitable, humble and affable, though subject to great eruptions of anger, but at the same time very placable and ready to be appeased, and altogether of too generous a nature to be really vindictive.

The Dissenters once got an agreeable surprise whilst Hacket was rector of St. Andrew's. Soon after the Restoration, having received notice of the interment of a Dissenter belonging to his parish, he got the burial service by heart. He was a fine elocutionist, and besides felt deeply the propriety and excellence of what he had to deliver; so he went through the service with such emphasis and grace as touched the hearts of all who were present, and particularly of the friends of the deceased, who unanimously gave it as their opinion that they had never heard a finer discourse. Their astonishment may be conceived when they learned that it was taken word for word from the Liturgy, a book which, though they had never read it, they affected to hold in contempt and detestation. Other clergymen, it is said, have been known to practise the same pious fraud as Mr. Hacket, and with a like success.

During Mr. Hacket's time St. Andrew's was old and decayed. He took in hand to rebuild it, and for that purpose got together a great sum of money, but on the breaking out of the Civil War the funds were seized by Parliament, as well as those which had been gathered for the repair of St. Paul's Cathedral, so that he was unable to carry out his praiseworthy intentions.

Another eminent rector of St. Andrew's was Stillingfleet, who was afterwards raised to the see of Worcester. Stillingfleet was truly a controversial divine, his life being one long warfare with Romanists, Nonconformists, Socinians, and the philosopher, John Locke. Among his Nonconformist opponents were Owen, Baxter, and Howe. He was born in 1635, and died in 1699. He was presented to the living of St. Andrew's, Holborn, in 1665, by Thomas, Earl of Southampton. His biographer describes his person as tall, graceful, and well-proportioned; his countenance as comely, fresh, and awful. "His apprehension was quick and sagacious; his judgment exact and profound; and his memory very tenacious; so that considering how intensely he studied, and how he read everything, it is easy to imagine him what he really was, one of the most universal scholars that ever lived."

Stillingfleet was at one time chaplain to King Charles II., and in that capacity exhibited considerable ability as a courtier. On one occasion it is told that his majesty asked him "how it came about that he always read his sermons before him, when he was informed he invariably preached without book elsewhere?" He told the king that "the awe of so noble an audience, where he saw nothing that was not greatly superior to him, but chiefly the seeing before him so great and wise a prince, made him afraid to trust himself." With this answer, which was not very becoming in a divine, the king was well content. "But pray," said Stillingfleet, "will your majesty give me leave to ask you a question, too? Why do you read your speeches, when you have none of the same reasons?" "Why, truly, doctor," said the king, "your question is a very pertinent one, and so will be my answer. I have asked them so often, and for so much money, that I am ashamed to look them in the face."

Amongst the rectors of St. Andrew's was the Rev. Charles Barton, who died in 1805, and of whom an anecdote worth repeating is given by the historian of the churches of London. He had acted diligently as curate of the church for several years, when the previous rector died, and presuming on length of service, he waited on the Duchess-Dowager of Buccleuch to ask for the living. "You have come soon, and yet too late," said her Grace; "for having made up my mind a dozen years ago as to whom I would give St. Andrew's, I have sent my servant with the presentation." Mr. Barton bowed in silence, and returned home, where he found his wife and family rejoicing over the duchess's letter. "Ah," said he, "her Grace loves a joke," and of course went back immediately to thank her. When he died the duchess continued her kindness to the family, and presented a living to his eldest son, who was also in the Church. Mr. Charles Barton was buried in St. Andrew's, and is commemorated by a tablet in the north gallery.

Under an Act of Parliament passed in the reign of Queen Anne, and in consequence of the proceedings that took place in connection with it, the parish of St. George the Martyr, Queen Square, which before had formed part of St. Andrew's, Holborn, was erected into a distinct parish for spiritual purposes, although still united with St. Andrew's as regards the poor, and other secular matters.

Newcourt informs us that a public grammar-school was among the adjuncts of the church. It was one of those erected by Act of Parliament in the reign of Henry VI., and, according to Maitland, stood on the right side of the church, and was taken down in 1737.

CHAPTER LVIII.

ELY PLACE.

Ely Place: its Builders and Bishops—Its Demolition—Seventy Years ago—"Time-honoured" Lancaster's Death—A King admonished—The Earl of Sussex in Ely Place—The Hatching of a Conspiracy—Ely Place Garden—The Duke of Gloucester's Dessert of Strawberries—Queen Elizabeth's Handsome Lord Chancellor—A Flowery Lease—A Bishop Extinguished—A Broken Heart—Love-making in Ely Place—"Strange Lady." Hatton shows her Temper—An Hospital and a Prison—Festivities in Ely Place—The Lord Mayor offended—Henry VII. and his Queen—A Five Days' Entertainment—The Last Mystery in England—A Gorgeous Anti-masque—Two Bailiffs baffled, and a Bishop taken in—St. Etheldreda's Chapel—Its Interior—The Marriage of Evelyn's Daughter—A Loyal Clerk.

A LITTLE north of St. Andrew's, Holborn, and running parallel to Hatton Garden, stand two rows of houses known as Ely Place. To the public it is one of those unsatisfactory streets which lead nowhere; to the inhabitants it is quiet and pleasant; to the student of Old London it is possessed of all the charms which can be given by five centuries of change and the long residence of the great and noble. The present Ely Place, and a knot of neighbouring tenements, streets, and alleys, occupy the site of the town house, or "hostell," of the Bishops of Ely. And to the history of the old mansion, and its sometimes gay and sometimes sober inmates, we shall devote the following chapter.

The earliest notice of Ely Place belongs to the close of the thirteenth century. John de Kirkeby, Bishop of Ely, died in the year 1290, and left to his successors in the see a messuage and nine cottages in Holborn. His intention was to found a London residence for the Bishops of Ely, suitable to their rank. Previous to this time they had their London residence in the Temple, but things do not seem to have gone smoothly with them there. In 1250 Bishop Balsham was denied entrance there by the master, when Hugh Bigod was Justiciary of England. He insisted, however, on the rights which his predecessors had enjoyed, from the Conquest, of using the hall, chapel, chambers, kitchen, pantry, buttery, and wine-cellar, with free ingress and egress, by land and water, whenever he came to London, and he laid his damages at £200. The master not being able to overthrow the claim, the bishop won the case. But this was not an agreeable way of obtaining town lodgings, so no wonder John de Kirkeby was induced to bequeath the Holborn property for the benefit of his successors. The next bishop, William de Luda, probably built the chapel of St. Etheldreda, and we find him adding a further grant to the bequest of John de Kirkeby, accompanied by the condition that "his next successor should pay one thousand marks for the finding of three chaplains" in the chapel there. The next benefactor to the episcopal residence was John de Hotham, another bishop, who added a vineyard,

kitchen-garden, and orchard, and, altogether, seems to have given the finishing touch to the premises; so that Camden speaks of Ely Place as "well beseeming bishops to live in; for which they are beholden to John de Hotham, Bishop of Ely under King Edward III." Other and subsequent prelates did their duty by building, altering, and repairing, and conspicuous amongst these was the well-known Arundel, afterwards Archbishop of Canterbury, who erected a large and handsome "gate-house or front," towards Holborn, in the stone-work of which his arms remained in Stow's time. Thus Ely Place, by the liberality of many successive prelates, came to be one of the most magnificent of metropolitan mansions.

In the reign of Elizabeth, Sir Christopher Hatton was the occupant of Ely Place; and we shall tell in a few words the interesting story of his coming in, and the bishop's going out. Meanwhile—pursuing our rapid notice of the history of the house—let us only say that Sir Christopher died, in Ely Place, in 1591, and was succeeded in his estates by his nephew, Newport, who took the name of Hatton. When he died, his widow, "the Lady Hatton," who married Sir Edward Coke, the famous lawyer, held the property. The Bishops of Ely, upon her death, came in again, though in what appears a confused and unsatisfactory sort of way; and the subsequent history has been thus summarised by Mr. Peter Cunningham:—"Laney, Bishop of Ely, died here in 1674-5, and in Bishop Patrick's time (1691-1707) a piece of ground was made over to the see for the erection of a new chapel, and the Hatton property saddled with a rent-charge of £100 per annum, payable to the see. In this way matters stood till the death, in 1762, of the last Lord Hatton, when the Hatton property in Holborn reverted to the Crown. An amicable arrangement was now effected, the see, in 1772, transferring to the Crown all its right to Ely Place, on an act (12 Geo. III., c. 43) for building and making over to the Bishops of Ely a spacious house in Dover Street, Piccadilly, still in possession of the see, with an annuity of £200 payable for ever."

In Ralph Aggas's map of London, in the reign of

Elizabeth, we see the vineyard, meadow, kitchen-garden, and orchard of Ely Place, extending northward from Holborn to the present Hatton Wall and Vine Street, and east and west from Saffron Hill to nearly the present Leather Lane. Except a cluster of houses—Ely Rents—standing on Holborn Hill, the surrounding ground was about that time entirely open and unbuilt upon. In the names of Saffron Hill, Field Lane, Turnmill and Vine Streets, we get a glimpse of the rural past. In the Sutherland View (1543) the gate-house, banqueting-hall, chapel, &c., of this house are shown.

During the imprisonment of Bishop Wren by the Long Parliament, most of the palatial buildings were taken down, and upon the garden were built Hatton Garden, Great and Little Kirby Streets, Charles Street, Cross Street, and Hatton Wall. The present Ely Place was not built till about 1773. We find a fragment of the old episcopal residence preserved in, and giving its name to, Mitre Court, which leads from Ely Place to Hatton Garden. Here, worked into the wall of a tavern known as "The Mitre," is a bishop's mitre, sculptured in stone, "which probably," Mr. Timbs conjectures, "once adorned Ely Palace, or the precinct gateway.

A writer in Knight's "London" has been at the pains to put together, from existing material, a description of Ely Place as it existed immediately before the bishop's residence was levelled to the ground. "Let us imagine ourselves," he says, "entering the precincts from Holborn. The original gate-house, where the bishop's armed retainers were wont to keep watch and ward in the old style, is now gone, and we enter from Holborn at once upon a small paved court, having on the right various offices, supported by a colonnade, and on the left a wall, dividing the court from the garden.

"Passing from the court, we reach the entrance to the great hall, which extends along in front, and to our left. This fine edifice, measuring about 30 feet in height, 32 in breadth, and 72 in length, was originally built with stone, and the roof covered with lead. The interior, lighted by six fine Gothic windows, was very interesting. It had its ornamental timber roof, its tiled and probably originally chequered floor, its oaken screen at one end, and its daïs at the other; and when filled with some of the brilliant and picturesque-looking crowds that have met under its roof, must have presented a magnificent spectacle.

"Beyond the hall, and touching it at the north-west corner, were the cloisters, enclosing a quadrangle nearly square, of great size, and having in the midst a small garden—made, perhaps, after the grant of the principal garden to Hatton. Over the cloisters were long, antique-looking galleries, with the doors and windows of various apartments appearing at the back; in the latter, traces of painted glass—the remnants of former splendour—were still visible. Lastly, at the north-west corner of the cloisters, *in a field* planted with trees and surrounded with a wall, stood the chapel—now all that remains of what we have described, and of the still more numerous buildings that at one time constituted the palace of the Bishops of Ely."

Having now got an idea of the appearance of Ely Place, and a notion of, at least, the skeleton of its history, we may proceed to add to our information, and to tell of the characters who have lived in it, and the incidents of which it has been the scene.

A famous character in English history—"Old John of Gaunt, time-honoured Lancaster"—resided here at the close of his eventful life. He died here in 1399. How this came to be his residence is unknown: it is conjectured by Cunningham, and with some show of probability, that the bishops occasionally let the house—or rather, perhaps, the greater part of it—to distinguished noblemen. Certainly John of Gaunt stood at this time in need of a town-house, for his palace of the Savoy had been burned to the ground by the insurgents during Wat Tyler's rebellion. Froissart thus speaks of his death:—"So it fell that, about the feast of Christmas, Duke John of Lancaster—who lived in great displeasure, what because the king had banished his son out of the realm for so little cause, and also because of the evil governing of the realm by his nephew, King Richard—(for he saw well, if he long persevered, and were suffered to continue, the realm was likely to be utterly lost)—with these imaginations and others, the duke fell sick,-whereon he died; whose death was greatly sorrowed by all his friends and lovers."

Shakespeare, in his play of *Richard II.*, Act ii., sc. 1, represents the dying nobleman in Ely House admonishing with his last breath his dissipated nephew, the king :—

> "A thousand flatterers sit within thy crown,
> Whose compass is no bigger than thy head ;
> And yet, incagèd in so small a verge,
> The waste is no whit lesser than thy land.
> Oh, had thy grandsire, with a prophet's eye,
> Seen how his son's son should destroy his sons,
> From forth thy reach he would have laid thy shame.
> Deposing thee before thou wert possessed,
> Which art possessed now to depose thyself.
> Why, cousin, wert thou regent of the world
> It were a shame to let this land by lease ;
> But, for thy world, enjoying but this land,

Is it not more than shame to shame it so ?
Landlord of England art thou, and not king."

Another nobleman who at one time resided in
Ely Place was Henry Radclyff, Earl of Sussex.
We find him writing to his countess "from Ely
Place, in Holborn," to tell her of the death of
Henry VIII.   And in Ely Place—then the resi-
dence of the Earl of Warwick (afterwards Duke of
Northumberland—the council met and planned

of the coronation of the young King Edward V.
The Duke of Gloucester, afterwards Richard III.,
enters, and after a few words exchanged with Buckingham, turns—possibly to conceal his deep and
bloody design—to the bishop :—

" My lord of Ely, when I was last in Holborn,
I saw good strawberries in your garden there ;
I do beseech you, send for some of them !
   Ely. Marry, I will, my lord, with all my heart."

WILLIAM WHISTON.   (See page 512.)

the remarkable conspiracy which resulted in the
execution of the Protector Somerset.

The pleasant gardens which surrounded Ely
House rejoiced in the growth of fine strawberries,
and it is in connection with this fruit that the name
of Ely Place has been enshrined in the memory of
all readers of Shakespeare.   No one needs to have
recalled the scene in the Tower which ended in
the execution of Hastings.   Buckingham, Hastings,
the Bishop of Ely, and others. are talking together

He goes out, and shortly returning, finds Gloucester gone.

" Ely. Where is my lord the Duke of Gloucester ?   I have
   sent for those strawberries.
   Hastings. His grace looks cheerful and smooth this
   morning.
There's some conceit or other likes him well,
When that he bids good morrow with such spirit."

Ill-judging Hastings ! Little did he guess that
a few minutes after he would hear the Lord

Protector thundering out, with reference to himself, "Thou'rt a traitor! Off with his head!" After the execution the cold-blooded Gloucester likely enough sat down with relish to a dessert of the bishop's strawberries.

How closely in this scene Shakespeare followed the historical truth we may see in this passage from Holinshed:—"On the Friday (being the 13th of June, 1483) many lords were assembled in the Tower, and there sat in council, devising the honourable solemnity of the king's (the young

better thing as ready to your pleasure as that.' And therewithal, in all haste, he sent his servant for a mess of strawberries."

In the time of Richard III., it may be added, strawberries were an article of ordinary consumption in London. In Lydgate's poem of "London Lyckpeny" we learn as much:—

> "Then unto London I did me hie,
> Of all the land it beareth the prize;
> 'Good peascod!' one began to cry—
> 'Strawberry ripe! and cherries in the rise.'"

ELY HOUSE—THE HALL. *From Grose's "Antiquities,"* 1772. (*See page* 515.)

Edward V.'s) coronation, of which the time appointed then so near approached, that the pageants and subtleties were in making day and night at Westminster, and much victuals killed therefore, that afterwards was cast away. These lords so sitting together, communing of this matter, the Protector (Gloucester) came in amongst them, just about nine of the clock, saluting them courteously, and excusing himself that he had been from them so long, saying merrily that he had been a sleeper that day. After a little talking with them, he said unto the Bishop of Ely, 'My lord, you have very good strawberries at your garden in Holborn; I require you let us have a mess of them.' 'Gladly, my lord,' quoth he. 'Would God I had some

To make clear the connection existing between Lord Chancellor Hatton and Ely Place, to which we alluded at the beginning of this chapter, it will be necessary to give a short sketch of that worthy man who, says Malcolm, was "the cause of infinite loss and trouble to the Bishops of Ely for upwards of an hundred years." He was the youngest of three sons of William Hatton, of Holdenby, a gentleman of good family. In early life he was entered at one of the inns of court, where he studied law, but as a gentleman lawyer only, and not with the view of deriving any advantage from it as a profession. Whilst engaged in this way he had the good fortune to attract the notice of Queen Elizabeth, and became in turn Gentleman Pensioner,

Gentleman of the Privy Chamber, Captain of the Guard, Vice-Chamberlain, Member of the Privy Council, and Lord Chancellor. It seems he was possessed of many graces of person, and had great ability as a dancer. Elizabeth's fancy for him grew to such a height, that Leicester did his best to make his rival ridiculous, by offering to introduce to the queen a dancing-master whose abilities far excelled those of Hatton. But his project was not successful. "No," said Elizabeth, "I will not see your man; it is his trade." She abandoned herself to her extravagant passion, and Hatton and she corresponded in the most fond and foolish style, of which there exists plenty of proof in the State Papers in the Record Office.

But it can hardly be said that by dancing alone he skipped up to position and influence. He had many good mental qualities, and his advancement is one of the numerous proofs the queen gave of her penetration in the choice of great State officers. On his becoming Lord Chancellor, the lawyers were unable to stifle their indignation. Some of the serjeants-at-law even refused to plead before him. But Hatton, though deficient in reading and practice as a lawyer, had common sense enough to hold his place, and at the same time to prove himself qualified for it. In all doubtful cases he was in the habit of consulting one or two learned legal friends, and the result was that his decisions were by no means held in low repute in the courts of law.

In 1576, to oblige Queen Bess, Richard Cox, Bishop of Ely, granted to her Majesty's handsome Lord Chancellor the gate-house of the palace (excepting "two rooms used as prisons for those who were arrested or delivered in execution to the bishop's bailiff, and the lower rooms used for the porter's lodge"), the first courtyard within the gate-house, the stables, the long gallery, with the rooms above and below it, and some other apartments. Hatton also obtained fourteen acres of ground, and the keeping of the gardens and orchards; and of this pleasant little domain he had a lease for twenty-one years. The rent was not a heavy one. A red rose was to be paid for the gate-house and garden, and for the ground ten loads of hay and ten pounds sterling per annum. The grumbling bishop had to make the best of a bad bargain; and the only modification he could obtain in the terms was the insertion of a clause giving him and his successors free access through the gate-house, and the right to walk in the garden and gather twenty baskets of roses yearly.

Once in possession of this property, Hatton began building and repairing, and soon contrived to expend £1,897 5s. 8d. (about £6,000 of our

money), part of which amount, we may as well say here, was borrowed from his royal mistress. As he went on, his views expanded; and, not satisfied with what he had, he petitioned Queen Elizabeth to alienate to him the whole house and gardens. This, in days when sovereigns laid greedy hands on so many acres of rich Church property, was no unusual request; and the queen wrote to the bishop requesting him to demise the lands to her till such time as the see of Ely should reimburse Sir Christopher for the money he had laid out, and was still expending, in the improvement of the property. The bishop wrote an answer befitting the dignity of his position. "In his conscience," he said, "he could not do it, being a piece of sacrilege. When he became Bishop of Ely he had received certain farms, houses, and other things, which former pious princes had judged necessary for that place and calling; that these he had received, by the queen's favour, from his predecessors, and that of these he was to be a steward, not a scatterer; that he could not bring his mind to be so ill a trustee for his successors, nor to violate the pious wills of kings and princes, and, in effect, rescind their last testaments." And he concluded by telling her that he could scarcely justify those princes who transferred things appointed for pious purposes to purposes less pious.

But arguments and moral reflections were thrown away on the queen, and the bishop had to consent to a conveyance of the property to her Majesty, who was to re-convey it to Hatton, but on condition that the whole should be redeemable on the payment of the sum laid out by Sir Christopher.

On the death of Dr. Cox, his successor, Dr. Martin Heton, seemed extremely unwilling to carry out this agreement, and in a fit of fury the queen sat down and wrote him one of her most characteristic epistles:—

"PROUD PRELATE !—I understand you are backward in complying with your agreement: but I would have you know that I, who made you what you are, can unmake you; and if you do not forthwith fulfil your engagement, by —— I will immediately unfrock you. "ELIZABETH."

According to some writers, this letter was addressed to Bishop Cox; but it is of no great consequence: the sender is of more interest here than the receiver.

The debt of the Lord Chancellor to the Queen had now reached some forty thousand pounds. His prudence had fallen asleep when he allowed her Majesty to become his principal creditor. She required a settlement of their account, and poor Hatton was unable to produce the necessary funds. It killed him. There is something pathetic in the quaint account which Fuller gives of the close of his prosperous life and fortunes. " It broke his heart," says the biographer of the " Worthies," " that the queen, which seldom gave loans, and never forgave due debts, rigorously demanded the present payment of some arrears which Sir Christopher did not hope to have remitted, and did only desire to have forborne : failing herein in his expectation, it went to his heart, and cast him into a mortal disease. The queen afterwards did endeavour what she could to recover him, bringing, as some say, cordial broths unto him with her own hands ; but all would not do. There's no pulley can draw up a heart once cast down, though a queen herself should set her hand thereunto." He died in Ely House in 1591.

The scenes in Ely Place during Hatton's days must often have been gay enough.

" Full oft within the spacious walls,
　　When he had fifty winters o'er him,
　My grave lord-keeper led the brawls—
　　The seal and maces danced before him.
　His bushy beard and shoe-strings green,
　　His high-crowned hat and satin doublet,
　Moved the stout heart of England's queen,
　　Though Pope and Spaniard could not trouble it."

So Gray, in his " Long Story," wrote of Hatton in his manor house of Stoke Poges ; and in his town residence we can picture him quite as eager as in the country to shake the light fantastic toe, and cutting quite as quaint a figure as there.

It was in Ely House that Sir Edward Coke courted the rich widow, Lady Hatton, relict of the nephew of Sir Christopher, Queen Elizabeth's Lord Chancellor. The lady was young, beautiful, eccentric, and, it would seem, possessed of a most vixenish temper. As she was rich, she had no scarcity of wooers, and among them were two celebrated men, Coke and Bacon. Many a curious scene must Hatton House have witnessed, as those two rivals in law pursued their rivalry in love, and cherished their long-felt enmity towards each other. Bacon's ever-faithful friend, the unfortunate Earl of Essex, pleads his cause hard with the enchanting widow and with her mother. To the latter he says, in one of his letters, " If she were my sister or my daughter, I protest I would as confidently resolve to further it as I now persuade you;" and in another epistle he adds, " If my faith be anything, I protest, if I had one as near me as she is to you, I had rather match her with him than with men of far greater titles." However, Sir Edward Coke carried off the prize, such as it was, and bitterly did he afterwards repent it.

That the marriage was not a happy one we have already said when speaking of the entries in the register-books of St. Andrew's Church, Holborn. After her quarrel with her husband, Lady Hatton betook herself again to Ely House, and there she effectually repelled the entrance of Sir Edward. In Howell's " Letters " we catch a sight of her in one of her peculiar humours. He is speaking of Gondomar, the Spanish Ambassador. " He hath waded already very deep," he says, " and ingratiated himself with divers persons of quality, ladies especially : yet he could do no good upon the Lady Hatton ; whom he desired lately, that in regard he was her next neighbour [at Ely House], he might have the benefit of her back-gate to go abroad into the fields, but she put him off with a compliment : whereupon, in a private audience lately with the king, among other passages of merriment, he told him that my Lady Hatton was a strange lady, for she would not suffer her husband to come in at her fore-door, nor him to go out at her back-door, and so related the whole business."

The " strange lady," as she is called by Howell, " dyed in London on the 3rd January, 1646, at her house in Holborne."

During the anxious period of the civil war, Ely Place was turned to good account, and made use of both as a hospital and a prison. We may show this by the following extracts from the Journals of the House of Commons :—

" 1642-3. Jan. 3. The palace was this day ordered to be converted into a prison, and John Hunt, sergeant-at-arms, appointed keeper during the pleasure of the House. He was at the same time commanded to take care that the gardens, trees, chapel, and its windows, received no injury. A sufficient sum for repairs was granted from the revenues of the see."

" 1660. March 1. Ordered, that it be referred to a committee to consider how and in what manner the said widows, orphans, and maimed soldiers at Ely House may be provided for and paid, for the future, with the least prejudice, and most ease to the nation, and how a weekly revenue may be settled for their maintenance ; and how the maimed soldiers may be disposed of, so as the nation may be eased of the charge, and how they may be provided of a preaching minister."

" March 13. £1,700 was voted for the above purpose, and for those at the Savoy, and certain members of the committee were named to inquire into the receipts and expenditures of the keepers of the *hospitals.*"

Malcolm gives a lamentable account of the inconvenience and mortification to which the bishops were in succession subjected in consequence of the unfortunate lease given to the Hatton family.

He is speaking of the latter part of the seventeenth century :—"The gate-house was taken down, and great part of the dwelling, and their lordships were compelled to enter the apartments reserved for their use by the old back way; several of the cellars, even under the rooms they occupied, were in possession of tenants; and those intermixed with their own, all of which had windows and passages into the cloisters.

"One half of the crypt under the chapel, which had been used for interments, was then frequented as a drinking place, where liquor was retailed; and the intoxication of the people assembled often interrupted the offices of religion above them. Such were the encroachments of the new buildings, that the bishop had his horses brought through the great hall, for want of a more proper entrance."

Some of the most memorable of feasts have been held here, the Bishops of Ely, in the true spirit of hospitality, having apparently been in the habit of lending their hall for the festive gatherings of the newly-elected serjeants of law. No doubt the halls of the Inns of Court were often too small to accommodate the number of guests. We shall notice three of these serjeants' merry-makings. The first took place in Michaelmas Term, 1464, and is noticeable for the fact that the Lord Mayor took great offence at a slight which the learned gentlemen unthinkingly put upon him. He came to the banquet, and found a certain nobleman— Grey of Ruthin, then Lord Treasurer of England —preferred before him, and sitting in the seat of state. That seat, by custom, he held, should have been occupied by himself; so, in high dudgeon, his lordship marched off, with his following of aldermen, to his own house, where he compensated his faithful adherents by a splendid entertainment, including all the delicacies of the season. He was wonderfully displeased, says Stow, at the way in which he had been treated, "and the new serjeants and others were right sorry therefore, and had rather than much good (as they said) it had not so happened."

Another banquet took place in 1495, and on this occasion Henry VII. was present, with his queen. This was one of the occasions, it has been pointed out, when the victor of Bosworth strove to correct a little the effect of his sordid habits, his general seclusion, and his gloomy, inscrutable nature, which altogether prevented him from obtaining the popularity which is agreeable to most monarchs—even to those the least inclined to purchase it at any considerable cost. "The king," says his great historian, Bacon, "to honour the feast, was present with his queen at the dinner,

being a prince that was ever ready to grace and countenance the professors of the law; having a little of that, that as he governed his subjects by his laws, so he governed his laws by his lawyers."

But the last feast we shall mention was the most splendid of all. Eleven serjeants had been created in November, 1531, and it was resolved to celebrate the event on an unparalleled scale of magnificence. The entertainment lasted five days, and on the fourth day the proceedings were graced by the presence of Henry VIII. and his queen, Catherine of Aragon; but these two dined "in two chambers," Stow parenthetically observes. At this very time the final measures were in progress for the divorce of the unfortunate queen, and Henry's marriage with Anne Boleyn. Besides these distinguished personages, the foreign ambassadors were there, and they also had a chamber to themselves. In the hall, at the chief table, sat Sir Nicolas Lambard, Lord Mayor of London, and with him were the judges, Barons of the Exchequer, and certain aldermen. The Master of the Rolls and the Master of the Chancery were supported at the board on the south side by many worshipful citizens, and on the north side of the hall there were other aldermen and merchants of the City. The remainder of the company, comprising knights, esquires, and gentlemen, were accommodated in the gallery and the cloisters, and, there being, apparently, a great scarcity of room, even in the chapel.

"It would be tedious," says Stow, to set down all "the preparation of fish, flesh, and other victuals, spent in this feast;" and he hints that no one would believe him if he did. To excite the wonder and the appetite of his readers, however, he gives a few particulars. There were twenty-four "great beefs," or oxen, at 26s. 8d. each, and one at 24s.; one hundred "fat muttons," at 2s. 10d.; fifty-one "great veals," at 4s. 8d.; thirty-four "porks," or boars, at 3s. 3d.; ninety-one pigs, at 6d.; ten dozen "capons of Greece of one poulter (for they had three)," at 1s. 8d.; nine dozen and six "capons of Kent," at 1s.; nineteen dozen "capons course," at 6d.; innumerable pullets, at 2d. and 2½d.; pigeons, at 10d. the dozen; larks, at 5d. the dozen; and fourteen dozen swans at a price not mentioned. And the feast, says the honest historian, "wanted little of a feast at a coronation."

No doubt it was at Ely Place that a ludicrous scene took place between the Bishop of Ely and two bailiffs, about the close of the seventeenth century—the conclusion of an adventure with the celebrated comedian, Joe Haines. Haines (who died in 1701) was always indulging in practical jokes and swindling tricks, and meeting with comical adventures. One day he was arrested by two bailiffs for a debt of twenty pounds, just as the Bishop of Ely was riding by in his carriage. Quoth Joe to the bailiffs, " Gentlemen, here is my cousin, the Bishop of Ely ; let me but speak a word to him, and he will pay the debt and costs." The bishop ordered his carriage to stop, whilst Joe—quite a stranger to him—whispered in his ear, " My lord, here are a couple of poor waverers, who have such terrible scruples of conscience that I fear they will hang themselves." " Very well," replied the bishop. So, calling to the bailiffs, he said, " You two men, come to me to-morrow, and I will satisfy you." The bailiffs bowed, and went their way. Joe, tickled in the midriff, and hugging himself with his device, took himself off. The next morning the bailiffs repaired to Ely Place. " Well, my good men," said his lordship, "what are your scruples of conscience ?" " Scruples !" replied they, " we have no scruples ; we are bailiffs, my lord, who yesterday arrested your cousin, Joe Haines, for twenty pounds. Your lordship promised to satisfy us to-day ; and we hope you will be as good as your word." The bishop, to prevent any further scandal to his name, immediately paid all that was owing.

A scene almost without a parallel was once arranged in Ely Place. This was a famous masque, with its attendant anti-masque, which came off during the brilliant part of the reign of the ill-fated Charles I. " Not the least interesting circumstances," it has been observed, " attending the splendid pageant, are the character and position of the men who had the management of the affair, and of him who has made himself its historian." This last was Whitelock, the learned and estimable lawyer, who, during the period preceding, comprising, and following the Commonwealth, enjoyed the respect of all parties, and has left us one of the most valuable records of the momentous events he witnessed and in which he took a part. That his heart was in this masque and anti-masque is evident from the enthusiasm with which he describes both, and the space which he devotes to them in his great work.

The year before this gorgeous display, the irrepressible Mr. Prynne had published his " Histrio-Mastix," in which he discharged a perfect broadside of abuse against plays and players, masques and masquers, and generally against all kinds of sport and pastime. The Queen Henrietta Maria, not long before, had engaged in some sort of theatrical performance with her maids of honour. The book was therefore offensive to the whole court, and no doubt to this circumstance the writer owed in part the extreme severity of his punish-

ment. But before he took his turn in the pillory, and lost his ears, the members of the four Inns of Court designed a masque, "as an expression of their love and duty to their majesties." It was whispered to them from the court that it would be well taken from them ; and some held it the more seasonable, because this action would manifest the difference of their opinion from Mr. Prynne's new learning, and serve to confute his " Histrio-Mastix " against interludes. It was therefore agreed by the benchers to have the solemnity performed in the most noble and stately manner that could be invented.

A committee was formed, consisting of two members from each House ; among the committee-men being Whitelock himself, Edward Hyde (who afterwards became Lord Clarendon), and the famous Selden. They set to work, and Whitelock's part in the arrangements was to superintend the music. This he did with energy. " I made choice," he says, " of Mr. Simon Ivy, an honest and able musician, of excellent skill in his art, and of Mr. Lawes (a name familiar to every lover of Milton) to compose the airs, lessons, and songs for the masque, and to be master of all the music, under me." He goes on to tell what meetings he had of " English, French, Italian, German, and other masters of music ; forty lutes at one time, beside other instruments in concert." At last everything was arranged, and one Candlemas, in the afternoon, " the masquers, horsemen, musicians, dancers, and all that were actors in this business, according to order, met at Ely House, in Holborn ; there the grand committee sat all day to order all affairs ; and when the evening was come, all things being in full readiness, they began to set forth in this order down Chancery Lane to Whitehall." And here we can picture to ourselves the crowded streets, the enthusiastic spectators, the loyal lawyers, and Prynne and his sympathisers scowling and muttering in the background, all on a sharp evening in February, 1633.

" The first that marched were twenty footmen in scarlet liveries, with silver lace, each one having his sword by his side, a baton in one hand, and a lighted torch in the other ; these were the marshal's men, who made way, and were about the marshal, waiting his commands. After them, and sometimes in the midst of them, came the marshal—then Mr. Darrel, afterwards knighted by the king : he was of Lincoln's Inn, an extraordinary handsome proper gentleman. He was mounted upon one of the king's best horses and richest saddles, and his own habit was exceeding rich and glorious, his horsemanship very gallant ; and besides his marshal's men, he had two lackeys who carried torches by him, and a page in livery that went by him carrying his cloak. After him followed one hundred gentlemen of the Inns of Court, five-and-twenty chosen out of each house, of the most proper and handsome young gentlemen of the societies. Every one of them was lackeys carried torches, and the page his master's cloak. The richness of their apparel and furniture, glittering by the light of a multitude of torches attending on them, with the motion and stirring of their mettled horses, and the many and various gay liveries of their servants, but especially the personal

ELY CHAPEL. *From a View by Malcolm,* 1800. (*See page* 525.)

mounted on the best horses, and with the best furniture that the king's stables, and the stables of all the noblemen in town, could afford; and they were forward on this occasion to lend them to the Inns of Court. Every one of these hundred gentlemen was in very rich clothes—scarce anything but gold and silver lace to be seen of them; and each gentleman had a page and two lackeys waiting on him, in his livery, by his horse's side; the beauty and gallantry of the handsome young gentlemen, made the most glorious and splendid show that ever was beheld in England.

"After the horsemen came the anti-masquers, and, as the horsemen had their music—about a dozen of the best trumpeters proper for them, and in their livery—sounding before them—so the first anti-masquers, being of cripples and beggars on horseback, had their music of keys and tongs,

ELY HOUSE. *From a Drawing made in 1772.* (*See page* 515.)

and the like, snapping, and yet playing in a concert, before them. These beggars were also mounted, but on the poorest, leanest jades that could be gotten out of the dirt-carts or elsewhere; and the variety and change from such noble music and gallant horses as went before them unto their proper music and pitiful horses, made both of them more pleasing. The habits and properties of these cripples and beggars were most ingeniously fitted (as of all the rest) by the committee's direction, wherein (as in the whole business) Mr. Attorney Noy, Sir John Finch, Sir Edward Herbert, Mr. Selden, those great and eminent persons, and all the rest of the committee, had often meetings, and took extraordinary care and pains in the ordering of this business, and it seemed a pleasure to them.

"After the beggars' anti-masque came men on horseback playing upon pipes, whistles, and instruments sounding notes like those of birds of all sorts, and in excellent concert, and were followed by the anti-masque of birds. This was an owl in an ivy-bush, with many several sorts of other birds in a cluster, gazing, as it were, upon her. These were little boys put into covers of the shapes of those birds, rarely fitted, and sitting on small horses, with footmen going by them with torches in their hands; and there were some, besides, to look unto the children; and this was very pleasant to the beholders.

"After this anti-masque came other musicians on horseback, playing upon bagpipes, hornpipes, and such kind of northern music, speaking the following anti-masque of projectors to be of the Scotch and northern quarters; and these, as all the rest, had many footmen, with torches, waiting on them. —First in this anti-masque rode a fellow upon a little horse with a great bit in his mouth, and upon the man's head was a bit, with headstall and reins fastened, and signified a projector, who begged a patent that none in the kingdom might ride their horses but with such bits as they would buy of him. Then came another fellow, with a bunch of carrots upon his head, and a capon on his fist, describing a projector who begged a patent of monopoly as the first inventor of the art to feed capons fat with carrots, and that none but himself might have use of that invention, and have the privilege for fourteen years, according to the statute. Several other projectors were in like manner personated in this anti-masque; and it pleased the spectators the more because by it an information was covertly given to the king of the unfitness and ridiculousness of these projects against the law; and the Attorney Noy, who had most knowledge of them,

had a great hand in this anti-masque of projectors."

Other anti-masques followed, and then came chariots with musicians, chariots with heathen gods and goddesses, then more chariots with musicians, "playing upon excellent and loud music," and going immediately before the first grand masquer's chariot. This "was not so large as those that went before, but most curiously framed, carved and painted with an exquisite art, and purposely for this service and occasion." Its colours were silver and crimson: "it was all over painted richly with these colours, even the wheels of it, most artificially laid on, and the carved work of it was as curious for that art, and it made a stately show. It was drawn with four horses, all on breast, and they were covered to their heels all over with cloth of tissue, of the colours of crimson and silver, huge plumes of red and white feathers on their heads and buttocks; the coachman's cap and feather, his long coat, and his very whip and cushion, of the same stuff and colour. In this chariot sat the four grand masquers of Gray's Inn, their habits, doublets, trunk-hose, and caps of most rich cloth of tissue, and wrought as thick with silver spangles as they could be placed; large white silk stockings up to their trunk-hose, and rich sprigs in their caps, themselves proper and beautiful young gentlemen. On each side of the chariot were four footmen, in liveries of the colour of the chariot, carrying huge flambeaux in their hands, which, with the torches, gave such a lustre to the paintings, the spangles, and habits, that hardly anything could be invented to appear more glorious." Similar chariots, similarly occupied, followed from each of the other three Inns of Court, the only difference being in the colours. And in this manner the procession reached Whitehall, where the king, from a window of the Banqueting House—it might possibly be the very one out of which he stepped to the scaffold— saw, with his queen Henrietta Maria, the whole pageant pass before him. The royal spectators were so pleased with the show, that they sent a message to the marshal requesting him to conduct his following round the Tilt Yard opposite, that they might see it a second time. This done, they entered the palace, where the masque, to which all this gorgeous spectacle was but a preliminary, began, and, says Whitelock, it was "incomparably performed, in the dancing, speeches, music, and scenes; the dances, figures, and properties; the voices, instruments, songs, airs, and composures; the words and actions were all of them exact, and none failed in their parts." Henrietta Maria was so charmed, that she resolved to have the whole repeated shortly afterwards. The festivities concluded with dancing, when the queen and her ladies of honour were led out by the principal masquers. The expense of this spectacle was not less than £21,000. Some of the musicians had £100 apiece for their blowing and fiddling.

The last "mystery" represented in England was that of "Christ's Passion," in the reign of James I.: this, Prynne tells us, was "performed at Elie House, in Holborne, when Gondomar lay there, on Good Friday, at night, at which there were thousands present."

This incident suggests one or two facts relating to the performance in England of miracle-plays and mysteries. These were founded on the lives of the saints, and on those parts of the Scriptures best represented by the latter term. About the earliest mention of a miracle-play is of the date of 1110, when one was performed in the Abbey of St. Albans. Whether Geoffrey, a learned Norman, who composed this religious drama, then first introduced the custom of acting such pieces, is by no means certain. London had plays representing the working of miracles and the sufferings of the saints about the year 1170; so we learn from the monk Fitz-Stephen. That these exhibitions "were well attended," says Malcolm, in his "Manners and Customs of London," "we cannot doubt for a moment, as there was a double inducement, compounded of curiosity and devotion. Piers Plowman and Chaucer both confirm the fact of the general approbation with which they were received." They were, it is certain, introduced into England from the Continent.

As an interesting specimen of the "mysteries," we may take the play of *Noah*, preserved in the Towneley collection. It will serve as an example of the corrupt and not very reverent manner in which the events of Scripture history were, during the Middle Ages, communicated to the common people. When Noah carries to his wife the news of the impending Flood, she is introduced abusing him for his credulity, sneering at him as an habitual bearer of bad tidings, and complaining of the hard life she leads with him. He tells her to "hold her tongue," but she only becomes more abusive, till he is provoked to strike her. She returns the blow with interest, and they fall to fighting, till Noah has had enough of it, and runs off as hard as he can to his work. When the ark is finished there is another quarrel, for Noah's wife laughs at the structure, and declares she will never go into it. But the water rises fast, and the danger becomes so great, that she changes her mind and jumps on board, only, however, to pick another quarrel with her husband. They fight again, but this time Noah comes off victorious, and his partner complains of being beaten "blue," whilst their three sons lament over the family discord.

The chapel of Ely Place, still standing, was dedicated to St. Etheldreda. And who was she? She was the daughter of Anna, King of the West Angles, and was born in Suffolk, about the year 630. She took part in the erection of the cathedral of Ely, and in course of time was elected to fill the position of its patron saint. She died, in 679, the abbess of the convent of Ely. Sometimes St. Etheldreda is called by the more homely name of St. Audry; and from this second appellation is derived the familiar adjective *tawdry*. It is a digression, but we may as well tell how this came about. At the fair of St. Audry, at Ely, in the olden time, a description of cheap necklaces used to be sold, which under the name of *tawdry laces*, were long very popular. In process of time the epithet *tawdry* came to be applied to any piece of glittering tinsel or shabby magnificence.

The builder of the chapel is unknown, but Malcolm conjectures that it is to Thomas Arundel that we are indebted for this beautiful but solitary fragment, "now left for the admiration of the antiquary and man of taste—the product of an architect familiar with the rich fancy of the Edwardian style, fully indulged in the grand east window."

"In spite of patchings and modernisings," says Mr. J. Saunders, in 1842, "St. Etheldreda's Chapel retains much of its original aspect. On looking at the exterior, if we shut our eyes to the lower portion, where a part of the window has been cut away, and an entrance made where evidently none was ever intended to exist, we perceive the true stamp of the days when men built the cathedrals—works which no modern art has rivalled, and which yet seemed so easy to them, that the names of the architects have failed to be preserved. And in the interior the effect of the two windows, alike in general appearance, yet differing in every respect in detail, is magnificent, although the storeyed panes, which we may be sure once filled them, are gone. The bold arch of the ceiling, plain and whitewashed though now be its surface, retains so much of the old effect, that, though we miss the fine oak carvings, we do not forget them. The noble row of windows on each side are in a somewhat similar condition. All their exquisite tracery has disappeared, but their number, height, and size tell us what they must have been in the palmy days of Ely Place; and if we are still at a loss, there is fortunately ample evidence remaining in the ornaments which surround the upper portions of the windows in the interior, and divide them from each other. We scarcely remember anything more exquisite in architecture than the fairy workmanship of the delicate, pinnacle-like ornaments which rise between and overtop these windows. Of the original entrances into the chapel one only remains, which is quite unused, and is situated at the south-west corner of the edifice. Stepping through the doorway into a small court that encloses it, we perceive that it has been a very beautiful, deeply-receding, pointed arch, but now so greatly decayed that even the character of its ornaments is but partially discoverable. Here, too, is a piece of the wall of one of the original buildings of the palace—a stupendous piece of brickwork and masonry ; and on looking up, one of the octagonal buttresses, with its conical top, which ornamented the angles of the building, is seen. Descending a flight of steps, we find a low window looking into the crypt. . . . It is now filled with casks, and we can but just catch a glimpse of the enormous chestnut posts and girders with which the floor of the chapel is supported."

In 1878-9 the chapel passed into other hands and was thoroughly restored, from the crypt below to the open oak roof above, and it is now used as a place of Roman Catholic worship.

The diarist, Evelyn, has two notices of Ely Place chapel which may be worth our attention. The first runs thus :—" November 14th, 1668. In London. Invited to the consecration of that excellent person, the Dean of Ripon, Dr. Wilkins, now made Bishop of Chester. It was at Ely House : the Archbishop of Canterbury, Dr. Cosin (Bishop of Durham), the Bishops of Ely, Salisbury, Rochester, and

others, officiating. Dr. Tillotson preached. Then we went to a sumptuous dinner in the hall, where were the Duke of Buckingham, Judges, Secretaries of State, Lord Keeper, Council, noblemen, and innumerable other company, who were honourers of this incomparable man, invariably beloved by all who knew him." The other is of a domestic character, and gives us a pleasant glimpse of the kindly parental feelings of this estimable man :— " 27th April, 1693. My daughter Susanna was married to William Draper, Esq., in the chapel of Ely House, by Dr. Tenison, Bishop of Lincoln (since Archbishop). I gave her in portion £4,000. Her jointure is £500 per annum. I pray God Almighty to give her his blessing on this marriage."

The chapel was at one time leased to the National Society for a school-room, after which it remained for a while untenanted ; but on the 19th of December, 1843, it was opened for the service of the Established Church in the Welsh language, being the first service of the kind ever attempted in London. In 1874 it was bought by the Roman Catholic Fathers of Charity.

An amusing incident took place in Ely Chapel on the arrival of the news of the defeat of the young Pretender by the Duke of Cumberland, in 1746. The clerk allowed his loyalty to overcome his devotion, and struck up a lively ditty in praise of the reigning family. Cowper thought this worthy of notice in his " Task : "—

" So in the chapel of old Ely House,
   When wandering Charles, who meant to be the third,
   Had fled from William, and the news was fresh,
   The simple clerk, but loyal, did announce,
   And eke did roar, right merrily, two staves
   Sung to the praise and glory of King George."

CHAPTER LIX.

HOLBORN, TO CHANCERY LANE.

The Divisions of Holborn—A Miry Thoroughfare—Oldbourne Bridge—In the Beginning of the Century—Holborn Bars—The Middle Row—On the Way to Tyburn—A Sweet Youth in the Cart—Clever Tom Clinch—Riding up Heavy Hill—The Hanging School—Cruel Whippings—Statue to the late Prince Consort—The " Rose " Tavern—Union Court—Bartlett's Buildings—Dyers' Buildings—A Famous Pastry-cook—Castle Street—A Strange Ceremony—Cursitor Street—Lord Chancellor Eldon—A Runaway Match—Southampton House—An old Temple—Southampton Buildings—Flying for Dear Life—Jacob's Coffee House—Ridiculous Enactments—Dr. Birkbeck and Mechanics' Institutions—An Extraordinary Well—Fulwood's Rents—Ned Ward and the " London Spy "—Selling a Horse—Dr. Johnson—A Lottery Office—Lotteries : Their History and Romance—Praying for Luck—A £20,000 Prize—Lucky Numbers—George A. Stevens—Gerarde, the old Herbalist, and his Garden—The Flying Pieman of Holborn Hill—An old Bellman of Holborn.

LEAVING the gates of Ely Place we turn westwards, and pursue our way along the main thoroughfare of Holborn. And, to begin, let us speak of the divisions of this street. From Farringdon Street to Fetter Lane used to be known as Holborn Hill ; from Fetter Lane to Brooke Street as Holborn, and from Brooke Street to Drury Lane

as High Holborn. Since the recent alterations and improvements, Holborn extends from Holborn Viaduct to Holborn Bars, and High Holborn from the Bars to Drury Lane.

One of the first great improvements effected in Holborn was its being paved, in 1417, at the expense of Henry V., when the highway, we learn from Rymer's "Fœdera," "was so deep and miry that many perils and hazards were thereby occasioned, as well to the king's carriages passing that way as to those of his subjects."

In Holborn, where is now Farringdon Street, there was of old a stone bridge over the Fleet, called "Oldbourne Bridge." Stow thus describes this locality:—"Old borne or Hilborne, breaking out about the place where now the Bars do stand, and it ran down the whole street till Oldborne Bridge, and into the river of the Wells or Turnemill Brook. This bourn was likewise long since stopped up at the head, and in other places where the same hath broken out, but yet till this day the said street is here called High Oldborne Hill, and both the sides thereof, together with all the grounds adjoining, that lie betwixt it and the river of Thames, remain full of springs, so that water is there found at hand, and hard to be stopped in every house."

Aggas's map of London, in the time of Elizabeth, represents Holborn as a very different sort of a place from what it is now. All the ground from Shoe Lane to Chancery Lane was then a garden with trees and shrubs; and long before Aggas's day part of that space was a rural region belonging to the see of Bangor.

Holborn in the beginning of this century is described by Malcolm, the careful compiler of "Londinium Redivivum." "Holborn," he says, writing in 1803, "is an irregular long street, narrow and inconvenient at the north end of Fleet Market, but widening from Shoe Lane, up the hill, westward; thence to Middle Row, or the south end of Gray's Inn Lane. It is an excellent broad and dry place, or oblong square." In the additional Act for rebuilding London, 1670, it was enacted "that the passage to Holborn Bridge is too strait and narrow, incommodious for the many passengers daily using and frequenting the same, and it is therefore necessary to be enlarged : that it may be lawful for the Mayor, &c., to make it run in a bevil line from a certain timber-house on the north side thereof, named the Cock, to the Swan Inn, on the north side of Holborn Hill."

Holborn was anciently of much consequence, not only on account of the many eminent people who resided here, but because of the Inns of Court, which graced both its north and south sides. Besides, it contained a hospital for the poor, and a cell to the house of Clugny in France, suppressed with the Priories Alien.

"Holborn Bars" used to stand a little west of Brooke Street. They marked the termination of the City Liberties in that direction. The spot is now shown by two granite obelisks bearing the City arms. The Corporation of London formerly received a penny and two-penny toll from the carts and carriages of non-freemen entering the City. These tolls were levied at the six bars, including Holborn Bars. The richest inlets were Temple Bar and Whitechapel Bar.

The Middle Row, Holborn, has disappeared, like the Bars. This was a block of houses which stood half blocking up the street at the south end of Gray's Inn Lane. For at least a couple of centuries it was considered an obstruction. Howel, in his "Perlustration of London," 1657 (p. 344), says :—"Southward of Gray's Inn Lane there is a row of small houses, which is a mighty hindrance to Holborn, in point of prospect, which if they were taken down there would be from Holborn Conduit to St. Giles-in-the-Fields one of the fairest rising streets in the world." The obstructive buildings were at last made an end of in 1868. There is a view of the old Row in Faithorne's ichnographical delineation of London in the reign of Charles I.

Holborn was the old road from Newgate and the Tower to the gallows at Tyburn. At regular and frequent intervals both sides of the way were lined and all the windows were covered with curious and often sympathising spectators to see light-fingered gentlemen, murderers, forgers, and such like, riding to their doom.

"Now I am a wretch indeed," says Polly, in the *Beggar's Opera*, alarmed on account of Captain Macheath; "methinks I see him already in the cart, sweeter and more lovely than the nosegay"—which he had received at St. Sepulchre's—"in his hand! I hear the crowd extolling his resolution and intrepidity ! What volleys of sighs are sent from the windows of Holborn that so comely a youth should be brought to disgrace ! I see him at the tree ! the whole circle are in tears ! even butchers weep ! Jack Ketch himself hesitates to perform his duty, and would be glad to lose his fee by a reprieve ! What then will become of Polly ?"

Swift gives us a picture of an execution procession in his "Clever Tom Clinch going to be hanged :"—

> "As clever Tom Clinch, while the rabble was bawling,
> Rode stately through Holborn to die in his calling,
> He stopt at the George for a bottle of sack,
> And promised to pay for it when he came back.
> His waistcoat and stockings and breeches were white,
> His cap had a new cherry ribbon to tie 't.
> The maids to the doors and the balconies ran,
> And said, 'Lack-a-day ! he's a proper young man !'
> But as from the windows the ladies he spied,
> Like a beau in the box he bowed low on each side !
> And when his last speech the loud hawkers did cry,
> He swore from his cart, 'It was all a d——d lie !'
> The hangman for pardon fell down on his knee,
> And clever Tom gave him a kick—for his fee !

MIDDLE ROW, HOLBORN. *From a Drawing taken short y before its Demolition, 1865.* (See page 527.)

Then said, 'I must speak to the people a little;
But I'll see you all —— before I will whittle.
My honest friend Wild (may he long hold his place!)
He lengthened his life with a whole year of grace.
Take courage, dear comrades, and be not afraid,
Nor slip this occasion to follow your trade;

procession ascending it, bound for Tyburn, in our old authors:—

"Sirrah," says Sir Sampson, in Congreve's *Love for Love* (1695), "you'll be hanged; I shall live to see you go up Holborn Hill."

STAIRCASE IN SOUTHAMPTON HOUSE. (*See page* 532.)

My conscience is clear, and my spirits are calm,
And thus I go off, without Prayer-book or Psalm;
Then follow the practice of clever Tom Clinch,
Who hung like a hero and never would flinch."

Holborn Hill, we mentioned in a previous page, was sometimes known as "Heavy Hill." To speak of any one having the privilege of riding in a cart up "the Heavy Hill," was equivalent, in the free and easy talk of our forefathers, to saying that he was sure to be hung.

There are many allusions to Heavy Hill, and the

"Daughter Pad," says Aldo, in Dryden's *Limberham* (1678), "you are welcome. What! you have performed the last Christian office to your keeper; I saw you follow him up the Heavy Hill to Tyburn."

And in Ben Jonson's *Bartholomew Fair* we have the following:—

"*Knockem:* What! my little lean Ursula! my she-bear! art thou alive yet with thy litter of pigs to grunt out another Bartholomew Fair? ha!

Ursula: Yes, and to a nble a-foot, when the Fair is

done; to hear you groan out of a cart up the Heavy
Hill——　　　·

　　Knockem : Of Holborn, Ursula, mean'st thou so ?"

It is told in Tom Brown's works that an old
counsellor who lived in Holborn used every execu-
tion-day to give his clerks a half-holiday, sending
them to see the show, and giving them this piece
of advice : "Go, ye young rogues, go to school,
and improve !"

The Holborn line of road was selected for the
whippings which Doctor Titus Oates and Dangerfield had to suffer, in the reign of James II. Titus
Oates, as every one knows, was the chief informer
in what was called the Popish plot—a plot, as
he pretended to prove, that was promoted for the
destruction of the Protestant religion in England.
Several persons of quality were tried and executed
chiefly on his evidence, and Oates, in return for
his kind and timely information, received a pension
of £1,200 a year, and was lodged in Whitehall.
Scarcely, however, had King James II. ascended
the throne, than he was cast into prison, and tried
for perjury with respect to what he had asserted
regarding the alleged plot. Being convicted, he
was sentenced to stand in the pillory five times a
year during his life, to be whipped from Aldgate
to Newgate, and from thence to Tyburn ; which
sentence, says Neal, was exercised with a severity
unknown to the English nation. "The impudence
of the man," says the historian Hume, "supported
itself under the conviction, and his courage under
the punishment. He made solemn appeals to
Heaven, and protestations of the veracity of his
testimony. Though the whipping was so cruel
that it was evidently the intention of the Court to
put him to death by that punishment, yet he was
enabled, by the care of his friends, to recover, and
he lived to King William's reign, when a pension
of £400 a year was settled upon him. A considerable number of persons adhered to him in his
distress, and regarded him as a martyr to the Protestant cause." He died in 1705. Hume describes him as the most infamous of mankind, and
tells us that in early life he had been chaplain to
Colonel Pride, and that he was afterwards chaplain
on board the fleet, whence he had been igno-
miniously dismissed. He then became a convert
to the Roman Catholics, but used to boast in
after years that his conversion was a mere pretence, which he made in order to get into their
secrets and betray them.

The gentle Evelyn saw the Holborn part of
Dates' punishment inflicted. He has this entry in
his "Diary," on the 22nd of May, 1685 : "Oates,
who had but two days before been pilloried at

several places, and whipped at the cart's tail from
Newgate to Aldgate, was this day placed on a
sledge, being not able to go, by reason of so late
scourging, and dragged from prison to Tyburn, and
whipped again all the way, which some thought
to be very severe and extraordinary : but if he was
guilty of the perjuries, and so of the death of so
many innocents, as I fear he was, *his punishment
was but what he deserved*. I chanced to pass just
as execution was doing on him—a strange revolution."

Dangerfield, who had been the inventor of the
"Meal-Tub Plot," was condemned, in the same
year, to about as severe a punishment as Oates.
He was ordered to stand twice in the pillory ; to
be whipped from Aldgate to Newgate on one day,
and from Newgate to Tyburn on another ; and
to pay a fine of £500. He was not made of
such tough material as his brother scoundrel, Oates.
He "was struck with such horror at this terrible
sentence, that he looked upon himself as a dead
man, and accordingly chose a text for his funeral
sermon, but persevered in asserting that all he had
delivered in evidence before the House of Commons was true. The whipping was executed with
full rigour, as before upon Oates, and was scarce
over before one Mr. Robert Francis, a barrister, of
Gray's Inn, gave him a wound with his cane in or
near the eye, which, according to the deposition of
the surgeon, was the cause of his death." This
furious barrister, Mr. Francis, was consequently
tried for the murder, and as it was found that the
popular feeling was very violent against him, it
was judged a politic proceeding to permit his conviction and execution.

So much for general observations upon Holborn.
The first object which catches the eye as we look
about for particulars on which to comment, is the
statue erected to the memory of the late Prince
Consort in Holborn Circus. This statue was un-
veiled on Friday the 9th of January, 1874. It was
a gift from a patriotic gentleman, who desired to
remain unknown, to the Corporation of London.
The prince is represented as responding to a salute.
The pedestal, which is composed of stones weighing
two to ten tons each, includes two sitting figures
illustrating History and Peace, and bas-reliefs illustrating important events in Prince Albert's life.
The statue is the work of Mr. Bacon. The
pedestal is the joint design of the sculptor and
Mr. William Haywood.

We must not forget to speak of an inn called
the "Rose," which stood formerly on Holborn
Hill, and disappeared only within the recollection
of the present generation. From it Taylor the

water-poet started in the Southampton coach for the Isle of Wight on the 19th of October, 1647, while Charles I. was there.

"We took one coach, two coachmen, and four horses,
  And merrily from London made our courses,
  We wheeled the top of the heavy hill called Holborn
  (Up which hath been full many a sinful soul borne),
  And so along we jolted past St. Giles's,
  Which place from Brentford six or seven miles is."

So says Taylor in the beginning of his "Travels from London to the Isle of Wight."

Union Court, situated over against St. Andrew's Church, was originally called Scroop's Court. It derived this name from the noble family of Scrope of Bolton, who had a town house here, which was afterwards let to the serjeants-at-law. It ceased, it is said, to be a serjeants' inn about the year 1498.

Bartlett's Buildings, on the south side of Holborn, is described by Strype as "a very handsome place, graced with good buildings of brick, with gardens behind the houses," and he adds, that it is a region "very well inhabited by gentry, and persons of good repute." Were Strype to come alive again, he would not recognise the locality. Bartlett's Buildings are mentioned in the register of St. Andrew's as far back as 1615. The place is now chiefly occupied by warehouses and offices, and by the Farringdon Dispensary and Lying-in Charity.

We read in Thoresby's Diary, 13th May, 1714:— "At the meeting of the Royal Society, where was Sir Isaac Newton, the president. I met there, also, with several of my old friends, Dr. Sloane, Dr. Halley, &c. But I left all to go with Mr. Chamberlayn to Bartlett's Buildings, to the other society, viz., that for promoting Christian Knowledge, which is to be preferred to all other learning."

In Dyers' Buildings, the site of some almshouses of the Dyers' Company, lived William Roscoe, when he published his edition of Pope's Works, with notes and a life of the poet, 10 vols. 8vo, 1824. One of the principal objects of this new edition was to give a fuller and more accurate life of the poet than had yet appeared. Of the various biographical notices of him, it is not unjust to say that there was not one worthy of the subject. The *Quarterly Review* (October, 1825), in summing up the merits of Mr. Roscoe's work, says, "His original criticism is not much, but is enlightened and liberal; and the candour with which that and the life are written, is quite refreshing after the blighting perversity of the preceding editors, whose misrepresentations and calumnies he has industriously examined and patiently refuted, with a lucid arrangement both of facts and arguments."

At the corner of Furnival's Inn, on the opposite side of the street from Dyers' Buildings, Edward Kidder, the famous pastry-cook, had a school. He had another establishment in St. Martin's-le-Grand, and in these two places is said to have taught, from first to last, nearly six thousand ladies the delightful art of making pastry. Kidder published his receipts, engraved on copper, in a thin 8vo volume, with his portrait as a frontispiece. He died in April, 1739, in his seventy-third year. His book is somewhat dull reading, being unenlivened by any of those touches of fancy and eccentricity which make a work like Dr. Kitchener's "Cook's Oracle" so delightful to spend half an hour over.

And now crossing the street again we come to Castle Street, which runs from Holborn into Cursitor Street. Its proper name is Castle Yard, perhaps from the name of Castle Inn, on the site of which it is built. Lord Arundel, the great collector of art and antiquities, was living in 1619-20 in "Castle Yard, in Holborn." And here died Lady Davenant, the first wife of Sir William Davenant, the poet.

And having by Castle Street reached Cursitor Street, we may as well say a little about it, having omitted to do so in the beginning of our pilgrimage when speaking of Chancery Lane, of which it is a tributary. It is named after the Cursitor's Office or Inn, founded by Sir Nicholas Bacon, Lord Keeper of the Great Seal of England, and father of the famous Lord Bacon. Stow, speaking of Chancery Lane, says, "In this street the first fair building to be noted on the east side is called the Cursitor's Office : built with divers fair lodgings for gentlemen, all of brick and timber, by Sir Nicholas Bacon, late Lord Keeper of the Great Seal." Cursitor is said to be a corruption of chorister, and this seemeth the more probable, because "anciently all or the most part of the officers and ministers of Chancery, or Court of Conscience (for so the Chancery hath been called) were churchmen, divines, and canonists." The business of the Cursitors is to make out and issue writs in the name of the Court of Chancery.

When passing once through Cursitor Street with his secretary, Lord Chancellor Eldon said : "Here was my first perch ; how often have I run down to Fleet Market with sixpence in my hand to buy sprats for supper."

It was here he lived with that pretty young wife whom he married so imprudently, though he used in after life to reflect upon the step as one of the most fortunate of his early career. "The romance of the law," says Mr. Jeaffreson, "contains few more pleasant episodes than the story of the elopement of Jack Scott (afterwards Lord Eldon) with Bessie

Surtees. There is no need to tell in detail how the comely Oxford scholar danced with the banker's daughter at the Newcastle assemblies; how his suit was at first recognised by the girl's parents, although the Scotts were but rich 'fitters,' whereas Aubone Surtees, Esquire, was a banker and gentleman of honourable descent; how, on the appearance of an aged and patrician suitor for Bessie's hand, papa and mamma told Jack Scott not to presume on their condescension, and counselled Bessie to throw her lover over, and become the lady of Sir William Blackett; how Bessie was faithful and Jack was urgent; how they had secret interviews on Tyne-side and in London, meeting clandestinely on horseback and on foot, corresponding privately by letters and confidential messengers; how, eventually, the lovers, to the consternation of 'good society' in Newcastle, were made husband and wife at Black-shiels, North Britain. Who is ignorant of the story? Does not every visitor to Newcastle pause before an old house in Sandhill, and look up at the blue pane which marks the window from which Bessie descended into her lover's arms?" After a short residence at Oxford, the future Lord Eldon naturally came (as mostly all talent does come) to London, and established himself in a humble little house in Cursitor Street. The pretty wife made it cheerful for him. He had in after life to regret her peculiarities, her stinginess, and her nervous repugnance to society; but he remained devoted in his attachment. "Poor Bessie!" he said, in his old age, after she was dead; "if ever there was an angel on earth, she was one. The only reparation which one man can make to another for running away with his daughter, is to be exemplary in his conduct towards her."

Returning to Holborn and proceeding west-ward, we come to Southampton Buildings, built on the site of Southampton House. They lie on the south side of Holborn, a little above Holborn Bars. Speaking of the old mansion-house, Peter Cunningham, in 1849, remarked that fragments still remained in his day. He was shown, in 1847, what was still called "the chapel" of the house, a building with rubble walls and a flat timbered roof. The occupant also told him that his father remem-bered a pulpit in the chapel, and that he himself, when forming the foundation of a workshop ad-joining, had seen portions of a circular building which he supposed to be part of the old temple mentioned in a passage from Stow, which we shall make the subject of the following paragraphs:—

"Beyond the Bars [Holborn Bars]," says Stow, "had ye in old time a temple built by the Templars, whose order first began in 1118, in the nineteenth of Henry I. This temple was left and fell to ruin since the year 1184, when the Templars had builded them a new Temple in Fleet Street, near to the river of Thames. A great part of this old temple was pulled down but of late, in the year 1595.

"Adjoining to this old temple was some time the Bishop of Lincoln's inn, wherein he lodged when he repaired to this city. Robert de Curars, Bishop of Lincoln, built it about the year 1147. John Russell, Bishop of Lincoln, Chancellor of England in the reign of Richard III., was lodged there. It hath of late years belonged to the Earl of Southampton, and therefore called Southampton House. Master Roper hath of late much built there, by means whereof part of the ruins of the old temple are seen to remain, built of Caen stone, round in form as the new Temple by Temple Bar, and other temples in England."

We must not forget that in Southampton House, Thomas, the last Earl of Southampton, the faithful and virtuous servant of Charles I., and Lord Trea-surer in the beginning of the reign of Charles II., ended his days. Pennant, the historian, when he comes to this point in his " Account of London," writes with all the pathos of an honest and feeling heart. "He died," he says, "in 1667, barely in possession of the white rod, which his profligate enemies were with difficulty dissuaded from wresting out of his dying hands. He had the happiness of marrying his daughter and heiress to a nobleman of congenial merit, the ill-fated Lord Russell. Her virtues underwent a fiery trial, and came out of the test if possible more pure. I cannot read of her last interviews with her devoted lord without the strongest emotions. Her greatness of mind appears to uncommon advantage. The last scene is beyond the power of either pen or pencil. In this house they lived many years. When his lord-ship passed by it, on the way to execution, he felt a momentary bitterness of death in recollecting the happy moments of the place. He looked towards Southampton House, the tear started into his eye, but he instantly wiped it away."

Southampton House was taken down and private tenements erected on the site in the middle of the seventeenth century. Howel, writing in 1657, mentioning this fact, breaks out in his quaint way: "If any one should ask what the Almighty doth now in London, he might (as the pulse of the times beats) give the same answer that was given by the pagan philosopher, who, being demanded what Jupiter did in heaven, he said, 'Jupiter breaks great vessels, and makes small ones of their pieces.'"

In Southampton Buildings, in the house of a relative, Ludlow, the Parliamentary general, lay concealed from the Restoration till the period of his escape. And a very narrow escape it was. When the proclamation was issued by Charles II., requiring all the late king's judges to surrender themselves in fourteen days, on pain of being left out of the act of indemnity, he determined to fly the country. He bade farewell to his friends, and went over London Bridge in a coach to St. George's Church in the borough of Southwark, where he took horse, and travelling all night, arrived at Lewes, in Sussex, by break of day next morning. Soon after, he went on board a small open vessel prepared for him; but the weather being very bad, he quitted that, and took shelter in a larger which had been got ready, but it stuck in the sands going down the river. He had hardly got on board this, when some persons came to search that which he had just left. After waiting a night and a day for the storm to abate (during which time the master of the vessel asked him whether he had heard that Lieutenant-General Ludlow was confined among the rest of the king's judges), he put to sea, and landed at Dieppe in the evening, before the gates were shut. Having thus got him out of the reach of danger, we shall leave him, only waiting to tell the reader that he died at Vevay, in Switzerland, in 1693, his last wishes being for the prosperity, peace, and glory of his country.

One of the earliest coffee-houses of London was established in Southampton Buildings. In the autobiography of Anthony à Wood (ii. 65) we come upon the following passage in connection with the year 1650:—"This year Jacob, a Jew, opened a coffey-house at the Angel in the parish of St. Peter, in the East Oxon, and there it was by some, who delighted in noveltie, drank. When he left Oxon, he sold it in old Southampton Buildings, in Holborne, near London, and was living there in 1671."

When coffee was first introduced into England, about the middle of the seventeenth century, the new beverage, as was to be expected, had its opponents as well as its advocates. There were broadsides against coffee, just as there had been counterblasts against tobacco; but in spite of opposition it became a favourite drink, and the shops where it was sold grew to be places of general resort. They were frequented by *quidnuncs*, and were the great marts for news of all kinds, true and false.

In 1675, a paternal Government issued a proclamation for shutting up and suppressing all coffee-houses. They found, however, that in making this proclamation they had gone a step too far. So early as this period the coffee-house had become a power

in the land—as Macaulay tells us—a most important political institution, when public meetings, harangues, resolutions, and the rest of the machinery of agitation, had not come into fashion, and nothing like a newspaper existed. In such circumstances the coffee-houses were the chief organs through which the public opinion of the metropolis vented itself. Consequently, on a petition of the merchants and retailers of coffee, permission was granted to keep the coffee-houses open for six months, under an admonition that the masters of them should prevent all scandalous papers, books, and libels from being read in them, and hinder every person from declaring, uttering, or divulging all manner of false and scandalous reports against Government or the ministers thereof. The absurdity of constituting every maker of a cup of coffee a censor of the press was too great even for those days: the proclamation was laughed at, and no more was heard of the suppression of coffee-houses.

Dr. Birkbeck, in 1823, founded in Southampton Buildings a Mechanics' Institution. for the dissemination of useful knowledge among the industrious classes of the community, by means of lectures, classes, and a library.

"In inquiring," says a writer from whom we have already quoted, "into the origin of that movement for popular instruction which has occupied so broad a space during this century, we are met by the name of George Birkbeck standing out in conspicuous characters. The son of a banker at Settle, in Yorkshire, and reared as a medical practitioner, he was induced at an early period of life to accept a professorship in what was called the Andersonian Institution of Glasgow, a kind of popular university which had just then started into being. Here Birkbeck found great difficulty in getting apparatus made for a course of lectures on Natural and Experimental Philosophy; and this suggested to him the establishment of popular lectures to working men, with a view to the spread of knowledge in various matters relating to the application of science to the practical arts. This was the germ from which Mechanics' Institutions afterwards sprung. The trustees of the Andersonian Institution had not Birkbeck's enthusiasm; they deemed the scheme visionary, and refused at first to support it. In the autumn of 1800 he went to Yorkshire for a vacation, and there digested a plan for forming a class solely for persons engaged in the practical exercise of the mechanical arts, men whose education in early life had precluded even the possibility of acquiring the smallest portion of scientific knowledge. This mechanics' class was to be held in one of the rooms of the Andersonian Institution,

"On his return to Glasgow, he opened communications with the chief owners of manufacturing establishments, offering to the more intelligent workmen free admission to his class. The first lecture was attended by seventy-five artisans; it excited so much interest, that two hundred came to the second lecture, three hundred to the third, and five hundred to the fourth. His grateful pupils presented him with a silver cup at the close of the course, as a token of their appreciation of his disinterested kindness. He repeated these labours

1821 a School of Arts was established in Edinburgh, chiefly through the instrumentality of Mr. Leonard Horner. In 1823 a Mechanics' Institution was founded at Glasgow, and another in London, of which last Dr. Birkbeck was very appropriately elected president, an office he filled till his death, eighteen years afterwards.

"On the 2nd of December, 1824, being the first anniversary of the formation of the London Mechanics' Institution, the foundation-stone was laid of an edifice to be used as a theatre for deliver-

ROOM OF A HOUSE IN FULWOOD'S RENTS. *After Archer.* (*See page* 536.)

year after year till 1804, when he resigned his position at Glasgow to Dr. Ure, who, like him, was at that time struggling into fame. Birkbeck married, came to London, and settled down as a physician.

"Many years elapsed during which Dr. Birkbeck was wholly absorbed in his professional duties. He did not, however, forget his early schemes, and as he advanced in life, he found or made opportunities for developing them. In 1820 he gave a gratuitous course of lectures at the London Institution. Gradually a wish spread in various quarters to put in operation the plan which had so long occupied the thoughts of Dr. Birkbeck—viz., to give instruction in science to working men. In

ing the lectures of the professors, on the premises occupied by the Institution in Southampton Buildings. The newly-established concern was at first highly successful. Men of great attainments offered their services as lecturers, and the lecture-hall very often contained a thousand persons listening with the greatest attention to discourses on astronomy, experimental philosophy, chemistry, physiology, the steam-engine, &c. Many persons who afterwards attained to a more or less distinguished position in society, owed their first knowledge of the principles of science to the London Mechanics' Institution. The novelty and success of the enterprise were so great that similar institu-

DRAWING THE STATE LOTTERY AT GUILDHALL.   *From a Print of about 1750.*   (*See page 537.*)

tions sprang up rapidly in various parts of the kingdom."

When the first enthusiasm wore off, Mechanics' Institutions hardly realised, perhaps, the expectations of their founders. The reasons for this have been thus set down by a careful observer :—" In large towns," he says, " the energy and enthusiasm that originated them carried them on for a time ; but as the novelty wore off the members and revenue decreased, modifications of plan had to be adopted, new features introduced, and radical changes made. If these proved acceptable to the public, the institution flourished ; if not, it decayed. If the original idea of giving scientific education only were strictly carried out, the number of members was small, while, if amusement took the place of study, the institution lived in jeopardy from the fickle and changing taste for amusement on the part of the public."

The Mechanics' Institution in Southampton Buildings has now departed considerably from the design of the founder, and flourishes under the title of the Birkbeck Literary and Scientific Institution.

A well by which wonderful cures were effected both on the blind and the lame was discovered in 1649 near Southampton House. It was known as the Soldier's Well, the finder having been of the military profession, and is mentioned in " Perfect Occurrences from August 24th to August 31st, 1649."

Fulwood's Rents, commonly called Fuller's Rents, in Holborn, is a narrow-paved court nearly opposite the end of Chancery Lane. It leads into Gray's Inn Walks, Gray's Inn Gardens. Strype, in 1720, describes it thus :—" Fulwood's Rents, opposite to Chancery Lane, runneth up to Gray's Inn, into which it hath an entrance, through the gate ; a place of a good resort, and taken up by coffee-houses, ale-houses, and houses of entertainment, by reason of its vicinity to Gray's Inn. On the east side is a handsome open place, with a free-stone pavement, and better built, and inhabited by private housekeepers. At the upper end of this court is a passage into the Castle Tavern, a house of considerable trade, as is the Golden Griffin Tavern, on the west side, which also hath a passage into Fulwood's Rents."

Here stood " John's," one of the earliest coffee-houses. " When coffee first came in (circ. 1656)," says Aubrey, in his " Lives," " he (Sir Henry Blount) was a great upholder of it, and hath ever since been a constant frequenter of coffee-houses, especially Mr. Farre's, at the Rainbow, by Inner Temple-gate, and lately John's Coffee-house, in Fuller's Rents."

Adjoining Gray's Inn Gate, on the west side, was Squire's Coffee-house, from whence several of the *Spectators* are dated.

Ned Ward, the author of the "London Spy," kept a punch-house within one door of Gray's Inn, and here he died, in the year 1731. This writer, whom, in the course of our rambles through Old London, we have already several times quoted, was of low extraction, and born in Oxfordshire, about 1667. His residence was not always in Fulwood's Rents, for we find him living a while in Gray's Inn, then, for some years after, keeping a public-house in Moorfields, and after that in Clerkenwell. In his last establishment, off Holborn, he would entertain any company who invited him with stories and adventures of the poets and authors he was acquainted with. Pope honoured him with a place in the " Dunciad," but Ward took his revenge, and retorted with some spirit. He died on the 20th of June, 1731, and, on the 27th of the same month, was interred in St. Pancras Churchyard, with one mourning coach for his wife and daughter to attend the hearse, as he had himself directed in a poetical will, written by him on the 24th of June, 1725. Ward is best known by his " London Spy," a coarse production, but, in some respects, a true representation of the metropolitan manners of his day.

The "Castle Tavern," of which Strype makes mention, was kept for many years by Thomas Winter, better known as "Tom Spring," the pugilist, who died here on the 20th of August, 1851.

A curious gabled and projecting house, of the time of James I., stands about the centre of the east side of Fulwood's Rents. A ground-floor room of this house is engraved by Mr. Archer, in his " Vestiges of Old London," and is given by us on page 534. The apartment was entirely panelled with oak, the mantelpiece being carved in the same wood, with caryatides and arched niches ; the ceiling-beams were carved in panels, and the entire room was original, with the exception of the window. On the first floor, a larger room contained another carved mantelpiece, of very florid construction. The front of the house is said to be covered with ornament, now concealed by plaster.

In the " Banquet of Jests " (1639) we find mention made of a tavern near this, called the "Sun :" —"A pleasant fellow, willing to put off a lame horse, rode him from the 'Sunne Tavern,' within Cripplegate, to the 'Sunne' in Holborn, neere the Fuller's Rents ; and the next day offering to sell him in Smithfield, the buyer asking him why he looked so leane, ' Marry, no marvell,' answered he, 'for but yesterday I rid him from sunne to sunne, and never drew bit."

Dr. Johnson, in 1748, lived at the "Golden Anchor," at Holborn Bars.

At the east corner of the Middle Row, Sir James Branscombe kept a lottery-office for forty years, He had been footman to the Earl of Gainsborough, and was knighted when Sheriff of London and Middlesex, in 1806.

The history of lotteries in England is an entertaining one. The earliest English lottery was drawn in 1569. The drawing began on the 11th of January, at the west door of St. Paul's, and continued day and night till the 6th of May. The scheme, which had been announced two years before, shows that the lottery consisted of 40,000 lots, or shares, at 10s. each, and that it comprehended "a great number of good prizes, as well of ready money as of plate, and certain sorts of merchandise." Any profit that might be derived from the scheme was to be devoted to the reparation of harbours and other useful public works. The second lottery, in 1612, was projected to benefit the new colony in Virginia, and there is a tradition that the principal prize—4,000 crowns—was gained by a poor tailor. Down to 1826 (except for a short time following upon an Act of Queen Anne) lotteries continued to be sanctioned by the English Government as a source of revenue. It seems strange, says a popular writer, that so glaringly immoral a project should have been kept up under such auspices so long. The younger people at the present day may be at a loss to believe that, in the days of their fathers, there were large and imposing offices in London, such as this one in Holborn, and pretentious agencies in the provinces, for the sale of lottery-tickets; while flaming advertisements on walls, in new books, and in the public journals, proclaimed the preferableness of such and such "lucky" offices—this one having sold two-sixteenths of the last £20,000 prize, another having sold an entire £30,000 ticket the year before, and so on. It was found possible to persuade the public, or a portion of it, that where a blessing had once lighted, it was the more likely to light again. The competition amongst the lottery-offices was intense. One firm, finding an old woman in the country of the name of Goodluck, gave her £50 a year, on condition she should join them as a nominal partner, for the sake of the attractive effect of her name. In their advertisements each was sedulous to tell how many of the grand prizes had in former years fallen to the lot of persons who had bought at *his* shop.

"The State lottery," Dr. Chambers remarks, "was founded on the simple principle that the State held forth a certain sum, to be repaid by a larger. The transaction was usually managed thus: —The Government gave £10 in prizes for every share taken, on an average. A great many blanks, or of prizes under £10, left, of course, a surplus for the creation of a few magnificent prizes, wherewith to attract the unwary public. Certain firms in the City, known as lottery-office keepers, contracted for the lottery, each taking a certain number of shares; the sum paid by them was always more than £10 per share, and the excess constituted the Government profit. It was customary, for many years, for the contractors to give about £16 to the Government, and then to charge the public from £20 to £22. It was made lawful for the contractors to divide the shares into halves, quarters, eighths, and sixteenths, and they always charged relatively more for these aliquot parts. A man with 30s. to spare could buy a sixteenth, and the contractors made a large portion of their profit out of such customers."

"The Government sometimes paid the prizes in terminable annuities, instead of cash, and the loan system and the lottery system were occasionally combined in a very odd way. Thus, in 1780, every subscriber of £1,000 towards a loan of £2,000,000, at four per cent., received a bonus of four lottery-tickets, the value of each of which was £10, and any one of which might be the fortunate number for a £20,000 or £30,000 prize."

The culminating point in the history of lottery gambling appears to have been the year 1772. The whole town then went crazed on the chance of making large gains by small ventures. There were lottery magazines, lottery tailors and dressmakers; lottery glovers, hat-makers, and tea-dealers; lottery snuff and pig-tail merchants; lottery barbers, who promised, on payment of 3d., to shave you and give you a chance of being paid £10; lottery shoe-blacks; lottery ordinaries, where one might obtain, for 6d., a plate of beef and the chance of winning sixty guineas; lottery oyster-stalls, where 3d. yielded a dozen of oysters and a very distant prospect of five guineas; and, lastly, a sausage-stall, in a blind alley, where you might, by purchasing a farthing's worth of sausages, should the fates prove propitious, gain a bonus of 5s.

The demoralising effect of this state of affairs may be readily imagined. By creating illusive hopes lotteries supplanted steady industry. Shopmen robbed their masters, servant-girls their mistresses, friends borrowed from each other under false pretences, and husbands stinted their wives and children of necessaries—all to raise the means for buying a portion or the whole of a lottery-ticket. There was no exaggeration in the report of a committee of the House of Commons, a considerable time prior to the abolition of lotteries in 1826, which remarked that "the foundation of the lottery is so radically vicious that under no system can it become an efficient source of gain, and yet be divested of the evils and calamities of which it has proved so baneful a source. Idleness, dissipation, and poverty are increased; sacred and confidential trusts are betrayed; domestic comfort is destroyed; madness often created; crimes subjecting the perpetrators to death are committed. No mode of raising money appears so burdensome, pernicious, and unproductive. No species of adventure is known where the chances are so great against the adventurers, none where the infatuation is more powerful, lasting, and destructive. In the lower classes of society the persons engaged are, generally speaking, either immediately or ultimately tempted to their ruin; and there is scarcely any condition of life so destitute and so abandoned but its distresses have not been aggravated by this allurement to gaming."

Amidst all this immoral and unhealthy excitement, however, many incidents occurred which, to read about at least, afford amusement. In 1767, for example, a lady in Holborn had a lottery-ticket presented to her by her husband, and on the Sunday preceding the drawing, her success was prayed for in the parish church—St. Andrew's, most probably—in this form : "The prayers of this congregation are desired for the success of a person engaged in a new undertaking." Possibly she was one of those who followed the lottery-loving clergy who used to defend the appeal to chance by reference to Scripture, urging that "by lot it was determined which of the goats should be offered to Aaron; by lot the land of Canaan was divided; by lot Saul was marked out for the kingdom; by lot Jonah was found to be the cause of the tempest; by lot the apostles filled up the vacant place of Judas." But "the devil can quote Scripture for his purpose."

In the same year (1767) the prize (or a prize) of £20,000 fell to the lot of a tavern-keeper at Abingdon. We are told, in the journals of the time—"The broker who went from town to carry him the news he complimented with £100. All the bells in the place were set a-ringing. He called his neighbours, and promised to assist this one with a capital sum, that one with another. He gave away plenty of liquor, and vowed to lend a poor cobbler money to buy leather to stock his

stall so full that he should not be able to get into it to work; and, lastly, he promised to buy a new coach for the coachman who brought him down the ticket, and to give a set of as good horses as could be bought for money."

The theory of "lucky numbers" attracted great attention in the days of lotteries. When the drawing took place, papers inscribed with as many different numbers as there were shares, or tickets, were placed in a hollow wheel; one of these was drawn out, usually by a Bluecoat boy, and the number was audibly announced. Another Bluecoat boy then drew out of another wheel a paper, representing either a "blank" or a prize for a certain sum of money, and the purchaser of that particular number got nothing or gained a prize accordingly. With a view to getting lucky numbers, one man would select his own age, or the age of his wife; another would select the date of the year, a third a row of odd or of even numbers. Some, in their excitement, dreamt of numbers, and purchased tickets in harmony with their dreams. There is an amusing paper in the *Spectator* (No. 191, October 9, 1711) in which the subject of lucky numbers is dealt with in a strain of pleasant banter. It tells of one man who selected 1711, because it was the year of our Lord; of another who sought for 134, because it constituted the minority on a celebrated bill in the House of Commons; and of a third who selected the number of the beast, 666, on the ground that wicked beings were often lucky. In 1790 a lady bought No. 17090, because it was the nearest *in sound* to 1790, which had been already sold to some other applicant. A story is told of a tradesman who, on one occasion, bought four tickets consecutive in number. He thought it foolish to have them so close together, and took one back to the office to be exchanged. The one thus taken back turned up a £20,000 prize!

The last "State lottery" was drawn in England on the 18th of October, 1826, at Cooper's Hall, Basinghall Street. Public suspicion had, however, by this time been aroused, and, though such numbers turned out to see the last of a long series of legalised swindles as to inconveniently crowd the hall, the lottery-office keepers could not dispose of all the tickets. The abolition of lotteries deprived the Government of a revenue equal to £250,000 or £300,000 per annum.

In Holborn was born the once popular lecturer and poet, George Alexander Stevens, "a man," says the late Mr. J. H. Jesse, "whose misfortunes were only equal to his misconduct—at one time the idol of a Bacchanalian club, and at another the inmate of a gaol; at one time writing a drinking-song, and at another a religious poem. Stevens is now, perhaps, best remembered from his 'Lectures on Heads,' a medley of wit and nonsense, to which no other person but himself could have given the proper effect. The lecture was originally designed for Shuter, who entirely failed in the performance. Stevens, however, no sooner attempted the task himself than it became instantly popular."

At the commencement of his career Stevens attempted the stage, a line of life which he soon abandoned. As an actor his merit was below mediocrity. As a humorous writer he acquired considerable fame, but his life being neither regulated by the rules of virtue nor of prudence, his health was soon impaired, his finances were often at a low ebb, and his person was not unfrequently in durance. His pecuniary position, however, was much improved by his happily conceived lecture, by means of which he soon amassed a large sum of money. After delivering it in England and Scotland, with extraordinary approbation, he visited America, and was well received in all the principal towns. In fact, in the course of a few years he became worth about £10,000; but the greater part of this sum had melted from his hands before his death. He died on the 6th of September, 1784, his mind having for some time previous been in a state of hopeless idiotic ruin.

Stevens is the first instance that can be produced of one man, single-handed, keeping an audience amused for the space of four hours. As he was the inventor of this species of entertainment, it may naturally be inquired by what means it was suggested to him. The first idea of his lecture, it is said, was got at a village, where he was manager of a theatrical company. He met there with a country mechanic, who described the members of the corporation with great force and humour. Upon this idea Stevens improved, and was assisted in making the heads by his friend, who little imagined what a source of profit he had established.

Gerarde, the herbalist, had a large physic-garden in Holborn. The site is uncertain, but we may as well notice it here. He dates his " Herbal" " From my house in London, within the suburbs of London, this first of December, 1597." He mentions in his famous work many rare plants which grew well in the garden behind his house.

Of his botanic garden in Holborn, says Chalmers, "Gerard published a catalogue in 1596, and again in 1599. Of this work scarcely an impression is known to exist, except one in the British Museum, which proved of great use in preparing the 'Hortus Kewensis' of Mr. Aiton, as serving to ascertain the time when many old plants were first culti-

vated. It contains, according to Dr. Pulteney, 1,033 species, or at least supposed such, though many, doubtless, were varieties; and there is an attestation of Lobel subjoined, vouching for his having seen nearly all of them growing and flowering. This was one of the earliest botanic gardens in Europe."

This last statement of Chalmers' is a little of an exaggeration. The fact is, there was a botanic garden in England, at Syon House, the seat of the Duke of Somerset, as early as the beginning of the sixteenth century. It was under the superintendence of Dr. Turner, whom Dr. Pulteney considers as the father of English botany. A great deal of interest seems to have been taken in botany during the reign of Queen Elizabeth, and many new plants were brought into the country. Gerarde mentions Nicholas Lete, a merchant in London, "greatly in love with rare and fair flowers, for which he doth carefully send into Syria, having a servant there at Aleppo, and in many other countries, for which myself and the whole land are much bound unto him." The same author also gives due honour to Sir Walter Raleigh; to Lord Edward Zouch, who, assisted by the celebrated Lobel, brought plants and seeds from Constantinople; and to Lord Hunsdon, Lord High Chamberlain of England, who, he says, "is worthy of triple honour for his care in getting, as also for his care in keeping, such rare and curious things from the farthest parts of the world."

Gerarde was born at Nantwich, in Cheshire, in 1545. He practised surgery in London, and rose to eminence in that profession. After the publication of his ' Herbal," he lived for about ten years, his death taking place in 1607. Many errors have been pointed out in Gerarde's work, but he had the great merit of a practical knowledge of plants, with unbounded zeal and indefatigable perseverance. He contributed greatly to forward the knowledge of plants in England, and his name will be remembered by botanists with esteem, when the utility of his " Herbal" is superseded. " He was patronised," says Pennant, " by several of the first characters of the time. During twenty years he superintended the garden of the great statesman, Lord Burleigh; on his death, he found in Sir Walter Raleigh another patron; and the same in Lord Edward Zouch and Lord Hunsdon, Lord High Treasurer of England. All of those noblemen were much smitten with the useful and agreeable study of botany."

Many districts of London have in past times had the good fortune to be haunted by characters of an original type, and a most interesting volume might be compiled of these metropolitan oddities. At present we shall notice one who used to frequent the region of Holborn, and who has been noticed by the *City Press* in "London Scenes and London People." This was Peter Stokes, known as "the Flying Pieman of Holborn Hill." He is thus described, dressed in all the finery of an old-fashioned costume, by Mr. Harvey, writing in 1863 :—" When I was a youngster, the steep road-way from Hatton Garden to Fleet Market was

tray or board, just large enough to receive an appetite-provoking pudding, about three inches thick. This was divided into twelve slices, which he sold at a penny a slice. A broad blunt spatula, brilliantly bright, which he carried in his left hand, enabled him to dispense his sweets without ever touching them. His countenance was open and agreeable, expressive of intellect and moral excellence."

And about this man, engaged in such a humble

OLD HOUSES IN HOLBORN, OPPOSITE GRAY'S INN ROAD. (*See page* 527.)

highly attractive to me on account of the 'Flying Pieman,' though he did not vend pies, but a kind of baked plum-pudding, which he offered smoking hot. He was a slim, active, middle-sized man, about forty years old. He always wore a black suit, scrupulously brushed, dress-coat and vest, knee-breeches, stout black silk stockings, and shoes with steel buckles, then rather fashionable. His shirt, remarkably well got up, had a wide frill, surmounted by a spotless white cravat. He never wore either hat or cap; his hair, cropped very close, was plentifully powdered, and he was decorated with a delicate lawn apron, which hardly reached to his knees. In his right hand he held a small circular

trade, shone the light of a somewhat romantic history. He was by profession a painter, and, it was believed, possessed considerable talent. When he was a very young man he married, "all for love." His practice as an artist did not keep pace with the growing wants of a small family, and at last, with an eccentricity which, in the circumstances, may be pardoned, he determined to begin a street-trade on Holborn Hill, and conducted this business for many a day. From twelve to four o'clock he was to be seen shouting, "Buy, buy, buy!" as he moved to and fro, from Fetter Lane to Ely Place, thence to Thavies Inn ·or to Field Lane, Hatton Garden or Fleet Market, rapidly getting rid of his tempting wares. After four o'clock he betook himself to genteel lodgings in Rathbone Place, where Stokes was himself again, resumed his palette and easel, and found sitters increase as his means made them less necessary, for the street business proved a money-making one.

Peter Stokes' history recalls that of a remarkable hawker of savoury patties, who might be con-

teenth century," writes Dr. Robert Chambers, "the bellman was the recognised term for what we would now call a night watchman, being derived from the handbell which the man carried in order to give alarm in case of fire. In the Luttrell Collection of Broadsides (British Museum) is one dated 1683–4, entitled, 'A Copy of Verses presented by Isaac Ragg, Bellman, to his Masters and Mistresses of Holbourn Division, in the Parish of St. Giles-in-the-

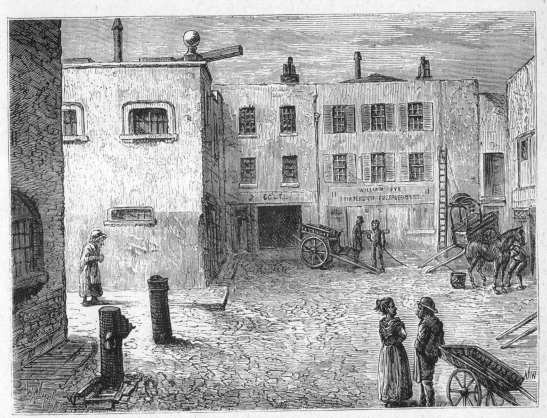

BLEEDING HEART YARD. (*See page* 544.)

stantly seen in the streets of Paris, during the earlier years of Louis XVI. He was of higher origin than our London "Flying Pieman," however, but reckless extravagance had reduced him to poverty while he was yet in the prime of life. His dress was fastidiously elegant, and while standing, basket in hand, on the steps of the Palais Royal, he wore round his neck the decoration of St. Croix. Sterne had seen him, and declares that his manners and address were those of a man of high rank.

Let us now speak about another character of this neighbourhood, namely, an old bellman of Holborn, and take the opportunity of saying a few words about bellmen in general. "In London, and probably in other English cities in the seven-

Fields.' It is headed by a woodcut representing Isaac in professional accoutrements—a pointed pole in the left hand, and in the right a bell, while his lantern hangs from his jacket in front. Below is a series of verses on St. Andrew's Day, King Charles the First's birthday, St. Thomas's Day, Christmas Day, St. John's Day, Childermas Day, New Year's Day, the 13th of January, &c., all of them being very proper, and very insufferable. The 'prologue' indeed is the only specimen worth giving, being the expression of Mr. Ragg's official duty. It runs as follows:—

'Time, master, calls your bellman to his task,
　To see your doors and windows all are fast,
　And that no villany or foul crime be done
　To you or yours in absence of the sun.

If any base lurker I do meet,
In private alley or in open street,
You shall have warning by my timely call ;
And so, God bless you, and give rest to all.'"

One of our Holborn bellman's professional brethren, Thomas Law, issued a similar but un- adorned broadside in 1666, which has had the good fortune to be preserved for our enlighten- ment. In it he greets his masters of " St. Giles, Cripplegate, within the Freedom," in no less than twenty-three dull stanzas, of which the last may be given here :—

"No sooner hath St. Andrew crowned November,
 But Boreas from the north brings cold December ;
 And I have often heard a many say
 He brings the winter month Newcastle way :
 For comfort here of poor distressed souls
 Would he had with him brought a fleet of coals."

At a fixed season of the year—most often, no doubt, Christmas—it seems to have been customary for the bellman to distribute copies of his broadside through the district of which he had the charge, expecting his masters to favour him in return with some small gratuity. The execrable character which usually belonged to these rhymed produc- tions is shown by the contempt with which the wits used to speak of " bellman's verses."

Robert Herrick has a little poem in which he wishes good luck to his friends in the form of the nightly addresses of the bellman. Like all Herrick's productions, it is daintily musical. With its good wishes applied to the reader, we shall leave him for the present, and conclude this chapter :—

" From noise of scare fires rest ye free,
  From murders benedicite ;
  From all mischances that may fright
  Your pleasing slumbers in the night ;
  Mercie secure ye all, and keep
  The goblin from ye, while ye sleep.
  Past one o'clock, and almost two :
  My masters all, ' good-day to you !' "

CHAPTER LX.

THE NORTHERN TRIBUTARIES OF HOLBORN.

Field Lane—A Description by Dickens—Saffron Hill—Old Chick Lane—Thieves' Hiding Places—Hatton Garden—A Dramatist's Wooing— The Celebrated Dr. Bate—Charles Street—Bleeding Heart Yard—Love or Murder—Leather Lane—George Morland, the Painter— Robbing One's Own House—Brooke Street—The Poet Chatterton—His Life in London, and his Death—The Great Lord Hardwicke— A Hard-working Apprenticeship—A Start in Life—Offices of the Prudential Assurance Company—Greville Street—Lord Brooke's Murder— A Patron of Learning—Gray's Inn Road—Tom Jones's Arrival in Town—"Your Money or Your Life"—Poets of Gray's Inn Road—James Shirley, the Dramatist—John Ogilby—John Langhorne—The " Blue Lion "—Fox Court—The Unfortunate Richard Savage.

IN speaking of the tributary streams of human activity which flow into Holborn from the north, we shall begin a little to the east of Ely Place, and mention one which has lately been improved out of existence, namely, Field Lane. Field Lane, extending from the foot of Holborn Hill north- ward, and in this way lying parallel with Fleet Ditch, used to be an infamous haunt of the " dan- gerous classes." Now, its site, entered off Charter- house Street, may be visited by the inquiring stranger with somewhat of a feeling of disappoint- ment that respectability is not half so picturesque as its opposite. In 1837, Field Lane was vividly sketched by Charles Dickens, in his " Oliver Twist." " Near to the spot," he says, " on which Snow Hill and Holborn meet, there opens, upon the right hand as you come out of the City, a narrow and dismal alley, leading to Saffron Hill. In its filthy shops are exposed for sale huge bunches of pocket-handkerchiefs of all sizes and patterns, for here reside the traders who purchase them from pickpockets. Hundreds of these hand- kerchiefs hang dangling from pegs outside the windows or flaunting from the door-posts, and the shelves within are piled with them. Confined as the limits of Field Lane are, it has its barber, its coffee-shop, its beer-shop, and its fried fish ware- house. It is a commercial colony of itself—the emporium of petty larceny, visited at early morning and setting-in of dusk by silent merchants, who traffic in dark back parlours and go as strangely as they come. Here the clothes-man, the shoe- vamper, and the rag-merchant, display their goods as sign-boards to the petty thief, and stores of old iron and bones, and heaps of mildewy fragments of woollen-stuff and linen, rust and rot in the grimy cellars."

Northward from Field Lane ran Saffron Hill, which once formed a part of the pleasant gardens of Ely Place, and derived its name from the crops of saffron which it bore. But the saffron disappeared, and in time there grew up a squalid neighbour- hood, swarming with poor people and thieves. Strype, in 1720, describes the locality as " of small account both as to buildings and inhabitants, and pestered with small and ordinary alleys and courts taken up by the meaner sort of people; others are," he says, "nasty and inconsiderable." Saffron Hill ran from Field Lane into Vine Street, in which we have a name recalling the vineyard of old Ely Palace. Cunningham (1849) mentions that so dangerous was this neighbourhood in his day that when the clergy of St. Andrew's, Holborn (the parish in which the purlieu lies), visited it, they had to be accompanied by policemen in plain clothes.

Old Chick Lane debouched into Field Lane. The beginning of its destruction was in 1844. The notorious thieves' lodging-house here, formerly the "Red Lion" tavern, we have already noticed. It had various cunning contrivances for enabling its inmates to escape from the pursuit of justice. Fleet Ditch lay in the rear, and across it by a plank the hunted vagabonds often ran to conceal themselves in the opposite knot of courts and alleys.

Moving westward, we come to Hatton Garden— so called after the Sir Christopher Hatton whom we have already met as Lord Chancellor in Elizabeth's reign, and after "Christopher Hatton, his godson, son of John Hatton, cousin and heir-male of the celebrated Sir Christopher Hatton, created Baron Hatton of Kirby, in the county of Northampton, July 29th, 1643, and died 1670."

Strype describes Hatton Garden as "a very large place, containing several streets—viz., Hatton Street, Charles Street, Cross Street, and Kirby Street, all which large tract of ground was a garden, and belonged to Hatton House, now pulled down, and built into houses."

We get a glimpse of active building operations going on here in the middle of the seventeenth century, in Evelyn's "Diary:"—"7th June, 1659. To London to take leave of my brother, and see the foundations now laying for a long streete and buildings in Hatton Garden, designed for a little towne, lately an ample garden."

In Dennis's "Letters," 1721, we come upon a passage relating to an almost-forgotten poet and playwright who, on matrimonial thoughts intent, once haunted this locality. "Mr. Wycherly visited her [the Countess of Drogheda] daily at her lodgings, while she stayed at Tunbridge, and after she went to London, at her lodgings in Hatton Garden, where, in a little time, he got her consent to marry her." This is part of a romantic story told in Cibber's "Lives of the Poets," in repeating which we must begin by informing the reader that one of Wycherly's most successful plays was entitled *The Plain Dealer*. The writer went down to Tunbridge, to take either the benefit of the waters or the diversions of the place, and when walking one day upon the Wells Walk with his friend Mr. Fair-

beard, of Gray's Inn, just as he came up to the bookseller's, the Countess of Drogheda, a young widow, rich and beautiful, came to the bookseller and inquired for *The Plain Dealer*. "Madam," says Mr. Fairbeard, "since you are for *The Plain Dealer*, there he is for you," pushing Mr. Wycherley towards her. "Yes," says Mr. Wycherley, "this lady can bear plain dealing, for she appears to be so accomplished, that what would be a compliment to others, when said to her would be plain dealing." "No, truly, sir," said the lady; "I am not without my faults, like the rest of my sex; and yet, notwithstanding all my faults, I love plain dealing, and never am more fond of it than when it tells me of a fault." "Then, madam," says Mr. Fairbeard, "you and 'The Plain Dealer' seem designed by Heaven for each other."

The upshot of the affair was that Mr. Wycherley accompanied the countess on her walks, waited on her home, visited her daily at her lodgings, followed her to town, and, as we have seen, at Hatton Garden brought his wooing to a successful close.

A gallant beginning should have a good ending. But it was not so here: the lady proved unreasonably jealous, and led the poor poet a sad life. Even from a pecuniary point of view he made a bad bargain of his marriage, for after her death her bequest to him was disputed at law, and, drowned in debt, he was immured in a gaol for seven years.

The celebrated physician, Dr. George Bate, who attended Oliver Cromwell in his last illness, died in Hatton Garden in 1668. He was born in 1608 at Maid's Morton, near Buckingham. He rose to great eminence in his profession, and when King Charles kept his court at Oxford, was his principal physician there. When the king's affairs declined, he removed to London, and adapted himself so well to the changed times that he became chief physician to the Lord Protector, whom he is said to have highly flattered. Upon the restoration he got into favour again with the royal party, and was made principal physician to Charles II., and Fellow of the Royal Society. This, we are told, was owing to a report, raised on very slender foundation, and asserted only by his friends, that he gave Cromwell a dose of poison which hastened his death.

Charles Street, which intersects Hatton Garden, is interesting as that in which Joseph Strutt, the antiquarian writer, died, on the 16th of October, 1802. We have already given some particulars regarding him, when speaking of St. Andrew's Churchyard, in which he was buried. There is a public-house of the name of the "Bleeding Heart" in this street. This is a sign dating from before the Reformation. It is the emblematical representation of the five sorrowful mysteries of the Rosary—viz., the heart of the Holy Virgin pierced with five swords. Bleeding Heart Yard, adjoining the public-house in Charles Street, is immortalised by Charles Dickens in " Little Dorrit."

Bleeding Heart Yard, says the novelist, "was a place much changed in feature and fortune, yet with some relish of ancient greatness about it. Two or three mighty stacks of chimneys, and a few large dark rooms, which had escaped being walled and subdivided out of the recognition of their old pro-portions, gave the yard a character. It was in-habited by poor people, who set up their rest among its faded glories as Arabs of the desert pitch their tents among the fallen stones of the Pyramids; but there was a family sentimental feeling prevalent in the yard, that it had a character. . . . . .

" The opinion of the Yard was divided re-specting the derivation of its name. The more practical of its inmates abided by the tradition of a murder; the gentler and more imaginative inhabi-tants, including the whole of the tender sex, were loyal to the legend of a young lady of former time closely imprisoned in her chamber by a cruel father for remaining true to her own true love, and refusing to marry the suitor he chose for her. The legend related how that the young lady used to be seen up at her window, behind the bars, murmuring a love-lorn song, of which the burden was 'Bleeding Heart, Bleeding Heart, bleeding away,' until she died. It was objected by the murderous party that this refrain was notoriously the invention of a tambour-worker, a spinster, and romantic, still lodging in the yard. But forasmuch as all favourite legends must be associated with the affections, and as many more people fall in love than commit murder—which, it may be hoped, howsoever bad we are, will continue until the end of the world to be the dispensation under which we live—the Bleeding-Heart, Bleeding-Heart, bleeding-away story, carried the day by a large majority. Neither party would listen to the antiquaries, who delivered learned lectures in the neighbourhood showing the bleeding heart to have been the heraldic cognisance of the old family to whom the property once be-longed. And considering that the hour-glass they turned from year to year was filled with the earthiest and coarsest sand, the Bleeding Heart Yarders had reason enough for objecting to be despoiled of the one little golden grain of poetry that sparkled in it."

The next Holborn tributary to be mentioned is Leather Lane, which runs from Holborn to Liquor-pond Street. "Then, higher up," says Stow, "is Lither Lane, turning also to the field, lately re-plenished with houses built, and so to the bar."

Strype, describing it in his own time, says, "The east side of this lane is best built, having all brick houses. . . . . In this lane is 'White Heart Inn,' 'Nag's Head Inn,' and 'King's Head Inn '—all indifferent."

Following Leather Lane northwards, we come to Eyre Street. It is too far removed from our main thoroughfare to be mentioned without an excuse. We make the excuse, however, for the sake of the eminent artist who breathed his last here. Here, in 1804, died George Morland, the celebrated painter. It was in a sponging-house. He had been taken in execution by a publican, for a debt amounting, with costs, to about ten pounds, and was conveyed to this place in Eyre Street Hill, overwhelmed with misfortune, debt, and neglect; every evil being aggravated by the bitterness of self-reproach.

"In this state of desperation," says his bio-grapher, "he drank great quantities of spirits, and more than once attempted to resume the exercise of those talents which hitherto had never failed to procure him the means of relief; but the period was arrived when even that resource failed him, for the next morning he dropped off his chair in a fit, while sketching a bank and a tree in a drawing. This proved to be the commencement of a brain fever; after which he never spoke intelligibly, but remained eight days delirious and convulsed, in a state of utter mental and bodily debility, and expired the 29th of October, 1804, in the forty-second year of his age.

With regard to the works of this unfortunate and dissipated artist, justly entitled to the appellation of " the English Teniers," it is certain that they will be esteemed so long as any taste for art remains in the kingdom. Even his ordinary productions will give pleasure to all who are charmed with an accu-rate representation of nature. His command over the implements of his profession was very great, so great, indeed, that the use of them became to him a second nature. Thus pictures flowed from his pencil with the most astonishing rapidity, and without that patience and industry which works even of inferior merit so often require. While he was in the prime of life, with a constitution unim-paired, his chief efforts were in picturesque land-scape, in which every circumstance was represented with the utmost accuracy and spirit; and it is such subjects as these, to which he devoted his attention for about seven years, that have secured him an im-perishable reputation. In such pieces, the figures he introduced were of the lowest order, but they retained a consistency appropriate to the surround-ings. When, from increasing depravity of manners, he left the green woodside, and became the constant inmate of the alehouse, his subjects were of a meaner cast, for he only painted what he saw. "In portraying drovers, stage-coachmen, postilions, and labourers of all descriptions," says Mr. F. W. Blagdon, "he shone in full glory; and his favourite animals, the ass, the sheep, and the hog, were represented with an accuracy peculiar to himself, though with a deficiency of that correctness which is requisite to form a *finished* picture; because a few strokes will represent a *picturesque* character, while beauty of form can only arise from repeated comparisons with and amendments from viewing the object delineated. Morland, however, made his sketches at once, and finished them from recollection, and hence his pictures afford the finest specimens of Nature in her roughest state, but nothing that in point of form can be called beautiful: it has even been said, though with what truth I cannot pretend to determine, that he was never able to draw a beautiful horse, like those delineated by Stubbs or Gilpin. But it will never be disputed that as a painter of old, rugged, and working cattle, together with all the localities of a farm-yard or stable, his equal does not, nor ever did, exist."

He was much given to mischievous amusement, and was fond of making a disturbance in the night, and alarming his neighbours. A frolic of this sort had nearly cost him dear:—Whilst living at Lambeth, he, with the assistance of a drunken companion, actually broke open his own house, and enjoyed beyond description the alarm it occasioned his family, some relations being at the time with him on a visit. He was at length taken up by some persons who witnessed the transaction, when it turned out that he had apprised the watchman of his intentions, and even bribed him to assist.

Brooke Street, Holborn, is familiar enough to the general public as leading to the church of St. Alban's—a church which, for its Ritualistic services, has been of late somewhat prominently before the world. Few, however, of those who pass up and down its well-trodden pavement are aware of the interesting memories which belong to the neighbourhood.

In a lodging in Brooke Street, on the 24th of August, 1770, the marvellous boy, Chatterton, put an end to his life by swallowing arsenic in water. The house was then in the occupation of a Mrs. Angel, a sackmaker. Nearly all the western side of the street was pulled down in 1880 for the purpose of being re-built on an improved scale.

With Chatterton's career in Bristol—where he was born on the 20th November, 1752—with his Rowley forgeries, with his communications with Horace

Walpole, and the discovery of their spurious nature, we shall not meddle at present. But we may profitably spend a short time here in speaking of his life from the time of his arrival in the great metropolis till his sad end. Dissatisfied with Bristol, and feeling certain that in London his talent would be duly honoured, he came here about the end of April, 1770. To his correspondents he boasted that he had had three distinct resources to trust to: one was to write, another was to turn Methodist parson, and the last was to shoot himself. The last resource, unfortunately, is in everybody's power. A friendly group saw him start; he arrived in town, and settled first in lodgings in Shoreditch, but afterwards removed to the above-mentioned address in Brooke Street. For the space of four months he struggled against fate, but the records we have of his doings are obscure and untrustworthy. It is true he sent flaming accounts to friends in Bristol of his rising importance; that he found money to purchase and transmit to his mother and sister useless articles of finery; and also that he did his best to form profitable connections: it may well be doubted, however, whether any large amount of success or remuneration rewarded his extraordinary efforts.

His first literary attempts were of a political kind, and he contrived to write on both sides of the question. He also produced numerous articles of a miscellaneous kind in prose and verse. At one time he seemed in a fair way for fortune, for Lord Mayor Beckford encouraged him, and accepted of the dedication of an essay; but before the essay could appear, Beckford died. He made a profit, however, on the Lord Mayor's death, and wrote down on the back of a MS., "I am glad he is dead, by £3 13s. 6d." Wilkes also took notice of him, but, likely enough, he was more ready with his praise than with his money.

At length, work failed the unfortunate poet, and he began to starve; his literary pursuits were abandoned, and he projected to go out to Africa as a naval surgeon's mate. He had picked up some knowledge of surgery from Mr. Barrett, the historian of Bristol, and now requested that gentleman's recommendation; but he thought proper to refuse. The short remainder of his days was spent in a conflict between pride and poverty.

"Mrs. Angel," says Dix, in his "Life of Chatterton," "stated that for two days, when he did not absent himself from his room, he went without sustenance of any kind. On one occasion, when she knew him to be in want of food, she begged he would take a little dinner with her; he was offended at the invitation, and assured her he was not hungry.	Mr. Cross also, an apothecary in Brooke Street, gave evidence that he repeatedly pressed Chatterton to dine or sup with him, and when, with great difficulty, he was one evening prevailed on to

burial-ground, as mentioned by us already (Vol. I., p. 134); but there is a story, also related by us elsewhere, to which some credit may perhaps be given, that his body was removed to Bristol, and secretly

LEATHER LANE.	(*See page* 544.)

partake of a barrel of oysters, he was observed to eat most voraciously."

When he was found lying on his bed, stiff and cold, on the 25th of August, there were remains of arsenic between his teeth. Previous to committing suicide, he seems to have destroyed all his manuscripts; for when his room was broken open, it was found littered with little scraps of paper.

He was interred, after the inquest, in a pauper's

stowed away in the churchyard of St. Mary Redcliffe. "There can be no more decisive proof," says Mr. Chalmers, " of the little regard he attracted in London, than the secrecy and silence which accompanied his death. This event, though so extraordinary—for young suicides are surely not common —is not even mentioned in any shape in the *Gentleman's Magazine*, the *Annual Register*, *St. James's* or *London Chronicles*, nor in any of the respectable publications of the day." And so perished in destitution, obscurity, and despair, one who, under happier circumstances, might have ranked among the first of his generation.

Of the house in which the poet terminated his strange career, Mr. Hotten, in his "Adversaria,"

as in 1770; for the walls were old and dilapidated, and the flooring decayed. It was a square and rather large room for an attic. It had two windows in it—lattice windows, or casements—built in a style which I think is called 'Dormer.' Outside ran the gutter, with a low parapet wall, over which

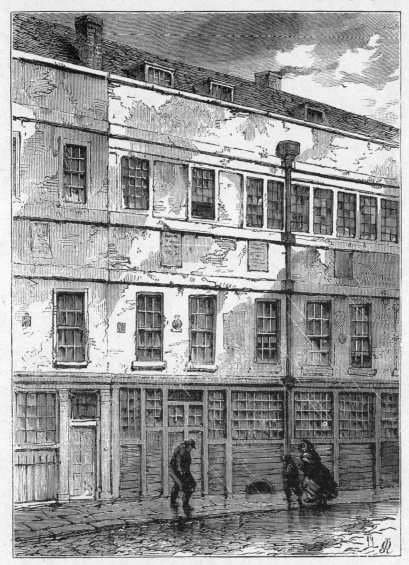

CHATTERTON'S HOUSE IN BROOKE STREET. (*See page* 545.)

gives some interesting reminiscences. At the date of Mr. Hotten's writing, the house was occupied by a plumber, of the name of Jefford. "We know," he says, "from the account of Sir Herbert Croft, that Chatterton occupied the garret—a room looking out into the street, as the only garret in this house does. I remember this room very well as it was twenty-six years ago, soon after which the occupier made some alterations in it. It must then have been substantially in the same condition

you could look into the street below. The roof was very low—so low that I, who am not a tall man, could hardly stand upright in it with my hat on; and it had a very long slope, extending from the middle of the room down to the windows. It is a curious fact that, in the well-known picture (the 'Death of Chatterton,' by Wallis) exhibited at Manchester, St. Paul's is visible through the window; I say a singular fact, because, although this is strictly in accordance with the truth, as now known, the story previously believed was that the house was opposite, where no room looking into the street could have commanded a view of St. Paul's. This, however, could only have been a lucky accident of the painter's. About the time I have mentioned, the tenant divided the garret into two with a partition, carried the roof up, making it horizontal, and made some other alterations which have gone far to destroy the identity of the room. It is a singular coincidence, seeing the connection between the names of Walpole and Chatterton, that my friend, Mrs. Jefford, the wife of the now occupier, who has resided there more than twenty years, was for some years in the service of Horace Walpole, afterwards Lord Orford. She is a very old lady, and remembers Lord Orford well, having entered his family as a girl, and continued in it till he died, near the end of the last century."

The epitaph adopted for Chatterton's monument in Bristol was one written by himself; and with it we leave him, to pass on to a happier subject :—

To the Memory of
THOMAS CHATTERTON.
Reader, judge not ; if thou art a Christian,
believe that he shall be judged by
a superior Power ; to that Power
alone he is answerable.

Philip Yorke, the great Lord Chancellor Hardwicke (born 1690), was articled, without a fee, it is said, to an attorney named Salkeld, in Brooke Street. It was rather against the wish of his mother, who was a rigid Presbyterian. She expressed a strong wish, " that Philip should be put apprentice to some ' honester trade ; ' " and sometimes she declared her ambition to be that " she might see his head wag in the pulpit." However, an offer having been made by Mr. Salkeld, she withdrew her objections, and Philip was transferred to the metroplis, to exhibit " a rare instance of great natural abilities, joined with an early resolution to rise in the world, and aided by singular good luck." He had received an imperfect education—his family being in narrow circumstances—and whilst applying to business here with the most extraordinary assiduity, he employed every leisure moment in endeavouring to supply the defects of his early training. "All lawyer's clerks," says Lord Campbell, in his " Lives of the Lord Chancellors," " were then obliged, in a certain degree, to understand Latin, in which many law proceedings were carried on ; but he, not content with being able to construe the ' chirograph of a fine,'* or to draw a

' Nar,' * took delight in perusing Virgil and Cicero, and made himself well acquainted with the other more popular Roman classics, though he never mastered the minutiæ of Latin prosody, and, for fear of a false quantity, ventured with fear and trembling on a Latin quotation. Greek he hardly affected to be acquainted with."

By these means he gained the entire good-will and esteem of his master, who, observing in him abilities and application that prognosticated his future eminence, entered him as a student in the Temple, and suffered him to dine in the Hall during the terms. But his mistress, a notable woman, thinking she might take some liberties with a gratis clerk, used frequently to send him from his business on family errands, and to fetch in little necessaries from Covent Garden and other markets. This, when he became a favourite with his master, and entrusted with his business and cash, he thought an indignity, and got rid of it by a stratagem which prevented complaints or expostulation. In his accounts with his master there frequently occurred " Coach hire for roots of celery and turnips from Covent Garden, and a barrel of oysters from the fishmonger's, &c." This Mr. Salkeld observed, and urging on his wife the impropriety and ill housewifery of such a practice, put an end to it.

There were at that time in Mr. Salkeld's office several young gentlemen of good family and connections, who had been sent there to be initiated in the practical part of the law. With these Philip Yorke, though an articled clerk, associated on terms of perfect equality, and they had the merit of discovering and encouraging his good qualities.

" But the young man," continues Lord Campbell, " still had to struggle with many difficulties, and he would probably have been obliged, from penury, to go upon the roll of attorneys, rising only to be clerk to the magistrates at petty sessions, or, perhaps, to the dignity of town clerk of Dover, had it not been for his accidental introduction to Lord Chief Justice Parker, which was the foundation of all his prosperity and greatness. This distinguished judge had a high opinion of Mr. Salkeld, who was respected by all ranks of the profession, and asked him one day if he could tell him of a decent and intelligent person who might assist as a sort of law-tutor for his sons—to assist and direct them in their professional studies. The attorney eagerly recommended his clerk, Philip Yorke, who was immediately retained in that capacity, and, giving the highest satisfaction by his assiduity and his

---

* The record of a fictitious suit, resorted to for the purpose of docking estates tail, and quieting the title to lands.

* Familiar contraction of Narratio, the " Declaration " or Statement of the plaintiff's grievance, or cause of action.

obliging manners, gained the warm friendship of the sons, and the weighty, persevering, and unscrupulous patronage of the father." In Brooke Street

> " Three years he sat his smoky room in,
> Pens, paper, ink, and pounce consumin' ; "

but he now bade adieu to that legal haunt, and had a commodious chamber assigned him in Lincoln's Inn Fields. Released from the drudgery, not only of going to Covent Garden Market, but of attending captions and serving process, he devoted himself with fresh vigour to the abstruse parts of the law, and to his more liberal studies. He rose, by gradual steps, to the Lord Chancellorship, an office which he held for twenty years. His reputation as a judge was very high ; during his Chancellorship not one of his decisions was set aside, and only three were tried on appeal.

At the corner of Brooke Street and Holborn, and occupying part of the site of old Brooke House, is the new office of the Prudential Assurance Company, a lofty and imposing edifice of red brick, built from the designs of Mr. Alfred Waterhouse, A.R.A. The style of architecture is a modification of the Gothic ; the noble pile of buildings rise to a height of 117 feet from the level of the street, and the area of the entire site is 30,000 square feet. Both externally and internally the two great objects of the architect seem to have been a judicious combination of elegance and convenience ; the building conveying the impression of a baronial castle or the hall of one of our wealthy city guilds, and at the same time being well adapted to the discharge of a large commercial undertaking.

Greville Street, running off Brooke Street, as well as Brooke Street itself, derives its name from Fulke Greville, Lord Brooke, "servant to Queen Elizabeth, counsellor to King James, and friend to Sir Philip Sidney." Brooke House was subsequently known as Warwick House, and stood, according to Mr. Cunningham, where Greville Street now stands.

It was in Brooke House that, on the 1st of September, 1628, Lord Brooke met with his tragical fate. He had been attended for many years by one Ralph Haywood, a gentleman by birth, who thought that the least his master could do for him would be to reward his long services by bequeathing him a handsome legacy. It fell out, however, that Lord Brooke not only omitted Haywood's name from his will, but unfortunately allowed him to become cognisant of the fact. Irritated at this, and, besides, at having been sharply reprimanded for some real or imaginary offence, Haywood determined to have his revenge. He entered Lord Brooke's chamber, had a violent dispute with him, and ended by stabbing him in the back. The assassin then retreated to his own apartment, locked himself in, and committed suicide, killing himself by the same weapon with which he had stabbed his master. Lord Brooke survived only a few days.

Lord Brooke was born at Beauchamp Court, in Warwickshire, in 1554, and was educated at Oxford. Upon his return to England, after a Continental tour to finish his education, he was introduced to the Court of Elizabeth by his uncle, Robert Greville. He speedily became a favourite with the Queen, though he did not fail to experience some of the capriciousness, as well as many of the delights, of royal favour. He and Sir Philip Sidney became fast friends, and when, in 1586, the latter unfortunately closed his earthly career, he left Lord Brooke (then simply Mr. Greville) one-half of his books. The reign of James I. opened happily for him. At the king's coronation he was made K.B., and an office which he held, in connection with the Council of the Court of Marches of Wales, was confirmed to him for life. In the second year of James I., he obtained a grant of Warwick Castle. This seems to have gratified him exceedingly ; and the castle being in a ruinous condition, he laid out £20,000 in repairing it. He afterwards occupied the posts of Under-Treasurer and Chancellor of the Exchequer, and Lord of the King's Bedchamber. On the death of King James, he continued in the privy council of Charles I., in the beginning of whose reign he founded a history lecture in the University of Cambridge, and endowed it with a salary of £100 a year. He did not long survive this last act of generosity ; for though he was a munificent patron of learning and learned men, he at last fell a victim to the extraordinary outrage, as we have seen, of a discontented domestic.

He was the author of several works ; but it is for his generosity to more successful authors than himself that he is chiefly to be remembered. "He made Sir Philip Sidney, his dear friend," says Chalmers, "the great exemplar of his life in everything ; and Sidney being often celebrated as the patron of the Muses in general, so, we are told, Lord Brooke desired to be known to posterity under no other character than that of Shakespeare's and Ben Jonson's master ; Lord Chancellor Egerton and Bishop Overall's patron. His lordship also obtained the office of Clarencieux-at-Arms for Mr. Camden, who very gratefully acknowledged it in his lifetime, and at his death left him a piece of plate in his will. He also raised John Speed from a mechanic to be an historiographer." His kindness to Sir William Davenant must also be mentioned.

He took a fancy to that poet when he was very young, and received him into his family, and it is quite likely that the plan of the earlier plays of Davenant was formed in Brooke House; they were published shortly after Lord Brooke's death.

Gray's 'Inn Road (formerly known as Gray's Inn Lane) is the last northern tributary we have to mention. It derives its name from the adjacent inn of court. "This lane," says Stow, "is furnished with fair buildings, and many tenements on both the sides leading to the fields towards Highgate and Hampstead."

To the novel-reader Gray's Inn Road will be always interesting. Tom Jones entered the great metropolis by its narrow, dingy thoroughfare, on his way to put up at the "Bull and Gate," in Holborn. Jones, as well as Partridge, his companion, writes Fielding, "was an entire stranger in London; and as he happened to arrive first in a quarter of the town the inhabitants of which have very little intercourse with the householders of Hanover or Grosvenor Square (for he entered through Gray's Inn Lane), so he rambled about some time before he could even find his way to those happy mansions where fortune segregates from the vulgar those magnanimous heroes, the descendants of ancient Britons, Saxons, or Danes, whose ancestors, being born in better days, by sundry kinds of merit have entailed riches and honour on their posterity."

It was there he hoped to find Sophia Western, but "after a successless inquiry, till the clock had struck eleven, Jones at length yielded to the advice of Partridge, and retreated to the 'Bull and Gate,' in Holborn, that being the inn where he had first alighted, and where he retired to enjoy that kind of repose which usually attends persons in his circumstances"—the unquiet sleep that lovers have.

We can picture to ourselves the excitement with which Fielding's hero and his companion first rode down Gray's Inn Road. They had, an hour or two before, had an adventure with a highwayman, an adventure told by the novelist in his chapter on "What happened to Mr. Jones on his Journey from St. Albans," and which we shall repeat here for the benefit of those who, though perhaps on nodding acquaintance with the "Foundling," have not yet had leisure to listen to all his long history. "They were got about two miles beyond Barnet, and it was now the dusk of the evening, when a genteel-looking man, but upon a very shabby horse, rode up to Jones, and asked him whether he was going to London, to which Jones answered in the affirmative. The gentleman replied, 'I shall be obliged to you, sir, if you will accept of my com-

pany; for it is very late, and I am a stranger to the road.' Jones readily complied with the request, and on they travelled together, holding that sort of discourse which is usual on such occasions. Of this, indeed, robbery was the principal topic; upon which subject the stranger expressed great apprehensions; but Jones declared he had very little to lose, and consequently as little to fear. Here Partridge could not forbear putting in his word. 'Your honour,' said he, 'may think it a little, but I am sure if I had a hundred pound bank-note in my pocket as you have, I should be very sorry to lose it. But, for my part, I was never less afraid in my life; for we are four of us"—the guide made the fourth of the party—"and if we all stand by one another, the best man in England can't rob us. Suppose he should have a pistol, he can kill but one of us, and a man can die but once; that's my comfort—a man can die but once.'

"Besides the reliance on superior numbers—a kind of valour which hath raised a certain nation among the moderns to a high pitch of glory—there was another reason for the extraordinary courage which Partridge now discovered, for he had at present as much of that quality as was in the power of liquor to bestow.

"Our company were now arrived within a mile of Highgate, when the stranger turned short upon Jones, and pulling out a pistol, demanded that little bank-note which Partridge had mentioned.

"Jones was at first somewhat shocked at this unexpected demand; however, he presently recollected himself, and told the highwayman all the money he had in his pocket was entirely at his service; and so saying, he pulled out upwards of three guineas, and offered to deliver it, but the other answered, with an oath, that would not do. Jones answered, coolly, he was very sorry for it, and returned the money into his pocket.

"The highwayman then threatened, if he did not deliver the bank-note that moment, he must shoot him; holding the pistol at the same time very near to his breast. Jones instantly caught hold of the fellow's hand, which trembled so that he could scarce hold the pistol in it, and turned the muzzle from him. A struggle then ensued, in which the former wrested the pistol from the hands of his antagonist, and both came from their horses on the ground together—the highwayman on his back, the victorious Jones upon him.

"The poor fellow now began to implore mercy of the conqueror, for, to say the truth, he was in strength by no means a match for Jones. 'Indeed, sir,' says he, 'I could have no intention to shoot you, for you will find the pistol was not loaded. This is the first robbery I ever attempted, and I have been driven by distress to this.'

"At this instant, about one hundred and fifty yards distant, lay another person on the ground, roaring for mercy in a much louder voice than the highwayman. This was no other than Partridge himself, who, endeavouring to make his escape from the engagement, had been thrown from his horse, and lay flat on his face, not daring to look up, and expecting every minute to be shot.

"In this posture he lay till the guide, who was no otherwise concerned than for his horse, having secured the stumbling beast, came up to him, and told him his master had got the better of the highwayman.

"Partridge leaped up at this news, and ran back to the place where Jones stood, with his sword drawn in his hand, to guard the poor fellow, which Partridge no sooner saw, than he cried out, 'Kill the villain, sir! Run him through the body! Kill him, this instant!'

"Luckily, however, for the poor wretch, he had fallen into more merciful hands; for Jones, having examined the pistol, and found it to be really unloaded, began to believe all the man had told him before Partridge came up—namely, that he was a novice in the trade, and that he had been driven to it by the distress he had mentioned, the greatest, indeed, imaginable—that of five hungry children, and a wife lying-in of the sixth, in the utmost want and misery; the truth of all which the highwayman most violently asserted, and offered to convince Mr. Jones of, if he would take the trouble to go to his house, which was not above two miles off, saying he desired no favour, but on condition of proving all he alleged.

"Jones at first pretended that he would take the fellow at his word, and go with him, declaring that his fate should depend entirely on the truth of his story. Upon this the poor fellow immediately expressed so much alacrity, that Jones was perfectly satisfied with his veracity, and began now to entertain sentiments of compassion for him. He returned the fellow his empty pistol, advised him to think of honester means of relieving his distress, and gave him a couple of guineas for the immediate support of his wife and family, adding, he wished he had had more, for his sake, for the hundred pounds that had been mentioned was not his own."

They parted, and Jones and Partridge rode on towards London, conversing of highwaymen. Jones threw out some satirical jokes on his companion's cowardice; but Partridge gave expression to a new philosophy:—"A thousand naked men," said he, "are nothing to one pistol; for though, it is true, it will kill but one at a single discharge, yet who can tell but that one may be himself?"

Among the famous residents in Gray's Inn Road were Hampden and Pym. It was here that they held their consultations, when the matter of the ship-money was pleaded in the Star-Chamber.

Three poets are also to be mentioned in connection with the lane. The first of these is James Shirley, the poet and dramatist. This once well-known writer was educated at St. John's College, Oxford, and was destined for the Church. Archbishop Laud advised him against carrying out the design, the reason being, according to Shirley's biographer, that the archbishop, who was a rigid observer of the canons of the Church, had noticed that the future poet had a large mole on one of his cheeks. Notwithstanding this, however, Shirley eventually took orders, and obtained a curacy near St. Albans. He was not, however, satisfied with his position; his religious opinions became unsettled, and leaving the Church of England, he soon went over to Rome. After trying to maintain himself by teaching, he made his way to London, took up his abode in Gray's Inn Road, and became a writer for the stage.

Happily, he lived in a golden age for dramatic genius. Charles I. appreciated him, and invited him to court, and Queen Henrietta Maria conferred on him an appointment in her household. But soon the Civil War broke out. The poet then bade adieu to wife and children, and accompanied the Duke of Newcastle in his campaigns. On the failure of the king's cause he returned to London, ruined and desponding. His patron had perished on the scaffold, and his occupation as a playwright was being denounced from every pulpit in the land. He did the most sensible thing possible in the circumstances—he resumed his occupation of schoolmaster. His success was considerable; and he showed his attention to his profession by publishing several works on grammar.

After a time came the Restoration, and with it the revival of his plays, but it brought no long career of prosperity to the poet. His death was remarkable. His house, which was at that time in Fleet Street, was burned to the ground in the Great Fire of 1666, and he was forced, with his wife, to retreat to the suburbs, where the fright and loss so affected them both, that they died within some hours of each other, and were buried in the same grave.

The second poet to be noticed is John Ogilby, whom the late Mr. Jesse terms "unfortunate," but whom Mr. Chalmers characterises by the juster terms of "a very industrious adventurer in literary speculation," and "an enterprising and honest man." He was in his youth bound apprentice to a dancing-master in Gray's Inn Road. In this line of life he soon made money enough to purchase his discharge from his apprenticeship. His talents as a dancer led to his introduction at court; but unluckily, at a masque given by the Duke of Buckingham, in executing a caper, he fell, and so severely sprained one of the sinews of his leg as to be incapacitated from such lively exhibitions for the future. He had, however, a resource still left for him, as he continued to teach dancing. After a time he became author by profession, and wrote, translated, and edited all the rest of his days. Towards the close of his career he was appointed cosmographer and geographic printer to Charles II.

The third and last poet is the Rev. John Langhorne, known to every school-boy and girl for his lines " To a Redbreast," beginning—

"Little bird with bosom red,
Welcome to my humble shed."

His favourite haunt was the "Peacock," in this lane, a house celebrated in the last century for its Burton ale. It is a pity that Langhorne was too fond of the pleasant beverage: over-indulgence in it is said to have hastened his end. Chalmers certainly suggests a lame excuse for his tippling habits—that he had twice lost a wife. Langhorne deserves remembrance, if for nothing else than the excellent translation of Plutarch's "Lives," which he executed in company with his brother William, and which has become so universally popular. To judge from his writings, he was a man of an amiable disposition, a friend to religion and morality ; and, though a wit, we never find him descending to grossness or indelicacy. He was born in 1735, and died on the 1st of April, 1779.

Numerous indeed are the spots in Gray's Inn Road about which some memory hovers, or concerning which some good anecdote might be unearthed. Towards the close of the eighteenth century there was in this lane a public-house called the " Blue Lion ; " but the lion being the work of an artist who had not given very deep study to the personal appearance of the monarch of beasts, the establishment was commonly spoken of by its humorous frequenters as the "Blue Cat." It bore no good character. A witness giving evidence, in the year 1835, before a Committee of the House of Commons, appointed to inquire into the state of education of the people of England and Wales, said, " I have seen the landlord of this place come into the long room with a lump of silver in his hand, which he had melted for the thieves, and paid them for it. There was no disguise about it ; it was done openly."

Walking up Gray's Inn Road, the first turning one comes to on the right is Fox Court. There is nothing attractive about its outward appearance, but, like nearly every nook and corner of old London, it has its own story to tell. " In this wretched alley," says Mr. Jesse, " the profligate Countess of Macclesfield was delivered of her illegitimate child, Richard Savage. In ' the Earl of Macclesfield's Case,' presented to the House of Lords, will be found some curious particulars respecting the *accouchement* of the countess, and the birth of the future poet. From this source it appears that Anne, Countess of Macclesfield, under the name of Madame Smith, was delivered of a male child in Fox Court, Holborn, by a Mrs. Wright, a midwife, on Saturday, the 16th of January, 1697, at six o'clock in the morning ; that the child was baptised on the Monday following, and registered by Mr. Burbridge, assistant curate of St. Andrew's, Holborn, as the son of John Smith ; that it was christened, on Monday, the 18th of February, in Fox Court, and that, from the privacy maintained on the occasion, it was supposed by Mr. Burbridge to be a ' by-blow.' During her delivery, Lady Macclesfield wore a mask. By the entry of the birth in the parish register of St. Andrew's, it appears that the child's putative father, Lord Rivers, gave his son his own Christian name : ' January 1696-7, Richard, son of John Smith and Mary, in Fox Court, in Gray's Inn Lane, baptised the 18th.' "

The life of Savage was a singular one, and, as narrated by his intimate friend, Dr. Johnson, has attracted great interest from all classes of readers. After undergoing experiences of the strangest diversity, at one time living in the most lavish luxury, at another on the brink of starvation ; a successful poet to-day, and standing in the felon's dock on a charge of murder to-morrow, he died in 1743, in the debtors' prison at Bristol, exhibiting, as Johnson observes, with characteristic solemnity of antithesis, a lamentable proof that " negligence and irregularity, long continued, will make knowledge useless, wit ridiculous, and genius contemptible."

Fox Court opens into Brooke Street, and Mr. Cunningham points out this strange coincidence between the career of Savage, and that of the equally unfortunate Chatterton : "Savage was born in Fox Court, Brooke Street ; Chatterton died in Brooke Street ; Savage died in Bristol, and Chatterton was born in Bristol."

THE HALL OF GRAY'S INN.   (*See page* 554.)

CHAPTER LXI.

THE HOLBORN INNS OF COURT AND CHANCERY.

Gray's Inn—Its History—The Hall—A Present from Queen Elizabeth—The Chapel—The Library—Divisions of the Inn—Gray's Inn Walks—Bacon on Gardens—Observing the Fashions—Flirts and Flirtations—Old Recollections—Gray's Inn Gateway—Two Old Booksellers—Alms for the Poor—Original Orders—Eggs and Green Sauce—Sad Livery—Hats Off!—Vows of Celibacy—Mootings in Inns of Court—Joyous Revels—Master Roo in Trouble—Rebellious Students—A Brick Fight—An Address to the King—Sir William Gascoigne—A Prince imprisoned—Thomas Cromwell—Lord Burleigh—A Call to Repentance—Simon Fish—Sir Nicholas Bacon—Lord Bacon—A Gorgeous Procession—An Honest Welsh Judge—Bradshaw—Sir Thomas Holt—A Riot suppressed—Sir Samuel Romilly.

HOLBORN has long been famous as a law quarter of London.   In it are situated Gray's Inn, Staple Inn, and Barnard's Inn, together with what used to be the old legal haunts of Thavie's Inn and Furnival's Inn.   Of these we have now to speak, and the most important of them demands the earliest and deserves a large share of our attention.

Gray's Inn, on the north side of Holborn, and to the west of Gray's Inn Road, is the fourth Inn of Court in importance and size.   It derives its name from the noble family of Gray of Wilton, whose

residence it originally was.   Edmund, Lord Gray of Wilton, in August, 1505, by indenture of bargain and sale, transferred to Hugh Denny, Esq., "the manor of Portpoole, otherwise called 'Gray's Inn,' four messuages, four gardens, the site of a windmill, eight acres of land, ten shillings of free rent, and the advowson of the Chauntry of Portpoole."

From Denny's hands the manor passed into the possession of the Prior and Convent of East Sheen, in Surrey, an ecclesiastical establishment celebrated as having been the nursery of Cardinal Pole, and of many other distinguished churchmen, in the six-teenth century. By the Convent the mansion of Portpoole was leased to certain students of law, who paid, by way of rent, £6 13s. 4d. per annum. This arrangement held good till that lively time when Henry VIII. seized all the monastic property he could lay hands on. The benchers of Gray's Inn were thenceforth entered in the king's books as the fee-farm tenants of the Crown, and paid annually into the Exchequer the same rent as was formerly due to the monks of Sheen. The domain of the society extends over a large tract of ground between Holborn and Theobald's Road.

The name of Portpoole still survives in Portpool Lane, which runs from the east side of Gray's Inn Road into Leather Lane; and Windmill Hill still exists to point out the site of the windmill mentioned in the deed of transfer we have just quoted.

The old buildings of Gray's Inn are spoken of by a contemporary writer as boasting neither of beauty, uniformity, nor capacity. They had been erected by different persons, each of whom followed the dictates of his own taste, and the accommodation was so scanty that even the ancients of the house had to lodge double.

The Hall of the Inn was begun to be built in the reign of Queen Mary. It was finished in the reign of Elizabeth (1560), and cost £863 10s. 8d. In appearance the Hall is acknowledged to be "a very handsome chamber, little inferior to Middle Temple Hall, and its carved wainscot and timber roof render it much more magnificent than the Inner Temple, or Lincoln's Inn Hall." Its windows are richly emblazoned with the armorial bearings of Burleigh, Lord Verulam, Sir Nicholas Bacon, Judge Jenkins, and others. "The roof of oak," we are told by the historian of the "Inns of Court and Chancery," "is divided into six bays, or compartments, by seven arched and moulded Gothic ribs or principals. The spandrels, or spaces, are divided by upright timbers, with a horizontal cornice in the centre. At the extremity of the projecting spandrels is a carved pendant ornament, partaking of the nature of an entablature. The screen of this Hall is supported by six pillars of the Tuscan order, with caryatides supporting the cornice, in accordance with the style of ornament prevalent at that time. The Hall is also lighted by a handsome louvre, on which was formerly a dial, with the motto *Lux Dei, lex Dei*. Paintings of King Charles I., King Charles II., King James II., Sir Nicholas Bacon, Lord Bacon, and Lord Raymond—Lord Chief Justice of the King's Bench—hang upon the walls."

There is a tradition in Gray's Inn that the Bench tables in the Hall were the gift of Queen Elizabeth, and that Her Majesty once honoured the society by partaking of a magnificent banquet here. "On every grand day," writes Mr. Pearce, in his "Guide to the Inns of Court and Chancery" (1855), "the glorious, pious, and immortal memory of Queen Elizabeth is drunk with much formality. Three benchers rise to drink the toast; when they sit down, three others rise; and in this manner the toast passes down the Bar table, and from thence to the Students' table. It deserves to be remarked, too, that this is the only toast drunk in the Hall, and from the pleasure which Elizabeth derived from witnessing the performances of the gentlemen of Gray's Inn at her own palaces, and the distinction with which she on several occasions received them, it seems probable that the tradition to which reference has been made is correct, more especially as the Cecils, the Bacons, the Sidneys, and other illustrious personages of her court, were members of this house."

The Chapel of Gray's Inn is of modern erection. Likely enough, it was built on the site of the "Chauntry of Portpoole" mentioned in the grant to Hugh Denny. Divine service was of old performed here daily, and masses sung for the repose of the soul of John, son of Reginald de Gray—certain lands having been left for this purpose to the Prior and Convent of St. Bartholomew's, Smithfield.

The Chapel was an important institution in the olden time. All gentlemen of the Inn were ordered, in 1600, to frequent it regularly at service-time, as well as at sermons, and to receive the communion every term yearly, if they were in commons or resided in the house. If they omitted to do so, they forfeited 3s. 4d. for every time they neglected to receive the communion; and if they did not receive it at least once a year, they were liable to be expelled.

The Library of the Inn was rebuilt and enlarged in 1839-41. It consists of three handsome apartments, ceiled and wainscoted with oak. One of these is appropriated to the benchers, and the two larger rooms to the barristers and students of the society. In the principal room is a bust of Lord Bacon. The Library contains a complete series of reports, from the commencement of the year-books to the present day, with a large collection of valuable legal treatises and authorities.

The Inn was originally divided into four courts—viz., Coney Court; Holborn Court, which lay to the south of the Hall; Field Court, between Fulwood's Rents and the shady Walks of the Inn; and Chapel Court, between Coney Court and the

Chapel. Now it comprises South Square, Gray's Inn Square, Field Court, Gray's Inn Place, Raymond Buildings, Verulam Buildings, and the Gardens. The chambers are well adapted for study and retirement; they are commodious, airy, and quiet, and free from the fogs which, in the winter season, afflict the region near the river. The whole Inn is extra-parochial.

Gray's Inn Walks, or Gray's Inn Gardens, form one of the most interesting features connected with this learned region. In Charles II.'s time, and in the days of the *Tatler* and *Spectator*, Gray's Inn Walks formed a fashionable promenade on pleasant summer evenings. As late as 1633 one could obtain from this spot a delightful and uninterrupted view of the rising ground of Highgate and Hampstead.

Gray's Inn Gardens had their principal entrance from Holborn by Fulwood's Rents, then a fashionable locality—very unlike what it is now.

"This spot," says the late Mr. J. H. Jesse, "was a favourite resort of the immortal Bacon during the period he resided in Gray's Inn. It appears, by the books of the society, that he planted the greater number of the elm-trees which still afford their refreshing shade; and also that he erected a summer-house on a small mound on the terrace, where it is not improbable that he often meditated, and passed his time in literary composition. From the circumstance of Lord Bacon dating his Essays from his 'Chambers in Graie's Inn,' it is not improbable that the charming essay in which he dwells so enthusiastically on the pleasure of a garden was composed in, and inspired by, the floral beauties of this his favourite haunt. 'God Almighty,' he says, 'first planted a garden; and, indeed, it is the purest of human pleasures. It is the greatest refreshment to the spirits of man, without which buildings and palaces are but gross handy-works.' And he adds, 'Because the breath of flowers is far sweeter in the air—where it comes and goes like the warbling of music—than in the hand, therefore nothing is more fit for that delight than to know what be the flowers and plants that do best perfume the air.' As late as the year 1754 there was standing in the Gardens of Gray's Inn an octagonal seat, covered with a roof, which had been erected by Lord Bacon to the memory of his friend, Jeremiah Bettenham."

Howell, writing from Venice, June 5th, 1621, to a friend at Gray's Inn, says, "I would I had you here with a wish, and you would not desire in haste to be at Gray's Inn; though I hold your Walks to be the pleasantest place about London, and that **you** have there the choicest society."

Our often-quoted Pepys had an eye to the "choicest society," and on the 4th of May, 1662, we find him coming here after church-time, with his wife, to observe the fashions of the ladies; the reason being that Mrs. Pepys was just then bent on making some new dresses. Here pretty Fanny Butler was, in her brief day, the belle of the ground, and perhaps Pepys was thinking about her quite as much as about the latest fashions. He used to express his admiration at Fanny's beauty with a fervid candour by no means agreeable to the fair young wife on his own arm.

Sir Roger de Coverley is mentioned by Addison as walking here on the terrace, "hemming twice or thrice to himself with great vigour, for he loves to clear his pipes in good air (to make use of his own phrase), and is not a little pleased with any one who takes notice of the strength which he still exerts in his morning hems."

In the old dramatists we not unfrequently come across Gray's Inn Walks as a place of fashionable rendezvous. For example, in Dryden's *Sir Martin Mar-all* (1668) there is this reference to Gray's Inn Walks :—

"*Sir John Shallow.* But where did you appoint to meet him?

Mrs. Millisent. In Gray's Inn Walks."

And in the *Miser*, by Thomas Shadwell (1672), Cheatly says : "He has fifteen hundred pounds a year, and his love is honourable too. Now, if your ladyship will be pleased to walk in Gray's Inn Walks with me, I will design it so that you shall see him, and he shall never know on't."

Walking in these Gardens, we may thus call up many old associations. In addition to those just mentioned, we may picture to ourselves how those trees once shaded from the hot summer sun young men who loitered here with Butler and Cleveland. We can imagine Mr. Palmer, of Gray's Inn—the ingenious mechanician—pacing up and down these broad Walks, considering the qualities of the last addition to his collection of "telescopes and mathematical instruments, choice pictures, and other curiosities;" or devising some new contrivance for the improvement of that marvellous clock which roused the diarist's wonder and enthusiasm; or listening to John Evelyn's description of the museum of natural curiosities belonging to Mr. Charlton, of the Middle Temple, which collection eventually passed, by purchase, into the hands of Sir Hans Sloane.

The Gardens became, in time, the resort of dangerous classes; expert pickpockets and plausible ring-droppers found easy prey there on crowded days; and there were so many meetings of clandestine lovers, that it was thought expedient to close them, except at stated hours.

Many a married barrister, long ago, had his wife and family residing with him within the precincts of the Inns of Court. When that was the case, the children must have been bound over to keep the peace, and the lady strictly forbidden, during business hours, to practise on the piano. "Under the trees of Gray's Inn Gardens," says Mr. Jeaffreson (1867), "may be seen two modest tenements, each of them comprising some six or eight rooms and a vestibule. At the present time they are occupied as offices by legal practitioners; and many a day has passed since womanly skill decorated their windows with flowers and muslin curtains; but a certain venerable gentleman, to whom the writer of this page is indebted for much information about the lawyers of the last century, can remember when each of those cottages was inhabited by a barrister, his young wife, and three or four lovely children."

The origin of Gray's Inn Gateway we may read of in the following extract from an old author of the beginning of the seventeenth century:—"In this present age there hath been great cost bestowed therein upon faire buildings, and very lately the gentlemen of this House [Gray's Inn] purchased a Messuage and a Curtillage, scituate uppon the south side of this House, and thereuppon have erected a fayre Gate, and a Gate-house, for a more convenient and more honourable passage into the high street of Holborn, whereof this House stood in much neede; for the other former Gates were rather Posterns than Gates.

The celebrated bookseller, Jacob Tonson, had his shop here, within Gray's Inn Gate, next Gray's Inn Lane. Here he published Addison's "Campaign;" and from this place also he wrote the following letter to Pope:—

"Gray's Inn Gate, April 20th, 1706.

"Sir,—I have lately seen a pastoral of yours, in Mr. Walsh's and Congreve's hands, which is extremely fine, and is approved of by the best judges in poetry. I remember I have formerly seen you at my shop, and am sorry I did not improve my acquaintance with you. If you design your poem for the press, no person shall be more careful in the printing of it, nor no one can give greater encouragement to it than, sir, yours, &c., "Jacob Tonson."

Tonson was the second son of Jacob Tonson, a barber-chirurgeon in Holborn. He was born in the year 1656; and by his father's will, which was executed July 10th, 1668, and proved in the following November, he and his elder brother, Richard, and their three sisters, were each to receive the sum of £100 on their attaining the age of twenty-one—the money to be paid in Gray's Inn Hall. On the 5th of June, 1670, we find him bound appren-

tice for eight years to a bookseller called Thomas Basset, and on the 20th of December, 1677, he was admitted a freeman of the Stationers' Company. His first shop was in Chancery Lane, very near Fleet Street, and was distinguished by the sign of the "Judge's Head." About 1697 he removed to Gray's Inn, where he remained till about 1712, when he removed to a house in the Strand, over against Catherine Street, and here he chose Shakespeare's head for a sign. He died, very rich, on the 18th of March 1735-6.

The successor of Tonson in the Gray's Inn shop was another eminent bookseller, Thomas Osborne, who is oftener than once introduced in the "Dunciad." Pope makes him contend for the prize among the booksellers, and prove the successful competitor:—

'Osborne, through perfect modesty o'ercome,
Crowned with the jorden, walks contented home."

Osborne is perhaps best remembered by his well-known feud with Dr. Johnson. Of this Boswell writes: "It has been confidently related with many embellishments, that Johnson one day knocked Osborne down in his shop with a folio, and put his foot upon his neck. The simple truth I had from Johnson himself—'Sir, he was impertinent to me, and I beat him; but it was not in his shop, it was in my own chamber.'" Johnson, in his life of Pope, speaks of Osborne as a man entirely destitute of shame—without sense of any disgrace but that of poverty. He is said to have combined the most lamentable ignorance with extraordinary expertness in all the petty tricks of his trade.

Alms were distributed thrice a week at Gray's Inn Gate, for the better relief of the poor in Gray's Inn Lane, in 1587, the 29th year of Elizabeth's reign. The alms consisted of the broken victuals of the Hall table. The third butler was instructed to see that due consideration was had to the poorest sort of aged and impotent persons, and in case the panyer-man and under-cook should appropriate any of the said alms to themselves, they were allowed, by way of lessening the temptation, three loaves a-piece. The panyer-man here mentioned was a waiter. The Inner Temple Hall waiters are still called *panniers*—according to Mr. Timbs, from the *panarii* who attended the Knights Templars.

Some of the orders for the government of Gray's Inn are very curious—a remark, however, which might be applied to the regulations of all the other Inns. Let us notice a few of the more remarkable of these orders, as given by Herbert in his "Antiquities of the Inns of Court and Chancery" (1804).

At a *pension*, or meeting, held in the beginning

of the reign of King James, it was intimated to be the royal pleasure that none but gentlemen of descent should be admitted to the society. The names of all candidates were therefore ordered to be delivered to the Bench, that inquiries might be made as to their "quality."

In the reign of Edward VI. it was ordered that double readers were to have in commons only two servants, and single readers one. If a reader was elected, and he refused to serve, he had to forfeit ten pounds. For his trouble he was allowed thirty-five shillings for a hogshead of wine, and he fared well also as regards venison. In 28 Elizabeth (6 June) the reader for that summer was allowed "for every week ten bucks, and no more." In 1615 the House allowed the then two readers two hogsheads of wine, thirty bushels of flour, thirty pounds of pepper, and a "reward for thirty bucks and two stags, which were to be equally divided between them."

To ensure the orderly management of the public table, many regulations were made. In 1581 there was a cupboard-agreement regarding Easter Day, from which we learn that the members who came to breakfast after service and communion were to have "eggs and green sauce" at the cost of the House, and that "no calves'-heads were to be provided by the cook." At dinner and supper-time all were to be on their good behaviour. No gentleman was to be served out of his proper course; and by a regulation made in 1598, if any one "took meat by 'strong hand' from such as should serve him, he was to be put out of commons ipso facto."

In the sixteenth year of Elizabeth, the subject of dress was discussed, and an order was made "that every man of this society should frame and reform himself for the manner of his apparel, according to the proclamation then last set forth, and within the time therein limited; else not to be accounted of this house;" and that no one should wear any gown, doublet, hose, or outward garment of any light colour, upon penalty of expulsion; and within ten days following it was also ordered that no one should wear any white doublet in the house after Michaelmas Term ensuing.

Hats were forbidden to be worn in the Hall at meal-time, in 27 Elizabeth, under a penalty of 3s. 4d. for each offence. In 1600 the gentlemen of the society were instructed not to come into the Hall with their hats, boots, or spurs, but with their caps, decently and orderly, "according to the ancient orders." When they walked in the City or suburbs, or in the fields, they had to go in their gowns, or they were liable to be fined, and at the third offence to be expelled, and lose their chamber.

One cannot, however, oppose fashion; and though the benchers might talk grandly, in their council-chamber, of its being frivolity, and issue instructions about wearing this, and not wearing that, it is to be feared they did not always get themselves attended to. Was it likely that handsome youngsters were going to make guys of themselves? "Even in the time of Elizabeth," says one writer, "when authority was most anxious that utter-barristers should, in matter of costume, maintain that reputation for 'sadness' which is the proverbial characteristic of apprentices of the law, counsellors of various degrees were conspicuous through the town for 'brave' attire. At Gray's Inn, Francis Bacon was not singular in loving rich clothes, and running into debt for satin and velvet, jewels and brocade, lace and feathers. Even of that contemner of frivolous men and vain pursuits, Edward Coke, biography assures us that 'the jewel of his mind was put into a fair case—a beautiful body with a comely countenance: a case which he did wipe and keep clean, delighting in good clothes well worn; being wont to say that the outward neatness of our bodies might be a monitor of purity to our souls.'"

Among other ancient constitutions of Gray's Inn were the following:—That no officer of this house shall hold or enjoy his office longer than he shall keep himself sole and unmarried, excepting the steward, the chief butler, and the chief cook; that no fellow of the society stand with his back to the fire; that no fellow of the society make any rude noise in the Hall at exercises, or at meal-time; that no fellow of the society, under the degree of an ancient, keep on his hat at readings or moots, or cases assigned; and that search be made every Term for lewd and dangerous persons, that no such be suffered to lodge in the house.

Mootings, or disputations, in the Inns of Court and Chancery have long been disused. Danby Pickering, Esq., of Gray's Inn, was the last who voluntarily resumed them, but they were not of long continuance. Indeed, the course of legal education has greatly changed, and scarcely any of the ancient customs mentioned by authors are known, except as matters of curiosity.

The Inns of Court were, in the olden time, the scene of many joyous masques and revels, thus following the example set by the nobility in their castles and palaces. During the reigns of Henry VIII. and Elizabeth, masques, and other goodly "disguisings" sanctioned by the "grave and reverend Bench," were frequently performed at Gray's Inn. The first entertainment of this kind of which we have specific notice was a masque performed here at Christmas, 1527. It was composed by John Roo, serjeant-at-law, and was chiefly remarkable for the great offence which it gave to Cardinal Wolsey, whose ambition and misgovernment it was supposed to satirise. The old chronicler, Hall, giving an account of the events of the eighteenth year of from him his coif, and sent him to the Fleet; and afterwards he sent for the young gentlemen that played in the play, and highly rebuked and threatened them, and sent one of them, called Master Moyle, of Kent, to the Fleet; but, by means of friends, Master Roo and he were delivered at

GRAY'S INN GARDENS, 1770. (*See page* 555.)

Henry VIII., thus speaks of it :—"This Christmas was a goodly disguising played at Gray's Inn, which was compiled by John Roo, serjeant-at-the-law, twenty year past, and long before the cardinal had any authority. . . . This play was so set forth with rich and costly apparel, and with strange devices of masks and morrishes, that it was highly praised of all men, except by the cardinal, who imagined that the play had been devised of him. In a great fury he sent for Master Roo, and took last. This play sore displeased the cardinal, and yet it was never meant for him, wherefore many wise men grudged to see him take it so to heart."

Perhaps Roo, when he wrote his comedy, did not intend any special reference to Wolsey. It seems, however, that the performers were aware that the cardinal would likely take it home to himself. We learn as much from Fox's notice, in his "Acts and Monuments," of a Mr. Simon Fish, one of the gentlemen who acted in the piece.

That the presentation of plays was a customary feature of the festivities at Gray's Inn, we may infer from a passage from Dugdale, in his notes on this society. He says:—"In 4 Edward VI. (November 17) it was also ordered that henceforth there should be no comedies, called interludes, in this

cember (St. Thomas's Eve) the prince (one Master Henry Holmes, a Norfolk gentleman) took up his quarters in the Great Hall of the Inn, and by the 3rd of January the grandeur and comicality of his proceedings had created so much talk throughout the town, that the Lord Treasurer, Burghley, the

BARNARD'S INN. (*See page* 573.)

house out of Term time but when the feast of the Nativity of our Lord is solemnly observed. And that when there shall be any such comedies, then all the society at that time in commons, to bear the charge of the apparel."

The Prince of Purpoole's revel at Gray's Inn, in 1594, was a costly entertainment, and, in point of riotous excess, not inferior to any similar festivity in the time of Elizabeth. "On the 20th of De-

Earls of Cumberland, Essex, Shrewsbury, and Westmoreland; the Lords Buckhurst, Windsor, Sheffield, Compton; and a magnificent array of knights and ladies, visited Gray's Inn Hall on that day, and saw the masque which the revellers put upon the stage. After the masque there was a banquet, which was followed by a ball. On the day after, the prince, attended by eighty gentlemen of Gray's Inn and the Temple (each of them wearing a plume on his head), dined in state with the Lord Mayor and aldermen of the City, at Crosby Place. The frolic continued for many days more, the royal Purpoole, on one occasion, visiting Blackwall with a splendid retinue; on another, (Twelfth Night) receiving a gallant assembly of lords, ladies, and knights at his court in Gray's Inn; and on a third (Shrovetide) visiting the Queen herself, at Greenwich, when Her Majesty warmly applauded the masque set before her by the actors, who were members of the prince's court.

"So delighted was Elizabeth with the entertainment, that she graciously allowed the masquers to kiss her right hand, and loudly extolled Gray's Inn as ' an house she was much indebted to, for it did always study for some sport to present unto her;' whilst to the mock prince she showed her favour by placing in his hand the jewel (set with seventeen diamonds and fourteen rubies) which he had won by valour and skill in a tournament which formed part of the Shrovetide sports."

When the Prince of Purpoole kept his court at Gray's Inn on this occasion, we are told that his champion rode into the dining-hall upon the back of a fiery charger, which, like the rider, was clothed in a panoply of steel.

In 1612 the gentlemen of Gray's Inn, in company with those of the other Inns of Court, acted in a great masque at Whitehall, given in honour of the marriage of the Princess Elizabeth to the Count Palatine. To cover the expense of this display an assessment was made of £4 from each reader; the ancients paying £2 10s., the barristers £2, and the students 20s. apiece.

The society of Gray's Inn took an active part in the gorgeous masque which we have described as starting from Ely Place at Allhallowtide, 1633 (see p. 521 *et seq.*). One of the representatives of Gray's Inn on that occasion was a Mr. Read, whom all the women, and some of the men, pronounced "as handsome a man as the Duke of Buckingham." The only accident that happened that day was an unfortunate display of temper towards a Gray's Inn member. "Mr. May," says Garrard, in one of his letters to Lord Strafford, "of Gray's Inn, a fine poet—he who translated Lucan—came athwart my Lord Chamberlain in the banqueting-house, and he broke his staff across his shoulders, not knowing who he was. The king was present, who knew him, for he calls him his poet, and told the Chamberlain of it, who sent for him next morning, and fairly excused himself to him, and gave him fifty pounds in pieces." This hot-headed Lord Chamberlain was Philip Herbert, Earl of Pembroke and Montgomery, the "memorable simpleton" of

Horace Walpole, and one of whom Anthony Wood quaintly observes that he broke many wiser heads than his own.

The students of the Inns were never the quietest members of the community. Among the disturbances of Gray's Inn is one mentioned by Pepys in his Diary, May, 1667:—"Great talk of how the barristers and students of Gray's Inn rose in rebellion against the benchers the other day, who outlawed them; a great to-do; but now they are at peace again."

A few years later we find them up in arms again; but this time their strength is turned against outsiders, and not expended in hitting each other hard knocks. When building operations commenced in Holborn Fields, and the country about Gray's Inn began to give place to streets and squares, the legal fraternity, anxious to preserve the rural character of their neighbourhood, were greatly displeased. Lawyers, it is true, were the earliest householders, but that did not serve to mend the matter. Under date of June 10th, 1684, Narcissus Luttrell wrote in his Diary: "Dr. Barebone, the great builder, having some time since bought the Red Lyon Fields, near Graie's Inn Walks, to build on, and having, for that purpose, employed severall workmen to goe on with the same, the gentlemen of Graie's Inn took notice of it, and thinking it an injury to them, went with a considerable body of a hundred persons; upon which the workmen assaulted the gentlemen, and flung bricks at them. So a sharp engagement ensued, but the gentlemen routed them at last, and brought away one or two of the workmen to Graie's Inn. In this skirmish one or two of the gentlemen and servants of the house were hurt, and severall of the workmen."

The various eminent members of the Inn now claim our notice. Sir William Gascoigne, whose name is familiar to all, was one of the lawyers of the olden time connected with this house. He was reader here till 1398, in which year he was called to the degree of King's Serjeant-at-law. About three years afterwards he was made Chief Justice of the King's Bench. His death took place on the 17th of December, 1413. For his integrity as a judge, as well as for his private virtues, he deserves to be ever held in remembrance.

He distinguished himself on many occasions, particularly in refusing to pass sentence on Archbishop Scroop as a traitor, though commanded to do so by the king; and still more by committing the Prince of Wales, afterwards Henry V., to prison for contempt of court. This latter incident suggested to Shakespeare one of his most effective scenes.

Here is the account given by one of our old chroniclers of the Prince's committal to prison. "It happened," he says, "that a servant of Prince Henry, afterwards the fifth English king of that Christian name, was arraigned before this judge, Sir William Gascoigne, for felony, whom the Prince, then present, endeavoured to take away, coming up in such fury that the beholders believed he would have stricken the judge. But he, sitting without moving, according to the majesty he represented, committed the Prince prisoner to the King's Bench, there to remain until the pleasure of the Prince's father were further known. Who, when he heard thereof by some pickthank courtier, who probably expected a contrary return, gave God thanks for His infinite goodness, who at the same instant had given him a judge who could administer and a son who could obey justice." The dramatist puts these words in his mouth:—

> "Happy am I, that have a man so bold
> That dares do justice on my proper son
> And not less happy, having such a son
> That would deliver up his greatness so
> Into the hands of justice."

It is a fine scene in Shakespeare's *Henry IV.* (Part II., v. 2), where the future conqueror of Agincourt, after his accession to the throne, meets the independent judge:—

> "*King.* You are right, Justice, and you weigh this well;
> Therefore still bear the balance and the sword;
> And I do wish your honours may increase,
> Till you do live to see a son of mine
> Offend you and obey you, as I did.
> .   .   .   .   You did commit me:
> For which, I do commit into your hand
> The unstained sword that you have used to bear,
> With this remembrance, that you use the same
> With the like bold, just, and impartial spirit
> As you have done 'gainst me."

Thomas Cromwell, afterwards Earl of Essex, a conspicuous enough individual in his day, and also kept in remembrance by Shakespeare, was another member of this Inn. He was a man of humble origin, and owed his rise in life to his having been admitted into the household of Cardinal Wolsey. He is said to have acted as law adviser to the Cardinal, who recognised his abilities, rewarded his devotion, and left him a parting counsel:—

> "Oh, Cromwell, Cromwell,
> Had I but served my God with half the zeal
> I served my king, he would not in my age
> Have left me naked to mine enemies."

Cromwell was admitted of Gray's Inn in 1524. Ten years afterwards he was one of the ancients of the society, and in 1535 he was raised to the offices of Secretary to the Privy Council, Chan-cellor of the University of Cambridge, Master of the Rolls, and Lord Privy Seal. The new doctrines in religion, it was well known, had his sympathy and support.

> "*Bishop Gardiner.* Do I not know you for a favourer
> Of this new sect? Ye are not sound.
>   *Cromwell.*   Not sound?
>   *Gardiner.* Not sound I say,
>   *Cromwell.* Would you were half so honest.
> Men's prayers then would see you, not their fears.
>   *Gardiner.* I shall remember this bold language.
>   *Cromwell.*   Do;
> Remember your bold life too."—*Henry VIII.*, v. 1.

His successful career did not last long. As often happens, wealth and honour created envious enemies: the clergy, too, viewed him with hatred, and to the nobility he was odious on account of his mean extraction. He fell into disfavour with King Henry, and on the 10th of June, 1540, was committed to prison. He was impeached before Parliament, the articles accusing him of being "the most false and corrupt traitor and deceiver that had been known in that reign;" of being a "detestable heretic," and of having acquired "innumerable sums of money and treasure by oppression, bribery, and extortion." He was not allowed to answer these charges in open court, and was sentenced to be beheaded. The sentence was carried into effect on Tower Hill on the 28th of July of the same year.

William Cecil, Lord Burleigh, was another eminent member of whom Gray's Inn can boast. He entered at Gray's Inn in 1540. "Whether this removal to Gray's Inn," says Dr. Nares, "were for the purpose of his being bred wholly up to the profession of the law, we are not able to say, since it was no unusual thing in those days for young men of family and talents, who had any prospect of becoming members of the legislature, to go through a course of law at some one of our Inns of Court, in order to become better acquainted with the laws and constitution of their country. It was regarded, indeed, as almost a necessary qualification."

An anecdote of Burleigh's Gray's-Inn days, as quaintly related by his old historian, may afford the reader some gratification. "A mad companion having enticed him to play, in a short time he lost all his money, bedding, and books to his companion, having never used play before. And being afterwards among his other company, he told them how such a one had misled him, saying he would presently have a device to be even with him. And with a long trouke he made a hole in the wall, near his playfellow's bedhead, and in a fearful voice spake thus through the trouke:—'O mortal man, repent! repent of thy horrid time consumed in play, cozenage, and lewdness, or else thou art damned and canst not be saved!' Which being spoken at midnight, when he was all alone, so amazed him, as drove him into a sweat for fear. Most penitent and heavy, the next day, in presence of the youths, he told with trembling what a fearful voice spake to him at midnight, vowing never to play again; and calling for Mr. Cecil, asked him forgiveness on his knees, and restored him all his money, bedding, and books. So two gamesters were both reclaimed with this merry device, and never played more. Many other the like merry jests I have heard him tell, too long to be here noted."

"Who Burleigh's 'playfellows' were," observes Charles Knight in his "London," "nowhere appears; but the future statesman himself was a married man during the greater part of his sojourn at Gray's Inn, and ought to have been more steady than to stake his 'books and bedding,' after losing his money. However, from many memoranda of Gray's Inn which have come down to our time, it would seem that the students of this society were rather an unruly set."

The most distinguished writer on the laws of England who flourished in the sixteenth century was Anthony Fitzherbert, Lord Chief Justice of the Court of Common Pleas in the reign of Henry VIII. He once filled the office of reader in Gray's Inn. "His books"—"De Naturâ Brevium," and others—says Fuller, "are monuments which will longer continue his memory than the flat blue stone in Norbury Church, under which he lieth interred." Fitzherbert assisted to draw up the articles of impeachment against Cardinal Wolsey, which concluded by praying King Henry "that he be so provided for, that he never have any power, jurisdiction, or authority, hereafter to trouble, vex, and impoverish the Commonwealth of this your realm, as he hath done heretofore, to the great hurt and damage of almost every man, high and low."

We have already referred to Simon Fish, a student of this inn, who, for taking part in a masque supposed to satirise Wolsey, had to fly the kingdom, in 1527. During his residence in Germany, he composed a work called "The Supplication of Beggars," attacking the monastic orders in England. It was shown by Anne Boleyn to Henry VIII., who was so pleased with it, as falling in with his projects of plunder, that he not only permitted the return of the author to his native land, but took him under his protection. Fish did not long enjoy his good fortune; he died in 1531.

Passing from him, however, we come to two much more celebrated members of our inn. Sir Nicholas Bacon, Lord Keeper of the Great Seal of England during the greater part of Elizabeth's reign, kept his terms here. In the year 1532 he was admitted a student of Gray's Inn; in 1536 he rose to the degree of ancient in the society, and in 1550 was created a bencher.

Sir Nicholas Bacon had much of that penetrating genius, solidity of judgment, persuasive eloquence, and comprehensive knowledge of law and equity, which afterwards shone forth with so great a lustre in his son, who was, it has been remarked, "as much inferior to his father, in point of prudence and integrity, as his father was to him in literary accomplishments." He was the first Lord Keeper who ranked as Chancellor.

Towards the end of his life he became very corpulent, which gave occasion to Elizabeth to make a jest once: "Sir Nicholas's soul lodged well," she said. To himself, however, his bulk was very cumbersome, insomuch that, after walking from Westminster Hall to the Star Chamber, which was but a little way, he was usually so much out of breath that the lawyers forbore speaking at the bar till he recovered himself and gave them notice of it by knocking with his staff. His death, in 1579, is reported to have happened through a cold, caught from having fallen asleep with his window open, after having been under the hands of his barber.

But the name of which, above all others, Gray's Inn is proud, is that of Francis Lord Bacon, the youngest son of Sir Nicholas Bacon. This great man's history is well known, so we shall not repeat it, but content ourselves with recording the dates of his admission as a student here, and of his various degrees in the society. He was admitted in 1576; became ancient, 21st November, 1576; became barrister, 27th June, 1582; became bencher, 1586; became reader, 1588, and was duplex reader in 1600.

The errors and foibles of this great man were, no doubt, exaggerated by the malice of his enemies, and they have died with him; but his writings will exercise an influence for good on mankind as long as our language lasts; and his "name and memory," which he proudly bequeathed "to foreign nations and to his own countrymen, after some time passed over," will long be regarded as one of the most valuable inheritances of this ancient and honourable legal society.

After his downfall, when he had parted with York House, he resided again at his old chambers at Gray's Inn, whence, in 1626, he went one day, with his physician, towards Highgate, to take the air. "It occurred to Bacon to inquire if flesh might not be preserved in snow as well as in salt. Pulling up at a small cottage, near the foot of Highgate Hill, he bought a hen from an old dame, plucked and drew it, gathered up snow in his palms, and stuffed it into the fowl." He was smitten by a sudden chill, became too ill to return to Gray's Inn, and was carried to the Earl of Arundel's house, close at hand, where he died within a week. In his brief will it was directed that the lease of his rooms, valued at £300, was to be sold, and the money given to poor scholars.

Francis Bacon's progress from Gray's Inn to Westminster, on the 7th of May, 1617, has been described by many writers, who, however widely they differ in estimating the moral worth of the new Lord Keeper, concur in celebrating the gorgeousness of his pageant:—"On the first day of Trinity Term, May 7th, says Mr. Hepworth Dixon, in his "Story of Lord Bacon's Life," "he rode from Gray's Inn, which he had not yet left, to Westminster Hall, to open the courts in state, all London turning out to do him honour, the queen sending the lords of her household, Prince Charles the whole of his followers—the lords of the council, the judges, and serjeants composing his immediate train. On his right hand rode the Lord Treasurer, on his left the Lord Privy Seal, behind them a long procession of earls and barons, knights and gentlemen. Every one, says George Gerard, who could procure a horse and a foot-cloth fell into the train, so that more than 200 horsemen rode behind him, through crowds of citizens and apprentice boys from Cheap, of players from Bankside, of the Puritan hearers of Burgess, of the Roman Catholic friends of Danvers and Armstrong; and he rode, as popular in the streets as he had been in the House of Commons, down Chancery Lane and the Strand, past Charing Cross, through the open courts of Whitehall, and by King Street into Palace Yard. He wore on that day, as he had worn on his bridal day, a suit of purple satin. Alighting at the gates of Westminster Hall, and passing into the Court, he took his seat on the bench; when the company had entered, and the criers commanded silence, he addressed them on his intention to reform the rules and practices of the court."

Lord Bacon's chambers, says Mr. Pearce, "were in No. 1, Coney Court, which formerly stood on the site of the present row of buildings at the west side of Gray's Inn Square, adjoining the gardens. The whole of Coney Court was burnt down by a fire which occurred in the inn about the year 1678."

Gray's Inn can boast of having had as one of its members the patriotic and honest Welsh judge, David Jenkins. He was a famous champion of the royal cause, and in the most troublous time of England's history displayed undaunted courage and unbending devotion to his lawful sovereign. He was admitted a student of Gray's Inn in the year 1602, was called to the Bar in 1609, and on the 28th of May, 1622, was advanced to the degree of ancient in this house. In the discharge of his official duty he imprisoned and condemned several persons bearing arms against King Charles. For this the parliamentarians laid violent hands upon him, and on Monday, 21st of February, 1647, the keeper of Newgate brought Judge Jenkins, described as "Mr. David Jenkins, judge in Wales, now a prisoner in that gaole," to the bar of the House of Commons, upon an impeachment of high treason. The Speaker asked him what he had to say for himself, and David Jenkins was not slow to reply. We are informed by a contemporaneous account of his arraignment, that he said "that they had no power to try him, and at the bar, and in the open house, gave very contemptuous words and reproaches against the Houses and power of Parliament. He threatened Parliament with the king's numerous issue, with divers other reproachful words, such as the like were never offered in the face of a parliament. After he came out of the House, he put off his hat, and spake to this effect before the soldiers of the guard, and divers gentlemen at the doore : 'Gentlemen, God bless you all, protect the laws of the kingdom !'"

His carriage was declared to be a high contempt and misdemeanour, and he was ordered to be fined £1,000, and sent back to Newgate. When in prison he expected daily to be hanged, and formed the original resolution of being suspended from the gallows-tree with a Bible under one arm and Magna Charta under the other. It never came to that, however; and Judge Jenkins escaped with his life.

Bradshaw, who sat as president at the trial of Charles I., was a bencher of Gray's Inn. He was "a stout man," to quote the words of Whitelock, "and learned in his profession; no friend to monarchy." He entered Gray's Inn in the year 1622, was called to the bar on the 23rd of April, 1627, and was advanced to the degree of ancient on the 23rd of June, 1645.

Sir Thomas Holt was once Treasurer of Gray's Inn, and his son, who became Lord Chief Justice, was entered upon the society's books before he was ten years old. Lord Chief Justice Holt is deservedly regarded as a bright ornament of this Inn, and his escutcheon holds a prominent place in the principal window of the hall. He was born at Thame, in Oxfordshire, about 1642. His rise as a lawyer was very rapid, and in 1689 we find him appointed by King William III. Lord Chief Justice of the King's Bench, an office which he held till his death. On the removal of Lord Somers he was offered the Chancellorship, but he declined it. On the bench he is said to have conducted himself

writer, "to lay before them the noble character of Verus the magistrate, who always sat in triumph over, and contempt of vice; he never searched after it or spared it when it came before him. At the same time he could see through the hypocrisy and disguise of those who have no pretence to virtue themselves, but by their severity to the vicious. This same Verus was, in times past, Chief Justice, as we call it in Felicia (Britain). He was a man of profound knowledge of the laws of his

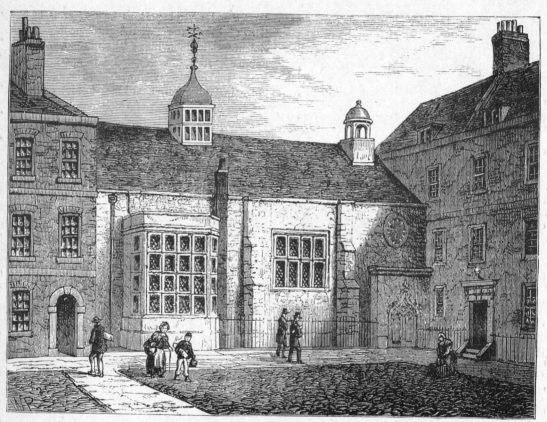

STAPLE INN. (See page 575.)

in a lofty and dignified manner, and to have set an example of spirit and temper which has continued since his day to adorn the English bench. On several occasions he was forced, in the conscientious discharge of his duty, to resist the encroachments of the Crown as well as of the Houses of Parliament. When he died, in March, 1709, he left behind him, says his biographer, "a reputation for learning, honour, and integrity, which has never been surpassed even among the many eminent individuals who have succeeded him in his dignified office."

There is a sketch of the character of Lord Chief Justice Holt in the 14th number of the *Tatler*. "It would become all men as well as me," remarks the

country, and as just an observer of them in his own person. He considered justice as a cardinal virtue, not as a trade for maintenance. Wherever he was judge, he never forgot that he was also counsel. The criminal before him was always sure he stood before his country, and, in a sort, a parent of it; the prisoner knew that, though his spirit was broken with guilt, and incapable of language to defend itself, all would be gathered from him which could conduce to his safety; and that his judge would wrest no law to destroy him, nor conceal any that could save him."

The following story concerning this eminent judge has appeared in many books of anecdote: —A party of the guards was once ordered from

Whitehall to put down a dangerous riot which had arisen in Holborn, from the practice of kidnapping, then carried to a great extent; and at the same time an officer was dispatched to inform the Chief Justice of what was doing, and to desire that he would send some of his people to attend and countenance the soldiers. "Suppose, sir," said Holt—"let us suppose that the populace should not disperse on your appearance, or at your com-

"This story," says Mr. Jeaffreson, in his "Book about Lawyers," "is very ridiculous, but it points to an interesting and significant event. Of course, it is incredible that Holt said, 'the laws of this kingdom are not to be executed by the sword.' He was too sound a constitutional lawyer to hold that military force could not be lawfully used in quelling civil insurrection. The interesting fact is this. On the occasion of a riot in Holborn, Holt

DOORWAY IN STAPLE INN. (*See page* 575.)

mand?" "Our orders are then to fire upon them." "Then mark, sir, what I say. If there should be a man killed in consequence of such orders, and you are tried before me for murder, I will take care that you and every soldier of your party shall be hanged. Return to those who sent you, and tell them that no officer of mine shall accompany soldiers; the laws of this kingdom are not to be executed by the sword. This affair belongs to the civil power, and soldiers have nothing to do here." Then ordering his tipstaves and some constables to accompany him, he proceeded to the scene of tumult; and the populace, on his assurance that justice should be done on the objects of their indignation, dispersed in a peaceable manner.

was formally required, as the supreme conservator of the king's peace, to aid the military; and instead of converting a street row into a massacre, he prevailed upon the mob to disperse, without shedding a single drop of blood. Declining to co-operate with soldiers on an unarmed multitude, he discharged the ancient functions of his office with words, instead of sabres—with grave counsels, instead of cruel violence. Under similar circumstances, Chief Justice Odo would have clad himself in mail, and crushed the rabble beneath the feet of his war-horse. At such a summons George Jeffreys, having fortified himself with a magnum of claret and a pint of strong water, would have accompanied the king's guards, and with noisy oaths would have bade them give the rascals a taste of cold steel. Wearing his judicial robes, and sustained by the majesty of the law, William III.'s chief justice preserved the peace without sacrificing life."

Sir Samuel Romilly, the celebrated English lawyer and M.P. for Westminster, was a member of Gray's Inn. As a student he seems to have had no anticipation of the brilliancy of his future career. We find him writing despondingly to a friend, in 1783—"I sometimes lose all courage, and wonder what fond opinion of my talents could ever have induced me to venture on so bold an undertaking; but it often happens (and I fear it has been in my case) that men mistake the desire for the ability of acting some distinguished part." He died by his own hand, in November, 1818, during an attack of brain fever, brought on by grief for the death of his wife.

CHAPTER LXII.

THE HOLBORN INNS OF COURT AND CHANCERY (continued).

Ecclesiastics of Gray's Inn—Stephen Gardiner—Whitgift—Bishop Hall, the "Christian Seneca"—Archbishop Laud—William Juxon—On the Scaffold—The "Bruised Reed"—Baxter's Conversion—Antiquaries and Bookworms—The Irritable Joseph Ritson—John Britton—Hall and his "Chronicles"—Rymer and his "Fœdera"—The Original of "Tom Folio"—George Chapman—A Celebrated Translation—Oliver Goldsmith—A Library of One Book—William Cobbett—Holborn Town Hall—What are Inns of Chancery?—Furnival's Inn—A Street Row—Sir Thomas More—Snakes and Eels—A Plague of a Wife—A Scene in the Tower—Scourges and Hair Shirts—No Bribery—Charles Dickens and "Pickwick"—Thavie's Inn—Barnard's Inn—The Old Hall—The Last of the Alchemists—A given Quantity of Wine—The "No Popery" Riots—Staple Inn—Stevens Correcting his Proof-Sheets—Dr. Samuel Johnson—A "Little Story Book"—Fire! Fire!

THE Inns of Court were instituted chiefly for the benefit of those desiring to devote themselves to the legal profession, but from an early period they were resorted to by Churchmen and sons of the nobility and gentry, to whom it was thought fitting to give some instruction in the principles and maxims of our municipal law. We shall mention a few of the more eminent ecclesiastics who have studied at Gray's Inn.

Stephen Gardiner, Bishop of Winchester, and Lord Chancellor of England, is the first of these. He was Cromwell's great adversary. His abilities it is impossible to over-rate, and one cannot but admire his inflexible courage in the most trying circumstances; but he was artful, ambitious, and revengeful, even to blood. He died in 1555. The dexterous equivocations by which he habitually endeavoured to secure the advantages and escape the penalties of untruthfulness gave rise to the remark, "My Lord of Winchester is like Hebrew, to be read backwards."

Whitgift, the third primate after the Reformation, was admitted to Gray's Inn on the 16th of March, 1592. He was distinguished for his learning, piety, and integrity, and is described by Fuller as "one of the worthiest men that ever the English hierarchy did enjoy." By his influence he obtained the mastership of the Temple for Hooker, and in gratitude for his kindness that famous divine dedicated to the Archbishop his "Ecclesiastical Polity."

In the books of Gray's Inn we find entered the name of another distinguished Churchman, Joseph Hall, Bishop successively of Exeter and Norwich.

His works have gained him the appellation of the "Christian Seneca." His "Meditations" are well known and much esteemed for the force and brilliancy of their language and the fervour of their piety. The knowledge of the world and depth of thought possessed by Bishop Hall place him nearer our own time than many of his contemporaries. He was born at Ashby-de-la-Zouch in 1574, and died in 1656. He rests in the churchyard of Heigham, near Norwich, and there he was interred without any memorial. In his will he says, "I leave my body to be buried without any funeral pomp, at the discretion of my executors, with this only monition, that I do not hold God's house a meet repository for the dead bodies of the greatest saints."

Another ecclesiastical member of Gray's Inn was Archbishop Laud. He was admitted on the 1st of November, 1615. Speaking of Laud, Fuller, in his characteristic style, remarks, "Indeed, I could instance in some kind of coarse venison, not fit for food when first killed; and therefore cunning cooks bury it for some hours in the earth, till the rankness thereof being mortified thereby, it makes most palatable meat. So the memories of some persons, newly deceased, are neither fit for a writer's or reader's repast, till some competent time after their interment. However, I am confident, that impartial posterity, on a serious review of all passages, will allow his name to be reposed among the heroes of our nation, seeing such as hold his expense on St. Paul's as but a cypher, will assign his other benefactions a very valuable significance, viz., his erecting and endowing an almshouse in Reading; his increasing of Oxford Library with books and St. John's College with beautiful buildings." He was beheaded January 10th, 1644.

William Juxon, Bishop of London, and afterwards Archbishop of Canterbury, was admitted a member of Gray's Inn on the 2nd of May, 1635. It was this prelate, the reader will remember, who attended Charles I. on the scaffold, and did his best, by suitable exhortations, to prepare the unfortunate king for his end. "There is, sir," said he, "but one stage more, which, though turbulent and troublesome, is yet a very short one. Consider, it will soon carry you a great way; it will carry you from earth to heaven; and there you shall find to your great joy the prize to which you hasten, a crown of glory." "I go," replied the king, "from a corruptible to an incorruptible crown;" and a moment afterwards his head, streaming with blood, was being exhibited to the assembled populace as "the head of a traitor."

The author of the "Bruised Reed," which led to the conversion of Richard Baxter, and which Izaak Walton bequeathed to his children, was once the preacher of Gray's Inn. He was Dr. Richard Sibbes. His death took place at his chambers here in 1635.

Baxter himself tells us of the happy influence which this book had upon him. His father was pious, but his surroundings generally were adverse to all religious impressions. The neighbourhood in which he passed his youth—a village near the foot of the Wrekin, in Shropshire — was all that Queen Elizabeth or King James could have wished; or, says one writer, "if it exceeded her Majesty's allowance — 'two preachers enough for one county,' in complying with her kinsman's 'Book of Sports,' it showed an excess of loyalty." The Maypole was erected beside a great tree, near the dwelling of Baxter's father, and as soon as the reader had rushed through the morning prayer the congregation turned out to the village green, and the lads and lasses began dancing. Young Baxter, however, seems to have been seriously inclined, and the religious teaching of his father was not wholly thrown away. When about fifteen years old, he had, with some other boys, been stealing apples, and whilst his mind was in a state of more than ordinary disquiet, he read a very awakening book called "Bunny's Resolution." He became filled with anxiety and foreboding. In the midst of those gloomy days a poor pedlar came to the door selling books. His stock consisted chiefly of ballads, but he chanced to have one good book, and that was the "Bruised Reed" of

Dr. Richard Sibbes. The elder Baxter bought it, and to the son it proved a messenger of salvation. The perusal of it, and one of Parkins's works, lent him by a servant, established his faith. "And thus," he says, "without any means but books, was God pleased to resolve me unto Himself." Nor is it wonderful, that, as he elsewhere remarks, "The use that God made of books above ministers to the benefit of my soul made me somewhat excessively in love with good books, so that I thought I had never enow, but scraped up as great a treasure of them as I could."

A few members of the picturesque race of antiquaries and bookworms—irritable, eccentric, and hermit-like—have resided in Gray's Inn. Joseph Ritson, for instance, had chambers here. He lived and died in No. 8, Holborn Court. The building stood against the south wall of the chapel, and has since been pulled down.

In that entertaining work, the "Bookhunter," by Mr. John Hill Burton, the historian of Scotland gives some curious particulars regarding Ritson. He was a man endowed with almost superhuman irritability of temper, and he had a genius fertile in devising means of giving scope to its restless energies. One of his obstinate fancies was, when addressing a letter to a friend of the male sex, instead of using the ordinary prefix of Mr. or the affix of Esq., to employ the term *Master*, as—when writing to two well-known fellow-workers in the ways of old antiquity—Master John Pinkerton, Master George Chalmers. The agreeable result of this eccentricity was that his communications on delicate and antiquarian disputes were invariably delivered to, and perused by, the young gentlemen of the family, so opening up new little delicate avenues, fertile in controversy and misunderstanding.

But he had another and more varied peculiarity. In his numerous books he insisted on a peculiar spelling. It was not phonetic, nor was it etymological, it was simply Ritsonian. To understand the efficacy of this arrangement as a source of controversy, it must be remembered that the instinct of a printer is to spell according to rule, and that every deviation from the ordinary method can only be carried out by a special contest over each word. Ritson, in seeing his works through the press, fought every step of the way, and such peculiarities as the following, profusely scattered over his books, may be looked upon as the names of so many battles or skirmishes with his printers: "Compilür," "writür," "wil," "kil," "onily," "probablely." Even when he condescended to use the spelling common to the rest of the nation he insisted on the employment of little irritating peculiarities ; as, for instance, in the word "ass," a word pretty often in his mouth, he would not follow the practice of his day, in the use of the long and short "fs," but inverted the arrangement thus, "sf."

"This strange creature," adds Mr. Burton, "exemplified the opinion that every one must have some creed—something from without having an influence over thought and action, stronger than the imperfect apparatus of human reason. Scornfully disdaining revelation from above, he groped below, and found for himself a little fetish made of turnips and cabbage. He was as fanatical a devotee of vegetarianism as others have been of a middle state or adult baptism ; and after having torn through a life of spiteful controversy with his fellow-men, and ribaldry of all sacred things, he thus expressed the one weight hanging on his conscience, that 'on one occasion, when, tempted by wet, cold, and hunger, in the south of Scotland, he ventured to eat a few potatoes dressed under the roast, nothing less repugnant to feelings being to be had.'"

Opposite Ritson's chambers lived John Britton, the eminent writer on topography and architecture, for three years clerk to one Simpson, an attorney, at the handsome salary of fifteen shillings a week. "Yet," he says, "with this small income, I felt comfortable and happy, as it provided me with a decent lodging, clothes, and food, and with the luxury of books." Britton's account of his master is a strange one, and gives an instructive picture of our legal friends at work amassing their six and eightpences. "At eleven o'clock he came to the office to receive business letters, each of which he read several times, with pauses between each sentence ; by which process six short letters would occupy at least an hour of his time. He devoted more than another hour to dictating equally laconic letters in reply ; whilst a third was employed in reading those answers when written. This vapid waste of time was the practice of every succeeding day for three years." Britton used occasionally to visit Ritson in his chambers.

Most of Britton's works were devoted to topography and architectural antiquities, biography, and the fine arts. Amongst these may be named his "Architectural Antiquities of Great Britain," and the "Cathedral Antiquities of England," works of national value, which will secure lasting fame for their author. A writer in the *Gentleman's Magazine*, to which Britton was a frequent contributor, thus speaks of him :—"To his labours, the architecture, and particularly the ecclesiastical and domestic architecture, of the country, is deeply indebted for the restoration of what was decayed,

and the improvement of what was defective ; and in his beautiful sketches and masterly engravings, extending through many volumes, he has given us a treasure-house of antiquarian art, and made the pencil and the graver not only perpetuate and preserve much that has long been mouldering into shapeless ruin, but has also supplied many a new model of improved beauty, suggested by his own genius, and carried into effect by his own zeal and perseverance." Britton was born in 1771, and died in 1857.

The well-known historian, Edward Hall, who wrote the "Chronicles," a work which furnished material for so many of the dramatic productions of the reign of Queen Elizabeth, was a reader, at one time, in Gray's Inn. We find his name mentioned in connection with a pension of the bench of Gray's Inn, held 16th May, 31 Henry VIII., when the king's command that all images of Thomas à-Becket, Archbishop of Canterbury in the reign of Henry II., should be removed from churches and chapels, was taken into consideration. It was then ordered that Edward Hall should see to the taking out of a certain window in the chapel of this house, "wherein the picture of the said archbishop was *gloriously* painted," and place another in its stead, descriptive of Christ praying on the mount. Hall was born about the last year of the fifteenth century, in the parish of St. Mildred's, London. He died in 1547, and was buried, but without any memorial, in the Church of St. Benet Sherehog, London. His "Chronicles" have been differently appreciated by antiquaries. Bishop Nicholson speaks of it disrespectfully, and says it is but a record of the fashions of summer clothes ; but Peck vindicates Hall with some energy. Hall was no favourer of the clergy.

Amongst other antiquarian members of Gray's Inn we may mention Rymer, whose work, the "Fœdera," has given him a European reputation. Rymer was born in Yorkshire, and after studying at Cambridge removed to Gray's Inn. He adopted the profession of the law, and in 1692 succeeded Shadwell in the post of historiographer to King William III. His death took place on the 10th of December, 1713, and he found a grave in St. Clement Danes.

In Gray's Inn lived Dr. Rawlinson, who stuffed four chambers so full of books that he had to sleep in the passage. He was the original of Tom Folio, so pleasantly described in No. 158 of the *Tatler*: "Tom Folio is a broker in learning, employed to get together good editions, and stock the libraries of great men. There is not a sale of books begins till Tom Folio is seen at the door. There is not an auction where his name is not heard, and that, too, in the very nick of time, in the critical moment, before the last decisive stroke of the hammer. There is not a subscription goes forward in which Tom is not privy to the first rough draft of the proposals, nor a catalogue printed that does not come to him wet from the press. He is an universal scholar, so far as the title-page of all authors; knows the manuscripts in which they were discovered, the editions through which they have passed, with the praises or censure which they have received from the several members of the learned world. He has a greater esteem for Aldus and Elzevir than for Virgil and Horace. If you talk of Herodotus, he breaks out into a panegyric upon Harvey Stephens. He thinks he gives you an account of an author when he tells you the subject he treats of, the name of the editor, and the year in which it was printed. Or, if you draw him into further particulars, he cries up the goodness of the paper, extols the diligence of the corrector, and is transported with the beauty of the letter. This he looks upon to be sound learning and substantial criticism. As for those who talk of the fineness of style and the justness of thought, or describe the brightness of any particular passages; nay, though they write themselves in the genius and spirit of the author they admire, Tom looks upon them as men of superficial learning, and flashy parts."

The quiet seclusion of Gray's Inn has, in bygone times, formed the retreat of many distinguished poets and literary men. It was the residence of George Chapman, the poet, who was born in 1557, and died, honoured and beloved, in 1634.

Chapman deserves best to be kept in remembrance for his translation of Homer, whom he speaks of as "the prince of poets, never before truly translated"—a production which has excited the admiration of many distinguished critics. Coleridge, in sending it to a friend for perusal, specially recommends the "Odyssey." "The 'Iliad,'" he says, "is fine, but less equal in the translation, as well as less interesting in itself. What is stupidly said of Shakespeare is really true and appropriate of Chapman — mighty faults, counterpoised by mighty beauties. Excepting his quaint epithets, which he affects to render literally from the Greek, . . . it has no look, no air of a translation. It is as truly an original poem as the 'Fairy Queen.' It will give you small idea of Homer, though a far truer one than Pope's epigrams or Cowper's cumbersome, most anti-Homeric Miltonism. For Chapman writes and feels as a poet—as Homer might have written had he lived in England in the reign of Queen Elizabeth. In short, it is an ex-

quisite poem, in spite of its frequent and perverse quaintnesses and harshnesses, which are, however, amply repaid by almost unexampled sweetness and beauty of language, all over spirit and feeling. In the main, it is an English heroic poem, the tale of which is borrowed from the Greek."

Sir Philip Sidney, the author of "Arcadia," and the gallant Governor of Flushing, was at one time a student here. And Butler, the immortal author of "Hudibras," seems also, says Mr. Pearce, "to have had a chamber some time in the inn, as one of his biographers has supposed he was a member of the house."

About the year 1756 Dr. Johnson was a resident in Gray's Inn, but for a short time only.

Oliver Goldsmith occupied chambers in Gray's Inn early in 1764, while his attic on the library staircase of the Temple was preparing. He was now at work for the Dodsleys, and we get a glimpse of his straitened circumstances in the following brief note to Mr. James Dodsley :—"Sir," it runs, being dated from "Gray's Inn," and addressed "to Mr. James Dodesley in Pall Mall," on the 10th of March, 1764, "I shall take it as a favour if you can let me have ten guineas per bearer, for which I promise to account. I am, sir, your humble servant, OLIVER GOLDSMITH. P.S. I shall call to see you on Wednesday next with copy, &c." Whether the money was advanced, or the copy supplied in time, does not appear.

A nephew of Goldsmith, when in town with a friend, proposed to call on Uncle Oliver, in Gray's Inn, when he was setting to work on his "Animated Nature." They expected to find him in a well-furnished library, with a host of books; when, greatly to their surprise, the only book they saw in the place was a well-thumbed part of Buffon's "Natural History."

The outspoken William Cobbett, the writer of the famous "Political Register," and as true a representative of the John Bull character as ever lived, was for some years a clerk in the chambers of a gentlemen of this inn.

At the corner of Gray's Inn Road and Clerkenwell Road (formerly Liquorpond Street), stands Holborn Town-hall. The building was erected in 1879, from the designs of Mr. Lewis H. Isaacs, at a cost of £50,000, including the site; it is constructed of red brick with stone dressings, and covers three sides of a quadrangle. The grand hall will contain upwards of 800 seats, and is used for public meetings, concerts, &c. At the angle formed by the junction of the two roads is a tower containing a clock, with a fine-toned bell for striking the hours and chimes for the quarter-hours.

Besides Gray's Inn, there lie in Holborn Furnival's Inn, Thavie's Inn, Barnard's Inn, and Staple Inn. Of these the first three have ceased to be directly representative of the law; the other, Staple Inn, still retains many legal features of interest.

To some an explanation of the nature and object of the Inns of Chancery may here be acceptable. These then will welcome the following extract from the interesting work of Mr. J. C.

Inn of Court higher admission fees were charged to students coming from Inns of Chancery over which it had no control, than to students who came from its own primary schools. If the reader bear in mind the difference in respect to age, learning, and privileges between our modern public school-boys, and university undergraduates, he will realise with sufficient nearness to truth the differences which existed between the Inns of Chancery

EXTERIOR OF FURNIVAL'S INN, 1754.

Jeaffreson, "A Book about Lawyers." "The Inns of Chancery," he says, "for many generations maintained towards the Inns of Court a position similar to that which Eton School maintains towards King's at Cambridge, or that which Winchester School holds to New College at Oxford. They were seminaries in which lads underwent preparation for the superior discipline, and greater freedom of the four colleges. Each Inn of Court had its own Inns of Chancery, yearly receiving from them the pupils who had qualified themselves for promotion to the status of Inns-of-Court-men. In course of time students, after receiving the preliminary education in an Inn of Chancery, were permitted to enter an Inn of Court, on which their Inn of Chancery was not dependent; but at every

students and the Inns of Court students in the fifteenth century; and in the students, utter-barristers, and benchers of the Inns of Court at the same period he may see three distinct orders of academic persons closely resembling the undergraduates, bachelors of arts, and masters of arts in our own universities."

Furnival's Inn, between Brooke Street and Leather Lane, was originally the town mansion of the Lords Furnival. It belonged some time, says Stow, "to William Furnivall, knight, who had in Holborn two messuages and thirteen shops, as appeareth by record of Richard II., in the 6th of his reign." It was an Inn of Chancery in the 9th of Henry IV., was held under lease in the time of Edward VI., and was sold, early in Elizabeth's

INTERIOR OF FURNIVAL'S INN (after Nichells), 1750.

reign, to the benchers of Lincoln's Inn, who appear to have formerly had the lease of it.

In Charles I.'s time the greater part of the old inn described by Stow was taken down and a new building erected in its stead. "The Gothic Hall," says Cunningham, "with its timber roof (part of the original structure), was standing in 1818, when the whole inn was rebuilt by Mr. Peto, the contractor, who obtained a lease of the ground." In the square is a statue of Peto. Furnival's Inn is let in chambers, but is no longer an Inn of Chancery. Part of its interior is occupied by an hotel. The Society of Furnival's Inn ceased to exist as a community about 1817.

The arms of Furnival's Inn are—argent, a bend between six martlets, with a bordure azure.

A street disturbance is mentioned by Stow, in his "Annals," in which the leading member of this Inn got into trouble:—"In the 32nd of Henry VI. a tumult betwixt the gentlemen of Inns of Court and Chancery and the citizens of London, happening in Fleet Street, in which some mischief was done, the principals of Clifford's Inn, Furnival's Inn, and Barnard's Inn were sent prisoners to Hartford Castle."

The famous Sir Thomas More was "reader by the space of three years and more" in this Inn. He was a member of Lincoln's Inn. Of this great Lord Chancellor of the reign of Henry VIII., one of the most illustrious men of that period, how much might be told! He was the son of Sir John More, an honest judge of the King's Bench, who had some humour in him, if what Camden records be true. Speaking of the lottery of marriage, he used to say, "I would compare the multitude of women which are to be chosen for wives unto a bag full of snakes, having among them a single eel. Now if a man should put his hand into this bag, he may chance to light on the eel, but it is a hundred to one he shall be stung by a snake." It has been observed, however, that he himself ventured to put his hand three times into the bag, for he married three wives; nor was the sting so hurtful as to prevent his arriving at the age of ninety, and even then he did not die of anything else than a surfeit, occasioned by eating grapes.

Sir Thomas was his son by his first wife. He also was not afraid of snakes. "Having determined," we are told, "by the advice and direction of his ghostly father, to be a married man, there was at that time a pleasant conceited gentleman, of an ancient family in Essex, one Mr. John Colt, of New Hall, that invited him into his house, being much delighted in his company, proffering unto him the choice of any of his daughters, who were

young gentlewomen of very good carriage, good complexions, and very religiously inclined; whose honest and sweet conversation, and virtuous education, enticed Sir Thomas not a little; and although his affection most served him to the second, for that he thought her the fairest and best favoured, yet when he thought within himself that it would be a grief and some blemish to the eldest to have the younger sister preferred before her, he, out of a kind of compassion, settled his fancy upon the eldest, and soon afterwards married her, with all his friends' good liking."

This marriage proved fairly happy, but, before many years had passed, Jane Colt died. More then put his hand a second time into the bag, and this time had the ill luck to draw out a scorpion. He proposed to a widow, named Alice Middleton, who would have done well enough for a superior domestic servant: his good judgment and taste deserted him when he decided to make her a closer companion. Bustling, loquacious, tart, the good dame scolded servants and petty tradesmen with admirable effect; but, even at this distance of time, the sensitive ear is pained by her sharp, garrulous tongue, when its acerbity and virulence are turned against her pacific and scholarly husband. She had no sympathy and no feelings in common with him; he had as little in common with her.

Both humorous and pathetic, it has been remarked, was that memorable interview between More and Mrs. Alice, in the Tower, when she, regarding his position by the light with which she had been endowed by Nature, advised him to yield even then to the king. "What the good-year, Mr. More!" cried she, bustling up to the tranquil and courageous man. "I marvel that you, who have been hitherto always taken for a wise man, will now so play the fool as to lie here in this close-fitting prison, and be content to be shut up thus with mice and rats, when you might be abroad at your liberty, with the favour and good will of the king and his council, if you would but do as the bishops and best learned of his realm have done. And seeing you have at Chelsea a right fair house, your library, your books, your gallery, and all other necessaries so handsome about you, where you might, in company with me, your wife, your children, and household, be merry, I muse what, in God's name, you mean here thus fondly to tarry." Having heard her out, preserving his good-humour, he said to her, with a cheerful countenance, "I pray thee, good Mrs. Alice, tell me one thing." "What is it?" saith she. "Is not this house as near heaven as my own?" The two were thinking of very different things. Sir Thomas More had his eye on heaven.   Mrs. Alice had hers on "the right fair house at Chelsea."

More, with all his talent, learning, and wit, was a devoted and earnest follower of the ancient faith. When about twenty years old he began to practise regular austerities, wearing a sharp shirt of hair next his skin, which he never left off entirely, even when he was Lord Chancellor. As a lay Carthusian he at one time disciplined his bare back with scourges, slept on the cold ground or a hard bench, with a log for a pillow, allowed himself but four or five hours' sleep in the night, and by a score of other strong measures sought to preserve his spiritual by ruining his bodily health.

He comes before us, very life-like and pleasing, in connection with the charges of bribery, which at the time of his fall were preferred against him before the Privy Council. One story of this period has been often repeated. A Mrs. Croker being opposed in a suit to Lord Arundel, sought to win Sir Thomas More's favour ; so she presented him with a pair of gloves containing forty angels. With a courteous smile he accepted the gloves, but constrained her to take back the gold. The gentleness of the rebuff is charming.

In Furnival's Inn Charles Dickens lived from shortly after his entering the reporters' gallery till 1837, and it was here that the proposal that originated " Pickwick " was made to him. Dickens has himself described to us what passed at an interview which must be regarded as a happy one by all admirers of the novelist. Mr. Seymour, the artist, had proposed to do a series of cockney sporting plates, which it was thought would take with the public, if accompanied by letterpress, and published in monthly parts. " The idea," says Dickens, "propounded to me was that the monthly something should be a vehicle for certain plates to be executed by Mr. Seymour ; and there was a notion, either on the part of that admirable humorous artist, or of my visitor, Mr. Hall, that a ' Nimrod Club,' the members of which were to go out shooting, fishing, and so forth, and getting themselves into difficulties through their want of dexterity, would be the best means of introducing these. I objected, on consideration, that although born and partly bred in the country, I was no great sportsman, except in regard to all kinds of locomotion ; that the idea was not novel, and had already been much used ; that it would be infinitely better for the plates to arise naturally out of the text; and that I would like to take my own way, with a freer range of English scenes and people, and was afraid I should ultimately do so in any case, whatever course I might prescribe to myself at starting. My

views being deferred to, I thought of ' Pickwick,' and wrote the first number ; from the proof-sheets of which Mr. Seymour made his drawing of the club and his happy portrait of its founder. I connected Mr. Pickwick with a club because of the original suggestion, and I put in Mr. Winkle expressly for the use of Mr. Seymour." Between the first and second number of " Pickwick," Mr. Seymour died by his own hand, and Mr. H. K. Browne was eventually chosen to fill his place as illustrator. But that is apart from Furnival's Inn history, so we may leave the rest of the story untold.

Thavie's Inn was formerly an Inn of Chancery, appertaining to Lincoln's Inn. It was sold, however, by that society in 1771 to a Mr. Middleton. Having been subsequently destroyed by fire, a range of private buildings was erected on its site. The name it bears is derived from John Thavie, a liberal-minded armourer, with whom we have already met when speaking of St. Andrew's. In 1348 he bequeathed certain houses in Holborn, returning a large rental, for the support of the fabric of that interesting edifice.

" I must and will begin with Thavie's Inne," says Sir George Buc, "for besides that at my first coming to London, I was admitted for probation into that good house, I take it to be the oldest Inn of Chancery, at the least in Holborn. It was before the dwelling of an honest citizen called John Thavie, an armourer, and was rented of him in the time of King Edward III. by the chief professors then of the law, viz., Apprentices, as it is yet extant in a record in the Hustings, and whereof my Lord Coke showed to me the transcript, but since that time it was purchased for the students and other professors of the Law of Chancery by the Benchers of Lincoln's Inn, about the reign of King Henry VII., and retaineth the name of the old landlord or owner, Master Thavie."

Barnard's Inn, an Inn of Chancery, appertained to Gray's Inn. Formerly it was called Mackworth's Inn, and in the days of Henry VI. we find it a messuage belonging to Dr. John Mackworth, Dean of Lincoln. When turned into an Inn of Chancery, it was in the occupation of one Barnard, and his name it retained till 1881, when it was sold. The arms of Barnard's Inn are those of Mackworth —party per pale, indented, ermine and sable, a cheveron, gules, fretted or.

The old hall of Barnard's Inn is the smallest of all the halls of the London Inns, being only thirty-six feet long, twenty-two feet wide, and thirty feet high. It contained a fine full-length portrait of the upright and learned Lord Chief Justice Holt, for some time principal of Barnard's Inn ; and also of Lord Burleigh, Lord Bacon, Lord Keeper Coventry, and other eminent men.

In the time of Elizabeth there were 112 students in this Inn in term, and 24 out of term ; in 1855 there were, including the principal, ancient, and companions, in all, 18 members.

A believer in alchemy, Mr. Peter Woulfe, F.R.S., lived, about seventy years ago, in Barnard's Inn, No. 2, second-floor chambers. He was an eminent chemist, and, according to Mr. Brande, "the last true believer in alchemy." But little is known of his life. " Sir Humphrey Davy tells us," says Mr. Timbs, in his "Century of Anecdotes," "that he used to hang up written prayers and inscriptions of recommendations of his processes to Providence. His chambers were so filled with furnaces and apparatus that it was difficult to reach the fireside. Dr. Babington told Mr. Brande that he once put down his hat and could never find it again, such was the confusion of boxes, packages, and parcels, that lay about the room. His breakfast hour was four in the morning ; a few of his friends were occasionally invited, and gained entrance by a secret signal, knocking a certain number of times at the inner door of the chamber. He had long vainly searched for the elixir, and attributed his repeated failure to the want of due preparation by pious and charitable acts. Whenever he wished to break with an acquaintance, he resented the supposed injuries by sending a present to the offender and never seeing him again. These presents sometimes consisted of an expensive chemical product or preparation. He had an heroic remedy for illness, which was a journey to Edinburgh and back by the mail-coach ; and a cold taken on one of these expeditions terminated in inflammation of the lungs, of which he died."

His last moments were remarkable. In spite of his serious illness, he strenuously resisted all medical advice. By his desire his laundress shut up his chamber, and left him. She returned at midnight, when he was still alive ; next morning, however, she found him dead, his countenance being calm and serene ; apparently he had not moved from the position in which she had seen him last.

A contemporary of Woulfe, also an alchemist, is mentioned by Sir Walter Scott, in his paper on astrology and alchemy, in the *Quarterly Review* (1821). About 1801 this enthusiast lived, or rather starved, in the metropolis, in the person of an editor of an evening journal. He expected to compound the alkahest, if he could only keep his materials digested in a lamp-furnace for the space of seven years. The lamp burnt brightly during six years, eleven months, and some odd days besides, and then unluckily it went out. Why it went out the adept never could guess ; but he was certain that if the flame could only have burnt to the end of the septennary cycle, his experiment must have succeeded.

An order made by the authorities of Barnard's Inn, in November, 1706, throws some light on legal manners in the beginning of the eighteenth century. This order named two quarts as the allowance of wine to be given to each mess of four men, on going through the ceremony of "initiation." Of course this amount of wine was an "extra" allowance, in addition to the ale and sherry allotted to members by the regular dietary of the house. " Even Sheridan," Mr. Jeaffreson remarks, " who boasted he could drink any *given* quantity of wine, would have thought twice before he drank so large a given quantity, in addition to a liberal allowance of stimulant. Anyhow, the quantity was fixed—a fact that would have elicited an expression of approval from Chief Baron Thomson, who, loving port wine wisely, though too well, expressed at the same time his concurrence with the words and his dissent from the opinion of a barrister who observed, ' I hold, my lord, that, after a good dinner, a certain quantity of wine does no harm.' With a smile, the Chief Baron rejoined, ' True, sir, it is the uncertain quantity that does the mischief.' "

During the " No Popery " riots of 1780, Barnard's Inn very nearly fell a sacrifice to one of those wild acts of incendiarism which at that time disgraced the metropolis. It stood next to the extensive premises of Langdale's distillery, and Mr. Langdale was both the object of indignation and interest to the mob : in the first place, he was a Roman Catholic ; and in the second, he had a plentiful store of tempting liquor in his hands. The attack on Langdale's distillery, and its subsequent destruction by fire, were among the most striking scenes of the famous riots. What ardent spirits escaped from the flames were swallowed by the rioters. Many of them are said to have literally drunk themselves dead ; women and children were seen drinking from the kennels, which flowed with gin and other intoxicating liquors ; and many of the rabble, who had drunk themselves into a state of insensibility, perished in the flames. A Dr. Warner, who had passed the night in his chambers in Barnard's Inn, writes thus on the following morning to George Selwyn :—" The staircase in which my chambers are is not yet burnt down, but it could not be much worse for me if it were. However, I fear there are many scores of poor creatures in this town who have suffered this night much more than I have, and with less ability to bear it. Will you give me leave to lodge the shattered remains of my little goods in Cleveland Court for a time? There can be no living here, even if the fire stops immediately, for the whole place is a wreck; but there will be time enough to think of this. But there is a circumstance which distresses me more than anything; I have lost my maid, who was a very worthy creature, and I am sure would never have deserted me in such a situation by her own will; and what can have become of her is horrible to think! I fervently hope that you and yours are free from every distress. . . . . Six o'clock. The fire, I believe, is nearly stopped, though only at the next door to me. But no maid appears. When I shall overcome the horror of the night, and its consequences, I cannot guess. But I know, if you can send me word that things go well with you, that they will be less sad with me."

Staple Inn is an Inn of Chancery appertaining to Gray's Inn. The tradition is that it derives its name from having been originally an inn or hostell of the merchants of the (wool) staple. With this explanation, until a better is given, we must rest satisfied. It became an Inn of Chancery in the time of Henry V., and the inheritance of it was granted, 20th Henry VIII., to the Society of Gray's Inn. The Holborn front is of the time of James I., and is worthy of notice as one of the oldest existing specimens of our metropolitan street architecture. The hall is of a later date, has a clock turret, and originally possessed an open timber roof. Some of the armorial glass in the windows of the hall dates as far back as 1500. There are a few portraits —amongst them are those of Charles II., Queen Anne, the Earl of Macclesfield, Lord Chancellor Cowper, and Lord Camden—and at the upper end is the woolsack, the arms of the Inn. Upon brackets are casts of the twelve Cæsars. In the garden adjoining used to be a fig-tree, which had spread itself over nearly all the south side of the hall. Upon a terrace opposite stands a row of buildings, occupied as offices and chambers, formerly used by the taxing-masters in Chancery. They were completed in 1843, and are in the purest style of the reign of James I. The arched entrances and semi-circular oriels are highly effective. The openwork parapet of the terrace, and the lodge and gate leading to Southampton Buildings, are very picturesque. The Inn is divided into two courts, with a pleasant garden behind.

The doorway shown in our illustration on page 365 is mentioned by Dickens in "Edwin Drood."

By it one entered the chambers of Mr. Grewgious. What P. J. T. meant, carved on the stone above the door—whether Possibly John Thomas, or Possibly Joe Tyler, or what—the reader will recollect occasionally formed an innocent subject of speculation to Mr. Grewgious.

In the reign of Queen Elizabeth, there were 145 students in Staple Inn, in term, and 69 out of term—the largest number in any of the houses of Chancery.

Reading and mootings were observed here with commendable regularity. Sir Simon d'Ewes mentions that, on the 17th of February, 1625, he went in the morning to Staple Inn, and there argued a moot point, or law case, with others, and they did not abandon the exercise till near three o'clock in the afternoon.

Isaac Reed, who died in 1807, had chambers here. It was in Reed's chambers that Steevens corrected the proof-sheets of his well-known edition of Shakespeare. His habits were peculiar. He used, says Peter Cunningham, to leave his house at Hampstead at one in the morning, and walk to Staple Inn. Reed, who went to bed at a reasonable hour, allowed his facetious fellow-commentator the luxury of a latch-key, so Steevens stole quietly to his work, without disturbing the repose of his friend.

Dr. Samuel Johnson removed to chambers in this Inn, on the breaking up of his establishment in Gough Square, Fleet Street, where he had resided for ten years. We find him writing, under date of 23rd March, 1759, to Miss Porter:—

"Dear Madam,—I beg your pardon for having so long omitted to write. One thing or other has put me off. I have this day moved my things, and you are now to direct to me at Staple Inn, London. . . . I am going to publish a little story-book, which I will send you, when it is out. Write to me, my dearest girl, for I am always glad to hear from you.—I am, my dear, your humble servant,

"SAM. JOHNSON."

The "little story-book" was "Rasselas," which he seems to have written here, at least, in part. Of this entertaining and at the same time profound performance, Boswell says:—"Johnson wrote it, that with the profits he might defray the expense of his mother's funeral, and pay some little debts which she had left. He told Sir Joshua Reynolds that he composed it in the evenings of one week, sent it to press in portions, as it was written, and had never since read it over. Mr. Strahan, Mr. Johnston, and Mr. Dodsley purchased it for £100, but afterwards paid him £25 more, when it came to a second edition."

"Considering the large sums which have been

received for compilations, and works requiring not much more genius than compilations, we cannot but wonder," adds Boswell, "at the very low price which he was content to receive for this admirable performance, which, though he had written nothing else, would have rendered his name immortal in the world of literature. None of his writings has been so extensively diffused over Europe; for it has been translated into most, if not all, of the modern languages. This tale, with all the charms of Oriental imagery, and all the force and beauty of which the English language is capable, leads us through the most important scenes of human life, and shows us that this stage of our being is full of 'vanity and vexation of spirit!' To those who look no further than the present life, or who maintain that human nature has not fallen from the state in which it was created, the instruction of this sublime story will be of no avail; but those who think justly, and feel with strong sensibility, will listen with eagerness and admiration to its truth and wisdom."

There was an alarming fire in Staple Inn, 27th November, 1756. It consumed several chambers, and two women and two children perished in the flames. The hall fortunately escaped destruction.

With this description of Holborn and the Inns of Court, which form its most interesting feature, we terminate our account of Old and New London east of Temple Bar. In the succeeding volumes we shall move westward, from the same starting point, along the Strand, through Westminster, and the western portions of London, and across the water into Southwark. The ground over which we shall travel will be found as replete with memories and associations of past history, and striking features of modern progress, as any of that which we have already surveyed.